CRIME
A SERIOUS
AMERICAN PROBLEM

ISSN 1532-2696

CRIME
A SERIOUS
AMERICAN PROBLEM

Jeffrey Ferro

INFORMATION PLUS® REFERENCE SERIES
Formerly published by Information Plus, Wylie, Texas

GALE®

THOMSON
™
GALE

Detroit • New York • San Diego • San Francisco • Cleveland • New Haven, Conn. • Waterville, Maine • London • Munich

Crime: A Serious American Problem

Jeffrey Ferro

Project Editor
Ellice Engdahl

Editorial
Paula Cutcher-Jackson, Kathleen Edgar, Christy Justice, Debra Kirby, Prindle LaBarge, Elizabeth Manar, Kathleen Meek, Charles B. Montney, Heather Price

Permissions
Margaret A. Chamberlain

Product Design
Michael Logusz

Composition and Electronic Prepress
Evi Seoud

Manufacturing
Keith Helmling

LIBRARY OF CONGRESS CATALOGING-IN-PUBLICATION DATA

ISBN 0-7876-5103-6 (set)
ISBN 0-7876-6062-0
ISSN 1532-2696

Printed in the United States of America
10 9 8 7 6 5 4 3 2 1

TABLE OF CONTENTS

Crime rates fell through the 1990s, but began to rise in 2001. This chapter examines arrest trends according to geographic location, age, gender, and race and ethnicity. The government's role in law enforcement is also explored.

In 2000 one crime was committed every 2.7 seconds in the United States. Crime rate statistics for murder, rape, robbery, assault, burglary, theft, and other offenses are discussed in this chapter.

Criminals target all types of people, but some are more affected than others. What groups are most affected by various types of crimes? This chapter examines the trends and laws associated with crime victimization. Also discussed are the costs of victimization as well as victim assistance and victims' rights.

Some crimes are motivated by racial discrimination, or by a hatred of people of a different gender, sexual orientation, or nationality. Federal and state governments have begun to create special laws to protect people from these types of crimes. A section on terrorism provides the latest statistics on its victims and perpetrators.

Juveniles commit and are arrested for crimes ranging from murder to curfew violations. Issues unique and not-so-unique to juvenile justice are explored in this chapter.

The judicial system is charged with the task of bringing justice to criminals. Prisons and jails are responsible for incarceration and rehabilitation. This chapter examines the demographics and effectiveness of the American criminal justice and penal systems.

White-collar crimes include embezzlement, counterfeiting, and fraud. While not violent, these crimes have financial and emotional costs. This chapter explores crimes involving greed and dishonesty.

The connection between criminal activity and the use of alcohol and drugs is undeniable. Many Americans are arrested on substance-related charges, while many arrested on other charges are found to be under the influence of these substances.

Law enforcement agencies take on the dangerous job of fighting crime. Other programs are designed to prevent crimes before they even occur. Also in this chapter, public opinion polls present the American public's views on crime.

PREFACE

Crime: A Serious American Problem is one of the latest volumes in the Information Plus Reference Series. Previously published by the Information Plus company of Wylie, Texas, the Information Plus Reference Series (and its companion set, the Information Plus Compact Series) became a Gale Group product when Gale and Information Plus merged in early 2000. Those of you familiar with the series as published by Information Plus will notice a few changes from the 2000 edition. Gale has adopted a new layout and style that we hope you will find easy to use. Other improvements include greatly expanded indexes in each book, and more descriptive tables of contents.

While some changes have been made to the design, the purpose of the Information Plus Reference Series remains the same. Each volume of the series presents the latest facts on a topic of pressing concern in modern American life. These topics include today's most controversial and most studied social issues: abortion, capital punishment, care for the elderly, crime, health care, the environment, immigration, minorities, social welfare, women, youth, and many more. Although written especially for the high school and undergraduate student, this series is an excellent resource for anyone in need of factual information on current affairs.

By presenting the facts, it is Gale's intention to provide its readers with everything they need to reach an informed opinion on current issues. To that end, there is a particular emphasis in this series on the presentation of scientific studies, surveys, and statistics. These data are generally presented in the form of tables, charts, and other graphics placed within the text of each book. Every graphic is directly referred to and carefully explained in the text. The source of each graphic is presented within the graphic itself. The data used in these graphics are drawn from the most reputable and reliable sources, in particular from the various branches of the U.S. government and from major independent polling organizations.

Every effort has been made to secure the most recent information available. The reader should bear in mind that many major studies take years to conduct, and that additional years often pass before the data from these studies are made available to the public. Therefore, in many cases the most recent information available in 2002 dated from 1999 or 2000. Older statistics are sometimes presented as well, if they are of particular interest and no more recent information exists.

Although statistics are a major focus of the Information Plus Reference Series, they are by no means its only content. Each book also presents the widely held positions and important ideas that shape how the book's subject is discussed in the United States. These positions are explained in detail and, where possible, in the words of their proponents. Some of the other material to be found in these books includes: historical background; descriptions of major events related to the subject; relevant laws and court cases; and examples of how these issues play out in American life. Some books also feature primary documents, or have pro and con debate sections giving the words and opinions of prominent Americans on both sides of a controversial topic. All material is presented in an even-handed and unbiased manner; the reader will never be encouraged to accept one view of an issue over another.

HOW TO USE THIS BOOK

The United States of America has among the highest crime and incarceration rates in the industrialized world. It comes as no surprise then that many Americans are very interested in crime, its causes, and how to prevent it. A tremendous number of studies are conducted every year on criminals, victims, law enforcement, the criminal justice system, and prisons and jails. This book gathers together and explains information from the largest, most recent, and most reputable of these studies, in order to provide a complete picture of crime in the United States.

Crime: A Serious American Problem consists of nine chapters and three appendices. Each of the chapters is devoted to a particular aspect of crime in the United States. For a summary of the information covered in each chapter, please see the synopses provided in the Table of Contents at the front of the book. Chapters generally begin with an overview of the basic facts and background information on the chapter's topic, then proceed to examine sub-topics of particular interest. For example, Chapter 6: Sentencing and Corrections begins with an overview of the types of sentences American criminals generally receive. It then closely examines the controversies surrounding the death penalty. Discussed next are growing incarceration rates and the demographic characteristics of prisoners. Probation, parole, and recidivism are covered, and the chapter ends with a discussion of the effectiveness of incarceration as a deterrent to crime. Readers can find their way through a chapter by looking for the section and sub-section headings, which are clearly set off from the text. Or, they can refer to the book's extensive index if they already know what they are looking for.

Statistical Information

The tables and figures featured throughout *Crime: A Serious American Problem* will be of particular use to the reader in learning about this issue. These tables and figures represent an extensive collection of the most recent and important statistics on crime, as well as related issues—for example, graphics in the book cover workplace homicides, hate crime offenses, arrest rates for juvenile criminals, international incarceration rates, and average length of imprisonment for possession of illegal drugs. Gale believes that making this information available to the reader is the most important way in which we fulfill the goal of this book: to help readers understand the issues and controversies surrounding crime in the United States and reach their own conclusions about them.

Each table or figure has a unique identifier appearing above it, for ease of identification and reference. Titles for the tables and figures explain their purpose. At the end of each table or figure, the original source of the data is provided.

In order to help readers understand these often complicated statistics, all tables and figures are explained in the text. References in the text direct the reader to the relevant statistics. Furthermore, the contents of all tables and figures are fully indexed. Please see the opening section of the index at the back of this volume for a description of how to find tables and figures within it.

Appendices

In addition to the main body text and images, *Crime: A Serious American Problem* has three appendices. The first is the Important Names and Addresses directory. Here the reader will find contact information for a number of government and private organizations that can provide further information on aspects of crime. The second appendix is the Resources section, which can also assist the reader in conducting his or her own research. In this section, the author and editors of *Crime: A Serious American Problem* describe some of the sources that were most useful during the compilation of this book. The final appendix is the index. It has been greatly expanded from previous editions, and should make it even easier to find specific topics in this book.

ADVISORY BOARD CONTRIBUTIONS

The staff of Information Plus would like to extend their heartfelt appreciation to the Information Plus Advisory Board. This dedicated group of media professionals provides feedback on the series on an ongoing basis. Their comments allow the editorial staff who work on the project to continually make the series better and more user-friendly. Our top priorities are to produce the highest-quality and most useful books possible, and the Advisory Board's contributions to this process are invaluable.

The members of the Information Plus Advisory Board are:

- Kathleen R. Bonn, Librarian, Newbury Park High School, Newbury Park, California
- Madelyn Garner, Librarian, San Jacinto College—North Campus, Houston, Texas
- Anne Oxenrider, Media Specialist, Dundee High School, Dundee, Michigan
- Charles R. Rodgers, Director of Libraries, Pasco-Hernando Community College, Dade City, Florida
- James N. Zitzelsberger, Library Media Department Chairman, Oshkosh West High School, Oshkosh, Wisconsin

COMMENTS AND SUGGESTIONS

The editors of the Information Plus Reference Series welcome your feedback on *Crime: A Serious American Problem.* Please direct all correspondence to:

Editors
Information Plus Reference Series
27500 Drake Rd.
Farmington Hills, MI, 48331-3535

ACKNOWLEDGMENTS

The editors wish to thank the copyright holders of material included in this volume and the permissions managers of many book and magazine publishing companies for assisting us in securing reproduction rights. We are also grateful to the staffs of the Detroit Public Library, the Library of Congress, the University of Detroit Mercy Library, Wayne State University Purdy/Kresge Library Complex, and the University of Michigan Libraries for making their resources available to us.

Following is a list of the copyright holders who have granted us permission to reproduce material in Information Plus: Crime. *Every effort has been made to trace copyright, but if omissions have been made, please let us know.*

For more detailed source citations, please see the sources listed under each individual table and figure.

Anti-Defamation League, New York. Reproduced by permission. All rights reserved: Figure 4.2, Table 4.1

Bureau of Alcohol, Tobacco and Firearms, Washington, DC: Figure 4.4, Figure 4.5, Figure 4.6, Figure 4.7

Death Penalty Information Center, Washington, DC: Figure 9.2, Figure 9.3

Federal Bureau of Investigation, Washington, DC: Figure 1.1, Figure 1.2, Figure 2.1, Figure 2.2, Figure 2.3, Figure 4.3, Figure 7.1, Figure 7.2, Table 1.1, Table 1.2, Table 1.3, Table 1.4, Table 1.5, Table 1.6, Table 1.7, Table 1.8, Table 1.9, Table 1.10, Table 2.1, Table 2.2, Table 2.3, Table 2.4, Table 2.5, Table 2.6, Table 2.7, Table 2.8, Table 2.9, Table 2.10, Table 2.11, Table 2.14, Table 2.15, Table 2.17, Table 2.18, Table 4.2, Table 4.3, Table 4.4, Table 4.5, Table 4.6, Table

5.2, Table 5.3, Table 5.5, Table 7.1, Table 7.2, Table 7.3, Table 7.4, Table 8.3, Table 9.1, Table 9.2, Table 9.3, Table 9.4, Table 9.5, Table 9.7

Federal Trade Commission, Washington, DC: Table 7.5, Table 7.6

The Gallup Organization, Inc., Princeton, NJ: Table 9.8, Table 9.9, Table 9.10, Table 9.11, Table 9.12, Table 9.14, Table 9.15, Table 9.16, Table 9.17, Table 9.18

Highway Loss Data Institute, Arlington, VA: Table 2.13

National Insurance Crime Bureau, Arlington, VA: Table 2.12

Office of Management and Budget, The White House, Washington, DC: Figure 1.3

Office of National Drug Control Policy, Washington, DC: Figure 8.6, Figure 8.8, Table 8.12, Table 8.14

The Sentencing Project, Washington, DC: Figure 6.2

Southern Poverty Law Center, Montgomery, AL: Figure 4.1

U.S. Department of Justice, Bureau of Justice Statistics, Washington, DC: Figure 3.1, Figure 3.3, Figure 3.4, Figure 6.1, Figure 8.1, Figure 8.2, Figure 8.3, Figure 8.4, Figure 8.5, Figure 9.1, Table 1.11, Table 1.12, Table 2.16, Table 3.1, Table 3.2, Table 3.3, Table 3.4, Table 3.5, Table 3.6, Table 3.7, Table 3.8, Table 6.2, Table 6.3, Table 6.4, Table 6.5, Table 6.6, Table 6.7, Table 6.8, Table 6.9, Table 6.10, Table 6.11, Table 8.1, Table 8.2, Table 8.4, Table 8.6, Table 8.7, Table 8.8, Table 8.9, Table 8.10, Table 8.11, Table 8.13, Table 8.15, Table 8.16, Table 9.6, Table 9.8, Table 9.9, Table 9.10,

Table 9.11, Table 9.12, Table 9.14, Table 9.15, Table 9.16, Table 9.17

U.S. Department of Justice, Office of Justice Programs: Table 6.12

U.S. Department of Justice, Office of Justice Programs, National Institute of Justice: Table 8.5

U.S. Department of Justice, Office of Justice Programs, Office of Juvenile Justice and Delinquency Prevention/National Center for Juvenile Justice: Figure 5.1, Figure 5.2, Figure 5.3, Figure 5.4, Figure 5.5, Figure 5.6, Figure 5.7, Figure 5.8, Figure 5.9, Figure 5.10, Figure 5.11, Figure 5.12, Figure 5.13, Figure 5.14, Figure 5.15, Figure 5.16, Figure 5.17, Figure 5.18, Figure 5.19, Table 5.1, Table 5.4, Table 5.7, Table 6.12

U.S. Department of Justice, Office of Justice Programs, Office of Juvenile Justice and Delinquency Prevention, Washington, DC: Figure 3.2, Table 5.6

U.S. Department of Justice, Washington, DC: Table 6.13, Table 6.14

U.S. Department of Labor, Bureau of Labor Statistics, Washington, DC: Figure 2.4, Table 6.1

U.S. Sentencing Commission, Washington, DC: Figure 8.7

University of Florida, Department of Sociology and the Center for Studies in Criminology and Law, Gainesville, FL: Figure 7.3, Figure 7.4, Figure 7.5, Figure 7.6

University of Michigan, Institute for Social Research, Ann Arbor, MI: Table 9.13

Violence Policy Center, Washington, DC: Table 2.19

CHAPTER 1

CRIME—AN OVERVIEW

CRIME

The U.S. Department of Justice defines crime as all behaviors and acts for which society provides formally approved punishments. Written law, both federal and state, defines which behavior is criminal and which is not. Some behaviors—murder, robbery, and burglary—have always been considered criminal. Other actions, such as domestic violence or driving under the influence of drugs or alcohol, were only recently added to the list of criminal offenses. Other changes in our society have also influenced crime. For example, the widespread use of computers provides new opportunities for white-collar crime, as well as adding a new word—"cybercrime"—to our vocabulary.

Two main government sources collect crime statistics. The Federal Bureau of Investigation (FBI) annually compiles the Uniform Crime Reports (UCR). The UCR collects data from about 17,000 city, county, and state law enforcement agencies, whose jurisdictions contain approximately 95 percent of the total U.S. population. The *National Crime Victimization Survey*, prepared by the Bureau of Justice Statistics (BJS), bases its findings on an annual survey of 100,000 people.

Crime can range from actions as simple as taking chewing gum from a store without paying, to those as tragic and violent as murder. Most people have broken the law, wittingly or unwittingly, at some time in their lives. Therefore, the true extent of criminality is impossible to measure; researchers can keep records only of what is reported by victims or known to the police.

FACTORS IN THE RATE OF CRIME

The FBI lists many factors that can influence the rate of crime in a particular area, including:

- Population density and degree of urbanization (big city growth).

- Variations in the makeup of the population, particularly where youth is most concentrated.

- Stability of the population—residents' tendencies to move around (mobility), commuting patterns, and length of time residing in the area (transient factors).

- Types and condition of transportation and highway systems available.

- Economic conditions, including average income, poverty, and job availability.

- Cultural conditions, such as educational, recreational, and religious characteristics.

- Family conditions with respect to divorce and family togetherness.

- Climate and weather.

- Effectiveness of law enforcement agencies.

- Policies of other parts of the criminal justice system (prosecutorial, judicial, correctional, and probational).

- Attitudes of residents toward crime.

- Crime-reporting practices of the citizens.

A DECADE OF CRIME ON THE DECLINE

In the 1990s much of the public believed the crime rate was increasing. The randomness of crime (drive-by shootings, driveway robberies), along with sensational news reporting, fed this belief. The BJS reported, in *Perceptions of Neighborhood Crime, 1995* (Carol J. DeFrances and Steven K. Smith, Washington, D.C., 1998), that about 7.3 percent of U.S. households reported crime as a major problem in their neighborhoods. Not surprisingly, households in central cities were twice as likely (14.5 percent) to feel that crime was a serious problem. In 1995, 19.6 percent of black central-city households

TABLE 1.1

Crime Index trends, January–June 2001 compared to January–June 2000

Population Group and Area	Number of agencies	Population (thousands)	Crime Index total	Modified total*	Violent crime	Property crime*	Murder	Forcible rape	Robbery	Aggravated assault	Burglary	Larceny-theft	Motor vehicle theft	Arson*
Total	9,224	203,224	-0.3	-0.3	-1.3	-0.2	+0.3	-1.7	+0.8	-2.4	-1.2	-0.4	+2.6	+2.9
Cities:														
Over 1,000,000	10	23,598	-1.3	-1.3	-2.6	-1.0	+1.8	-0.7	-3.0	-2.5	-4.0	+0.8	-4.0	+4.0
500,000 to 999,999	21	13,726	+0.1	+0.1	-2.2	+0.6	-9.7	-8.8	+2.6	-4.4	+1.7	-0.1	+1.8	-9.1
250,000 to 499,999	34	11,721	+1.9	+2.0	-0.5	+2.3	+6.9	-1.9	+1.8	-1.8	+0.2	+0.9	+11.5	+7.7
100,000 to 249,999	164	24,162	+0.6	+0.5	+1.9	+0.4	+1.3	-2.3	+3.5	+1.5	-1.7	+0.1	+4.9	-1.5
50,000 to 99,999	294	20,044	-1.7	-1.6	-0.4	-1.9	+10.5	-30	+3.1	-1.8	-2.7	-2.2	+1.5	+10.3
25,000 to 49,999	553	19,085	-0.3	-0.3	+0.7	-0.4	-0.8	+3.9	+2.1	-0.2	-0.2	-0.7	+2.3	-1.9
10,000 to 24,999	1,238	19,681	-1.3	-1.3	-2.3	-1.3	-9.2	+1.9	-3.2	-2.5	-0.6	-1.9	+4.1	+3.9
Under 10,000	4,263	14,627	+0.1	+0.2	+0.5	+0.1	+11.9	+4.3	+2.8	-0.5	+1.4	-0.5	+3.7	+8.9
Counties:														
Suburban [1]	898	36,817	-0.6	-0.5	-3.2	-0.3	+7.2	+2.0	+4.2	-5.6	-1.1	-0.8	+5.3	+5.8
Rural [2]	1,749	19,763	-1.9	-1.8	-6.7	-1.3	-11.6	-8.9	-3.5	-6.6	-2.7	-0.6	-0.5	+5.2
Areas:														
Suburban Area [3]	4,540	73,998	-0.4	-0.4	-1.2	-0.3	+4.5	+3.6	+3.4	-3.1	-0.2	-1.0	+4.8	+4.5
Cities outside Metropolitan Areas	2,412	16,212	-1.0	-1.0	-2.4	-0.9	-1.4	+0.5	-4.1	-2.4	-1.2	-0.9	+0.3	+3.8
Region:														
Northeast			-4.1	-4.1	-3.0	-4.3	+0.4	+0.7	-6.8	-1.0	-6.7	-3.5	-5.0	+1.3
Midwest			-1.9	-1.9	-1.9	-1.9	+2.8	-3.4	-1.0	-2.3	-2.9	-1.6	-2.2	-1.1
South			+0.8	+0.7	+0.2	+0.8	-6.4	-0.6	+6.4	-2.2	1.8	+0.1	+4.1	-0.3
West			+1.6	+1.6	-1.7	+2.1	+9.6	-3.2	+2.1	-3.4	-1.5	+1.8	+8.3	+8.9
Years:														
1998/1997			-5.1	-5.2	-7.1	-4.8	-7.6	-5.1	-11.2	-5.1	-3.3	-4.6	-8.4	-12.1
1999/1998			-9.5	-9.5	-8.1	-9.7	-12.6	-8.4	-10.0	-7.1	-13.7	-8.1	-12.0	-11.0
2000/1999			-0.3	-0.3	-0.3	-0.3	-1.8	+0.7	-2.6	+0.7	-2.4	+0.1	+1.2	-2.7
2001/2000			-0.3	-0.3	-1.3	-0.2	+0.3	-1.7	+0.8	-2.4	-1.2	-0.4	+2.6	+2.9

* The Modified total is the sum of the Crime Index offenses, including arson. Data for arson are not included in the property crime totals.

[1] Includes crimes reported to sheriffs' departments, county police departments, and state police within Metropolitan Statistical Areas.

[2] Includes crimes reported to sheriffs' departments, county police departments, and state police outside Metropolitan Statistical Areas.

[3] Includes crimes reported to city, county, and state law enforcement agencies within Metropolitan Statistical Areas, but outside the central cities.

SOURCE: Adapted from "Table 1: Crime Index Trends by Population Group and Area," "Table 2: Crime Index Trends by Geographic Region," and "Table 3: Crime Index Trends, Two-year Trends" *Crime in the United States, Uniform Crime Reports January–June 2001,* Federal Bureau of Investigation, Washington, DC, 2001

identified crime as a neighborhood problem, compared to 13 percent of white central-city households.

According to FBI, state, and city reports, however, the crime rate dropped steadily from 1991 to 2000. During that period the number of crimes in the United States declined from 14.9 million crimes in 1991 to 11.6 million in 2000. The 2000 national total was the lowest since 1978 and remained statistically unchanged from 1999. The 2000 crime rate (the number of crimes per 100,000 persons) was the lowest in 20 years and reflected nearly a 30 percent drop from 1991. This reduction appeared in all types of crime.

That general trend continued through the first six months of 2001, although more modestly than in previous years, according to preliminary UCR data released by the FBI. The overall crime index total was down by 0.3 percent in 2001 from the same time period in 2000. By comparison, the crime index total declined by almost 10 percent from 1998 to 1999, and by 5 percent from 1997 to 1998. (See Table 1.1.) While these trends were encouraging, many believed it was probably much too early to celebrate a victory over crime. As James Alan Fox, dean of the College of Criminal Justice at Boston's Northeastern University, notes, "We're moving in the right direction, but we have a long way to go still before we can claim victory over our crime problem."

Why the Decline?

Experts have attempted to identify key factors contributing to the marked trend. The statistics suggest that as the baby boomers (the generation born between 1946 and 1965) outgrew their prime crime years, the crime rate began to decline. Some observers also attribute this decline to other factors, including:

• More money spent on law enforcement.

• Stiffer sentences handed down by the courts.

- The growing number of neighborhood watch programs.

- The declining number of neighborhood bars.

Others argue the decline in crime was due to the increases in incarcerations (being jailed). From 1980 through 1995 the population in federal and state prisons more than tripled from 329,821 to 1,104,074. In June 2001 the number of prisoners, including city and county jail inmates, reached 1.97 million. Between 1990 and 2001 the annual incarceration rate—the number of persons in custody per 100,000 residents—rose from 458 to 690, an increase from a rate of 686 in 2000 but down slightly from a rate of 691 in 1999.

Urban police officers attribute the decline in crime to the hiring of more police officers and creation of gang and violent-crime task forces. They also praise citizens who joined crime watch organizations. In a 1995 Chicago study, researchers found that urban neighborhoods with a strong sense of community and shared values had markedly lower rates of violence (Robert J. Sampson et al., "Neighborhoods and Violent Crime: A Multilevel Study of Collective Efficacy," *Science,* vol. 277, August 15, 1997). Of special importance, the study noted, was the "willingness of residents to intervene in the lives of children," especially in the areas of truancy, graffiti, and teenage gang participation, such as hanging out on neighborhood street corners.

Others posit that the booming economy of the 1990s, with its low unemployment figures and rising wages, had some effect on crime. The theory is that the benefits of a strong economy reduced the incidence of crimes committed for financial gain, such as burglary or robbery. In addition, with more people employed the number of people with time to commit crimes declined. Other theories maintain that it is a combination of these or other factors.

Causes of the Earlier Crime Increase

If crime actually declined through the 1990s, what factors lay behind the apparent increase in crime starting in the 1960s and continuing through the 1980s? Experts continue to debate whether the increase in reported crime for that period was real. Some believe the increase only reflected better record-keeping and participation of more local law enforcement agencies in the FBI reporting system. Others attribute the long-term increase in the crime rate to the growing up of the baby boom generation. As this population bulge entered its juvenile years, it was only natural, they argue, that the crime rate would increase. Generally males between the ages of 15 and 24 commit the most crimes.

Neither the FBI nor the BJS has provided official interpretations as to why the crime rate increased in the late 1980s. Unofficial observations generally attributed the increase to the influence of drug use and drug trafficking, especially involving "crack" cocaine. A large proportion of convicted offenders were on drugs while committing the crimes for which they were sentenced.

Many crimes, including murder, are committed during drug transactions. While several theories may explain why youth gangs exist, many support themselves through drug trafficking. For some, the marketing of drugs is their sole reason for existence. The development of crack (a less expensive, more marketable form of cocaine) in the 1980s provided gangs throughout the United States with a money-making commodity. Gang wars over "turf" led to many deaths of gang members and innocent bystanders. Some gangs, often with strong ethnic ties such as the Chinese "tongs" or the Jamaican "posses," became dedicated to the drug trade and participated in brutal crimes.

INCREASES PREDICTED

Some criminologists predict that all crime rates will increase through the early years of the twenty-first century, as the children of the baby boomers (the "boomerang" or "boomlet" generation) become teenagers and young adults. Experts such as Dr. James Alan Fox think that a resurgence in juvenile crime, in particular, may be imminent based on the projected growth of the juvenile population. According to estimates by the U.S. Census Bureau, the population of juveniles 15 to 17 years of age—the group responsible for two-thirds of all juvenile arrests—will increase by 19 percent by 2007. Recent statistics indicate a diminishing rate of decline in juvenile crime. Juvenile crime declined by 50 percent from 1994 to 1999, and declined 5 percent from 1999 to 2000. For the first two months of 2002, gang homicides in Los Angeles tripled from the same period in 2001, as reported in *The New York Times.*

INCREASES NOTED IN 2001

The general trend of a declining crime rate in recent years appeared to reverse itself in 2001, according to preliminary UCR data released by the FBI in 2002. Despite the observation of a slight decrease in the first 6 months of 2001, year-end 2001 data indicated a 2 percent increase in the nation's Crime Index since 2000. (See Table 1.2.) The Crime Index includes the crimes of murder, forcible rape, robbery, aggravated assault, burglary, larceny-theft, and motor vehicle theft. The Modified Crime Index also includes the crime of arson. The FBI advised that the figures reflecting the offenses from the terrorist events of September 11, 2001, are not included in the trend data reflected in Table 1.2 because they are statistical outliers that will affect current and future crime trends.

According to the preliminary data for 2001 for violent crimes, there was a slight 0.3 percent increase from 2000.

TABLE 1.2

Crime Index trends, January–December 2001 compared to figures reported in 2000

Population Group and Area	Number of agencies	Popu-lation (thou-sands)	Crime Index total	Modi-fied total	Vio-lent crime	Prop-erty crime	Murder	For-cible rape	Rob-bery	Aggra-vated assault	Bur-glary	Larceny-theft	Motor vehicle theft	Arson
Total	10,329	223,320	+2.0	+2.0	+0.3	+2.2	+3.1	+0.2	+3.9	-1.4	+2.6	+1.4	+5.9	+2.0
Cities :														
Over 1,000,000	10	24,330	+1.8	+1.8	+1.4	+1.9	+6.7	+1.1	+2.4	+0.6	+1.1	+1.4	+4.3	+5.7
500,000 to 999,999	21	13,914	+2.3	+2.3	-1.0	+2.9	+1.5	-6.4	+3.5	-3.3	+6.5	+1.4	+4.6	-4.1
250,000 to 499,999	38	13,294	+3.9	+3.9	+1.9	+4.3	+9.0	+4.9	+4.0	+0.1	+2.9	+2.9	+11.1	+4.2
100,000 to 249,999	162	24,086	+1.8	+1.7	+0.7	+1.9	-0.8	-3.2	+4.5	-1.1	+1.1	+1.6	+4.5	-6.1
50,000 to 99,999	332	22,724	+1.5	+1.5	+0.6	+1.6	+3.1	-1.8	+4.5	-0.9	+1.9	+1.1	+4.3	+3.7
25,000 to 49,999	613	21,354	+2.4	+2.3	-0.6	+2.7	-3.1	+3.1	+3.9	-2.7	+4.0	+1.9	+6.4	-0.2
10,000 to 24,999	1,350	21,554	+0.9	+0.9	-0.6	+1.0	-0.4	+4.9	+2.7	-2.3	+2.9	*	+7.2	+4.9
Under 10,000	4,820	16,637	+0.8	+0.9	-2.7	+1.2	+3.3	-1.6	+7.2	-4.6	+3.4	+0.5	+3.9	+4.4
Counties:														
Suburban [1]	987	42,384	+2.4	+2.5	+0.2	+2.7	+5.3	+2.6	+8.3	-2.3	+2.9	+1.7	+8.3	+5.4
Rural [2]	1,996	23,043	+0.6	+0.7	-1.4	+0.9	-5.8	-0.1	+2.2	-1.8	*	+1.2	+2.2	+3.0
Areas:														
Suburban Area [3]	4,940	82,284	+2.2	+2.2	-0.1	+2.4	+5.0	+3.5	+7.0	-2.8	+3.8	+1.3	+7.7	+3.7
Cities outside Metropolitan Areas	2,830	19,644	+0.7	+0.7	-2.0	+1.0	-5.9	+0.7	+0.8	-2.9	+1.5	+0.6	+3.9	+5.1
Region:														
Northeast			-1.2	-1.1	-2.3	-1.0	+7.7	+1.9	-2.3	-2.9	-0.5	-1.5	+1.1	+5.2
Midwest			+0.9	+0.8	-1.0	+1.1	+4.1	-0.3	+0.5	-2.0	+2.0	+0.8	+1.5	-1.7
South			+1.9	+1.9	+1.7	+1.9	-2.1	+0.5	+7.1	-0.5	+4.0	+0.9	+4.4	+2.0
West			+4.5	+4.5	+1.0	+5.0	+8.0	-0.7	+7.1	-1.5	+2.5	+4.1	+12.2	+2.9
Years:														
1998/1997			-5.4	-5.5	-6.4	-5.3	-7.1	-3.2	-10.4	-4.8	-5.3	-4.8	-8.4	-6.6
1999/1998			-6.8	-6.8	-6.7	-6.8	-8.5	-4.3	-8.4	-6.2	-10.0	-5.7	-7.7	-3.6
2000/1999			-0.2	-0.2	-0.1	-0.3	*	+0.9	-0.4	-0.1	-2.4	+0.2	+1.2	+0.4
2001/2000			+2.0	+2.0	+0.3	+2.2	+3.1	+0.2	+3.9	-1.4	+2.6	+1.4	+5.9	+2.0

*Less than one-tenth of 1 percent.
[1] Includes crimes reported to sheriffs' departments, county police departments, and state police within Metropolitan Statistical Areas.
[2] Includes crimes reported to sheriffs' departments, county police departments, and state police outside Metropolitan Statistical Areas.
[3] Includes crimes reported to city, county, and state law enforcement agencies within Metropolitan Statistical Areas, but outside the central cities.

SOURCE: Adapted from "Table 1: Crime Index Trends by Population Group and Area," "Table 2: Crime Index Trends by Geographic Region," and "Table 3: Crime Index Trends, Two-year Trends," *Uniform Crime Reports January–December 2001*, U.S. Department of Justice, Federal Bureau of Investigation, Clarksburg, WV, 2002

Robbery increased by 3.9 percent, murder rose by 3.1 percent, and forcible rape increased slightly, by 0.2 percent. Aggravated assault, the most frequently occurring violent crime included in the Crime Index, was the only offense to show a decrease (of 1.4 percent) from 2000 levels.

Among property crimes, the FBI's 2001 preliminary data showed an increase of 2.2 percent from 2000 figures. There was an increase of 5.9 percent in motor vehicle theft, followed by a 2.6 percent increase in burglary, a 2 percent increase in arson, and an increase of 1.4 percent in larceny-theft since 2000.

By region, preliminary Crime Index totals for 2001 increased by 4.5 percent in the nation's West, followed by 1.9 percent in the South, 1.2 percent in the Northeast, and 0.9 percent in the Midwest, compared to 2000 levels. Preliminary Crime Index offenses increased in the nation's cities, as well, with the largest increase of 3.9 percent recorded in cities with populations of 250,000 to 499,000. The smallest rise was recorded in the smallest cities—those with populations under 10,000.

If the offenses surrounding the events of September 11, 2001, are included in the crime trends for 2001, preliminary data show that the 2001 Crime Index would remain at the 2.0-percent increase from the 2000 figure. Yet with the events included, the volume of violent crime would increase 0.6 percent and the murder volume would increase by 26.4 percent.

THE UNIFORM CRIME REPORTS

The FBI compiles various sets of crime statistics. In one category the FBI tracks the number of crimes by type as reported by local police. The more serious crime types are included in the Crime Index. A second category tracks cleared offenses. Cleared offenses are crimes for which at least one person is arrested, charged, and turned over to the court for prosecution. This does not necessarily mean the person arrested is guilty or will be convicted for the crime.

The Crime Index includes the violent crimes of murder, forcible rape, robbery, and aggravated assault, and the property crimes of burglary, larceny-theft, motor vehicle

TABLE 1.3

Index of crime, 2000

Area	Population[1]	Crime Index total	Modified Crime Index total[2]	Violent crime[3]	Property crime[3]	Murder and non-negligent man-slaughter	Forcible rape	Robbery	Aggravated assault	Burglary	Larceny-theft	Motor vehicle theft	Ar-son[2]
United States Total	281,421,906	11,605,751		1,424,289	10,181,462	15,517	90,186	407,842	910,744	2,049,946	6,965,957	1,165,559	
Rate per 100,000 inhabitants		4,124.0		506.1	3,617.9	5.5	32.0	144.9	323.6	728.4	2,475.3	414.2	
Metropolitan Statistical Area	224,805,902												
Area actually reporting[4]	92.6%	9,397,904		1,206,574	8,191,330	12,889	68,359	378,602	746,724	1,602,509	5,547,197	1,041,624	
Estimated totals	100.0%	9,954,479		1,261,958	8,692,521	13,368	74,660	388,817	785,113	1,696,990	5,916,697	1,078,834	
Rate per 100,000 inhabitants		4,428.0		561.4	3,866.7	5.9	33.2	173.0	349.2	754.9	2,631.9	479.9	
Cities Outside Metropolitan Area	22,738,278												
Area actually reporting[4]	80.7%	833,503		76,568	756,935	718	6,467	11,430	57,953	142,304	576,717	37,914	
Estimated totals	100.0%	1,019,808		91,290	928,518	873	8,013	13,622	68,782	172,636	710,592	45,290	
Rate per 100,000 inhabitants		4,485.0		401.5	4,083.5	3.8	35.2	59.9	302.5	759.2	3,125.1	199.2	
Rural Counties	33,877,726												
Area actually reporting[4]	79.8%	530,110		60,873	469,237	1,018	5,929	4,662	49,264	151,037	283,512	34,688	
Estimated totals	100.0%	631,464		71,041	560,423	1,276	7,513	5,403	56,849	180,320	338,668	41,435	
Rate per 100,000 inhabitants		1,864.0		209.7	1,654.3	3.8	22.2	15.9	167.8	532.3	999.7	122.3	

[1] Populations are Bureau of the Census 2000 decennial census counts and are subject to change.

[2] Although arson data are included in the trend and clearance tables, sufficient data are not available to estimate totals for this offense.

[3] Violent crimes are offenses of murder, forcible rape, robbery, and aggravated assault. Property crimes are offenses of burglary, larceny-theft, and motor vehicle theft.

[4] The percentage reported under "Area actually reporting" is based upon the population covered by agencies providing 3 months or more of crime reports to the FBI.

SOURCE: "Table 2: Index of Crime, United States, 2000," *Crime in the United States, 2000: Uniform Crime Reports*, Federal Bureau of Investigation, Washington, DC, 2001

theft, and arson. Arrest statistics include information on many different crimes, such as drug violations, fraud, runaways, and vagrancy. Various trends and patterns can be interpreted from these statistical categories.

Highest Rates in the Cities

While crime is certainly not limited to the cities, it is far more likely to occur in urban areas than in rural areas. In 2000 the Index crime rate in metropolitan statistical areas was 4,428.0 per 100,000 inhabitants. (As defined by the U.S. Census Bureau, a "metropolitan statistical area," or MSA, is an urbanized area including a central city of 50,000 residents or more, or a Census Bureau-defined urbanized area of at least 50,000 inhabitants and a total metropolitan population of 75,000 in New England and at least 100,000 elsewhere.) In cities outside the metropolitan areas (a city or urbanized area not meeting the qualifications for an MSA) the rate was 4,485.0 per 100,000, nearly 2.5 times higher than in rural areas (1,864 per 100,000 inhabitants). (See Table 1.3.) The crime with the greatest disparity between MSAs and rural rates, robbery, occurred about 11 times more often in metropolitan areas than in rural areas. The incidence of motor vehicle theft was about 4 times higher in MSAs than in rural areas.

Crime Index total rates in smaller cities, while just slightly higher than those in metropolitan areas, displayed different characteristics. In 2000 the overall rate of violent crime was higher in metropolitan areas (561.4 per 100,000 residents) than in smaller cities (401.5). In each category of violent crime other than forcible rape, the rate was higher in metropolitan areas. However, the rate of property crime was higher in cities outside metropolitan areas than within metropolitan areas (4,083.5 and 3,866.7 per 100,000, respectively). Among property crimes, larceny-theft occurred at a significantly higher rate in smaller cities (3,125 per 100,000 residents) than in metropolitan areas (2,631.9).

URBAN RATES. According to the Crime Index, the nation's largest cities (over one million in population) reported a 2.6 percent decrease in violent crimes from January to June 2001. By comparison, during that same period, the rate of violent crime was up by 1.9 percent in cities with populations between 100,000 and 249,999. (See Table 1.1.)

In the first six months of 2001, murders were up by 1.8 percent in cities with over one million in population, compared to the same period in 2000. The largest increase in murders during this time was 11.9 percent in cities under 10,000, closely followed by a 10.5 percent increase in murders in cities with between 50,000 and 99,999 in population. In contrast, murders declined by almost 10

FIGURE 1.1

Violent and property crime rates by region, 2000

PER 100,000 INHABITANTS

WEST
3,701.5
520.9
Violent Property

MIDWEST
3,517.2
427.8
Violent Property

NORTHEAST
2,620.9
443.4
Violent Property

SOUTH
4,162.8
580.6
Violent Property

SOURCE: "Figure 2.4: Regional crime rates 2000: violent & property crimes," *Crime in the United States, 2000: Uniform Crime Reports*, Federal Bureau of Investigation, Washington, DC, 2001

TABLE 1.4

Number of arrests by crime, 2000

Total[1, 2]	**13,980,297**	Other assaults	1,312,169	Offenses against the family and children	147,663
		Forgery and counterfeiting	108,654	Driving under the influence	1,471,289
Murder and nonnegligent manslaughter	13,227	Fraud	345,732	Liquor laws	683,124
Forcible rape	27,469	Embezzlement	18,952	Drunkenness	637,554
Robbery	106,130	Stolen property; buying,		Disorderly conduct	638,740
Aggravated assault	478,417	receiving, possessing	118,641	Vagrancy	32,542
Burglary	289,844	Vandalism	281,305	All other offenses	3,710,434
Larceny-theft	1,166,362	Weapons; carrying, possessing, etc.	159,181	Suspicion	5,682
Motor vehicle theft	148,225	Prostitution and commercialized vice	87,620	Curfew and loitering law violations	154,711
Arson	16,530	Sex offenses (except forcible rape		Runaways	141,975
Violent crime[3]	625,132	and prostitution)	93,399		
Property crime[4]	1,620,928	Drug abuse violations	1,579,566		
Crime Index total[5]	2,246,054	Gambling	10,842		

[1] Does not include suspicion.
[2] Because of rounding, the figures may not add to total.
[3] Violent crimes are offenses of murder, forcible rape, robbery, and aggravated assault.
[4] Property crimes are offenses of burglary, larceny-theft, motor vehicle theft, and arson.
[5] Includes arson.

SOURCE: "Table 29: Estimated Arrests, United States, 2000," *Crime in the United States, 2000: Uniform Crime Reports*, Federal Bureau of Investigation, Washington, DC, 2001

percent in cities with populations of between 500,000 and 999,999. The percentage of forcible rapes during the first six months of 2001 was highest in cities under 10,000 in population (4.3 percent), while forcible rapes were down by 8.8 percent in cities of 500,000 to 999,999.

Property crimes such as burglary and motor vehicle theft also declined in large cities of one million or more residents, while rising in smaller cities. The largest increase in burglaries (1.7 percent) occurred in cities with populations between 500,000 and 999,999, closely followed by a 1.4 percent increase in burglaries in cities with under 10,000 residents. Motor vehicle thefts were up by 11.5 percent in cities with populations between 250,000 and 499,000, followed by an increase of 4.9 percent in cities with populations between 100,000 and 249,999, and 4.1 percent in cities with between 10,000 and 24,999 residents.

Regional Differences

Distinct crime patterns are also commonly evident between different regions of the nation. In 2000 the South had the highest crime rates for both violent crimes (580.6 per 100,000 residents) and property crimes (4,162.8 per 100,000). The Northeast had the lowest property crime rate (2,620.9 per 100,000), and the Midwest had the lowest violent crime rate (427.8 per 100,000). (See Figure 1.1.)

ARRESTS

In 2000 law enforcement agencies nationwide made nearly 14 million arrests for all criminal infractions excluding traffic violations. This figure includes all offenses reported by local law enforcement agencies to the FBI, including crimes not counted in the FBI's tabulations on specific crimes. These arrests represent an overall decrease of 2.2 percent from 1999, and a 3.7 percent decrease in arrests for Crime Index offenses. There were 625,132 arrests for Crime Index violent crimes and 1.6 million arrests for Crime Index property crimes in 2000, for a total of 2.2 million arrests. Of the arrests for Crime Index offenses, larceny-theft arrests accounted for the greatest number (1.2 million), followed by aggravated assault (478,417), burglary (289,844) and motor vehicle theft (148,225). Non-Crime Index arrests for drug abuse violations (1.6 million), driving under the influence (1.5 million), and public drunkenness (637, 554) accounted for over one-fourth (26.4 percent) of all arrests in 2000. (See Table 1.4.)

Age

In 2000 arrestees under the age of 25 accounted for 46 percent of persons arrested for all criminal offenses nationwide, and 55.1 percent of persons arrested for Crime Index offenses. (See Table 1.5.) Arrestees under 21 accounted for 32.1 percent of all arrests and 43.1 percent of arrests for Crime Index offenses. Persons under 18 comprised 17.1 percent of all arrests and 27.5 percent of arrests for Crime Index offenses in 2000, while persons under 15 accounted for 5.5 percent of all arrests. Overall, persons in the under-25 age group accounted for 47.5 percent of arrests in the cities and about 41 percent each in suburban counties and rural counties.

In 2000 persons under 25 accounted for 44.4 percent of violent crime arrests and 59.2 percent of property crime arrests. People in this young age group represented a large percentage of those arrested for many crimes:

• Arson (71.6 percent)

TABLE 1.5

Arrests of persons under 15, 18, 21, and 25 years of age, 2000

[9,017 agencies; 2000 estimated population 182,090,101]

Offense charged	Total all ages	Number of persons arrested				Percent of total all ages			
		Under 15	Under 18	Under 21	Under 25	Under 15	Under 18	Under 21	Under 25
TOTAL	9,116,967	498,219	1,560,289	2,927,221	4,196,971	5.5	17.1	32.1	46.0
Murder and nonnegligent manslaughter	8,709	104	806	2,675	4,464	1.2	9.3	30.7	51.3
Forcible rape	17,914	1,142	2,937	5,552	8,139	6.4	16.4	31.0	45.4
Robbery	72,320	4,863	18,288	34,401	45,508	6.7	25.3	47.6	62.9
Aggravated assault	316,630	15,889	43,879	81,125	126,387	5.0	13.9	25.6	39.9
Burglary	189,343	24,152	62,557	98,180	120,863	12.8	33.0	51.9	63.8
Larceny-theft	782,082	97,017	243,723	363,895	445,236	12.4	31.2	46.5	56.9
Motor vehicle theft	98,697	8,680	33,816	52,951	65,642	8.8	34.3	53.7	66.5
Arson	10,675	3,677	5,635	6,838	7,639	34.4	52.8	64.1	71.6
Violent crime[1]	415,573	21,998	65,910	123,753	184,498	5.3	15.9	29.8	44.4
Property crime[2]	1,080,797	133,526	345,731	521,864	639,380	12.4	32.0	48.3	59.2
Crime Index total[3]	1,496,370	155,524	411,641	645,617	823,878	10.4	27.5	43.1	55.1
Other assaults	858,385	66,960	154,914	243,403	356,261	7.8	18.0	28.4	41.5
Forgery and counterfeiting	71,268	527	4,225	15,887	27,984	0.7	5.9	22.3	39.3
Fraud	213,828	1,168	6,645	30,258	64,808	0.5	3.1	14.2	30.3
Embezzlement	12,577	72	1,299	3,971	6,037	0.6	10.3	31.6	48.0
Stolen property; buying, receiving, possessing	78,685	5,239	18,373	34,066	45,457	6.7	23.4	43.3	57.8
Vandalism	184,500	32,672	74,837	105,477	127,196	17.7	40.6	57.2	68.9
Weapons; carrying, possessing, etc.	105,341	8,281	24,877	44,862	62,220	7.9	23.6	42.6	59.1
Prostitution and commercialized vice	61,383	120	924	5,385	12,332	0.2	1.5	8.8	20.1
Sex offenses (except forcible rape and prostitution)	61,172	5,933	11,399	17,658	24,076	9.7	18.6	28.9	39.4
Drug abuse violations	1,042,334	22,237	134,580	335,529	505,057	2.1	12.9	32.2	48.5
Gambling	7,197	183	1,009	2,254	3,456	2.5	14.0	31.3	48.0
Offenses against the family and children	91,297	2,201	5,798	12,326	23,286	2.4	6.4	13.5	25.5
Driving under the influence	915,931	454	13,081	94,608	242,107	[4]	1.4	10.3	26.4
Liquor laws	435,672	10,281	101,637	302,763	334,662	2.4	23.3	69.5	76.8
Drunkenness	423,310	1,855	14,421	52,918	111,223	0.4	3.4	12.5	26.3
Disorderly conduct	421,542	41,381	109,355	172,986	236,540	9.8	25.9	41.0	56.1
Vagrancy	21,988	565	2,036	4,837	7,077	2.6	9.3	22.0	32.2
All other offenses (except traffic)	2,411,162	76,181	269,134	601,714	982,074	3.2	11.2	25.0	40.7
Suspicion	3,704	182	783	1,381	1,919	4.9	21.1	37.3	51.8
Curfew and loitering law violations	105,683	30,045	105,683	105,683	105,683	28.4	100.0	100.0	100.0
Runaways	93,638	36,158	93,638	93,638	93,638	38.6	100.0	100.0	100.0

[1] Violent crimes are offenses of murder, forcible rape, robbery, and aggravated assault.
[2] Property crimes are offenses of burglary, larceny-theft, motor vehicle theft, and arson.
[3] Includes arson.
[4] Less than one-tenth of 1 percent.

SOURCE: "Table 41: Arrests of Persons Under 15, 18, 21, and 25 Years of Age, 2000," *Crime in the United States, 2000: Uniform Crime Reports*, Federal Bureau of Investigation, Washington, DC, 2001

- Burglary (63.8 percent)

- Liquor law violations (76.8 percent)

- Motor vehicle theft (66.5 percent)

- Robbery (62.9 percent)

- Vandalism (68.9 percent)

Arrests of persons under 18 years of age (considered juveniles by most states) fell 4.8 percent from 1999 to 2000, but increased by 3.4 percent from 1991 to 2000. This compares to a slight decline in arrestees over 18 years of age during the same 10-year period. (See Table 1.6.) Drug abuse violations accounted for the largest increase (144.8 percent) in arrests of persons under 18 between 1991 and 2000, followed by an increase of 131.9

percent in under-18 arrests for embezzlement and 81.2 percent for curfew and loitering law violations. Because curfew/loitering and running away are considered status offenses (crimes for juveniles but not for adults), they are not measured for persons over 18 years of age. Despite these increases, Crime Index arrests for juveniles declined. Arrests for violent crimes like murder and rape dropped significantly in this age group (64.6 and 26.4 percent respectively), as did some types of property crime, like motor vehicle theft (50.5 percent).

Gender

In 2000 men were arrested 3.5 times more often than women. Overall, males accounted for about 5.8 million arrests in 2000, compared to 1.6 million arrests of females. However, from 1991 to 2000, the number of

TABLE 1.6

Ten-year arrest trends, 1991–2000

[6,422 agencies; 2000 estimated population 149,828,555; 1991 estimated population 133,490,609]

| | Number of persons arrested | | | | | | | | |
| | Total all ages | | | Under 18 years of age | | | 18 years of age and over | | |
Offense charged	1991	2000	Percent change	1991	2000	Percent change	1991	2000	Percent change
TOTAL[1]	7,394,878	7,412,294	+0.2	1,214,753	1,255,623	+3.4	6,180,125	6,156,671	-0.4
Murder and nonnegligent manslaughter	11,950	7,012	-41.3	1,811	641	-64.6	10,139	6,371	-37.2
Forcible rape	20,716	14,538	-29.8	3,211	2,364	-26.4	17,505	12,174	-30.5
Robbery	88,660	60,812	-31.4	21,504	15,310	-28.8	67,156	45,502	-32.2
Aggravated assault	270,787	265,385	-2.0	37,842	35,307	-6.7	232,945	230,078	-1.2
Burglary	248,292	157,665	-36.5	83,933	52,157	-37.9	164,359	105,508	-35.8
Larceny-theft	879,815	641,370	-27.1	265,806	202,933	-23.7	614,009	438,437	-28.6
Motor vehicle theft	118,867	77,070	-35.2	52,761	26,099	-50.5	66,106	50,971	-22.9
Arson	10,508	8,824	-16.0	5,068	4,712	-7.0	5,440	4,112	-24.4
Violent crime[2]	392,113	347,747	-11.3	64,368	53,622	-16.7	327,745	294,125	-10.3
Property crime[3]	1,257,482	884,929	-29.6	407,568	285,901	-29.9	849,914	599,028	-29.5
Crime Index total[4]	1,649,595	1,232,676	-25.3	471,936	339,523	-28.1	1,177,659	893,153	-24.2
Other assaults	554,987	676,319	+21.9	88,226	120,488	+36.6	466,761	555,831	+19.1
Forgery and counterfeiting	53,853	58,493	+8.6	4,349	3,500	-19.5	49,504	54,993	+11.1
Fraud	188,100	155,231	-17.5	4,891	4,755	-2.8	183,209	150,476	-17.9
Embezzlement	7,458	10,730	+43.9	470	1,090	+131.9	6,988	9,640	+38.0
Stolen property; buying, receiving, possessing	91,166	66,772	-26.8	26,281	15,641	-40.5	64,885	51,131	-21.2
Vandalism	175,632	150,132	-14.5	77,182	60,951	-21.0	98,450	89,181	-9.4
Weapons; carrying, possessing, etc.	125,722	86,620	-31.1	27,360	20,133	-26.4	98,362	66,487	-32.4
Prostitution and commercialized vice	57,335	47,481	-17.2	832	27	-12.6	56,503	46,754	-17.3
Sex offenses (except forcible rape and prostitution)	60,035	51,643	-14.0	10,162	9,707	-4.5	49,873	41,936	-15.9
Drug abuse violations	563,776	842,532	+49.4	43,289	105,993	+144.8	520,487	736,539	+41.5
Gambling	7,124	4,020	-43.6	551	404	-26.7	6,573	3,616	-45.0
Offenses against the family and children	50,869	68,740	+35.1	2,088	4,015	+92.3	48,781	64,725	+32.7
Driving under the influence	971,628	775,392	-20.2	9,563	10,888	+13.9	962,065	764,504	-20.5
Liquor laws	300,147	341,047	+13.6	67,729	81,223	+19.9	232,418	259,824	+11.8
Drunkenness	492,720	358,041	-27.3	12,562	12,151	-3.3	480,158	345,890	-28.0
Disorderly conduct	336,418	295,597	-12.1	58,394	77,396	+32.5	278,024	218,201	-21.5
Vagrancy	23,995	17,008	-29.1	1,937	1,296	-33.1	22,058	15,712	-28.8
All other offenses (except traffic)	1,534,628	2,000,927	+30.4	157,261	212,849	+35.3	1,377,367	1,788,078	+29.8
Suspicion	8,563	2,768	-67.7	2,614	640	-75.5	5,949	2,128	-64.2
Curfew and loitering law violations	50,472	91,453	+81.2	50,472	91,453	+81.2	–	–	–
Runaways	99,218	81,440	-17.9	99,218	81,440	-17.9	–	–	–

[1] Does not include suspicion.
[2] Violent crimes are offenses of murder, forcible rape, robbery, and aggravated assault.
[3] Property crimes are offenses of burglary, larceny-theft, motor vehicle theft, and arson.
[4] Includes arson.

SOURCE: "Table 32: Ten-Year Arrest Trends, Totals 1991–2000," *Crime in the United States, 2000: Uniform Crime Reports*, Federal Bureau of Investigation, Washington, DC, 2001

males arrested for all offenses declined by 3.8 percent, while female arrests for all offenses increased by 17.6 percent. The increase in female arrests was more pronounced among juvenile arrestees. While arrests for males under 18 declined by 3.2 percent, arrests for females under 18 increased by 25.3 percent between 1991 and 2000. (See Table 1.7.)

From 1991 to 2000 drug abuse violations accounted for the largest percentage increase in non-status offense arrests for all males (47.5 percent) and all females (59.2 percent). For males and females under the age of 18, arrests for drug abuse violations between 1991 and 2000 increased by 135.1 percent and 219.7 percent, respectively. Offenses against family and children (domestic violence and child abuse) increased by 93.6 percent for all females

and 24.3 percent for all males between 1991 and 2000. In 2000 men were arrested most often for drug abuse violations (690,873) and driving under the influence (649,243). Women were arrested most often for larceny-theft (231,793), although the number of women arrested for larceny-theft declined by 18.1 percent from 1991 to 2000.

Race and Ethnicity

Although whites are arrested more often in total numbers, African Americans are over-represented in almost all areas of arrests in relation to their proportion of the general population. Hispanics are counted by the government as an ethnic group, not a race, and therefore do not always appear as a separate category in statistics. Hispanics are counted as either white or black, although usually counted

TABLE 1.7

Ten-year arrest trends by gender, 1991–2000

[6,422 agencies; 2000 estimated population 149,828,555; 1991 estimated population 133,490,609]

| | Males | | | | | | Females | | | | | |
| | Total | | | Under 18 | | | Total | | | Under 18 | | |
Offense charged	1991	2000	Percent change	1991	2000	Percent change	1991	2000	Percent change	1991	2000	Percent change
TOTAL[1]	6,000,210	5,771,866	-3.8	934,971	904,927	-3.2	1,394,668	1,640,428	+17.6	279,782	350,696	+25.3
Murder and nonnegligent manslaughter	10,772	6,237	-42.1	1,737	568	-67.3	1,178	775	-34.2	74	73	-1.4
Forcible rape	20,475	14,382	-29.8	3,158	2,335	-26.1	241	156	-35.3	53	29	-45.3
Robbery	81,000	54,624	-32.6	19,712	13,877	-29.6	7,660	6,188	-19.2	1,792	1,433	-20.0
Aggravated assault	234,479	212,297	-9.5	32,165	27,130	-15.7	36,308	53,088	+46.2	5,677	8,177	+44.0
Burglary	224,420	135,735	-39.5	76,452	45,777	-40.1	23,872	21,930	-8.1	7,481	6,380	-14.7
Larceny-theft	596,714	409,577	-31.4	188,274	127,254	-32.4	283,101	231,793	-18.1	77,532	75,679	-2.4
Motor vehicle theft	106,545	64,825	-39.2	46,604	21,651	-53.5	12,322	12,245	-0.6	6,157	4,448	-27.8
Arson	9,161	7,539	-17.7	4,624	4,176	-9.7	1,347	1,285	-4.6	444	536	+20.7
Violent crime[2]	346,726	287,540	-17.1	56,772	43,910	-22.7	45,387	60,207	+32.7	7,596	9,712	+27.9
Property crime[3]	936,840	617,676	-34.1	315,954	198,858	-37.1	320,642	267,253	-16.7	91,614	87,043	-5.0
Crime Index total[4]	1,283,566	905,216	-29.5	372,726	242,768	-34.9	366,029	327,460	-10.5	99,210	96,755	-2.5
Other assaults	462,154	519,812	+12.5	67,254	83,182	+23.7	92,833	156,507	+68.6	20,972	37,306	+77.9
Forgery and counterfeiting	34,813	35,738	+2.7	2,870	2,292	-20.1	19,040	22,755	+19.5	1,479	1,208	-18.3
Fraud	101,764	84,743	-16.7	3,342	3,152	-5.7	86,336	70,488	-18.4	1,549	1,603	+3.5
Embezzlement	4,381	5,300	+21.0	291	557	+91.4	3,077	5,430	+76.5	179	533	+197.8
Stolen property; buying, receiving, possessing	80,275	55,068	-31.4	23,599	13,173	-44.2	10,891	11,704	+7.5	2,682	2,468	-8.0
Vandalism	156,310	126,935	-18.8	70,764	53,400	-24.5	19,322	23,197	+20.1	6,418	7,551	+17.7
Weapons; carrying, possessing, etc.	116,884	79,704	-31.8	25,629	18,099	-29.4	8,838	6,916	-21.7	1,731	2,034	+17.5
Prostitution and commercialized vice	21,901	18,542	-15.3	396	292	-26.3	35,434	28,939	-18.3	436	435	-0.2
Sex offenses (except forcible rape and prostitution)	55,799	47,792	-14.3	9,575	8,986	-6.2	4,236	3,851	-9.1	587	721	+22.8
Drug abuse violations	468,519	690,873	+47.5	38,296	90,032	+135.1	95,257	151,659	+59.2	4,993	15,961	+219.7
Gambling	6,322	3,555	-43.8	531	381	-28.2	802	465	-42.0	20	23	+15.0
Offenses against the family and children	42,901	53,311	+24.3	1,378	2,539	+84.3	7,968	15,429	+93.6	710	1,476	+107.9
Driving under the influence	844,043	649,243	-23.1	8,263	9,050	+9.5	127,585	126,149	-1.1	1,300	1,838	+41.4
Liquor laws	244,596	264,267	+8.0	49,458	55,923	+13.1	55,551	76,780	+38.2	18,271	25,300	+38.5
Drunkenness	442,460	312,278	-29.4	10,616	9,857	-7.1	50,260	45,763	-8.9	1,946	2,294	+17.9
Disorderly conduct	269,039	225,501	-16.2	46,119	55,055	+19.4	67,379	70,096	+4.0	12,275	22,341	+82.0
Vagrancy	20,933	13,403	-36.0	1,674	1,016	-39.3	3,062	3,605	+17.7	263	280	+6.5
All other offenses (except traffic)	1,264,657	1,584,206	+25.3	123,297	158,794	+28.8	269,971	416,721	+54.4	33,964	54,055	+59.2
Suspicion	7,126	2,220	-68.8	2,063	494	-76.1	1,437	548	-61.9	551	146	-73.5
Curfew and loitering law violations	36,947	62,901	+70.2	36,947	62,901	+70.2	13,525	28,552	+111.1	13,525	28,552	+111.1
Runaways	41,946	33,478	-20.2	41,946	33,478	-20.2	57,272	47,962	-16.3	57,272	47,962	-16.3

[1] Does not include suspicion.
[2] Violent crimes are offenses of murder, forcible rape, robbery, and aggravated assault.
[3] Property crimes are offenses of burglary, larceny-theft, motor vehicle theft, and arson.
[4] Includes arson.

SOURCE: "Table 33: Ten-Year Arrest Trends, by Sex, 1991–2000," *Crime in the United States, 2000: Uniform Crime Reports*, Federal Bureau of Investigation, Washington, DC, 2001

as white. Hispanics, like African Americans, are also arrested more often in relation to their proportion of the population than are non-Hispanics.

According to the U.S. Census Bureau, in 2001 whites comprised 77 percent of the population, while African Americans and Hispanics accounted for 12.9 and 12.5 percent respectively. In 2000, of some 9.1 million arrests nationwide, about 69.7 percent of those arrested were white and 27.9 percent were African American. (See Table 1.8.) American Indians and Asians/Pacific Islanders each accounted for another 1.2 percent of arrests. About 49 percent of those arrested for murder were African American, almost the same percent as whites. Sixty-three percent of those arrested for rape

were white, while 34 percent were African American. Similarly, 63.5 percent of those arrested for aggravated assault were white, while 34 percent were African American. Of those arrested for burglary in 2000, 69 percent were white and 28 percent African American. Sixty-seven percent of arrestees for larceny-theft were white, while 30 percent were African American.

Whites were much more likely to be arrested for driving under the influence, other liquor law violations, and running away. American Indians comprised 1.1 percent of all arrests for drunkenness, while Asian or Pacific Islanders accounted for less than 1 percent of such arrests. Driving under the influence accounted for the highest rate of arrests among whites (88.2 percent), while robbery

TABLE 1.8

Number of arrests by race, 2000

[9,017 agencies; 2000 estimated population 182,090,101]

	Total arrests					Percent distribution[1]				
Offense charged	Total	White	Black	American Indian or Alaskan Native	Asian or Pacific Islander	Total	White	Black	American Indian or Alaskan Native	Asian or Pacific Islander
TOTAL	**9,068,977**	**6,324,006**	**2,528,368**	**112,192**	**104,411**	**100.0**	**69.7**	**27.9**	**1.2**	**1.2**
Murder and nonnegligent manslaughter	8,683	4,231	4,238	87	127	100.0	48.7	48.8	1.0	1.5
Forcible rape	17,859	11,381	6,089	197	192	100.0	63.7	34.1	1.1	1.1
Robbery	72,149	31,921	38,897	445	886	100.0	44.2	53.9	0.6	1.2
Aggravated assault	315,729	200,634	107,494	3,542	4,059	100.0	63.5	34.0	1.1	1.3
Burglary	188,726	131,049	53,573	1,787	2,317	100.0	69.4	28.4	0.9	1.2
Larceny-theft	779,166	519,671	236,801	9,916	12,778	100.0	66.7	30.4	1.3	1.6
Motor vehicle theft	98,318	54,490	40,886	1,099	1,843	100.0	55.4	41.6	1.1	1.9
Arson	10,634	8,121	2,305	99	109	100.0	76.4	21.7	0.9	1.0
Violent crime[2]	414,420	248,167	156,718	4,271	5,264	100.0	59.9	37.8	1.0	1.3
Property crime[3]	1,076,844	713,331	333,565	12,901	17,047	100.0	66.2	31.0	1.2	1.6
Crime Index total[4]	1,491,264	961,498	490,283	17,172	22,311	100.0	64.5	32.9	1.2	1.5
Other assaults	855,536	564,571	269,736	11,695	9,534	100.0	66.0	31.5	1.4	1.1
Forgery and counterfeiting	70,828	48,197	21,227	421	983	100.0	68.0	30.0	0.6	1.4
Fraud	211,984	142,684	66,672	1,173	1,455	100.0	67.3	31.5	0.6	0.7
Embezzlement	12,539	7,975	4,281	51	232	100.0	63.6	34.1	0.4	1.9
Stolen property; buying, receiving, possessing	78,429	46,233	30,690	579	927	100.0	58.9	39.1	0.7	1.2
Vandalism	184,010	139,662	39,779	2,573	1,996	100.0	75.9	21.6	1.4	1.1
Weapons; carrying, possessing, etc.	104,996	64,410	38,596	776	1,214	100.0	61.3	36.8	0.7	1.2
Prostitution and commercialized vice	61,347	35,567	24,222	514	1,044	100.0	58.0	39.5	0.8	1.7
Sex offenses (except forcible rape and prostitution)	60,936	45,317	14,149	668	802	100.0	74.4	23.2	1.1	1.3
Drug abuse violations	1,039,086	667,485	358,571	5,547	7,483	100.0	64.2	34.5	0.5	0.7
Gambling	7,149	2,195	4,607	29	318	100.0	30.7	64.4	0.4	4.4
Offenses against the family and children	90,502	61,212	26,805	931	1,554	100.0	67.6	29.6	1.0	1.7
Driving under the influence	900,089	793,696	86,194	11,855	8,344	100.0	88.2	9.6	1.3	0.9
Liquor laws	433,637	371,186	46,107	13,091	3,253	100.0	85.6	10.6	3.0	0.8
Drunkenness	421,859	357,283	57,806	4,633	2,137	100.0	84.7	13.7	1.1	0.5
Disorderly conduct	419,408	273,884	136,573	6,030	2,921	100.0	65.3	32.6	1.4	0.7
Vagrancy	21,967	11,772	9,524	562	109	100.0	53.6	43.4	2.6	0.5
All other offenses (except traffic)	2,400,906	1,579,231	758,669	31,441	31,565	100.0	65.8	31.6	1.3	1.3
Suspicion	3,675	2,535	1,086	11	43	100.0	69.0	29.6	0.3	1.2
Curfew and loitering law violations	105,563	76,233	26,065	1,165	2,100	100.0	72.2	24.7	1.1	2.0
Runaways	93,267	71,180	16,726	1,275	4,086	100.0	76.3	17.9	1.4	4.4

[1] Because of rounding, the percentages may not add to total.
[2] Violent crimes are offenses of murder, forcible rape, robbery, and aggravated assault.
[3] Property crimes are offenses of burglary, larceny-theft, motor vehicle theft, and arson.
[4] Includes arson.

SOURCE: Adapted from "Table 43: Arrests by Race, 2000," *Crime in the United States, 2000: Uniform Crime Reports*, Federal Bureau of Investigation, Washington, DC, 2001

accounted for the highest proportion of arrests among African Americans (53.9 percent). Among American Indians, liquor law violations accounted for the highest proportion of arrests (3 percent of all arrests for this offense). Gambling was the crime for which the most Asians/Pacific Islanders were arrested.

Offenses Cleared by Arrest

The more violent the crime, the more likely it is that a suspect will be arrested. For the crimes reported to law enforcement agencies nationwide in 2000, 63.1 percent of all murders, 56.9 percent of all aggravated assaults, 46.9 percent of forcible rapes, and 25.7 percent of robberies were cleared by arrest. Property crimes, such as larceny-theft (18.2 percent), motor vehicle theft (14.1 percent), and burglary (13.4 percent), were least likely to be cleared by arrest in 2000. (See Figure 1.2.) The fact that a crime is cleared by arrest does not mean that the individual arrested is guilty of the crime or will be convicted of the offense in criminal or juvenile court.

FIGURE 1.2

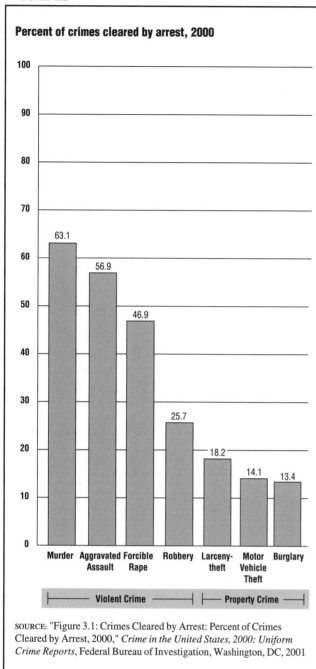

Percent of crimes cleared by arrest, 2000

SOURCE: "Figure 3.1: Crimes Cleared by Arrest: Percent of Crimes Cleared by Arrest, 2000," *Crime in the United States, 2000: Uniform Crime Reports*, Federal Bureau of Investigation, Washington, DC, 2001

THE "TAKE" FROM EACH CRIME

In 2000, the value of the goods taken in the average crime varied. Generally, the value of goods taken is very low compared to the risk and consequences of the crime. The majority of crimes in 2000 netted less than $200. In 37.7 percent of cases the value of the goods taken was under $50 and in 23.4 percent of cases it was between $50 and $200. It was over $200 in 38.9 percent of property crimes. Motor vehicle thefts, which are calculated separately, had the highest average loss of all property crimes in 2000—$6,682—up by 2.1 percent from 1999. The average bank robbery in 2000 netted $4,437, up by 1.4 percent from 1999. Robberies of convenience stores

resulted in an average of $544 taken in 2000. The average burglary in 2000 resulted in a loss of $1,462, while pocket-picking and purse-snatching accounted for losses averaging $408 and $356, respectively. (See Table 1.9.)

When a criminal steals money, as in the case of a bank robber or purse-snatcher, he or she can usually spend the stolen cash. However, in the case of burglary or motor vehicle theft the criminal almost never collects the total value of the stolen property. While the value of the stolen goods in a typical burglary might be $1,462, the thief has no way to sell it for its real value. He or she usually takes it to a fence (a person who buys and sells stolen goods). The fence may pay as little as 10 percent of the value of the item or items, depending on how easily he or she feels it will be to find a buyer for the stolen property. Thus, a $400 VCR could be worth as little as $40 to the thief.

Studies in 1996 showed the "take" from a murder ($125) or rape ($25) is far below other crimes, since stealing is not usually the primary objective of these types of crime. Taking money or property is an afterthought, and the 2000 study assigned no monetary value to these crimes.

Recovery Rate

In 2000 only 34.8 percent of the value of stolen property was recovered. The recovered value of motor vehicles in 2000 was highest, at 62.2 percent, followed by clothing and furs (13.5 percent), consumable goods (13 percent), and firearms (9.3 percent). Recovery rates for jewelry, precious metals, and office equipment averaged around 5 percent in 2000, while theft victims recovered televisions, stereos, and other electronics only 4.1 percent of the time. (See Table 1.10.)

THE FEDERAL GOVERNMENT'S ROLE

Federal spending accounts for only about 10 percent of all law enforcement resources. State and local governments have always played the central role in controlling crime. The federal government is required to enforce only laws within its jurisdiction, such as forgery and espionage, and to operate prisons for those convicted of federal crimes. Yet the federal government at times has responded to increased public concern over violent crime (like after the terrorist attacks on the Pentagon and the World Trade Center in New York on September 11, 2001) by expanding its law enforcement role. Federal agencies can encourage cooperation among state and local governments and act with foreign governments to curb threats such as the spread of terrorism, drug-related crime, and organized crime. The federal government is better able than the states to collect national crime statistics and give out information. It also develops and promotes new technologies, such as crime databases, fingerprint facilities, and DNA-testing laboratories, to serve both national and local needs.

TABLE 1.9

Number of crimes, 2000, and percent change between 1999 and 2000

[11,084 agencies; 2000 estimated population 217,569,490]

Classification	Number of offenses 2000	Percent change over 1999	Percent distribution[1]	Average value
Murder	11,171	+0.2	–	
Forcible rape	68,158	+0.8	–	
Robbery:				
Total	286,150	-0.1	100.0	$1,170
Street/highway	131,657	-3.6	46.0	879
Commercial house	39,782	-0.2	13.9	1,705
Gas or service station	8,192	+11.3	2.9	693
Convenience store	18,351	+2.0	6.4	544
Residence	34,868	+2.0	12.2	1,358
Bank	6,026	+1.4	2.1	4,437
Miscellaneous	47,274	+6.1	16.5	1,298
Burglary:				
Total	1,572,093	-2.5	100.0	1,462
Residence (dwelling):	1,023,673	-3.9	65.1	1,381
Night	306,104	-2.6	19.5	1,154
Day	472,825	-2.6	30.1	1,453
Unknown	244,744	-7.8	15.6	1,524
Nonresidence (store, office, etc.):	548,420	+0.3	34.9	1,615
Night	229,770	-0.9	14.6	1,404
Day	168,676	+4.4	10.7	1,641
Unknown	149,974	-2.2	9.5	1,907
Larceny-theft (except motor vehicle theft):				
Total	5,267,454	-0.3	100.0	735
By type:				
Pocket-picking	26,921	-2.0	0.5	408
Purse-snatching	28,093	-1.1	0.5	356
Shoplifting	725,059	-5.0	13.8	181
From motor vehicles (except accessories)	1,326,444	-0.5	25.2	712
Motor vehicle accessories	512,110	-3.5	9.7	445
Bicycles	236,004	-8.9	4.5	276
From buildings	690,793	+0.2	13.1	1,176
From coin-operated machines	34,535	-2.6	0.7	500
All others	1,687,495	+4.6	32.0	977
By value:				
Over $200	2,049,910	-0.1	38.9	1,793
$50 to $200	1,231,950	-0.8	23.4	124
Under $50	1,985,594	[2]	37.7	21
Motor vehicle theft	877,513	+2.1	–	6,682

[1] Because of rounding, the percentages may not add to total.
[2] Less than one-tenth of 1 percent.

SOURCE: "Table 23: Offense Analysis: Number and Percent Change, 1999–2000," *Crime in the United States, 2000: Uniform Crime Reports*, Federal Bureau of Investigation, Washington, DC, 2001

Nonetheless, the Federal Budget for fiscal year 2002 allocated a proposed $4.2 billion to assist state and local governments in fighting crime. Although this level of spending was $1 billion less than in fiscal year 2001, federal assistance to state and local governments for criminal justice expenditures increased by 500 percent from 1992 to 2001.

Proposed Federal Budget

Of the nearly $30 billion in the Federal budget proposed for administration of justice in fiscal year 2002, nearly half was allocated for law enforcement. (See Figure 1.3.) Some of the highlights of the proposed FY 2002 budget included:

- $902 million allocated to prevent, mitigate, and investigate acts of terrorism.

- 570 new border patrol agents.

- Additional funding to reduce the incidence of violent crime, with an emphasis on dismantling violent gangs.

- $5 million to evaluate the effectiveness of faith-based prison pre-release programs in reducing the recidivism rate.

- $154 million to assist state and local governments in protecting youth from gun violence.

TABLE 1.10

Property stolen and recovered by type and value, 2000

[10,567 agencies; 2000 estimated population 209,155,140]

Type of property	Value of property		Percent recovered
	Stolen	Recovered	
Total	$11,905,789,142	$4,141,042,418	34.8
Currency, notes, etc.	785,032,155	43,751,660	5.6
Jewelry and precious metals	894,164,680	55,938,661	6.3
Clothing and furs	210,943,777	28,375,547	13.5
Locally stolen motor vehicles	5,746,074,858	3,572,319,332	62.2
Office equipment	413,338,013	22,114,063	5.4
Televisions, radios, stereos, etc.	799,413,419	32,700,712	4.1
Firearms	80,496,218	7,447,121	9.3
Household goods	197,503,939	10,796,021	5.5
Consumable goods	98,035,074	12,710,464	13.0
Livestock	32,086,625	1,871,155	5.8
Miscellaneous	2,648,700,384	353,017,682	13.3

SOURCE: "Table 24: Property Stolen and Recovered, by Type and Value, 2000," *Crime in the United States, 2000: Uniform Crime Reports*, Federal Bureau of Investigation, Washington, DC, 2001

The administration's 2002 budget also proposed $1 billion in new funding for prison construction, modernization, and the activation of newly-constructed federal prisons. See Table 1.11 for a detailed look at the allocation of Office of Justice Programs' funds from 1990 to 2001, which shows that budget requests for 2001 were about 5.5 times those for 1990. Spending by Federal criminal justice budget authorities is expected to increase from some $26.7 billion in 2000 (actual dollars) to a projected $37.7 billion by 2006. (See Table 1.12.)

Violent Crime Control and Law Enforcement Act of 1994

The Violent Crime Control and Law Enforcement Act of 1994 (PL 103-322) included several "get tough on crime" provisions:

• A ban on some semiautomatic assault-style rifles.

• A "three strikes and you're out" provision. This provision requires a mandatory life sentence without parole when an offender has been convicted of at least three serious or violent felony crimes and/or serious or violent drug-related crimes.

• Resources for more police, and grants to help involve community organizations in crime prevention programs.

The act also expanded the federal death penalty to apply to more than 50 offenses and provided funding for prison construction projects. A new trust fund—the Violent Crime Reduction Trust Fund—supported these new programs.

VIOLENCE AGAINST WOMEN. As part of the Violent Crime Reduction Trust Fund, the 2001 Federal budget proposed some $274 million to support various programs created by the Violence Against Women Act (PL 103-322). The largest portion of that amount ($209.7 million) was allocated for grants to assist the states in the apprehension and prosecution of offenders.

STATE CORRECTIONS BUDGETS

According to the National Association of State Budget Officers, total state spending for corrections in fiscal year 2000 was $36.1 billion, an increase of some 6.1 percent from FY 1999. Corrections accounted for about 7 percent of all state general-fund spending in 2000. Despite a declining crime rate, the rise in state prison populations accounted for much of the increase from 1999 to 2000, with about $2 billion allocated for the construction of new correctional facilities.

States in New England had the largest increase in spending for corrections in 2000, at 12.6 percent, followed by the Mid-Atlantic states and Rocky Mountain states (10.4 percent each). States in the Southeast spent only 2.4 percent more on corrections in FY 2000 than in FY 1999.

FIGURE 1.3

Federal justice expenditures, 1992–2002

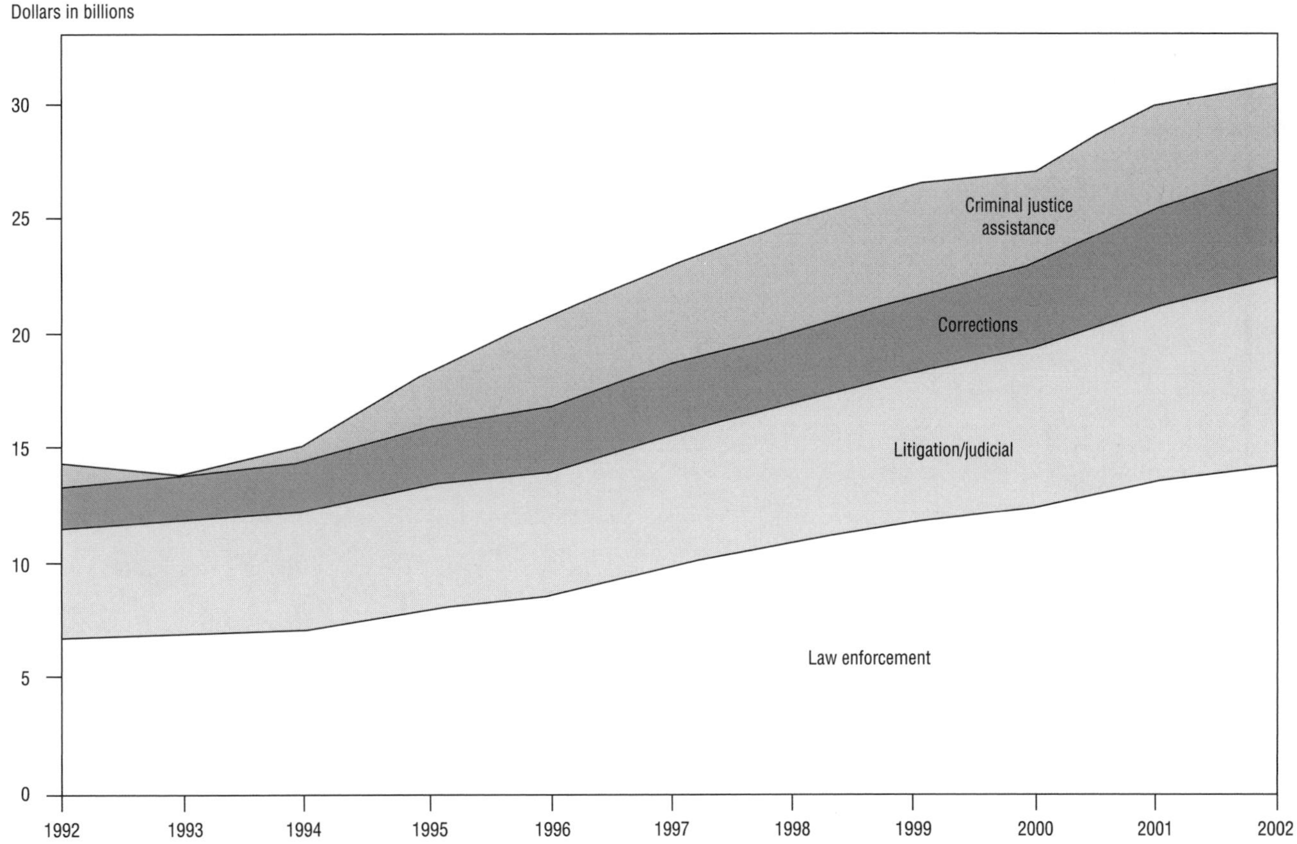
Dollars in billions
30
25
20
15
10
5
0
1992
1993
1994
1995
1996
1997
1998
1999
2000
2001
2002
Criminal justice assistance
Corrections
Litigation/judicial
Law enforcement

Note: Data includes discretionary expenditures only.

SOURCE: "Chart 17-2. Federal Justice Expenditures," in *Budget of the United States, Fiscal Year 2002,* Office of Management and Budget, The White House, Washington, DC, 2002

TABLE 1.11

Allocation of Office of Justice programs' funds by type of justice activity, fiscal years 1990–2001[a]

In thousands of dollars

Type of budget activity	1990[b]	1991[b]	1992	1993	1994	1995	1996	1997	1998[c]	1999[c]	2000[c]	2001[d]
Total	**$762,358**	**$845,021**	**$865,689**	**$997,023**	**$848,960**	**$1,267,660**	**$2,702,011**	**$3,251,347**	**$3,733,066**	**$3,743,045**	**$3,919,611**	**$4,175,721**
Executive direction and control	24,240	25,169	26,641[e]	27,219	29,600	31,702	28,696	30,579	35,039	38,103	44,103	47,728
Research, evaluation, and demonstration programs	22,766	23,929	23,739	22,995	22,500	27,000	30,000	30,000	41,148	46,148	43,448	69,846
Justice statistical programs	20,879	22,095	22,095	21,373	20,943	21,379	21,379	21,379	21,529	25,029	25,505	28,991
State and local assistance programs												
Alcohol and crime in Indian country	NA	NA	NA	NA	NA	NA	NA	NA	NA	NA	NA	4,989
Anti-drug abuse formula (Byrne grants)	395,101	423,000	423,000	423,000	358,000	450,000	475,000	500,000	505,000	505,000	500,000	498,900
Anti-drug abuse discretionary	49,636	66,994	73,500	223,000[f]	116,500	62,000	60,000	60,000	46,500	47,000	52,000	78,377
Counterterrorism	NA	NA	NA	NA	0	NA	NA	17,000	19,000	0	152,000	220,494
Criminal records upgrade	NA	NA	NA	NA	0	100,000	25,000	50,000	45,000	45,000	0	0
DNA identification State grants	NA	NA	NA	NA	NA	NA	1,000	3,000	12,500	15,000	0	0
Drug courts	NA	NA	NA	NA	NA	11,900	0	30,000	30,000	40,000	40,000	49,890
Family support	NA	NA	NA	NA	NA	NA	1,000	1,000	1,000	1,500	1,500	1,497
Indian tribal courts program	NA	NA	NA	NA	NA	NA	NA	NA	NA	5,000	5,000	7,982
Law enforcement block grants	NA	NA	NA	NA	NA	NA	503,000	523,000	523,000	523,000	497,885[g]	521,849
Motor vehicle theft prevention	NA	NA	NA	NA	NA	NA	500	750	750	1,300	1,300	1,297
Public Safety Officers' Benefits Program	24,818	26,075	27,144	28,524	30,821	29,717	30,608	32,276	33,003	31,809	32,541	35,619
Regional Information Sharing System[h]	13,402	14,000	14,500	14,491	14,491	14,500	14,500	14,500	20,000	20,000	20,000	24,945
State and local correctional facilities grants	NA	NA	NA	NA	0	24,500	617,500	670,000	720,500	720,500	653,533[g]	684,990
State criminal alien assistance program	NA	NA	NA	NA	NA	130,000	300,000	330,000	420,000	420,000	420,000	399,120
State prison drug treatment	NA	NA	NA	NA	NA	NA	27,000	30,000	63,000	63,000	63,000	62,861
Telemarketing fraud prevention	NA	NA	NA	NA	NA	NA	NA	2,000	2,500	2,000	2,000	1,996
Televised testimony of child abuse victims	NA	NA	1,000	0	0	0	50	550	1,000	1,000	1,000	998
Weed and Seed program	NA	NA	NA	NA	NA	NA	NA	0	33,500	33,500	33,500	33,925
White Collar Crime Information Center[i]	NA	NA	NA	NA	0	1,400	3,850	3,850	5,350	7,350	9,250	9,230
Juvenile justice programs												
Block grants	NA	NA	NA	NA	NA	NA	NA	0	250,000	250,000	237,994[g]	249,450
Child abuse investigation and prosecution	NA	NA	1,500	1,500	3,000	4,500	4,500	4,500	7,000	7,000	7,000	8,481
Court appointed special advocates	NA	NA	NA	NA	4,500	6,000	6,000	6,000	7,000	9,000	10,000	11,475
Judicial child abuse training	NA	NA	500	500	500	750	750	1,000	2,000	2,000	2,000	1,996
Juvenile justice discretionary programs	21,044	22,796	22,823[e]	23,372[e]	44,640	70,600	70,600	80,100	130,850	193,394	196,910	207,452
Juvenile justice formula grants	48,361	49,255	49,733[e]	50,078	58,310	68,600	68,600	85,100	95,100	77,556	76,540	76,372
Missing Alzheimer's program	NA	NA	NA	NA	NA	NA	900	900	900	900	900	898
Missing children	3,971	7,971	8,471	8,471	6,621	6,721	5,971	5,971	12,256	17,168	19,952	22,997

TABLE 1.11

Allocation of Office of Justice programs' funds by type of justice activity, fiscal years 1990–2001[a] [CONTINUED]

In thousands of dollars

Type of budget activity	1990[b]	1991[b]	1992	1993	1994	1995	1996	1997	1998[c]	1999[c]	2000[c]	2001[d]
Violence against women programs												
Encouraging arrest policies	NA	NA	NA	NA	NA	NA	28,000	33,000	59,000	34,000	34,000	33,925
Law enforcement and prosecution grants	NA	NA	NA	NA	NA	26,000	130,000	145,000	172,000	206,750	206,750	209,717
Rural domestic violence and child abuse enforcement	NA	NA	NA	NA	NA	NA	7,000	8,000	25,000	25,000	25,000	24,945
Violence against women training programs	NA	NA	NA	NA	NA	NA	1,000	1,000	2,000	5,000	5,000	4,989
Crime Victims Fund[l]	123,250	126,750	127,968	150,000	138,534	178,891	227,707	528,942	362,891	324,038	500,000[k]	537,500[l]
Programs previously funded by OJP[m]												
Emergency assistance[n]	9,927	0	1,000	0	0	0	0	0	0	0	0	0
High intensity drug trafficking areas[o]	NA	32,024	37,110	0	0	0	0	0	0	0	0	0
Mariel Cuban[p]	4,963	4,963	4,963	2,500	0	0	0	0	0	0	0	0
Other Crime Bill programs	NA	NA	NA	NA	NA	1,500	11,900	1,950	27,750	0	0	0

[a] Detail may not add to total because of rounding.
[b] Includes effect of Gramm-Rudman-Hollings reductions.
[c] Appropriations.
[d] Includes rescission per Public Law 106-554.
[e] Reflects the total program level, which includes unused carryover earmarked by Congress for addition to appropriated amount.
[f] Includes $150 million supplemental appropriation for the Police Hiring Program.
[g] Includes rescission per Public Law 106-113.
[h] A program to aid State and local law enforcement agencies in the exchange of intelligence information.
[i] This previously was part of the Regional Information Sharing System.
[j] Represents amount deposited in previous year.
[k] Collections totaled $985.2 million, however, an obligation limitation of $500 million was placed on total collections.
[l] Collections totaled $777 million, however, an obligation limitation of $537.5 million was placed on total availability.
[m] Previously funded OJP programs may still be operational for either of the following reasons: (1) the program may be operating on funds appropriated in prior fiscal years; (2) the program may be subsumed under another program that is currently funded.
[n] A program authorized to provide funds, equipment, intelligence information, and/or personnel to a requesting State in the event of a law enforcement emergency.
[o] Funds transferred from the Office of National Drug Control Policy.
[p] Refers to an appropriation to be allocated to States housing Mariel Cuban refugees in State correctional facilities.

SOURCE: "Table 1.11. Allocation of Office of Justice Programs' funds," in *Sourcebook of Criminal Justice Statistics 2000*, U.S. Department of Justice, Bureau of Justice Statistics, Washington, DC, 2001

TABLE 1.12

Federal criminal justice budget authorities, 2000 (actual) and 2001–06 (estimated)

(In millions of dollars)

Type of program	2000 actual	Estimated					
		2001	2002	2003	2004	2005	2006
Total[1]	**$26,730**	**$30,379**	**$32,836**	**$32,585**	**$35,423**	**$36,539**	**$37,726**
Discretionary, total	27,056	29,955	31,031	31,994	33,038	34,114	35,234
Federal law enforcement activities, total	12,437	13,607	14,179	14,661	15,191	15,737	16,307
Criminal investigations[2]	4,467	4,600	4,810	4,983	5,171	5,367	5,572
Bureau of Alcohol, Tobacco and Firearms	564	771	805	832	863	895	928
Border enforcement activities[3]	4,898	5,540	5,764	5,954	6,162	6,378	6,603
Equal Employment Opportunity Commission	281	303	317	328	340	353	366
Tax law, criminal investigations[4]	379	374	394	409	428	446	465
Other law enforcement activities	1,848	2,019	2,089	2,155	2,227	2,298	2,373
Federal litigative and judicial activities, total	6,896	7,434	7,672	7,908	8,160	8,422	8,696
Civil and criminal prosecution and representation	2,788	2,974	3,067	3,170	3,278	3,392	3,513
Representation of indigents in civil cases	304	329	336	343	350	358	365
Federal judicial and other litigative activities	3,804	4,131	4,269	4,395	4,532	4,672	4,818
Correctional activities[5]	3,670	4,307	4,475	4,620	4,779	4,943	5,112
Criminal justice assistance[6]	4,053	4,607	4,705	4,805	4,908	5,012	5,119
Mandatory, total	-326	424	1,805	591	2,385	2,425	2,492
Federal law enforcement activities, total	-301	-614	-346	-360	1,419	1,444	1,496
Assets Forfeiture Fund	480	377	337	344	351	359	366
Border enforcement activities[3]	1,568	2,061	2,412	2,354	2,241	2,249	2,286
Immigration and Naturalization Service fees	-1,483	-2,262	-2,240	-2,176	-1,686	-1,681	-1,676
Customs fees	-1,282	-1,303	-1,343	-1,395	-3	-3	-3
Other mandatory law enforcement programs	416	513	488	513	516	520	523
Federal litigative and judicial activities[7]	468	491	538	521	535	551	565
Correctional activities	-3	-3	-3	-4	-4	-5	-5
Criminal justice assistance, total	-490	550	1,616	434	435	435	436
Crime victims' fund	-523	517	1,583	400	400	400	400
Public safety officers' benefits	33	33	33	34	35	35	36

Note: These data are from the budget submitted by the President to Congress in 2001. The "budget authority" (actual or estimated) is the authority becoming available during the year to enter into obligations that will result in immediate or future outlays of Government funds. Spending is divided into two categories: discretionary spending and mandatory (direct) spending. Discretionary spending is controlled through the annual appropriations process and includes items such as funding for salaries and other operating expenses of Government agencies. Mandatory spending is controlled by authorizing legislation; the major entitlement programs such as Social Security, Medicare and Medicaid payments, unemployment insurance benefits, and farm price supports are examples of mandatory spending because payments for these programs are authorized in permanent laws. The negative figures appearing in the table represent Governmental receipts and collections such as court fines, customs duties, certain licensing fees, and various other collections from the public. These figures are deducted from the gross budget authority.

[1] Detail may not add to total because of rounding.
[2] Includes Drug Enforcement Administration, Federal Bureau of Investigation, Financial Crimes Enforcement Network, and interagency crime and drug enforcement programs.
[3] Includes U.S. Customs Service and Immigration and Naturalization Service.
[4] Internal Revenue Service.
[5] Federal prison system and detention trustee program.
[6] Law enforcement assistance, community policing, and other justice programs.
[7] Federal judicial officers' salaries and expenses, and other mandatory programs.

SOURCE: "Table 1.10: Federal criminal justice budget authorities," *Sourcebook of Criminal Justice Statistics 2000*, U.S. Department of Justice, Bureau of Justice Statistics, Washington, DC, 2001

CHAPTER 2
TYPES OF CRIME

In 2000 one Crime Index offense was committed every 2.7 seconds in the United States. Property crimes were committed more frequently (one every 3.1 seconds) than violent crimes (one every 22.1 seconds), down from one every 19 seconds in 1996. The Crime Clock does not imply these crimes were committed with regularity; instead it represents the relative frequency of occurrence. Note this frequency of occurrence does not take into account population increases, as does the per capita crime rate.

The Federal Bureau of Investigation (FBI), in its annual *Crime in the United States* report, publishes data for serious crimes in the Crime Index. The Index includes murder, rape, robbery, aggravated assault, burglary, larceny-theft, motor vehicle theft, and arson.

Although the number of crimes in the United States in 2000 remained high, at over 11 million, the total of Crime Index offenses remained relatively unchanged from 1999, declining slightly by 0.2 percent. Violent crimes comprised 12.3 percent of all Crime Index offenses in 2000, while property crimes accounted for 87.7 percent. Larceny-theft (a property crime) was the offense most often reported to law enforcement, while murder was reported least often in 2000. (See Figure 2.1.)

FIGURE 2.1

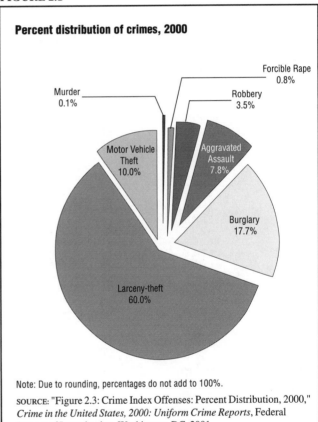

Note: Due to rounding, percentages do not add to 100%.

SOURCE: "Figure 2.3: Crime Index Offenses: Percent Distribution, 2000," *Crime in the United States, 2000: Uniform Crime Reports*, Federal Bureau of Investigation, Washington, DC, 2001

MURDER

The FBI defines murder and non-negligent manslaughter as "the willful (non-negligent) killing of one human being by another." The figures do not include suicides, accidents, or justifiable homicides either by citizens or law enforcement officers. In 2000 a murder was committed every 33.9 minutes, at a rate of 5.5 murders for every 100,000 inhabitants, the lowest rate since 1965. In 2000, murders were most likely to occur in July and least likely to occur in February.

Murder Rate Decline

The total of homicides in 2000 was 15,517, compared to 15,522 in 1999. (See Table 2.1.) The difference between 1999 and 2000 is statistically insignificant and represents the first year since 1993 when there has not been a measurable decline in homicides compared to the previous year. Murder and non-negligent manslaughter declined by 21 percent from 1996 to 2000, and by 37.2 percent from 1991, when a peak of 24,703 offenses were committed.

TABLE 2.1

Index of crime, 1981–2000

Population[1]	Crime Index total	Modified Crime Index total[2]	Violent crime[3]	Property crime[3]	Murder and non-negligent man-slaughter	Forcible rape	Robbery	Aggravated assault	Burglary	Larceny-theft	Motor vehicle theft	Arson[2]
					Number of Offenses							
Population by year:												
1981-229,465,714	13,423,800		1,361,820	12,061,900	22,520	82,500	592,910	663,900	3,779,700	7,194,400	1,087,800	
1982-231,664,458	12,974,400		1,322,390	11,652,000	21,010	78,770	553,130	669,480	3,447,100	7,142,500	1,062,400	
1983-233,791,994	12,108,630		1,258,087	10,850,543	19,308	78,918	506,567	653,294	3,129,851	6,712,759	1,007,933	
1984-235,824,902	11,881,755		1,273,282	10,608,473	18,692	84,233	485,008	685,349	2,984,434	6,591,874	1,032,165	
1985-237,923,795	12,430,357		1,327,767	11,102,590	18,976	87,671	497,874	723,246	3,073,348	6,926,380	1,102,862	
1986-240,132,887	13,211,869		1,489,169	11,722,700	20,613	91,459	542,775	834,322	3,241,410	7,257,153	1,224,137	
1987-242,288,918	13,508,708		1,483,999	12,024,709	20,096	91,111	517,704	855,088	3,236,184	7,499,851	1,288,674	
1988-244,498,982	13,923,086		1,566,221	12,356,865	20,675	92,486	542,968	910,092	3,218,077	7,705,872	1,432,916	
1989-246,819,230	14,251,449		1,646,037	12,605,412	21,500	94,504	578,326	951,707	3,168,170	7,872,442	1,564,800	
1990-249,464,396	14,475,613		1,820,127	12,655,486	23,438	102,555	639,271	1,054,863	3,073,909	7,945,670	1,635,907	
1991-252,153,092	14,872,883		1,911,767	12,961,116	24,703	106,593	687,732	1,092,739	3,157,150	8,142,228	1,661,738	
1992-255,029,699	14,438,191		1,932,274	12,505,917	23,760	109,062	672,478	1,126,974	2,979,884	7,915,199	1,610,834	
1993-257,782,608	14,144,794		1,926,017	12,218,777	24,526	106,014	659,870	1,135,607	2,834,808	7,820,909	1,563,060	
1994-260,327,021	13,989,543		1,857,670	12,131,873	23,326	102,216	618,949	1,113,179	2,712,774	7,879,812	1,539,287	
1995-262,803,276	13,862,727		1,798,792	12,063,935	21,606	97,470	580,509	1,099,207	2,593,784	7,997,710	1,472,441	
1996-265,228,572	13,493,863		1,688,540	11,805,323	19,645	96,252	535,594	1,037,049	2,506,400	7,904,685	1,394,238	
1997-267,783,607	13,194,571		1,636,096	11,558,475	18,208	96,153	498,534	1,023,201	2,460,526	7,743,760	1,354,189	
1998-270,248,003	12,485,714		1,533,887	10,951,827	16,974	93,144	447,186	976,583	2,332,735	7,376,311	1,242,781	
1999-272,690,813	11,634,378		1,426,044	10,208,334	15,522	89,411	409,371	911,740	2,100,739	6,955,520	1,152,075	
2000-281,421,906	11,605,751		1,424,289	10,181,462	15,517	90,186	407,842	910,744	2,049,946	6,965,957	1,165,559	
Percent change, number of offenses:												
2000/1999	-0.2		-0.1	-0.3	[4]	+0.9	-0.4	-0.1	-2.4	+0.2	+1.2	
2000/1996	-14.0		-15.6	-13.8	-21.0	-6.3	-23.9	-12.2	-18.2	-11.9	-16.4	
2000/1991	-22.0		-25.5	-21.4	-37.2	-15.4	-40.7	-16.7	-35.1	-14.4	-29.9	
					Rate per 100,000 Inhabitants							
Year:												
1981	5,850.0		593.5	5,256.5	9.8	36.0	258.4	289.3	1,647.2	3,135.3	474.1	
1982	5,600.5		570.8	5,029.7	9.1	34.0	238.8	289.0	1,488.0	3,083.1	458.6	
1983	5,179.2		538.1	4,641.1	8.3	33.8	216.7	279.4	1,338.7	2,871.3	431.1	
1984	5,038.4		539.9	4,498.5	7.9	35.7	205.7	290.6	1,265.5	2,795.2	437.7	
1985	5,224.5		558.1	4,666.4	8.0	36.8	209.3	304.0	1,291.7	2,911.2	463.5	
1986	5,501.9		620.1	4,881.8	8.6	38.1	226.0	347.4	1,349.8	3,022.1	509.8	
1987	5,575.5		612.5	4,963.0	8.3	37.6	213.7	352.9	1,335.7	3,095.4	531.9	
1988	5,694.5		640.6	5,054.0	8.5	37.8	222.1	372.2	1,316.2	3,151.7	586.1	
1989	5,774.0		666.9	5,107.1	8.7	38.3	234.3	385.6	1,283.6	3,189.6	634.0	
1990	5,802.7		729.6	5,073.1	9.4	41.1	256.3	422.9	1,232.2	3,185.1	655.8	
1991	5,898.4		758.2	5,140.2	9.8	42.3	272.7	433.4	1,252.1	3,229.1	659.0	
1992	5,661.4		757.7	4,903.7	9.3	42.8	263.7	441.9	1,168.4	3,103.6	631.6	
1993	5,487.1		747.1	4,740.0	9.5	41.1	256.0	440.5	1,099.7	3,033.9	606.3	
1994	5,373.8		713.6	4,660.2	9.0	39.3	237.8	427.6	1,042.1	3,026.9	591.3	
1995	5,274.9		684.5	4,590.5	8.2	37.1	220.9	418.3	987.0	3,043.2	560.3	
1996	5,087.6		636.6	4,451.0	7.4	36.3	201.9	391.0	945.0	2,980.3	525.7	
1997	4,927.3		611.0	4,316.3	6.8	35.9	186.2	382.1	918.8	2,891.8	505.7	
1998	4,620.1		567.6	4,052.5	6.3	34.5	165.5	361.4	863.2	2,729.5	459.9	
1999	4,266.5		523.0	3,743.6	5.7	32.8	150.1	334.3	770.4	2,550.7	422.5	
2000	4,124.0		506.1	3,617.9	5.5	32.0	144.9	323.6	728.4	2,475.3	414.2	
Percent change, rate per 100,000 inhabitants:												
2000/1999	-3.3		-3.2	-3.4	-3.1	-2.3	-3.5	-3.2	-5.4	-3.0	-2.0	
2000/1996	-18.9		-20.5	-18.7	-25.6	-11.7	-28.2	-17.2	-22.9	-16.9	-21.2	
2000/1991	-30.1		-33.2	-29.6	-43.7	-24.2	-46.9	-25.3	-41.8	-23.3	-37.2	

[1] Populations are Bureau of the Census provisional estimates as of July 1 for each year except 1990 and 2000 which are the decennial census counts. The 1981 through 1999 population and Crime Index offense and rate counts have been adjusted.
[2] Although arson data are included in the trend and clearance tables, sufficient data are not available to estimate totals for this offense.
[3] Violent crimes are offenses of murder, forcible rape, robbery, and aggravated assault. Property crimes are offenses of burglary, larceny-theft, and motor vehicle theft.
[4] Less than one-tenth of 1 percent.

SOURCE: "Table 1: Index of Crime, United States, 1981–2000," *Crime in the United States, 2000: Uniform Crime Reports*, Federal Bureau of Investigation, Washington, DC, 2001

TABLE 2.2

Offense and population distribution by region, 2000

Region	Population	Crime Index total	Modified Crime Index total[1]	Violent crime[2]	Property crime[2]	Murder and non-negligent man-slaughter	Forcible rape	Robbery	Aggravated assault	Burglary	Larceny-theft	Motor vehicle theft	Arson[1]
United States Total[3]	100.0	100.0		100.0	100.0	100.0	100.0	100.0	100.0	100.0	100.0	100.0	
Northeastern States	19.0	14.2		16.7	13.8	13.9	13.2	20.5	15.4	12.5	14.0	14.8	
Midwestern States	22.9	21.9		19.3	22.2	21.2	25.0	20.0	18.4	20.8	22.9	20.9	
Southern States	35.6	41.0		40.9	41.0	44.0	38.0	37.4	42.6	44.2	40.9	35.9	
Western States	22.5	23.0		23.1	23.0	21.0	23.8	22.0	23.6	22.5	22.2	28.4	

[1] Although arson data are included in the trend and clearance tables, sufficient data are not available to estimate totals for this offense.
[2] Violent crimes are offenses of murder, forcible rape, robbery, and aggravated assault. Property crimes are offenses of burglary, larceny-theft, and motor vehicle theft.
[3] Because of rounding, the percentages may not add to total.

SOURCE: "Table 3: Index of Crime Analysis, Offense and Population Distribution by Region, 2000," *Crime in the United States, 2000: Uniform Crime Reports*, Federal Bureau of Investigation, Washington, DC, 2001

Murder Rate by Area

The South, the nation's most populous region, had the highest incidence of murder in 2000, accounting for 44 percent of all homicides in the United States. Midwestern states were next, at 21.2 percent, followed by the West at 21 percent, and the Northeast at 13.9 percent. (See Table 2.2.) These proportions are nearly identical to 1998 figures, when 44 percent of murders in the nation occurred in the South, 22 percent occurred in Western states, 21 percent occurred in Midwestern states and 13 percent were in Northeastern states.

In 2000 metropolitan areas reported a murder rate of 5.9 victims per 100,000 population, down from 6.7 victims per 100,000 persons in 1998. (As defined by the U.S. Census Bureau, a "metropolitan statistical area," or MSA, is an urbanized area including a central city of 50,000 residents or more, or a Census Bureau-defined urbanized area of at least 50,000 inhabitants and a total metropolitan population of 75,000 in New England and at least 100,000 elsewhere.) Rates for murder in 2000 were almost equal in cities outside metropolitan areas and in rural counties, at 3.8 victims per 100,000 population.

Sex, Race, and Age

In 2000 about two-thirds of the accused murder offenders were reported to be male (65.1 percent), though in 27.9 percent of cases, the sex of the offender was not given. (See Table 2.3.) Of 14,697 murder offenders, 3,134 males and 242 females were under the age of 22, while 751 males and 81 females were under the age of 18. Of murder offenders in 2000 for whom race was known, 36.5 percent were black, 32.7 percent were white, and 1.8 percent were of other racial origins. The remainder were persons of unknown races.

The offender and the victim were usually of the same race. Of 3,352 white murder victims, 2,860 were killed by white offenders in 2000. Similarly, of 2,927 black victims of homicide, almost all (2,723) were killed by black offenders. (See Table 2.4.) Males and females were the victims of male offenders in most cases, though female murder offenders were more likely to kill males than females in 2000.

Murder Circumstances

In 2000 relatives, acquaintances, or others with personal relationships to the victims committed more than half of all murders in which the relationship of the victim to the offender was known. (Almost 43 percent of the relationships were unknown.) Of 12,943 murders in 2000, 598 wives were the victims of their husbands and 417 girlfriends were the victims of their boyfriends. (See Table 2.5.) Arguments resulted in 3,681 murders in 2000, down from 5,047 in 1996. Robbery was the felony offense most likely to result in murder in 2000, as it was in each of the previous four years from 1996 through 1999. Juvenile gang killing accounted for 650 murders in 2000, up from 580 in 1999 and 628 in 1998. Juvenile gang killing accounted for about 5 percent of all murders in 2000. (See Table 2.6.)

Sixty-five percent of all murders were committed with firearms. (See below for more information on firearms and crime.) Knives were used in 13.3 percent of murders; blunt instruments in 5.3 percent; personal weapons (fists, feet, and the like) in 6.7 percent; and other weapons, such as poisons and explosives, in the remaining 9.7 percent.

Firearms killed 65.6 percent of murder victims in 2000, followed by knives or cutting instruments (13.5 percent), personal weapons such as hands for feet (7 percent), and blunt objects such as clubs or hammers (4.7 percent). Less common were poison, narcotics, strangula-

TABLE 2.3

Murder offenders by age, gender, and race, 2000

Age	Total	Sex			Race			
		Male	Female	Unknown	White	Black	Other	Unknown
Total	14,697	9,562	1,039	4,096	4,809	5,361	270	4,257
Percent distribution[1]	100.0	65.1	7.1	27.9	32.7	36.5	1.8	29.0
Under 18[2]	832	751	81	–	345	444	35	8
Under 22[2]	3,378	3,134	242	2	1,382	1,856	107	33
18 and over [2]	8,785	7,861	919	5	4,261	4,232	229	63
Infant (under 1)	–	–	–	–	–	–	–	–
1 to 4	1	–	1	–	–	1	–	–
5 to 8	2	1	1	–	–	2	–	–
9 to 12	13	12	1	–	9	3	–	1
13 to 16	415	370	45	–	171	226	16	2
17 to 19	1,651	1,540	109	2	651	922	61	17
20 to 24	2,571	2,397	174	–	1,064	1,427	58	22
25 to 29	1,481	1,342	139	–	647	796	30	8
30 to 34	947	811	136	–	510	408	26	3
35 to 39	792	664	127	1	462	294	31	5
40 to 44	629	507	122	–	359	253	11	6
45 to 49	426	367	58	1	260	152	13	1
50 to 54	270	232	37	1	168	92	6	4
55 to 59	140	114	26	–	101	31	7	1
60 to 64	93	86	7	–	68	24	–	1
65 to 69	59	54	5	–	37	22	–	–
70 to 74	42	37	5	–	31	9	2	–
75 and over	85	77	8	–	68	14	3	–
Unknown	5,080	951	38	4,091	203	685	6	4,186

[1]Because of rounding, the percentages may not add to total.
[2]Does not include unknown ages.

SOURCE: "Table 2.6: Murder Offenders, by Age, Sex, and Race, 2000," *Crime in the United States, 2000: Uniform Crime Reports*, Federal Bureau of Investigation, Washington, DC, 2001

TABLE 2.4

Murder victim/offender relationship by race and gender, 2000

[Single Victim/Single Offender]

Race of victim	Total	Race of offender				Sex of offender		
		White	Black	Other	Unknown	Male	Female	Unknown
White victims	3,352	2,860	417	40	35	2,985	332	35
Black victims	2,927	178	2,723	5	21	2,565	341	21
Other race victims	169	43	22	103	1	150	18	1
Unknown race	66	30	19	1	16	48	2	16

Sex of victim	Total	Race of offender				Sex of offender		
		White	Black	Other	Unknown	Male	Female	Unknown
Male victims	4,542	2,004	2,397	100	41	3,983	518	41
Female victims	1,906	1,077	765	48	16	1,717	173	16
Unknown sex	66	30	19	1	16	48	2	16

SOURCE: "Table 2.8: Murder Victim/Offender Relationship, by Race and Sex, 2000," *Crime in the United States, 2000: Uniform Crime Reports*, Federal Bureau of Investigation, Washington, DC, 2001

tion, and other weapons. Of the 8,493 murder victims killed by firearms in 2000, 616 were under the age of 18 (7 percent) and 2,163 were under 22 years of age (25 percent). Almost 50 percent of murder victims under the age of 18 and over two-thirds of those under age 22 were killed by firearms.(See Table 2.7.)

Arrests

Because murder is considered the most serious crime, it receives the most police attention and, therefore, has the highest arrest rate of all felonies. About 63.1 percent of murders in 2000 were cleared by arrest. The rate was somewhat lower in cities, with 61 percent of murders and

TABLE 2.5

Murder circumstances by relationship of victim to offender, 2000

Circumstances	Total	Husband	Wife	Mother	Father	Son	Daughter	Brother	Sister	Other family	Acquaintance	Friend	Boyfriend	Girlfriend	Neighbor	Employee	Employer	Stranger	Unknown
Total*	**12,943**	**164**	**598**	**100**	**120**	**235**	**173**	**90**	**23**	**235**	**3,022**	**286**	**151**	**417**	**109**	**10**	**7**	**1,688**	**5,515**
Felony type total:	2,157	4	7	9	7	20	30	3	6	29	552	30	2	21	17	1	2	551	866
Rape	58	—	—	—	—	—	2	—	1	1	12	1	—	3	—	—	—	14	24
Robbery	1,048	—	—	—	3	—	1	2	3	9	195	11	—	4	7	1	—	376	435
Burglary	73	—	1	—	—	—	—	—	—	3	16	1	—	4	2	—	—	15	31
Larceny-theft	23	—	—	—	—	—	—	—	—	1	7	—	—	1	—	—	—	5	9
Motor vehicle theft	22	—	—	—	—	—	—	—	—	—	—	1	1	1	—	—	1	13	5
Arson	81	1	2	4	2	3	3	—	—	—	21	1	1	2	1	—	—	2	38
Prostitution and commercialized vice	5	—	—	—	—	—	—	—	—	—	1	—	—	—	—	—	—	4	—
Other sex offenses	10	—	—	—	1	—	—	1	—	2	2	—	—	—	—	—	—	3	2
Narcotic drug laws	572	—	—	2	—	—	—	—	—	5	230	12	—	1	3	—	—	69	249
Gambling	11	—	—	—	—	—	—	—	—	—	8	—	—	—	—	—	—	3	—
Other - not specified	254	3	4	3	1	17	24	—	2	8	60	3	—	5	4	—	1	47	73
Suspected felony type	60	—	—	—	—	—	—	—	—	—	8	—	—	—	—	—	—	1	50
Other than felony type total:	6,696	145	538	75	98	197	123	75	14	183	2,076	221	135	332	77	9	5	868	1,525
Romantic triangle	122	1	10	—	1	2	—	1	—	1	74	5	2	10	1	1	—	8	5
Child killed by babysitter	30	—	—	2	—	1	—	—	—	3	24	—	—	—	—	1	—	—	1
Brawl due to influence of alcohol	181	—	3	2	2	—	—	1	—	4	79	26	1	2	1	—	—	35	25
Brawl due to influence of narcotics	97	1	1	5	1	—	—	—	—	6	49	3	1	3	—	—	—	10	21
Argument over money or property	206	1	3	—	4	3	—	1	—	12	111	5	1	1	7	1	—	19	32
Other arguments	3,475	117	364	38	59	34	25	63	8	103	1,129	137	114	249	48	4	4	449	530
Gangland killings	63	—	—	—	—	—	—	—	—	—	23	3	—	—	—	—	—	13	27
Juvenile gang killings	650	—	—	—	—	—	—	—	—	—	187	—	—	—	—	—	—	129	331
Institutional killings	10	—	—	—	—	—	—	—	—	—	7	—	—	—	—	—	—	1	2
Sniper attack	8	—	—	—	—	—	—	—	—	—	1	—	—	—	1	—	—	—	6
Other - not specified	1,854	25	157	28	31	157	98	9	6	54	392	42	17	67	19	2	1	204	545
Unknown	4,030	15	53	16	15	18	20	12	3	23	386	35	14	64	14	—	—	268	3,074

*Total murder victims for whom supplemental homicide data were received.

SOURCE: "Table 2.12: Murder Circumstances, by Relationship, 2000," *Crime in the United States, 2000: Uniform Crime Reports*, Federal Bureau of Investigation, Washington, DC, 2001

TABLE 2.6

Murder circumstances, 1996–2000

Circumstances	1996	1997	1998	1999	2000
Total[1]	16,967	15,837	14,276	13,011	12,943
Felony type total:	3,186	2,968	2,514	2,215	2,157
Rape	70	67	62	47	58
Robbery	1,618	1,509	1,244	1,057	1,048
Burglary	123	101	92	81	73
Larceny-theft	24	16	17	14	23
Motor vehicle theft	23	18	17	12	22
Arson	105	92	83	66	81
Prostitution and commercialized vice	8	7	15	8	5
Other sex offenses	27	23	20	19	10
Narcotic drug laws	843	802	682	581	572
Gambling	12	19	12	17	11
Other - not specified	333	314	270	313	254
Suspected felony type	74	153	104	65	60
Other than felony type total:	8,597	7,666	7,232	6,880	6,696
Romantic triangle	189	176	187	137	122
Child killed by babysitter	29	24	23	34	30
Brawl due to influence of alcohol	256	239	213	203	181
Brawl due to influence of narcotics	195	106	117	127	97
Argument over money or property	328	287	241	213	206
Other arguments	4,719	4,476	4,129	3,471	3,475
Gangland killings	84	86	73	122	63
Juvenile gang killings	858	783	628	580	650
Institutional killings	13	19	15	13	10
Sniper attack	8	8	16	5	8
Other - not specified	1,918	1,462	1,590	1,975	1,854
Unknown	5,110	5,050	4,426	3,851	4,030

[1] Total number of murder victims for whom supplemental homicide data were received.

SOURCE: "Table 2.14: Murder Circumstances, 1996–2000," *Crime in the United States, 2000: Uniform Crime Reports*, Federal Bureau of Investigation, Washington, DC, 2001

non-negligent manslaughter offenses cleared by arrest in 2000. Because an arrest is made does not mean that the alleged offender is guilty or will be convicted in criminal or juvenile court.

RAPE

The FBI defines forcible rape as "the carnal knowledge of a female forcibly and against her will. Assaults or attempts to commit rape by force or threat of force are included; however, statutory rape (without force) [intercourse with a consenting minor]...and other sex offenses are excluded." Rape is a crime of violence in which the victim may suffer serious physical injury and long-term psychological pain. In 2000, 90,186 forcible rapes were reported to law enforcement agencies, an increase of less than one percent from 1999, but the first increase in rape totals since 1992. Forcible rape totals still show a decrease of 6.3 percent from 1996 to 2000, and 15.4 percent from 1991 to 2000. The rate of forcible rape in 2000 was 32 per 100,000 inhabitants, but since the FBI defini-

tion of rape only includes females, this means that 62.7 women in 100,000 were raped in 2000. This represents a decline of 1.6 percent from 1999, and 11.3 percent from 1996 to 2000.

For several reasons, the statistics on rape are difficult to interpret. The crime often goes unreported. The Bureau of Justice Statistics (BJS) estimates that only about one-third of the cases of completed or attempted rape are ever reported to the police. Because their data are collected through interviews, the BJS recognizes an underreporting in its statistics as well. Homosexual rape and "date rape" (sex forced upon a woman by her escort) are not included in BJS data.

Public attitudes and legal definitions of rape are changing to encompass an ever-widening range of sexual events. These actions can include varying degrees of violence, submissiveness, and injury, but all involve women having sex against their will. (By the Uniform Crime Reports definition, the victims of forcible rape are always female. The number of reported cases of rapes of males is so small that no statistics are available.) A majority of cases involve acquaintance rape. By the late 1990s most states also recognized marital rape, for which a husband could be charged with raping his wife. David Beatty, public policy director of the National Victims Center, commented that acquaintance rape is far more common than stranger rape. Most experts conclude that in 80 to 85 percent of all rape cases, the victim knows the defendant.

From 1979 through 1992 the rape rate increased 23 percent. Most experts attributed at least part of the increase in reported rape cases to a more sympathetic attitude by law enforcement authorities and a greater awareness of women's rights. After peaking in 1992, however, the rate steadily declined. Excluding 1999, the number of reported rape cases in 2000 (90,186) was the lowest since 1986, when 84,233 cases of forcible rape were reported.

When and Where

In keeping with a five-year trend, rapes in 2000 occurred most frequently during the summer months of July and August. (See Table 2.8.) The rate of rape in metropolitan statistical areas in 2000 was 65.0 per 100,000 females, a decline of 28.6 percent since 1991. The rate of rape was highest in cities outside of metropolitan areas, at 69 per 100,000 females, an increase of 3 percent from the previous year. While the rate of rape was lower in rural counties, at 43.3 per 100,000 females, the rate of decline 1991 to 2000 was much lower, at 6.5 percent. Regionally, though the highest total volume of rapes (38 percent of all rapes) were in the South (the most populated region in the United States) the highest rape rate occurred in the Midwestern states (68.4 victims per 100,000 women). By comparison, the rate of rape per 100,000 females in Southern states was 66.9; Western states, 66.5; and Northeastern states, 43.5. From 1991 to 2000, the rate of rape

TABLE 2.7

Murder victims by age and weapon, 2000

Age	Total	Weapons										
		Firearms	Knives or cutting instruments	Blunt objects (clubs, hammers, etc.)	Personal weapons (hands, fists, feet, etc.)[1]	Poison	Explosives	Fire	Narcotics	Strangulation	Asphyxiation	Other weapon or weapon not stated[2]
Total	12,943	8,493	1,743	604	900	8	9	128	20	166	89	783
Percent distribution[3]	100.0	65.6	13.5	4.7	7.0	0.1	0.1	1.0	0.2	1.3	0.7	6.0
Under 18[4]	1,300	616	103	63	300	1	4	34	5	22	32	120
Under 22[4]	3,247	2,163	308	98	344	1	4	45	7	43	37	197
18 and over[4]	11,380	7,750	1,611	527	575	7	4	87	15	141	56	607
Infant (under 1)	217	12	9	16	117	1	1	–	3	3	16	39
1 to 4	279	26	11	33	139	–	2	13	–	5	10	40
5 to 8	84	30	9	2	15	–	–	11	1	1	2	13
9 to 12	61	30	11	3	6	–	–	1	–	3	2	5
13 to 16	367	286	30	7	14	–	–	6	–	10	2	12
17 to 19	1,192	954	122	18	31	–	1	9	2	6	2	47
20 to 24	2,388	1,906	251	42	58	1	–	12	2	23	6	87
25 to 29	1,845	1,458	199	35	44	1	–	7	1	14	6	80
30 to 34	1,486	1,051	204	40	73	1	2	10	1	18	4	82
35 to 39	1,249	791	225	50	77	–	2	13	1	16	10	64
40 to 44	1,140	645	219	75	87	1	–	12	4	22	6	69
45 to 49	757	427	117	66	62	2	–	9	–	10	6	56
50 to 54	486	267	85	44	42	1	–	5	–	9	1	32
55 to 59	338	179	65	38	23	–	–	5	–	6	2	20
60 to 64	217	109	42	27	16	–	–	3	1	3	1	15
65 to 69	153	68	29	23	11	–	–	–	2	3	2	15
70 to 74	156	55	30	31	21	–	–	–	–	1	2	16
75 and over	265	72	56	40	39	–	–	5	–	10	8	35
Unknown	263	127	29	14	25	–	1	7	–	3	1	56

[1] Pushed is included in personal weapons.
[2] Includes drowning.
[3] Because of rounding, the percentages may not add to total.
[4] Does not include unknown ages.

SOURCE: "Table 2.11: Murder Victims by Age, by Weapon, 2000," *Crime in the United States, 2000: Uniform Crime Reports*, Federal Bureau of Investigation, Washington, DC, 2001

declined by 26.4 percent in the West, compared to 24.6 percent in the Northeast, 23.9 percent in the South, and 23.6 percent in the Midwest.

Arrests

Less than half (46.9 percent) of reported forcible rapes were cleared by arrest in 2000. Of persons arrested for forcible rape, 45.4 percent were under the age of 25 and 63.7 percent were white. Juveniles (under 18) arrested for forcible rape in 2000 accounted for 12.1 percent of those cleared by arrest.

ROBBERY

The FBI defines robbery as "the taking or attempting to take anything of value from the care, custody, or control of a person or persons by force or threat of force or violence and/or by putting the victim in fear." Robbery is a particularly threatening crime; its thousands of victims each year suffer psychological and physical trauma, and even non-victims experience anxiety from the fear of robbery. This fear can cause people to change their lives in ways destructive to social life and the sense of community, especially in urban areas.

TABLE 2.8

Forcible rape by month, percent distribution, 1996–2000

Month	1996	1997	1998	1999	2000
January	7.9	7.9	7.9	8.1	8.0
February	7.9	7.0	7.4	7.3	7.6
March	8.1	8.0	8.6	8.2	8.4
April	8.1	8.2	8.2	8.2	8.0
May	9.0	9.1	8.8	8.6	9.1
June	8.8	9.5	8.7	8.8	9.1
July	9.5	9.7	9.6	9.6	9.5
August	9.1	9.4	9.3	9.5	9.2
September	8.8	8.8	8.8	8.3	8.4
October	8.5	8.2	7.9	8.3	8.4
November	7.4	7.4	7.6	7.9	7.5
December	6.9	6.7	7.1	7.2	6.8

SOURCE: "Table 2.18: Forcible Rape by Month, Percent distribution, 1996–2000," *Crime in the United States, 2000: Uniform Crime Reports*, Federal Bureau of Investigation, Washington, DC, 2001

Robbery is the only one of the seven traditional FBI Index crimes that is both a property crime and a violent crime. It shares with other crimes of property the primary motivation (money) and the likelihood that the perpetra-

TABLE 2.9

Robbery, types of weapons used, percent distribution by region, 2000

Region	Total all weapons[1]	Armed			Strong-arm
		Firearms	Knives or cutting instruments	Other weapons	
Total	100.0	40.9	8.4	10.3	40.4
Northeastern States	100.0	35.0	9.9	8.3	46.8
Midwestern States	100.0	43.7	6.2	11.1	39.0
Southern States	100.0	45.8	7.5	10.9	35.7
Western States	100.0	34.9	10.2	10.1	44.8

[1] Because of rounding, the percentages may not add to total.

SOURCE: "Table 2.22: Robbery, Types of Weapons Used, Percent distribution by region, 2000," *Crime in the United States, 2000: Uniform Crime Reports*, Federal Bureau of Investigation, Washington, DC, 2001

tors do not know their victims. Robbery shares with other types of violent crime a relatively high probability of victim injury or death.

An estimated 407,842 robberies were reported during 2000, less than one percent fewer than in 1999. The number of robberies declined by 23.9 percent from 1996 to 2000, and by 40.7 percent since 1991, when the number of robberies during the past decade peaked at 687,732. The 2000 estimate represents the lowest figure in 27 years.

Rate

The robbery rate in 2000 was 144.9 per 100,000 inhabitants, a 3.5 percent decrease from 1999. The rate of robberies declined by 28.2 percent from 1996 to 2000, and by 46.9 percent from 1991 to 2000.

Robbery is largely a big-city crime. Of 407,842 total robberies reported by law enforcement agencies nationwide in 2000, some 378,602 occurred in metropolitan areas—a rate of 173 per 100,000 people. In those cities with populations of more than 250,000, the rate was 413.4, and in cities with more than 1 million, the robbery rate was 440.2. By comparison, the rate of robberies in cities outside metropolitan areas in 2000 was 59.9, and the rate was 15.9 in rural counties.

Average Losses

Over $477 million was stolen from robbery victims in 2000. The average value of items stolen during a robbery was estimated at $1,170 per incident. Average dollar losses in 2000 ranged from $4,437 for a bank robbery to $544 for a convenience-store robbery. Nearly half (46 percent) of robberies occurred on the streets or highways. Robberies of commercial and financial establishments accounted for an additional 13.9 percent and those occurring at residences, 12.2 percent.

The impact of robbery on its victims cannot be measured simply in terms of monetary loss. While the intention of a robber is to obtain money or property, the crime always involves the use or threat of force. Many victims suffer serious psychological and/or physical injury, sometimes even death. Firearms accounted for 40.9 percent of the weapons used in robberies in 2000. Strong-arm tactics (actual or threatened physical force) were used in 40.4 percent and knives or cutting instruments in 8.4 percent. (See Table 2.9.)

Arrests

In 2000 law authorities cleared about one-fourth (25.7 percent) of reported robbery offenses nationwide. Rural counties reported the highest clearance rate in 2000, at 40.2 percent, compared to 29.6 percent in suburban counties and 25.1 percent in cities. Of those arrested, 62.9 percent were under 25 years of age. Males comprised 89.9 percent of those arrested for robbery in 2000. Blacks accounted for 54.9 percent of arrestees for robbery, compared to 44.2 percent who were white. Of those cleared by arrest for robbery in 2000, 15.5 percent were juveniles under the age of 18.

AGGRAVATED ASSAULT

The FBI defines aggravated assault as "an unlawful attack by one person upon another for the purpose of inflicting severe or aggravated bodily injury. This type of assault is usually accompanied by the use of a weapon or by means likely to produce death or great bodily harm." In 2000, 910,744 offenses of aggravated assault were reported to law enforcement agencies nationwide. The aggravated assault rate of 323.6 per 100,000 inhabitants declined by 3.2 percent from 1999. By comparison, the rate of aggravated assault declined by 22.9 percent between 1996 and 2000, and by 25.3 percent from 1991 to 2000.

In 2000 metropolitan areas reported a rate of aggravated assault of 349.2 per 100,000 people, compared to 302.5 per 100,000 in cities outside metropolitan areas, and 167.8 per 100,000 in rural counties. Aggravated assault was more likely to occur in the South (42.6 percent of the cases) followed by the West (23.6 percent), the Midwest (18.4 percent), and the Northeast (15.4 percent). The highest rate of aggravated assault was in July while the lowest rates were in November through February.

Weapons Used

About one-third (35.9 percent) of all aggravated assaults in 2000 were committed with weapons such as clubs or other blunt objects. Personal weapons—hands, fists, and feet—were used in 28 percent of the offenses, firearms in 18.1 percent, and knives or cutting instruments in 18 percent. Almost 20 percent of assaults were committed with firearms in Midwestern states, compared to 19.7

TABLE 2.10

Aggravated assault, types of weapons used, percent distribution by region, 2000

Region	Total all weapons[1]	Firearms	Knives or cutting instruments	Other weapons (clubs, blunt objects, etc.)	Personal weapons
Total	100.0	18.1	18.0	35.8	28.1
Northeastern States	100.0	13.5	17.7	32.9	35.8
Midwestern States	100.0	19.9	18.3	35.5	26.3
Southern States	100.0	19.7	19.9	39.0	21.4
Western States	100.0	16.4	14.9	32.1	36.7

[1] Because of rounding, the percentages may not add to total.

SOURCE: "Table 2.24: Aggravated Assault, Types of Weapons Used, Percent distribution by region, 2000," *Crime in the United States, 2000: Uniform Crime Reports*, Federal Bureau of Investigation, Washington, DC, 2001

percent in Southern states, 16.4 percent in Western states, and 13.5 percent in Northeastern states. (See Table 2.10.)

Arrests

Law enforcement agencies cleared an average of 56.9 percent of the reported cases of aggravated assault in 2000. Three of every four violent crime arrests (76.2 percent) were for aggravated assault. Almost 40 percent of those arrested for aggravated assault were under 25 years of age. Males (79.9 percent of all offenders) were far more likely to be arrested than females. Among those arrested for aggravated assault, 63.5 percent were white and 34 percent were black.

BURGLARY

The FBI defines burglary as "the unlawful entry of a structure to commit a felony or theft. The use of force to gain entry is not required to classify an offense as burglary." An estimated 2.05 million burglaries were reported in 2000, down 2.4 percent from 1999. By comparison, burglaries declined by 18.2 percent between 1996 and 2000 (See Figure 2.2.), and by 35.1 percent between 1991 and 2000. The 2000 total was the lowest figure in over 30 years.

In 2000 the burglary rate was 728.4 per 100,000 persons, a 5.4 percent decrease from 1999. Burglary rates declined by 22.9 percent from 1996 to 2000, and by 41.8 percent from 1991 to 2000. The burglary rate in 2000 was highest in cities outside metropolitan areas (759.2 per 100,000 inhabitants), followed by metropolitan areas (754.9 per 100,000). Rural counties reported the lowest rate, at 532.3 per 100,000 population. The highest burglary volume was in the South (44.2 percent of total burglaries) and the South also had the highest burglary rate,

FIGURE 2.2

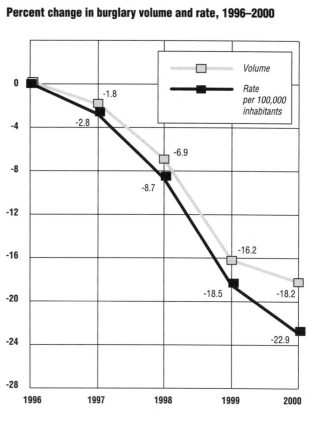

Percent change in burglary volume and rate, 1996–2000

SOURCE: "Figure 2.13: Burglary: Percent Change from 1996," *Crime in the United States, 2000: Uniform Crime Reports*, Federal Bureau of Investigation, Washington, DC, 2001

at 903 per 100,000 inhabitant. Total burglary volume was lower in the West (22.5 percent of all burglaries) and Midwest (20.8 percent), and lowest in the Northeast (12.5 percent). The highest burglary rates in 2000 occurred in July and August, while the lowest occurred in February.

Losses

Of the 1.57 million burglaries reported in 2000, 1.02 million occurred in residences and 548,420 involved non-residences such as stores and offices. Most residential burglaries occurred during daylight hours (60.7 percent) and non-residential burglaries occurred at night (57.7 percent). The average value lost in burglaries was $1,462 per incident. Non-residential losses from burglary averaged $1,615, compared to $1,381 for residential burglaries.

These dollar amounts indicate the value of goods lost to the property owner. The burglar may collect as little as 10 cents on the dollar from the fence, the person who buys the stolen goods. A television set worth $400 might net the burglar only about $40. These statistics indicate that most burglars are commonly risking arrest for about $100 to $200.

FIGURE 2.3

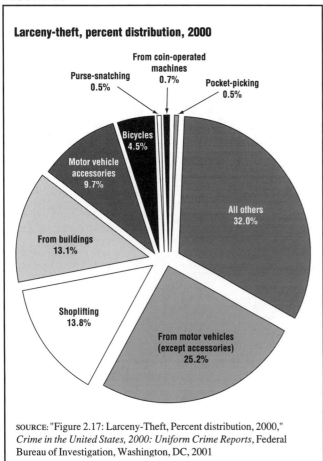

Larceny-theft, percent distribution, 2000

From coin-operated machines 0.7%

Purse-snatching 0.5%

Pocket-picking 0.5%

Bicycles 4.5%

Motor vehicle accessories 9.7%

All others 32.0%

From buildings 13.1%

Shoplifting 13.8%

From motor vehicles (except accessories) 25.2%

SOURCE: "Figure 2.17: Larceny-Theft, Percent distribution, 2000," *Crime in the United States, 2000: Uniform Crime Reports*, Federal Bureau of Investigation, Washington, DC, 2001

TABLE 2.11

Motor vehicle theft, percent distribution by month, 1996–2000

Month	1996	1997	1998	1999	2000
January	8.8	9.0	9.1	8.5	8.2
February	8.0	7.6	7.9	7.3	7.5
March	8.2	8.2	8.5	7.9	8.0
April	7.9	7.9	7.9	7.7	7.6
May	8.1	8.2	8.3	8.0	8.2
June	8.0	8.1	8.1	8.2	8.3
July	8.8	8.7	8.7	8.8	8.9
August	8.6	8.7	8.8	9.0	9.1
September	8.2	8.3	8.3	8.5	8.5
October	8.6	8.6	8.4	8.8	8.7
November	8.3	8.2	7.9	8.5	8.5
December	8.6	8.3	8.1	8.8	8.6

SOURCE: "Table 2.29: Motor Vehicle Theft by Month, Percent distribution, 1996–2000," *Crime in the United States, 2000: Uniform Crime Reports*, Federal Bureau of Investigation, Washington, DC, 2001

Arrests

Law officers cleared 13.4 percent of burglaries reported to law enforcement in 2000 through arrest. In 2000 juveniles under 18 accounted for 33 percent of all burglary arrests and were involved in 19.2 percent of burglary offenses cleared by law enforcement agencies. The percentage of juveniles arrested for burglary is higher than the clearance rate because more than one individual may be arrested in connection with the clearance of a single offense. About 63.8 percent of those arrested for burglary in 2000 were under the age of 25. Whites accounted for 69.4 percent of all persons arrested for burglary, and blacks comprised 28.4 of all such arrestees. About 86.7 percent of those arrested for burglary in 2000 were males. Arrests of juveniles and adults for burglary in 2000 declined by 5.0 and 2.6 percent, respectively.

LARCENY-THEFT

The FBI defines larceny-theft as "the unlawful taking, carrying, leading, or riding away of property from the possession ... of another" in which no use of force or fraud occurs. This crime category includes offenses such as shoplifting, pocket-picking, purse-snatching, thefts from motor vehicles, bicycle thefts, and so on. It does not include embezzlement, "con" games, forgery, and passing bad checks. (See Figure 2.3.)

In 2000 law enforcement agencies reported almost 7 million larceny-theft offenses for a rate of 2,475.3 per 100,000 people. This crime category amounted to 60 percent of the Crime Index total and over two-thirds of all property crimes. The rate of larceny-theft declined by 3 percent from 1999 to 2000, compared to declines of 16.9 percent from 1996 to 2000, and 23.3 percent from 1991 to 2000.

The larceny-theft rate in 2000 was 3,125.1 per 100,000 inhabitants in cities outside metropolitan areas, and 2,631.9 per 100,000 in metropolitan areas. Rural counties reported an average rate for larceny-theft of 999.7 per 100,000 residents. The South, the most populous area of the nation, accounted for 40.9 percent of the total number of larceny-theft offenses, with the West (22.2 percent), Midwest (22.9 percent), and Northeast (14.0 percent) making up the rest. Larceny-theft occurred most frequently in July and August and least often in February.

Losses

The average value of property stolen (excluding motor vehicles) in 2000 was $735, and the estimated total amount stolen was $5.1 billion. The estimated loss is considered conservative because many larceny-thefts of small amounts are never reported to authorities. The average amount taken differed depending on the specific crime. For example, the average value for pickpocket offenses was $408; the average purse-snatching, $356. Shoplifting resulted in an average loss of $181.

Miscellaneous thefts from buildings and thefts from motor vehicles (except accessories) averaged $1,176 and $712, respectively. The average loss for bicycle theft was $276 per incident and from coin-operated machines, $500. The largest proportion of larceny was thefts from motor vehicles (except accessories), which accounted for 25.2 percent of larceny-thefts in 2000, while thefts from buildings and shoplifting accounted for 13.1 percent and 13.8 percent, respectively. Bicycle theft accounted for 4.5 percent.

Arrests

About 18.2 percent of larceny-thefts reported in 2000 were cleared. Almost half (46.5 percent) of those arrested for larceny-theft were under 21 years of age, and 31.2 percent were under 18 years of age.

Females were arrested more often for larceny-theft than for any other offense in 2000, and comprised 35.9 percent of all arrestees for larceny-theft. About two-thirds (66.7 percent) of those arrested for larceny theft in 2000 were white, compared to 30.4 percent who were black.

MOTOR VEHICLE THEFT

The FBI defines motor vehicle theft as "the theft or attempted theft of a motor vehicle." In 2000 about 1.2 million cases of auto theft were reported in the United States. For the first time since 1990 the number of motor vehicle thefts increased from the previous year, up by 1.2 percent from 1999 to 2000. However, the rate of motor vehicle thefts decreased by 2 percent from 1999 to 2000, for a rate of 414.2 per 100,000 inhabitants. The 2000 rate shows a decline of 21.2 percent from 1996 to 2000, and 37.2 percent from 1991 to 2000.

Among the various regions in the country in 2000, motor vehicle theft totals increased by 7.1 percent in Western states, compared to an increase of less than 1 percent in Midwestern states. Motor vehicle theft declined in total numbers in both Northeastern states (2.9 percent) and in Southern states (1.3 percent). The Bureau of Justice Statistics found that the most common victims were African American and Hispanic households headed by people under age 25 in inner-city low-income housing. Overall, cities across the nation had a 1.4 percent increase in motor vehicle thefts from 1999 to 2000. Cities with populations of 100,000 to 249,999 had a 4.1 percent rise in motor vehicle thefts, similar to the 4.0 percent increase in cities with populations of 250,000 to 499,999. In suburban counties in 2000, motor vehicle thefts were up by 2.9 percent, and rural counties reported a 1.6 percent rise in motor vehicle thefts.

Losses

The total value of motor vehicles stolen in 2000 was approximately $7.8 billion. The average loss per vehicle was $6,682. Many stolen cars are recovered, and insurance covers a portion of the loss for most victims. Motor vehicle thefts in 2000 occurred most often in

TABLE 2.12

Most commonly stolen vehicles, 2000

1. Toyota Camry

2. Honda Accord

3. Oldsmobile Cutlass

4. Honda Civic

5. Jeep Cherokee/Grand Cherokee

6. Chevrolet Full Size C/K pick-up

7. Toyota Corolla

8. Chevrolet Caprice

9. Ford Taurus

10. Ford F150 pick-up

SOURCE: "Auto Theft Rises for First Time in 10 Years" (news release), National Insurance Crime Bureau, Arlington, VA, December 11, 2001

August, and were least likely to occur in February. (See Table 2.11.)

Types of Vehicles Stolen

Some 74.5 percent of all motor vehicles reported stolen in 2000 were automobiles. Approximately 19 percent were trucks or buses, and the remainder were other types of vehicles. In the Northeast, 88.2 percent of stolen vehicles were automobiles, and only 6.2 percent were trucks or buses. In the West, South, and Midwest, trucks made up a larger proportion of vehicles stolen (24.2 percent, 20.1 percent, and 13.7 percent, respectively). The Highway Loss Data Institute lists the make and series of cars for which the most theft claims are made. In 2000 the Toyota Camry was the most commonly stolen vehicle in the United States, followed by the Honda Accord, Oldsmobile Cutlass, and Honda Civic. (See Table 2.12.) Of passenger vehicles with the worst theft losses, between 1998 and 2000 the Audi Quatro Pro ranked highest, at $22,433, followed by the Chevrolet Corvette ($22,073), the BMW 7-series ($21,113), and the Lexus GS 300/400 ($18,594). (See Table 2.13.)

Arrests

In 2000 law enforcement agencies reported that 14.1 percent of motor vehicle thefts were cleared by arrest. In many cases, the stolen vehicle was found abandoned, and no arrest was made. Young males most often committed motor vehicle theft. Eighty-four percent of those arrested were male. Some 66.5 percent of persons arrested for motor vehicle theft in 2000 were under 25 years of age, and 34.3 percent were under 18. Whites comprised 55.4 percent of those arrested and African Americans comprised 41.6 percent.

ARSON

The FBI defines arson as "any willful or malicious burning or attempt to burn, with or without intent to defraud, a dwelling house, public building, motor vehicle or aircraft, personal property of another, etc." Arson statistics have only been collected since 1979. Not included in the arson statistics are fires of suspicious or unknown origins. In 2000 about 78,280 arson offenses were reported by law enforcement agencies nationwide, an increase of less than one percent from 1999. However, because not all agencies reported arson statistics, the data for arson collected by the FBI for 2000 represents approximately 76 percent of the population.

Rate

The rate of arson in the United States in 2000 was 36.9 offenses per 100,000 people nationwide. In cities with a population from 250,000 to 499,999, the arson rate was highest, at 69.5 per 100,000 inhabitants. Overall, cities reported an arson rate of 40.3 per 100,000 inhabitants in 2000. By comparison, suburban counties reported an arson rate of 33.9, while rural counties reported 17.7 arsons per 100,000. Arson occurred in the West at a rate of 39.5 per 100,000 inhabitants. The Midwest and the South had the next highest rates, 39.1 and 35.5 per 100,000, respectively. The Northeast reported the lowest rate, 31.6 arsons per 100,000 population.

What Is Being Burned?

In 2000 structural arson accounted for 43.8 percent of all arson offenses, or 30,116 reported incidents out of a total of 68,756. Residential property accounted for 26.4 percent of all arsons. Mobile property comprised about one-third (31.2 percent) of all reported incidents of arson in 2000, with motor vehicles accounting for about 95 percent of all mobile property arsons and 29.7 percent of all

TABLE 2.13

Passenger vehicles with worst theft losses, 1998–2000 models

Make & series	Vehicle size & type	Average loss payment per insured vehicle year	Theft claim frequency	Average loss payments per claim
Acura Integra	Small 2-door car	$230	21.6	$10,676
Acura Integra	Small 4-door car	$182	16.1	$11,336
Chevrolet Corvette	Small sports convertible	$73	3.3	$22,073
Cadillac Escalade 4-wheel-drive	Large 4-door utility vehicle	$71	6.5	$10,976
Lexus GS 300/400	Large 4-door luxury car	$65	3.5	$18,594
Mitsubishi Montero Sport 4-wheel-drive	Midsize 4-door utility vehicle	$64	4.7	$13,496
BMW 7 series long-wheel-base	Very large 4-door luxury car	$60	2.9	$21,113
Mercedes CLK class	Midsize 2-door luxury car	$58	3.3	$17,634
Audi A6 Quatro	Midsize 4-door luxury car	$58	2.6	$22,433
Lincoln Navigator 4-wheel-drive	Large 4-door utility vehicle	$54	4.4	$12,176
	AVERAGE FOR ALL CARS	$15	2.6 claims per 1,000 insured vehicle years	$5,998

SOURCE: "Passenger vehicles with worst theft losses, 1998–2000 models," in "Worst Theft Losses Are for Two Acura Models; Next Are Chevrolet Corvette, Cadillac Escalade" (news release), Highway Loss Data Institute, Arlington, VA, May 23, 2001

TABLE 2.14

Arson by type of property, 2000

[11,903 agencies; 2000 estimated population 213,171,039]

Property classification	Number of offenses	Percent distribution[1]	Percent not in use	Average damage	Total clearances	Percent cleared[2]	Percent under 18
Total	**68,756**	**100.0**		**$11,042**	**11,344**	**16.5**	**45.0**
Total structure:	30,116	43.8	18.2	19,479	6,637	22.0	44.6
Single occupancy residential	12,715	18.5	21.8	17,998	2,856	22.5	35.5
Other residential	5,447	7.9	13.1	18,081	1,181	21.7	37.3
Storage	2,249	3.3	19.3	10,727	408	18.1	60.3
Industrial/manufacturing	354	0.5	22.0	136,134	164	46.3	43.9
Other commercial	3,200	4.7	14.9	37,695	509	15.9	36.0
Community/public	3,622	5.3	10.5	12,572	1,059	29.2	72.9
Other structure	2,529	3.7	24.5	8,759	460	18.2	49.6
Total mobile:	21,442	31.2		5,803	1,528	7.1	23.5
Motor vehicles	20,396	29.7		5,516	1,360	6.7	20.8
Other mobile	1,046	1.5		11,387	168	16.1	45.2
Other	17,198	25.0		2,706	3,179	18.5	56.2

[1] Because of rounding, the percentages may not add to total.
[2] Includes offenses cleared by arrest or exceptional means.

SOURCE: "Table 2.32: Arson, by Type of Property, 2000," *Crime in the United States, 2000: Uniform Crime Reports*, Federal Bureau of Investigation, Washington, DC, 2001

TABLE 2.15

Murder victims by weapon used, 1996–2000

Weapons	1996	1997	1998	1999	2000
Total	16,967	15,837	14,276	13,011	12,943
Total firearms:	11,453	10,729	9,257	8,480	8,493
Handguns	9,266	8,441	7,430	6,658	6,686
Rifles	561	638	548	400	396
Shotguns	685	643	633	531	468
Other guns	20	35	16	92	51
Firearms, type not stated	921	972	630	799	892
Knives or cutting instruments	2,324	2,055	1,899	1,712	1,743
Blunt objects (clubs, hammers, etc.)	792	724	755	756	604
Personal weapons (hands, fists, feet, etc.)[1]	1,037	1,010	964	885	900
Poison	8	6	6	11	8
Explosives	15	8	10	–	9
Fire	170	140	132	133	128
Narcotics	33	37	35	26	20
Drowning	24	34	28	28	15
Strangulation	248	224	213	190	166
Asphyxiation	92	88	101	106	89
Other weapons or weapons not stated	771	782	876	684	768

[1] Pushed is included in personal weapons.

SOURCE: "Table 2.10: Murder Victims, by Weapon, 1996–2000," *Crime in the United States, 2000: Uniform Crime Reports*, Federal Bureau of Investigation, Washington, DC, 2001

arsons. The remaining 25 percent of incidents of arson were directed at property such as crops, fences, signs, timber, etc. (See Table 2.14.)

The average loss per incident in 2000 was $11,042. The overall average for all types of structures was $19,479. The lowest number of offenses (354) was against industrial/manufacturing structures, but their average loss per offense was the highest ($136,134). Mobile properties averaged $5,803 per incident, and other targets averaged $2,706.

Arrests

About 16.5 percent of all reported arsons were cleared by arrest in 2000. The highest clearance rate was 28.5 percent by cities under 10,000 in population. Cities overall had a clearance rate of 15.5 percent, while rural counties reported a 24.2 percent clearance by arrest. In 2000 juveniles under the age of 18 accounted for 52.8 percent of all arson arrests, and persons under 25 comprised 76.4 percent of arson arrests. Of all arson incidents cleared by arrest in 2000, some 45 percent were attributed to juveniles, the highest of any of the Index crimes. Juveniles comprised 44.6 percent of clearances by arrest for structural arson, compared to 23.5 percent of clearances for mobile property and 56.2 percent for all other property. Most persons arrested for arson in 2000 were male (84.9 percent), and 76.4 percent were white.

GUNS AND CRIME

There are enough guns in private hands to provide every adult in America with one.

—Bulletin Reports, Federal Bureau of Investigation, September 2, 1997

Based on a survey funded by a National Institute of Justice (NIJ) grant, the Police Foundation estimated that private citizens owned 192 million firearms in the United States in 1994. During the year, about 211,000 handguns and 382,000 long guns (rifles and shotguns) were stolen from the nation's homes or vehicles. Not surprisingly many stolen guns wound up in the hands of criminals.

In 2000, of the 12,943 weapons used to commit murder, 8,493 were firearms. Of those, 6,686 were handguns. (See Table 2.15.) About one-fourth (26 percent) of victims of violent crime in 2000 reported that a weapon was used in the commission of the offense. Among robbery victims, 55 percent reported the use of a weapon, as did 23 percent of victims of simple or aggravated assault. (See Table 2.16.)

Weapons Offenses and Offenders

Weapons offenses are violations of statutes or regulations that seek to control deadly weapons. Deadly weapons include firearms and their ammunition, silencers, explosives, and certain knives. From 1991 to 2000 the number of arrests for weapons offenses dropped from 125,722 to 86,620, a decline of 31.3 percent. The decline was less marked (26.4 percent) among juveniles

TABLE 2.16

Presence of weapons in violent crimes, 2000

Presence of offender's weapon	Violent crime		Rape or sexual assault		Robbery		Simple and aggravated assault	
	Number	Percent	Number	Percent	Number	Percent	Number	Percent
Total	6,322,730	100%	260,950	100%	731,780	100%	5,330,010	100%
No weapon	4,218,260	67%	218,710	84%	269,700	37%	3,729,850	70%
Weapon	1,642,760	26%	14,840	6%*	403,180	55%	1,224,740	23%
Firearm	533,470	8	6,550	3*	187,060	26	339,870	6
Knife	414,740	7	8,300	3*	104,580	14	301,870	6
Other	608,040	10	0	0*	88,430	12	519,610	10
Type not ascertained	86,510	1	0	0*	23,120	3*	63,390	1
Don't know	461,720	7%	27,390	10%	58,900	8%	375,420	7%

Note: Percentages may not total to 100% because of rounding. If the offender was armed with more than one weapon, the crime is classified based on the most serious weapon present.
* Based on 10 or fewer sample cases.

SOURCE: Callie Marie Rennison, "Table 5. Presence of weapons in violent crimes, 2000," in *Criminal Victimization 2000,* U.S. Department of Justice, Bureau of Justice Statistics, Washington, DC, 2001

under the age of 18 arrested for weapons offenses from 1991 to 2000, than among adults over 18 (32.4 percent).

In 2000 just over 1 percent of arrests nationwide were for weapons offenses. The FBI reported that state and local law enforcement agencies made 104,996 arrests for weapons offenses. Of those persons arrested, 59 percent were white and 39 percent were black.

Crimes Committed with Firearms

From 1974 to 1993 the number of violent offenses (murders, robberies, and aggravated assaults) committed with firearms increased 78 percent. From 1994 to 1998 the total number of all crimes committed with firearms steadily decreased, but this trend leveled off in 2000.

According to *Firearm Use by Offenders* (Caroline Wolf Harlow, Ph.D., Bureau of Justice Statistics Special Report, November 2001), some 18 percent of state prisoners and 15 percent of federal prisoners in 1997 reported that they carried a firearm at the time of their offenses. Of those, 9 percent of state prisoners and 2 percent of federal prisoners in 1997 said that they fired a gun during the commission of the offense for which they were incarcerated. Most reported carrying a handgun (83 percent of state prisoners and 87 percent of federal prisoners).

Among prisoners in 1997 who reported carrying a firearm during the commission of a crime, some 23 percent of state inmates and 5 percent of federal inmates either killed or injured their victim as the result of discharging the firearm. Nonetheless, between 1993 and 1997, gunshot wounds from any type of crime declined by some 40 percent according to *Firearm Injury and Death from Crime, 1993–97,* by Marianne W. Zawitz and Kevin J. Strom (Bureau of Justice Statistics, 2000). During the

same period, firearm-related homicides fell by 27 percent, from 18,300 in 1993 to 13,300 in 1997.

Crimes committed with firearms usually carry a higher penalty. About 40 percent of all state prisoners and 56 percent of all federal prisoners who used firearms were given more severe sentences. On average, state inmates who used a firearm received 18 years in prison, while those who committed similar crimes without firearms received 12 years.

Firearm-Related Deaths

From 1991 to 1999 the percentage of firearm-related homicides declined from 47 percent of all firearm-related deaths to 38 percent, according to the Bureau of Justice Statistics. The reduction in the overall number of firearm-related homicides was even more dramatic, from 17,986 in 1991 to 10,828 in 1999. Though the FBI estimated that 66 percent of the 15,517 murders in 2000 were committed with firearms, this still shows a decline, with about 10,241 homicides attributed to firearms. The National Center for Health Statistics estimated that of the other deaths caused by firearms in 1999, 57 percent were suicides, 3 percent were unintentional, and the intent in the remaining 1 percent of deaths was undetermined. The proportion of firearm-related deaths ruled to be suicides showed an increase between 1991 and 1999, rising from 48 percent to 57 percent. Although the rate of firearm-related suicides rose during that period, the overall number of such suicides declined from 18,526 in 1991 to 16,599 in 1999.

Among persons 19 years of age and younger, 59 percent (1,990) of the 3,385 firearm-related deaths in 1999 were homicides and 32 percent (1,078) were suicides. The remaining deaths were either unintentional or undetermined. Among adults 20 years of age or older, 35 percent of the 25,469 firearm-related deaths in 1999 were homicides and 61 percent were suicides.

Sources for Firearms Used in Crimes

Among prisoners in 1997 who reported carrying a firearm during their crimes, 14 percent said they bought or traded the gun from a legitimate retail outlet (store, pawn shop, flea market or gun show), a decline from the 21 percent of inmates in 1991 who reported purchasing a firearm from legitimate sources. Part of this decline may be attributed to the Brady Handgun Violence Prevention Act's requirement for criminal history checks for firearm purchases. According to the Bureau of Justice Statistics, since the law's enactment in 1994, some 689,000 of the nearly 30 million applicants for gun purchases were rejected by the FBI. Of the 7.8 million applicants for firearm permits or transfers in 2000, some 153,000 were rejected. State agencies rejected 2.5 percent of the 3.5 million criminal background checks conducted in 2000, while the FBI rejected 1.6 percent of 4.3 million checks they conducted. Friends, family, street buys, theft, and other illegal means of acquiring a gun accounted for 80 percent of firearms used in crimes.

Defensive Use of Guns

The number of justifiable homicides by private citizens (when a citizen kills a felon during the commission of a criminal offense) declined from 192 in 1999 to 163 in 2000. This is a sharp decrease from a five-year high of 280 in 1997. (See Table 2.17.) According to the FBI, in 2000 about 137 firearms were used in cases of justifiable homicide in the United States. Of those, most (122) were handguns. Among law enforcement officers, there were 297 incidents of justifiable homicide in 2000, most of which (265) involved the use of handguns. Justifiable homicides by law enforcement officers declined from a five-year high of 369 in 1998, to 308 in 1999, to the 2000 figure of 297. (See Table 2.18.)

WORKPLACE VIOLENCE

In 1999 the Society for Human Resource Management (SHRM) surveyed human resource professionals concerning violence in the workplace. Over half (57 percent) of those responding reported at least one violent incident between 1996 and 1999, an increase from the 48 percent of respondents who reported at least one violent incident in the workplace between 1994 and 1996.

Although violent attacks with firearms, knives, and other weapons receive the most media attention, they are rare in the workplace. Only 1 percent of the SHRM respondents reported shootings, and the same proportion reported stabbings. Verbal threats were the most frequently cited type of workplace violence (39 percent). Pushing and shoving (22 percent) and fistfights (13 percent) were the next most commonly reported incidents. Only 1 percent of respondents said that rape or sexual assault had occurred at work.

Each year the Bureau of Labor Statistics (BLS) gathers data about fatalities from job-related injuries, includ-

TABLE 2.17

Justifiable homicide by private citizens[1], by weapon, 1996–2000

Year	Total	Total firearms	Handguns	Rifles	Shotguns	Firearms, type not stated	Knives or cutting instruments	Other dangerous weapons	Personal weapons
1996	261	222	184	12	18	8	28	7	4
1997	280	238	197	16	14	11	28	6	8
1998	196	170	150	6	14	–	17	5	4
1999	192	158	137	5	10	6	18	9	7
2000	163	137	122	4	7	4	15	8	3

[1] The killing of a felon, during the commission of a felony, by a private citizen.

SOURCE: "Table 2.17: Justifiable Homicide, by Weapon, Private Citizen, 1996–2000," *Crime in the United States, 2000: Uniform Crime Reports*, Federal Bureau of Investigation, Washington, DC, 2001

TABLE 2.18

Justifiable homicide by law enforcement personnel[1], by weapon, 1996–2000

Year	Total	Total firearms	Handguns	Rifles	Shotguns	Firearms, type not stated	Knives or cutting instruments	Other dangerous weapons	Personal weapons
1996	357	354	326	10	10	8	–	1	2
1997	366	363	315	14	20	14	–	1	2
1998	369	367	322	15	18	12	–	–	2
1999	308	305	274	11	15	5	–	1	2
2000	297	297	265	13	12	7	–	–	–

[1] The killing of a felon by a law enforcement officer in the line of duty.

SOURCE: "Table 2.16: Justifiable Homicide, by Weapon, Law Enforcement, 1996–2000," *Crime in the United States, 2000: Uniform Crime Reports*, Federal Bureau of Investigation, Washington, DC, 2001

FIGURE 2.4

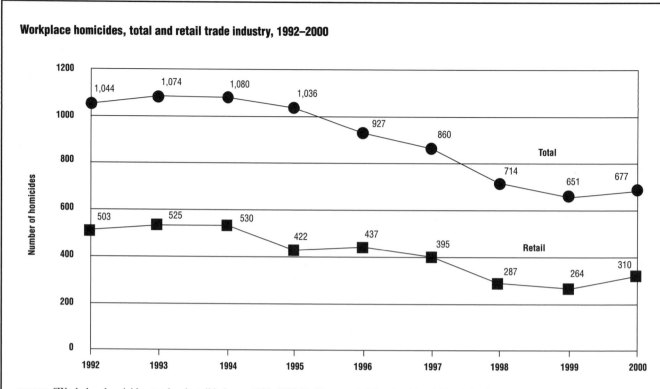

Workplace homicides, total and retail trade industry, 1992–2000

SOURCE: "Workplace homicides, total and retail industry, 1992–2000," in "Increase in job-related homicides in 2000," *MLR: The Editor's Desk, Monthly Labor Review Online*, U.S. Department of Labor, Bureau of Labor Statistics, August 28, 2001 [Online] http://www.bls.gov/opub/ted/2001/Aug/wk4/art02.htm [accessed April 9, 2002]

ing homicides. According to the BLS, workplace homicides rose from 651 in 1999 to 677 in 2000, the first such increase in six years. Nonetheless, the total number of workplace homicides in 2000 was 37 percent lower than the high of 1,080 such homicides in 1994. Firearms were used in almost 82 percent of these homicides. Workplace homicides in which robbery was the initial motive accounted for 367 of the 677 incidents in 2000, down from 387 in 1999. (See Figure 2.4.)

The Violence Prevention Center reported on the use of firearms in 65 high-profile shootings between 1963 and 2001. In 71 percent of incidents, a handgun was used, while a shotgun or rifle was used in the remaining 29 percent of incidents. In over half of such shootings (62 percent), the handguns were acquired legally, and in 71 percent of incidents the rifles or shotguns were legal. From 1999 to 2001 there were 25 high-profile shootings in the United States, 12 of which occurred at workplaces and 7 at schools. (See Table 2.19.)

TABLE 2.19

Selected high profile shootings, 1998–2001

Description	Casualties	Firearm(s)	Status of Firearm(s)
Santee High School Santana, California March 5, 2001	2 dead 13 wounded	.22 Arminius eight- shot revolver	Legal
The White House Washington, DC February 7, 2001	1 wounded	.38 revolver	Legal
Navistar International Corporation Melrose Park, Illinois February 5, 2001	5 dead 4 wounded	SKS 1954R rifle Remington 12-gauge shotgun Winchester .30 rifle .38 revolver	Legal
Edgewater Technology office Wakefield, Massachusetts December 26, 2000	7 dead	AK-47 assault rifle 12-gauge pump- action shotgun .32 pistol	Legal
Backstreet Café Roanoke, Virginia September 22, 2000	1 dead 6 wounded	Ruger 9mm pistol	Legal
Santos Linguisa sausage factory San Leandro, California June 21, 2000	3 dead	Beretta 9mm pistol Walther .380 pistol	Legal
Lake Worth Middle School Lake Worth, Florida May 26, 2000	1 dead	Raven .25 pistol	Legal
Wendy's Restaurant Queens, New York May 24, 2000	5 dead 2 wounded	Bryco .380 pistol	Illegal
Pittsburgh Suburbs Pittsburgh, Pennsylvania April 28, 2000	5 dead 1 wounded	Smith & Wesson .357 revolver	Legal
National Zoo Washington, DC April 24, 2000	7 wounded	9mm pistol	Illegal
Mi-T-Fine Car Wash Irving, Texas March 20, 2000	5 dead 1 wounded	9mm pistol	Illegal
Theo J. Buell Elementary School Mt. Morris Township, Michigan February 29, 2000	1 dead	Davis Industries .32 pistol	Illegal
Radisson Bay Harbor Inn Tampa, Florida December 30, 1999	5 dead 3 wounded	Lorcin 9mm pistol Charter Arms .38 revolver	Legal
Fort Gibson Middle School Fort Gibson, Oklahoma December 6, 1999	4 wounded	Taurus 9mm pistol	Legal
Northlake Shipyard Seattle, Washington November 3, 1999	2 dead 2 wounded	Glock 9mm pistol .32 pistol .22 rifle	Illegal
Xerox Office Building Honolulu, Hawaii November 2, 1999	7 dead	Glock Model 17 9mm pistol	Legal
Wedgewood Baptist Church Fort Worth, Texas September 15, 1999	8 dead 7 wounded	Ruger P85 9mm pistol .380 pistol	Legal
Laurel, Maryland September 9, 1999	2 dead	Smith & Wesson 9mm pistol	Illegal

TABLE 2.19

Selected high profile shootings, 1998–2001 [CONTINUED]

Description	Casualties	Firearm(s)	Status of Firearm(s)
North Valley Jewish Community Center Los Angeles, California August 10, 1999	1 dead 5 wounded	Fully automatic Uzi machine gun Glock Model 26 9mm pistol	Illegal
Atlanta brokerage offices Atlanta, Georgia July 29, 1999	13 dead 13 wounded	Glock Model 17 9mm pistol Colt 1911A1 .45 pistol	Legal
Illinois and Indiana July 4th weekend, 1999	3 dead 9 wounded	Bryco .380 pistol Ruger .22 pistol	Illegal
Heritage High School Conyers, Georgia May 20, 1999	6 wounded	.22 rifle .357 Magnum revolver	Legal
Columbine High School Littleton, Colorado April 20, 1999	15 dead 23 wounded	Intratec TEC-DC9 assault pistol Hi-Point 9mm Carbine Savage 67H pump-action shotgun Savage 311-D 12-gauge shotgun	Illegal
LDS Church Family History Library Salt Lake City, Utah April 15, 1999	3 dead 4 wounded	Ruger .22 pistol	Legal
Triad Center Salt Lake City, Utah January 13, 1999	1 dead 1 wounded	9mm pistol	Legal
U.S. Capitol Building Washington, DC July 24, 1998	2 dead 2 wounded	Smith & Wesson .38 revolver	Legal
Los Angeles, California May 28, 1998	2 dead	Two .38 revolvers	Legal
Thurston High School Springfield, Oregon May 21, 1998	4 dead 25 wounded	Glock 9mm pistol Ruger .22 rifle Ruger .22 pistol	Legal
Westside Middle School Jonesboro, Arkansas March 24, 1998	5 dead 10 wounded	Remington Model 742 .30-06 rifle Universal .30 M1 Carbine replica Davis Industries .38 two-shot derringer Double Deuce Buddie .22 two-shot derringer Charter Arms .38 revolver Star .380 pistol FIE .380 pistol Ruger Security Six .357 revolver Smith & Wesson .38 revolver	Legal
Connecticut State Lottery Headquarters Newington, Connecticut March 6, 1998	5 dead	9mm pistol	Legal

Note: Information for the chart has been gathered from a wide variety of publicly available news sources, which are often unclear and contradictory. Although every effort has been made to obtain the most accurate information possible, contradictions may exist between this chart and other sources. The determination as to whether a gun was obtained legally or illegally was made based on the law in effect at the time the firearm was acquired.

SOURCE: "Selected High-Profile Shootings in the United States, 1963–2001," in *Where'd They Get Their Guns? An Analysis of the Firearms Used in High-Profile Shootings, 1963 to 2001,* Violence Policy Center, Washington, DC, 2001

CHAPTER 3
VICTIMS OF CRIME

THE TRAUMA OF BEING VICTIMIZED

Becoming a crime victim can have serious consequences—outcomes the victim neither asks for nor deserves. A victim rarely expects to be victimized and seldom knows where to turn. Victims may end up in the hospital to be treated and released, or they may be confined to bed for days, weeks, or longer. Injuries may be temporary, or they may be permanent and forever change the way the victim lives. Victims may lose money or property, or they may even lose their lives—the ultimate cost for which a victim and his or her family can never be repaid.

The effects of crime are not limited to the victim. The family is frequently devastated, and the psychological trauma may affect everyone connected to a victim. Victims and their families may experience feelings of fear, anger, shame, self-blame, helplessness, and depression—emotions that can scar life and health for years after the event. Those who were attacked in their homes or whose homes were entered may no longer feel secure anywhere. They often blame themselves, feeling that they could have handled themselves better, or done something different to prevent being victimized.

In the aftermath of crime, when victims most need support and comfort, there is often no one available who understands. Parents or spouses may be dealing with their own feelings of anger or guilt for not being able to protect their loved ones. Friends may withdraw, not knowing what to say or do. As a result victims may lose their sense of self-esteem and no longer trust other people.

FEAR OF BECOMING A VICTIM

The fear of becoming a victim is often much greater than the likelihood of being one. Fear of crime has permeated our society so completely that it plays a daily role in our lives. In *Perceptions of Neighborhood Crime, 1995* (Carol J. DeFrances and Steven K. Smith, Washington, D.C., 1998), the Bureau of Justice Statistics (BJS) report-ed that about 7.3 percent of U.S. households believed that crime was a major problem in their neighborhoods.

Households in central cities (14.5 percent) were twice as likely as other households to feel that crime was a serious problem. In 1995, 19.6 percent of black central-city households identified crime as a neighborhood problem, compared to 13 percent of white central-city households.

In 2000, despite a steadily declining crime trend, 34 percent of respondents to a Gallup Poll felt that there was more crime in their area than the year before. Of those, a third lived in urban areas, 31 percent in suburban areas, and 41 percent resided in rural areas. About 34 percent of white respondents felt that crime was worse than the year before, compared to 31 percent of black respondents. Thirty-six percent of females and 32 percent of males who responded felt that there was more crime in their area than in the previous year.

THE NATIONAL CRIME VICTIMIZATION SURVEY

In 1972 the Law Enforcement Assistance Administration established the *National Crime Victimization Survey* (NCVS). The survey is an annual federal statistical study that measures the levels of victimization resulting from criminal activity in the United States. The survey was previously known as the *National Crime Survey*, but it was renamed to emphasize the measurement of victimization experienced by citizens.

Sponsored by the BJS, the survey was created because of a concern that the FBI's Uniform Crime Reports (UCR) did not fully portray the true volume of crime. The UCR provided data on crimes reported to law enforcement authorities, but it did not estimate how many crimes went unreported.

The NCVS is designed to complement the FBI's Uniform Crime Reports. It measures the levels of criminal victimization of persons and households for the crimes of rape,

TABLE 3.1

Rates of criminal victimization and percent change, 1993–2000

Type of crime	Victimization rates (per 1,000 persons age 12 or older or per 1,000 households)								
	1993	1994	1998	1999	2000	Percent change[3]			
						1993-00	1994-00	1998-00	1999-00
Personal crimes[4]	52.2	54.1	37.9	33.7	29.1	-44.3%[1]	-46.2%[1]	-23.2%[1]	-13.6%[1]
Crimes of violence	49.9	51.8	36.6	32.8	27.9	-44.1[1]	-46.1[1]	-23.8[1]	-14.9[1]
Completed violence	15.0	15.4	11.6	10.1	9.0	-40.0[1]	-41.6[1]	-22.4[1]	-10.9[2]
Attempted/threatened violence	34.9	36.4	25.0	22.6	18.9	-45.8[1]	-48.1[1]	-24.4[1]	-16.4[1]
Rape/sexual assault	2.5	2.1	1.5	1.7	1.2	-52.0[1]	-42.9[1]	-20.0	-29.4[1]
Rape/attempted rape	1.6	1.4	0.9	0.9	0.6	-62.5[1]	-57.1[1]	-33.3[1]	-33.3[1]
Rape	1.0	0.7	0.5	0.6	0.4	-60.0[1]	-42.9[1]	-20.0	-33.3[2]
Attempted rape	0.7	0.7	0.4	0.3	0.2	-71.4[1]	-71.4[1]	-50.0[1]	-33.3
Sexual assault	0.8	0.6	0.6	0.8	0.5	-37.5[2]	-16.7	-16.7	-37.5[1]
Robbery	6.0	6.3	4.0	3.6	3.2	-46.7[1]	-49.2[1]	-20.0[1]	-11.1
Completed robbery	3.8	4.0	2.7	2.4	2.3	-39.5[1]	-42.5[1]	-14.8	-4.2
With injury	1.3	1.4	0.8	0.8	0.7	-46.2[1]	-50.0[1]	-12.5	-12.5
Without injury	2.5	2.6	2.0	1.5	1.6	-36.0[1]	-38.5[1]	-20.0	6.7
Attempted robbery	2.2	2.3	1.2	1.2	0.9	-59.1[1]	-60.9[1]	-25.0	-25.0
With injury	0.4	0.6	0.3	0.3	0.3	-25.0	-50.0[1]	0.0	0.0
Without injury	1.8	1.7	0.9	0.9	0.6	-66.7[1]	-64.7[1]	-33.3[1]	-33.3[1]
Assault	41.4	43.3	31.1	27.4	23.5	-43.2[1]	-45.7[1]	-24.4[1]	-14.2[1]
Aggravated	12.0	11.9	7.5	6.7	5.7	-52.5[1]	-52.1[1]	-24.0[1]	-14.9[2]
With injury	3.4	3.3	2.5	2.0	1.5	-55.9[1]	-54.5[1]	-40.0[1]	-25.0[1]
Threatened with weapon	8.6	8.6	5.1	4.7	4.2	-51.2[1]	-51.2[1]	-17.6[1]	-10.6
Simple	29.4	31.5	23.5	20.8	17.8	-39.5[1]	-43.5[1]	-24.3[1]	-14.4[1]
With minor injury	6.1	6.8	5.3	4.4	4.4	-27.9[1]	-35.3[1]	-17.0[1]	0.0
Without injury	23.3	24.7	18.2	16.3	13.4	-42.5[1]	-45.7[1]	-26.4[1]	-17.8[1]
Personal theft[5]	2.3	2.4	1.3	0.9	1.2	-47.8[1]	-50.0[1]	-7.7	33.3
Property crimes	318.9	310.2	217.4	198.0	178.1	-44.2%[1]	-42.6%[1]	-18.1%[1]	-10.1%[1]
Household burglary	58.2	56.3	38.5	34.1	31.8	-45.4[1]	-43.5[1]	-17.4[1]	-6.7
Completed	47.2	46.1	32.1	28.6	26.9	-43.0[1]	-41.6[1]	-16.2[1]	-5.9
Forcible entry	18.1	16.9	12.4	11.0	9.6	-47.0[1]	-43.2[1]	-22.6[1]	-12.7[2]
Unlawful entry without force	29.1	29.2	19.7	17.6	17.3	-40.5[1]	-40.8[1]	-12.2[1]	-1.7
Attempted forcible entry	10.9	10.2	6.4	5.5	4.9	-55.0[1]	-52.0[1]	-23.4[1]	-10.9
Motor vehicle theft	19.0	18.8	10.8	10.0	8.6	-54.7[1]	-54.3[1]	-20.4[1]	-14.0[2]
Completed	12.4	12.5	7.8	7.5	5.9	-52.4[1]	-52.8[1]	-24.4[1]	-21.3[1]
Attempted	6.6	6.3	3.0	2.4	2.7	-59.1[1]	-57.1[1]	-10.0	12.5
Theft	241.7	235.1	168.1	153.9	137.7	-43.0[1]	-41.4[1]	-18.1[1]	-10.5[1]
Completed[6]	230.1	224.3	162.1	149.0	132.0	-42.6[1]	-41.2[1]	-18.6[1]	-11.4[1]
Less than $50	98.7	93.5	58.6	53.2	43.4	-56.0[1]	-53.6[1]	-25.9[1]	-18.4[1]
$50-$249	76.1	77.0	57.8	54.0	48.9	-35.7[1]	-36.5[1]	-15.4[1]	-9.4[1]
$250 or more	41.6	41.8	35.1	31.7	29.3	-29.6[1]	-29.9[1]	-16.5[1]	-7.6
Attempted	11.6	10.8	6.0	5.0	5.7	-50.9[1]	-47.2[1]	-5.0	14.0

Note: Victimization rates may differ from those reported previously because the estimates are now based on data collected in each calendar year rather than data about events within a calendar year. Completed violent crimes include rape, sexual assault, robbery with or without injury, aggravated assault with injury, and simple assault with minor injury. In 1993 the total population age 12 or older was 211,524,770; in 1994, 213,135,890; in 1998, 221,880,960; in 1999, 224,568,370 and in 2000, 226,804,610. The total number of households in 1993 was 99,927,410; in 1994, 100,568,060; in 1998, 105,322,920; in 1999, 107,159,550 and in 2000, 108,352,960.

[1]The difference between the indicated years is significant at the 95%-confidence level.
[2]The difference between the indicated years is significant at the 90%-confidence level.
[3]Differences in annual rates shown in each column do not take into account any changes that may have occurred during interim years.
[4]The NCVS is based on interviews with victims and therefore cannot measure murder.
[5]Includes pocket picking, purse snatching, and attempted purse snatching.
[6]Includes thefts with unknown losses.

SOURCE: Callie Marie Rennison, "Table 8. Rates of criminal victimization and percent change, 1993–2000," in *Criminal Victimization 2000: Changes 1999–2000 with Trends 1993–2000*, U.S. Department of Justice, Bureau of Justice Statistics, National Crime Victimization Survey, Washington, DC, 2001

robbery, assault, burglary, motor vehicle theft, and larceny. Murder is not included because the NCVS data is gathered through interviews with victims. Definitions for these crimes are the same as those established in the FBI's UCR.

Many observers believe the NCVS is a better indicator of the volume of crime in the United States than the FBI statistics. Nonetheless, like all surveys, it is subject to error. The survey depends on people's memories of incidents that happened up to six months before. Many times,

a victim is not sure what happened, even moments after the crime occurred.

Errors can come from other factors as well. Victims repeatedly victimized—by spousal or parental abuse, for example—may not remember individual incidents, or may remember only the most recent event. For instance, the NCVS found that a disproportionately large number of incidents are reported to have occurred at the end of the time period covered by the survey when the memory was perhaps fresher. In addition, the NCVS limits the data to victims age 12 and older, an admittedly arbitrary age selection. Despite these factors, however, the BJS claims a 90 to 95 percent confidence level in the data reported in the NCVS.

The NCVS and the FBI's UCR are generally considered the primary sources of statistical information on crime in the United States. Like all reporting systems, both have their shortcomings, but each provides valuable insights into the status of crime in the United States. Over the years some significant differences have occurred in their findings. For example, the Uniform Crime Reports saw a 15 percent increase in crime from 1982 to 1991, while the NCVS reported a leveling off of crime and, in 1990, a decrease. These differences require the reader to evaluate both sets of statistics carefully, not relying solely on one or the other.

Redesigned Survey

Beginning in 1979 the NCVS underwent a thorough, decade-long redesign. The new design was expected to improve the survey's ability to measure victimization in general and particularly for difficult-to-measure crimes, such as rape, sexual assault, and domestic violence. Improvements included the introduction of "short cues" or techniques to jog respondents' memories of events. Generally the redesign, as anticipated, resulted in an increased number of crimes counted by the survey. Therefore the 1991 and earlier data cannot be directly compared to the 1992 and later data.

A GENERAL DOWNTURN IN CRIME

Despite the continuing media spotlight on the high crime rate in the nation's cities, the findings from the 1996 NCVS indicated that overall crime victimization had declined from its peak in 1981. These findings support the FBI's Uniform Crime Reports, published in *Crime in the United States.*

Continuing the decline from 1997 to 1998, the rates of violent crime, personal theft, and property crime fell 6.6 percent, 18.8 percent, and 12.4 percent, respectively. Overall from 1993 to 1998 the violent victimization rate dropped 26.7 percent, the personal theft rate plummeted by 43.5 percent, and the property crime rate fell 31.8 percent. From 1998 to 2000 rates of criminal victimization (personal crimes) declined by 23.2 percent, while the overall rate for victims of property crimes dropped by 18.1 percent. (See Table 3.1.)

HOW MANY VICTIMIZATIONS IN 2000?

In 2000 U.S. residents of ages 12 and older were the victims of approximately 25.9 million crimes, down by 13.6 percent from the 28.8 million victimizations in 1999.

About 19.3 million were property crimes. Another 6.3 million were violent crimes, down by 15 percent from 1999, marking the largest single-year percent decrease ever measured by the NCVS. Approximately 274,000, or about 1 percent, were victims of personal thefts, marking a 33 percent increase from 1999. This was one of only two personal crimes, the other being robbery without injury (pocket-picking, purse-snatching, etc.), for which the rate actually increased from 1999 to 2000. (See Table 3.2.)

Victims of Violent Crimes

The 6.3 million violent victimizations in 2000 included 261,000 rapes/sexual assaults, 732,000 robberies, 1.3 million aggravated assaults, and 4 million simple assaults. Attempted or threatened violent crimes accounted for 4.3 million of all crimes of violence. The NCVS reported 27.9 violent victimizations per 1,000 persons of ages 12 and older. For every 1,000 persons ages 12 and older, there were 1.2 rapes/sexual assaults and 0.2 attempted rapes. In 2000, there were 2.3 completed robberies, resulting in injury to 0.7 victims per 1,000 persons ages 12 and over. The rate for victims of aggravated assault was 5.7 per 1,000, and 17.8 for simple assaults in 2000.

According to the Bureau of Justice Statistics, homicide rates for all age groups showed a general decline from 1976–2000, though rates rose from 1986 to 1991 for the age groups under age 35. From 1991 to 2000 the murder rates dropped by almost half for all age groups. In 2000 persons age 18–24 were murdered at a rate higher than all other age categories. Since 1986 this age group has consistently had the highest rate of homicides. Prior to 1986 the age group from 25–30 had the highest rate.(See Figure 3.1.)

Victims of Property Crimes

In 2000 property crimes accounted for about 75 percent of all victimizations. The NCVS reported 19.3 million property crimes, including household burglaries, motor vehicle thefts, and thefts of other property. Households experienced 642,000 completed vehicle thefts, 2.9 million completed household burglaries, and 14.3 million completed thefts of other property. For every 1,000 households in the United States, 31.8 households were burglarized, 5.9 had a motor vehicle stolen, and 132.0 suffered other thefts.

In 2000 about 58 percent of all crimes were thefts. Of the 14.3 million completed thefts, 4.7 million were thefts of less than $50. Another 5.3 million were between $50 and $249, and 3.2 million were of $250 or more. The value of the loss in the remaining thefts was unknown.

Reporting Crime to Police

Fewer than five of every ten violent crimes (47.9 percent) committed in 2000 were reported to the police.

TABLE 3.2

Criminal victimization, 1999–2000

Type of crime	Number of victimizations (1,000's)		Victimization rates (per 1,000 persons age 12 or older or per 1,000 households)		
	1999	2000	1999	2000	Percent change, 1999-2000
All crimes	28,780	25,893	. . .	. . .	
Personal crimes[3]	7,565	6,597	33.7	29.1	-13.6%[1]
Crimes of violence	7,357	6,323	32.8	27.9	-14.9[1]
Completed violence	2,278	2,044	10.1	9.0	-10.9[2]
Attempted/threatened violence	5,079	4,279	22.6	18.9	-16.4[1]
Rape/sexual assault	383	261	1.7	1.2	-29.4[1]
Rape/attempted rape	201	147	0.9	0.6	-33.3[1]
Rape	141	92	0.6	0.4	-33.3[2]
Attempted rape	60	55	0.3	0.2	-33.3
Sexual assault	182	114	0.8	0.5	-37.5[1]
Robbery	810	732	3.6	3.2	-11.1
Completed/property taken	530	520	2.4	2.3	-4.2
With injury	189	160	0.8	0.7	-12.5
Without injury	341	360	1.5	1.6	6.7
Attempted to take property	280	212	1.2	0.9	-25.0
With injury	78	66	0.3	0.3	0.0
Without injury	202	146	0.9	0.6	-33.3[1]
Assault	6,164	5,330	27.4	23.5	-14.2[1]
Aggravated	1,503	1,293	6.7	5.7	-14.9[2]
With injury	449	346	2.0	1.5	-25.0[1]
Threatened with weapon	1,054	946	4.7	4.2	-10.6
Simple	4,660	4,038	20.8	17.8	-14.4[1]
With minor injury	998	989	4.4	4.4	0.0
Without injury	3,662	3,048	16.3	13.4	-17.8[1]
Personal theft[4]	208	274	0.9	1.2	33.3
Property crimes	21,215	19,297	198.0	178.1	-10.1%[1]
Household burglary	3,652	3,444	34.1	31.8	-6.7
Completed	3,064	2,909	28.6	26.9	-5.9
Forcible entry	1,175	1,038	11.0	9.6	-12.7[2]
Unlawful entry without force	1,890	1,872	17.6	17.3	-1.7
Attempted forcible entry	587	534	5.5	4.9	-10.9
Motor vehicle theft	1,068	937	10.0	8.6	-14.0[2]
Completed	808	642	7.5	5.9	-21.3[1]
Attempted	260	295	2.4	2.7	12.5
Theft	16,495	14,916	153.9	137.7	-10.5[1]
Completed[5]	15,964	14,300	149.0	132.0	-11.4[1]
Less than $50	5,700	4,707	53.2	43.4	-18.4[1]
$50-$249	5,789	5,297	54.0	48.9	-9.4[1]
$250 or more	3,394	3,177	31.7	29.3	-7.6
Attempted	532	616	5.0	5.7	14.0

Note: Completed violent crimes include rape, sexual assault, robbery with or without injury, aggravated assault with injury, and simple assault with minor injury. The total population age 12 or older was 226,804,610 in 2000 and 224,568,370 in 1999. The total number of households was 108,352,960 in 2000 and 107,159,550 in 1999.
. . .Not applicable.
[1]The difference from 1999 to 2000 is significant at the 95%-confidence level.
[2]The difference from 1999 to 2000 is significant at the 90%-confidence level.
[3]The NCVS is based on interviews with victims and therefore cannot measure murder.
[4]Includes pocket picking, purse snatching, and attempted purse snatching.
[5]Includes thefts with unknown losses.

SOURCE: Callie Marie Rennison, "Table 1. Criminal victimization, 1999–2000," in *Criminal Victimization 2000: Changes 1999–2000 with Trends 1993–2000*, U.S. Department of Justice, Bureau of Justice Statistics, National Crime Victimization Survey, Washington, DC, 2001

Victims reported 48.1 percent of rapes, attempted rapes, and sexual assaults to the authorities. Law enforcement agencies received reports about 56.7 percent of aggravated assaults, 43.6 percent of simple assaults, and 56.3 percent of robberies. (See Table 3.3.)

Victims reported 35.7 percent of all property crimes. Motor vehicle theft was the most reported property crime (80.4 percent), while theft of other property was the least reported (29.5 percent). There were slight increases of 1 percent or less in the reporting of crimes to police between 1993 and 2000.

REASONS FOR REPORTING. BJS reports indicated several factors in reporting or not reporting a crime. For example, victims are more likely to report incidents to police if:

- Violent crimes were committed.

- The crime resulted in an injury.

- Items valued at $250 or more were stolen.

- Forcible entry occurred.

Victims of violent incidents most often cited the desire to prevent future acts of violence as a reason for reporting the crime. They also reported incidents because they thought it was the right thing to do. Victims of personal and property thefts frequently reported the incidents to enable recovery of their stolen property and to collect insurance. More females than males reported violent crime, with 55 percent of all violence experienced by females being reported and 43 percent of all violence against males being reported. This disparity between genders was significantly higher for whites than other races or ethnic groups, though a somewhat higher percentage of black females than males reported violent crimes.

Among victims who chose not to report a violent crime to the police, many indicated they felt the incident was private or personal in nature. In other cases, the incidents had not been completed, the stolen property had been recovered, or the victim feared retaliation from the criminal.

CHARACTERISTICS OF VICTIMS

The most likely victims of crime are male, young, poor, and residents of urban areas. Table 3.4 shows the 2000 violent victimization rates by type of crime, sex, age, race, and ethnicity. Table 3.5 displays similar property crime data. Table 3.6 shows violent victimization rates by income, marital status, region, and victims' area of residence.

Gender

Males are more likely than females to become victims of violent crime. In 2000, 32.9 of every 1,000 males were victimized by violent crime, compared to 23.2 per 1,000 females. In every category except rape/sexual assault and personal theft, men were more likely than women to be victimized.

Age

Teenagers and young adults were more likely than older persons to become victims of violent crime. In 2000 the rate for teenagers 12 to 15 years of age was 60.1 per 1,000; the rate for 16- to 19-year olds was 64.4 per 1,000, and the rate for 20- to 24-year olds was 49.5. Persons ages 12 to 19 were on average almost twice as likely as persons ages 25 to 34 and almost three times as likely as persons ages 35 to 49 to be victims of violent crime. The rate for 16- to 19-year olds was more than 17 times the rate for those ages 65 and older. (See Table 3.7.)

According the Office of Juvenile Justice and Delinquency Prevention (Washington, DC), research has shown that there can be long-term consequences to being victimized as an adolescent. When compared to adults who were not victimized as adolescents, adults who were adolescent victims were more likely to have drug problems and more likely to perpetrate violence. (See Figure 3.2.) They also committed more acts of domestic violence and were more often victims of domestic violence

FIGURE 3.1

Rate of homicide per 100,000 persons in each age category, 1976–2000

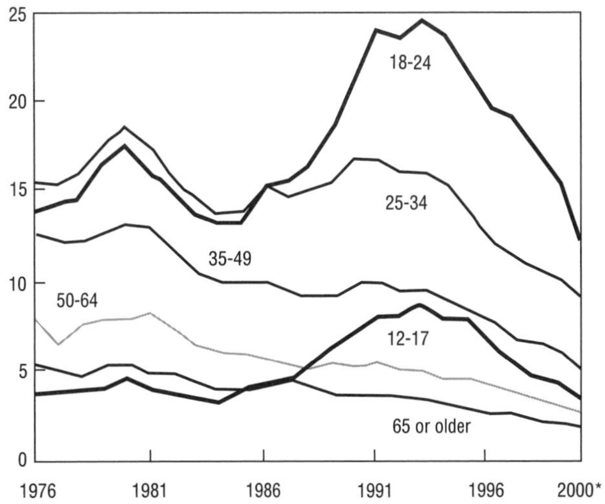

*Preliminary estimates

Age category	1991-2000 percent change
12-17	-59%
18-24	-50%
25-34	-47%
35-49	-52%
50-64	-53%
65 or older	-51%

SOURCE: Patsy Klaus and Callie Marie Rennison, "Rate of homicide per 100,000 persons in each age category," in *Age Patterns in Violent Victimization, 1976–2000,* Crime Data Brief, U.S. Department of Justice, Bureau of Justice Statistics, February 2002

than adults who were not victimized as adolescents. In addition, they were almost twice as likely to become adult victims of violent crime.

Race and Ethnicity

In 2000 African Americans were more likely than whites or persons of other races to be victims of most types of violent crimes. Of every 1,000 African Americans ages 12 and older, 35.3 percent were victims of violent crimes, while 27.1 per 1,000 whites and 20.7 percent of people of other races of the same ages were victimized. There were 7.7 aggravated assaults per 1,000 African American persons, 5.4 per 1,000 whites, and 5.2 per 1,000 persons in other racial categories. Hispanics experienced higher levels of violent victimization rates than non-Hispanics for robberies and personal theft, but lower rates in rape/sexual abuse and assaults. (See Table 3.4.)

For every 1,000 households in 2000, 173.3 white households, 212.2 African American households, and 171.3 households of other races were victims of property

TABLE 3.3

Violent crimes reported to the police, 1993–2000

	Percent of violent crime reported to the police, 1993-2000								Change in the percent reported to police, 1993-2000[3]
	1993	1994	1995	1996	1997	1998	1999	2000	
Violent crime	43.2%	40.4%	42.0%	42.8%	44.5%	45.9%	43.9%	47.9%	0.4
Rape/sexual assault	29.8	30.6	30.9	30.7	30.5	31.6	28.3	48.1[4]	0.6[2]
Robbery	59.5	53.9	55.7	53.9	55.8	62.0	61.2	56.3	0.2[2]
Aggravated assault	53.8	51.6	53.9	54.6	59.1	57.6	55.2	56.7	0.7
Simple assault	36.8	34.2	36.3	37.3	38.4	40.3	38.5	43.6	0.8[1]
Personal theft	25.8%	29.9%	35.0%	37.6%	30.5%	34.0%	25.9%	35.0%	0.2[2]
Property crime	33.5%	33.2%	33.6%	34.8%	35.1%	35.3%	33.8%	35.7%	0.2
Burglary	50.2	48.5	51.4	50.6	51.8	49.4	49.3	50.7	0.0
Motor vehicle theft	74.7	79.0	76.2	76.5	79.8	79.7	83.7	80.4	1.0[1]
Theft	26.2	25.9	26.4	28.4	27.9	29.2	27.1	29.5	0.4

The 1993-2000 difference is significant at the [1]95%-confidence level or [2]90%-confidence level.
[3]Values shown are the regression coefficient (*b*), the slope of the regression line, 1993-2000, based on a linear trend test, taking into account fluctuations in intervening years.
[4]The increase in the percentage of rapes/sexual assaults reported to the police, 1999-2000, was based on 10 or fewer sample cases.

SOURCE: Callie Marie Rennison, "Table 7. Violent crimes reported to the police, 1993–2000," in *Criminal Victimization 2000: Changes 1999–2000 with Trends 1993–2000*, U.S. Department of Justice, Bureau of Justice Statistics, National Crime Victimization Survey, Washington, DC, 2001

TABLE 3.4

Rates of violent crime and personal theft by gender, age, race, and Hispanic origin, 2000

		Victimizations per 1,000 persons age 12 or older						
		Violent crimes						
					Assault			Per-
Characteristic of victim	Population	All	Rape/ sexual assault	Robbery	Total	Aggra- vated	Simple	sonal theft
Gender								
Male	109,816,970	32.9	0.1*	4.5	28.3	8.3	19.9	1.0
Female	116,987,650	23.2	2.1	2.0	19.0	3.2	15.8	1.4
Age								
12-15	16,064,090	60.1	2.1	4.2	53.8	9.9	43.9	1.8
16-19	16,001,650	64.3	4.3	7.3	52.7	14.3	38.3	3.0
20-24	18,587,790	49.4	2.1	6.2	41.2	10.9	30.3	1.1*
25-34	37,757,070	34.8	1.3	3.9	29.5	6.8	22.7	1.5
35-49	64,927,820	21.8	0.8	2.7	18.4	4.7	13.7	0.9
50-64	40,764,000	13.7	0.4*	2.1	11.1	2.8	8.4	0.5*
65 or older	32,702,210	3.7	0.1*	0.7*	2.9	0.9	2.0	1.2
Race								
White	189,308,050	27.1	1.1	2.7	23.3	5.4	17.9	1.1
Black	27,978,180	35.3	1.2	7.2	26.9	7.7	19.2	1.9
Other	9,518,390	20.7	1.1*	2.8	16.7	5.2	11.5	1.8*
Hispanic origin								
Hispanic	24,513,290	28.4	0.5*	5.0	23.0	5.6	17.4	2.4
Non-Hispanic	200,294,810	27.7	1.2	3.0	23.5	5.7	17.8	1.1

Note: The National Crime Victimization Survey includes as violent crime rape, sexual assault, robbery, and assault. Because the NCVS interviews persons about their victimizations, murder and manslaughter cannot be included.
* Based on 10 or fewer sample cases.

SOURCE: Callie Marie Rennison, "Table 2. Rates of violent crime and personal theft , by gender, age, race, and Hispanic origin, 2000," in *Criminal Victimization 2000: Changes 1999–2000 with Trends 1993–2000*, U.S. Department of Justice, Bureau of Justice Statistics, National Crime Victimization Survey, Washington, DC, 2001

crimes. Hispanic households (227 per 1,000) were more likely than non-Hispanic households (173.4 per 1,000) to be victimized by property crimes. (See Table 3.5.)

The highest rate of burglaries occurred among African American households (47.6 per 1,000), while the rates for white households (29.4 per 1,000) and households of other races (32.4 per 1,000) were considerably lower. African American households also experienced more motor vehicle thefts and general thefts. Hispanic households (19.7 per 1,000) were more than twice as

TABLE 3.5

Property crime victimization by race, Hispanic origin, household income, region, locality, and home ownership of households victimized, 2000

Characteristic of household or head of household	Number of households, 2000	Victimizations per 1,000 households			
		Total	Burglary	Motor vehicle theft	Theft
Race					
White	90,887,030	173.3	29.4	7.9	136.0
Black	13,537,890	212.2	47.6	13.2	151.4
Other	3,928,040	171.3	32.4	10.4	128.6
Hispanic origin					
Hispanic	9,546,830	227.0	41.7	19.7	165.6
Non-Hispanic	98,070,420	173.4	31.0	7.6	134.7
Household income					
Less than $7,500	6,198,560	220.9	61.7	7.9	151.2
$7,500 - $14,999	9,966,270	167.1	41.1	9.1	116.8
$15,000 - $24,999	13,286,510	193.1	39.3	9.9	143.8
$25,000 - $34,999	12,612,950	192.2	33.3	9.5	149.4
$35,000 - $49,999	14,742,930	192.9	32.0	9.6	151.4
$50,000 - $74,999	14,509,310	181.9	24.0	10.0	147.9
$75,000 or more	15,493,460	197.2	27.7	7.0	162.5
Region					
Northeast	20,906,950	143.7	21.8	7.3	114.6
Midwest	26,132,460	181.9	31.4	9.3	141.2
South	38,866,820	167.8	33.2	6.9	127.8
West	22,446,720	223.4	39.1	12.3	172.0
Residence					
Urban	31,742,790	222.1	40.9	13.1	168.1
Suburban	49,919,960	163.7	27.2	8.1	128.4
Rural	26,690,210	152.6	29.5	4.4	118.7
Home ownership					
Owned	72,660,440	153.4	26.2	6.7	120.6
Rented	35,692,510	228.3	43.2	12.6	172.5

SOURCE: Callie Marie Rennison, "Table 6: Property crime victimization by race, Hispanic origin, household income, region, locality, and home ownership of households victimized, 2000," in *Criminal Victimization 2000: Changes 1999–2000 with Trends 1993–2000*, U.S. Department of Justice, Bureau of Justice Statistics, National Crime Victimization Survey, Washington, DC, 2001

likely as non-Hispanic households (7.6 per 1,000) to suffer a motor vehicle theft.

Income, Marital Status, and Area

INCOME. The less money that people or households earn, the more likely they will become victims of violent crime. In 2000 the very poor (earning less than $7,500 annually) suffered violent crime at a higher rate (60.3 per 1,000 persons) than any other income group and nearly three times as often as those earning $75,000 or more (22.3 per 1,000). (See Table 3.6.) Property crime rates for those earning less than $7,500 per year were also more elevated than those in higher income categories.

MARITAL STATUS. In 2000 the violent crime rate for persons who never married (51.4 per 1,000) was nearly four times higher than the rate for married people (12.8 per 1,000). The rate for divorced or separated persons (42.2 per 1,000) was over three times higher than the rate for married people. The victimization rates for rape/sexual assault, robbery, and both kinds of assault (aggravated and simple) were significantly higher for never-married, divorced, or separated persons than for married or widowed persons. (See Table 3.6.) The data for property crimes do not include marital status, since either married or unmarried people may head households.

REGIONS AND TYPES OF RESIDENCE. Those living in the West and in urban areas are more likely to be victimized both by property crimes and by violent crimes. In 2000, 223.4 of every 1,000 households in the West, and 222.1 per 1,000 urban households experienced property crimes. Rates in all categories of property crime in the West and in urban locations were higher than the rates in other regions and locations. The property crime rate for those who rented their homes was 228.3 per 1,000 households compared to 153.4 for those who owned their homes. (See Table 3.5.)

Residents in the West (33.9 per 1,000) and in urban locations (35.1 per 1,000) were also more likely to suffer violent crime incidents in 2000. Violence rates in all categories were generally higher in the West than in other regions. Victims in the Midwest (30.4 per 1,000) reported more violent crime than the Northeast (23.5) and South (24.9). Residents of rural areas (23.6 per 1,000) reported the lowest rate of violent crime. (See Table 3.6.)

Victim/Offender Relationship

In 2000, 45 percent of violent crime victims did not previously know their assailants. Strangers committed about 7 of 10 robberies compared to only about 3 of 10 rapes/sexual assaults. People either well known or casually known to the

TABLE 3.6

Rates of violent crime and personal theft by household income, marital status, region, and location of residence of victims, 2000

		Victimizations per 1,000 persons age 12 or older						
		Violent crimes						
					Assault			Per-
Characteristic of victim	Population	All	Rape/ sexual assault	Robbery	Total	Aggra- vated	Simple	sonal theft
Household income								
Less than $7,500	9,895,920	60.3	5.2	7.1	48.1	14.7	33.4	2.3*
$7,500 - $14,999	17,571,010	37.8	1.7	4.7	31.3	9.5	21.8	2.1
$15,000 - $24,999	25,931,570	31.8	1.4	3.2	27.2	6.1	21.2	1.2
$25,000 - $34,999	26,183,560	29.8	1.9	4.2	23.7	6.2	17.5	1.4
$35,000 - $49,999	32,930,980	28.5	0.8	2.3	25.3	6.2	19.2	0.6*
$50,000 - $74,999	34,619,880	23.7	1.0	3.6	19.1	3.8	15.3	1.0
$75,000 or more	38,258,270	22.3	0.2*	2.0	20.2	4.4	15.7	1.2
Marital status								
Never married	71,391,530	51.4	2.6	5.7	43.0	10.7	32.3	2.3
Married	116,032,860	12.8	0.1*	1.8	10.8	2.6	8.2	0.5
Divorced/separated	24,406,470	42.2	2.3	3.8	36.2	7.8	28.3	1.3
Widowed	13,657,920	8.1	0.2*	1.3*	6.6	2.3	4.3	1.3*
Region								
Northeast	43,839,990	23.5	1.5	3.3	18.8	4.0	14.7	2.3
Midwest	53,969,330	30.4	1.1	3.1	26.3	5.4	20.9	1.2
South	80,434,830	24.9	0.9	3.0	21.0	5.7	15.3	0.6
West	48,560,470	33.9	1.4	3.6	28.8	7.4	21.4	1.3
Residence								
Urban	63,598,980	35.1	1.5	6.0	27.6	7.1	20.4	2.3
Suburban	107,684,800	25.8	0.8	2.6	22.4	5.4	17.0	1.0
Rural	55,520,830	23.6	1.4	1.3	20.9	4.6	16.3	0.4*

Note: The National Crime Victimization Survey includes as violent crime rape, sexual assault, robbery, and assault. Because the NCVS interviews persons about their victimizations, murder and manslaughter cannot be included.
*Based on 10 or fewer sample cases.

SOURCE: Callie Marie Rennison, "Table 3: Rates of violent crime and personal theft, by household income, marital status, region, and location of residence of victims, 2000," in *Criminal Victimization 2000: Changes 1999–2000 with Trends 1993–2000*, U.S. Department of Justice, Bureau of Justice Statistics, National Crime Victimization Survey, Washington, DC, 2001

victim committed about two-thirds of all rapes/sexual assaults. Non-strangers committed 43 percent of aggravated and 61 percent of simple assaults. (See Table 3.8.)

WHEN AND WHERE DOES VIOLENT CRIME HAPPEN?

According to the Bureau of Justice Statistics, crime happens at all times of the day and night, though particular crimes exhibit different patterns. Fifty-three percent of violent crimes occur between 6 a.m. and 6 p.m. About two-thirds of simple assaults, compared to one-third of aggravated assaults, take place during these hours. Approximately two-thirds of rapes/sexual assaults occur at night.

Crime may also occur in any place. According to the NCVS, in 1995 some 25 percent of violent crime incidents occurred at or near the victim's residence. Of those, about 73 percent took place within five miles of the victim's home. Half took place within a mile of the victim's residence. Only 4 percent of victims of violent crime reported that the crime took place over 50 miles from their home.

Other common locales for crime were streets (19 percent), schools (14 percent), and commercial establishments (12 percent).

Victims' Activities

Twenty-three percent of violent crime victims reported being involved in some form of leisure activity away from home when victimized. Twenty-two percent said they were at home, and another 22 percent mentioned they were at work or traveling to or from work when the crime occurred. Robberies took place in a variety of situations:

- One in five (21 percent) during leisure activities.

- One in five (20 percent) during travel.

- One in six (17 percent) at home.

- One in six (17 percent) at work or while commuting to/from work.

- One in nine (11 percent) while shopping.

TRENDS IN VICTIMIZATION

Trends, 1973–2000

The NCVS, like the FBI's Uniform Crime Reports, found that the overall level of crime decreased from 1973 to 2000. (Although the 1993–2000 survey results cannot be directly compared to earlier statistics, adjusted data can be

TABLE 3.7

Violent victimization rates by age, 1973–2000

Violent crime rate per 1,000 persons in age group

	Age of victim						
	12-15	16-19	20-24	25-34	35-49	50-64	65+
1973	81.8	81.7	87.6	52.4	38.8	17.2	9.1
1974	77.5	90.6	83.5	58.6	37.5	15.5	9.5
1975	80.3	85.7	80.9	59.5	36.9	17.8	8.3
1976	76.4	88.8	79.7	61.5	35.9	16.1	8.1
1977	83.0	90.2	86.2	63.5	35.8	16.8	8.0
1978	83.7	91.7	91.1	60.5	35.8	15.0	8.4
1979	78.5	93.4	98.4	66.3	38.2	13.6	6.2
1980	72.5	91.3	94.1	60.0	37.4	15.6	7.2
1981	86.0	90.7	93.7	65.8	41.6	17.3	8.3
1982	75.6	94.4	93.8	69.6	38.6	13.8	6.1
1983	75.4	86.3	82.0	62.2	36.5	11.9	5.9
1984	78.2	90.0	87.5	56.6	37.9	13.2	5.2
1985	79.6	89.4	82.0	56.5	35.6	13.0	4.8
1986	77.1	80.8	80.1	52.0	36.0	10.8	4.8
1987	87.2	92.4	85.5	51.9	34.7	11.4	5.2
1988	83.7	95.9	80.2	53.2	39.1	13.4	4.4
1989	92.5	98.2	78.8	52.8	37.3	10.5	4.2
1990	101.1	99.1	86.1	55.2	34.4	9.9	3.7
1991	94.5	122.6	103.6	54.3	37.2	12.5	4.0
1992	111.0	103.7	95.2	56.8	38.1	13.2	5.2
1993	115.5	114.2	91.6	56.9	42.5	15.2	5.9
1994	118.6	123.9	100.4	59.1	41.3	17.6	4.6
1995	113.1	106.6	85.8	58.5	35.7	12.9	6.4
1996	95.0	102.8	74.5	51.2	32.9	15.7	4.9
1997	87.9	96.3	68.0	47.0	32.3	14.6	4.4
1998	82.5	91.3	67.5	41.6	29.9	15.4	2.9
1999	74.5	77.6	68.7	36.4	25.2	14.4	3.9
2000	60.1	64.4	49.5	34.9	21.8	13.7	3.7

Note: Because of changes made to the victimization survey, data prior to 1992 are adjusted to make them comparable to data collected under the redesigned methodology. Estimates for 1993 and beyond are based on collection year while earlier estimates are based on data year. Due to changes in the methods used, these data differ from earlier versions.

Violent crimes included are homicide, rape, robbery, and both simple and aggravated assault.

SOURCE: "Violent victimization rates by age, 1973–00," in *Key Facts at a Glance,* U.S. Department of Justice, Bureau of Justice Statistics, Washington, DC, 2002 [Online] http://www.ojp.usdoj.gov/bjs/glance/tables/vagetab.htm [Accessed April 30, 2002]

FIGURE 3.2

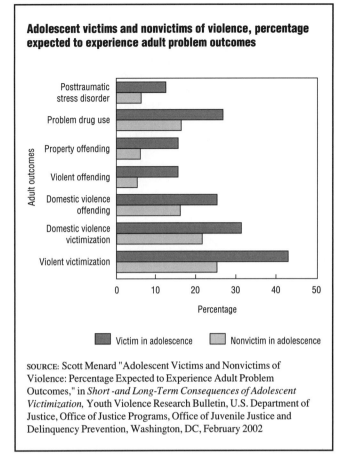

Adolescent victims and nonvictims of violence, percentage expected to experience adult problem outcomes

SOURCE: Scott Menard "Adolescent Victims and Nonvictims of Violence: Percentage Expected to Experience Adult Problem Outcomes," in *Short -and Long-Term Consequences of Adolescent Victimization,* Youth Violence Research Bulletin, U.S. Department of Justice, Office of Justice Programs, Office of Juvenile Justice and Delinquency Prevention, Washington, DC, February 2002

used to highlight trends.) Over 41 million personal and household crimes were committed in 1981. The 1981 adjusted rate of approximately 52.5 violent crimes per 1,000 persons was significantly higher than any time before 1977. The victimization rate for violent crimes increased between 1977 and 1981 and then declined until 1986. From 1986 to 1994 the violent crime rate increased, reaching 51.8 per 1,000 in 1994. From 1994 to 2000, however, violent crime rates fell 44.1 percent, and property crime rates declined by 44.2 percent. Figure 3.3 shows the adjusted trend of violent crime rates from 1973 through 2000.

Property crime rates fell dramatically between 1973 (adjusted data) and 1995. After a slight increase from 1973 to 1975, the rates dropped more or less consistently through 1995. Only motor vehicle theft remained relatively stable over this period. See Figure 3.4 for the adjusted trend of property crime rates between 1973 and 2000.

Violent victimizations by age dropped from 1973 to 2000. The proportion of victimizations across age groups has varied. For example, in 1973, 16- to 19-year-olds were about twice as likely to be victimized by violent crime as persons 35 to 49 years of age, but about three times as likely in 2000. For those ages 16–19, the violent victimization rate dropped by one-fifth between 1973 and 2000. For 12- to 15-year-olds, the rate of violent victimization dropped by one-quarter. For those ages 20–24, the rate fell over 40 percent. Rates of victimization remained within a much narrower range for those 50 to 64 years of age, yet still dropped 20 percent between 1973 and 2000. (See Table 3.7.)

Trends, 1994–2000

The 2000 rates of violent victimization continued the general decline of the previous several years. From 1994 to 2000 the rate of violent crime decreased by 46.1 percent. In 1994, there were 51.8 violent victimizations per 1,000 population compared to 27.9 per 1,000 in 2000. The robbery rate fell 49.2 percent and the aggravated assault rate dropped 52.1 percent. Personal theft declined 50 percent from 1994 to 2000.

The rates of all property crime categories continued to decrease from 1994 to 2000. Motor vehicle theft

TABLE 3.8

Crime victimization by victim and offender relationship, 2000

Relationship with victim	Violent crime Number	Violent crime Percent	Rape or sexual assault Number	Rape or sexual assault Percent	Robbery Number	Robbery Percent	Aggravated assault Number	Aggravated assault Percent	Simple assault Number	Simple assault Percent
All victims										
Total	6,322,730	100%	260,950	100%	731,780	100%	1,292,510	100%	4,037,500	100%
Nonstranger	3,376,520	53%	162,160	62%	203,630	28%	550,190	43%	2,460,530	61%
Intimate	655,350	10	45,100	17	38,000	5	66,350	5	505,900	13
Other relative	339,930	5	4,730	2*	20,650	3*	67,610	5	246,940	6
Friend/acquaintance	2,381,240	38	112,330	43	144,980	20	416,230	32	1,707,690	42
Stranger	2,829,840	45%	89,180	34%	507,170	69%	720,940	56%	1,512,540	38%
Relationship unknown	116,380	2%	9,600	4%*	20,970	3%*	21,380	2%*	64,420	2%
Male victims										
Total	3,612,390	100%	14,770	100%*	494,650	100%	915,970	100%	2,187,000	100%
Nonstranger	1,585,130	44%	9,260	63%*	113,430	23%	329,190	36%	1,133,250	52%
Intimate	98,850	3	0	0*	0	0*	18,380	2*	80,470	4
Other relative	107,970	3	0	0*	2,310	1*	36,930	4	68,730	3
Friend/acquaintance	1,378,310	38	9,260	63*	111,110	23	273,870	30	984,060	45
Stranger	1,945,980	54%	5,510	37%*	365,730	74%	565,410	62%	1,009,340	46%
Relationship unknown	81,280	2%	0	0%*	15,500	3%*	21,380	2%*	44,400	2%
Female victims										
Total	2,710,340	100%	246,180	100%	237,130	100%	376,540	100%	1,850,500	100%
Nonstranger	1,791,390	66%	152,900	62%	90,210	38%	221,010	59%	1,327,280	72%
Intimate	556,500	21	45,100	18	38,000	16	47,970	13	425,430	23
Other relative	231,960	9	4,730	2*	18,340	8*	30,680	8	178,220	10
Friend/acquaintance	1,002,930	37	103,070	42	33,870	14	142,360	38	723,630	39
Stranger	883,860	33%	83,680	34%	141,450	60%	155,530	41%	503,200	27%
Relationship unknown	35,090	1%	9,600	4%*	5,470	2%*	0	0%*	20,020	1%*

Note: Percentages may not total to 100% because of rounding. *Based on 10 or fewer sample cases.

SOURCE: Callie Marie Rennison, "Table 4. Victim and offender relationship, 2000," in *Criminal Victimization 2000: Changes 1999–2000 with Trends 1993–2000*, U.S. Department of Justice, Bureau of Justice Statistics, National Crime Victimization Survey, Washington, DC, 2001

showed a 52.8 percent decline. Theft rates fell 41.2 percent, continuing a steady decline that began in 1979.

COST OF VICTIMIZATION

Several different ways are available for a crime victim to consider his or her loss. Direct costs to the victim are easy to pinpoint, but indirect costs must be shared by the entire society (the expenses of the criminal justice system, for instance). While material costs (actual loss of property and medical expenses) are very important, emotional costs can affect the victim the rest of his or her life, sometimes producing radical and permanent changes in his or her lifestyle.

A National Institute of Justice Study

In *Victim Costs and Consequences: A New Look* (National Institute of Justice, Washington, D.C., 1996), Ted R. Miller, Mark A. Cohen, and Brian Wiersema estimated that from 1987 to 1990 personal crime cost $105 billion per year in medical costs, lost earnings, and public program expenses related to victim assistance. This amounts to about $425 per person (including children) in the United States. These tangible losses, however, do not account for the full impact of crime on victims. If the intangible factors of pain, suffering, reduced quality of life, and risk of death are included, victims' costs increase to an estimated $450 billion annually, or $1,800 per person.

The study excluded several crimes that also have large cost impacts, such as many forms of white-collar crime, personal fraud, and drug crimes. Also excluded were the costs of operating the nation's correctional institutions, an additional expense of approximately $40 billion annually.

VIOLENT CRIME. Violent crime, including drunk driving and arson, accounted for $426 billion of this annual total. Property crime accounted for $24 billion. Rape was considered the costliest crime, accounting for $127 billion annually. Rape and sexual abuse costs represented 28.2 percent of the total costs.

The study estimated that violent crime accounts for 3 percent of all U.S. medical spending and 14 percent of injury-related medical spending. The wage losses caused by violent crime are equivalent to 1 percent of American earnings. Violent crime may also account for as much as 10 to 20 percent of expenditures for mental health care,

FIGURE 3.3

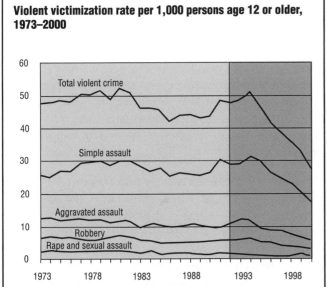

Violent victimization rate per 1,000 persons age 12 or older, 1973–2000

Note: From 1973 through 1991 data were collected under the National Crime Survey (NCS) and made comparable to data collected under the redesigned methods of the methods of the NCVS that began in 1992.

SOURCE: Callie Marie Rennison, "Violent victimization rate per 1,000 persons age 12 or older, 1973–2000," in *Criminal Victimization 2000: Changes 1999–2000 with Trends 1993–2000*, U.S. Department of Justice, Bureau of Justice Statistics, National Crime Victimization Survey, Washington, DC, 2001

FIGURE 3.4

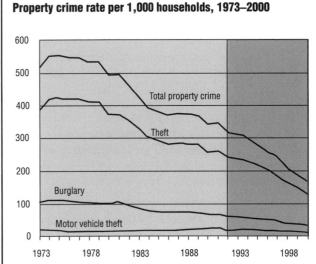

Property crime rate per 1,000 households, 1973–2000

Note: From 1973 through 1991 data were collected under the National Crime Survey (NCS) and made comparable to data collected under the redesigned methods of the methods of the NCVS that began in 1992.

SOURCE: Callie Marie Rennison, "Property crime rate per 1,000 households, 1973–2000," in *Criminal Victimization 2000: Changes 1999–2000 with Trends 1993–2000*, U.S. Department of Justice, Bureau of Justice Statistics, National Crime Victimization Survey, Washington, DC, 2001

primarily to treat victims. About half of these expenditures are for child abuse victims who are receiving treatment for abuse experienced years earlier. These estimates do not include any treatment for the perpetrators of violence.

PERSONAL CRIME. The study claimed that, by conservative estimates, personal crime reduced the average American's quality of life by 1.8 percent. Violence alone caused a 1.7 percent loss. These estimates include only costs to victimized households, ignoring the broader impact of crime-induced fear on society.

WHO PAYS THE CRIME BILL? The National Institute of Justice (NIJ) study found that crime victims and their families pay the bill for some crimes, while the public largely pays the bill for others. Insurers pay $45 billion annually due to crime, about $265 per every American adult. The federal government pays $8 billion annually for restorative and emergency services for crime victims, plus perhaps one-fourth of the $11 billion paid in health insurance payments. For arson and drunk driving, taxpayers and insurance purchasers cover almost all the tangible costs (for example, property damage and loss, medical care, police and fire services, and victim services).

Victims pay about $44 billion of the $57 billion in tangible non-service expenses for traditional crimes of violence (murder, rape, robbery, assault, abuse, and neglect). Employers pay almost $5 billion, primarily in health insur-

ance premiums, because of these crimes. (This estimate excludes sick leave and disability insurance costs other than workers' compensation.) Government bears the remaining costs through lost tax revenues and Medicare and Medicaid payments. Crime victim compensation accounts for 38 percent of homeowners' insurance payments and 29 percent of auto insurance payments.

Alfred Blumstein, a criminal justice expert and professor at Carnegie Mellon University (Pennsylvania), believes the report gives too high an estimate to intangible factors. He worries that the figures will cause people to demand more prisons and longer or mandatory sentences for certain crimes, and notes that although rates of incarceration have gone up as much as 450 percent in some cities, the violent crime rate has not dropped as dramatically. Blumstein says that there has been a considerable push by politicians to create "tough on crime" policies due to the public's perceptions. Also, Blumstein argues that the costs of prevention plans are more difficult to calculate, as their benefits cannot be known for 10 or 15 years. As a result, useful efforts such as prevention and rehabilitation for juveniles have largely been abandoned.

VICTIM SERVICES AND ASSISTANCE

Interest in assisting victims first developed in the United States as a desire for restitution (monetary compensation) to be paid to a victim by the offender. Restitution for criminal acts has a long history, dating back to biblical times. The Bible often cites money payments for injuries and this practice continued well into the Middle Ages. Around 1100, England's Henry I began to take a part of the restitution as a charge for holding a trial and for injury inflicted on the state because a criminal act had disturbed the peace of the kingdom. Eventually assault upon an individual became considered as an assault upon society, and the king took the entire payment.

For many years, a victim was often victimized again by the very system to which he or she turned for help. In 1982 Lois Haight observed in the "Statement of the Chairman," as part of the *President's Task Force on Victims of Crime* (Washington, D.C., 1982), that somewhere along the way, the system began to cater to lawyers, judges, and defendants. Meanwhile, the victim was treated with institutionalized disinterest.

The "revictimization" may begin with an insensitive police officer that questions whether a victim was really raped or whether she had enticed the rapist. The rape victim may sit alone in a hospital emergency room waiting to be treated. She may even have to pay for the rape examination herself. An assault victim may find the hospital is more concerned with whether he or she can pay for treatment. Judges and lawyers may seem to be more involved with the accused than with the victim. In fact, victims may never know when the trial takes place. If they do take part in a trial, victims may sit all day in a bare hallway outside the courtroom, waiting to testify as a witness, and may never even be called to the witness stand.

Changing Attitudes Toward Victims

Attitudes toward victims improved through the 1980s and 1990s. State and federal governments, the judicial system, and private groups grew more eager to help victims. By 1996 approximately 10,000 organizations offered services to victims of crime. These organizations included domestic violence shelters, rape crisis centers, and child abuse programs. Law enforcement agencies, hospitals, and social services agencies also provided victim services. The types of services provided include:

- Crisis intervention

- Counseling

- Emergency shelter and transportation

- Legal services

Victim Compensation

Victim compensation is a program that pays money from a public fund to help victims with expenses incurred because of a violent crime. Margery Fry, a British magistrate and legal reformer, began advocating a victim-compensation program during the 1950s. In her book, *Arms of the Law* (London, 1951), Fry wondered if we

have neglected restitution customs adopted by our earlier ancestors. She noted that making up for a wrong done held wide currency in earlier societies, and that it might be wise to revisit this form of punishment.

Her book and articles advocating compensation programs aroused considerable discussion in the United Kingdom and New Zealand. As a result, New Zealand's legislature passed a law permitting the government to award compensation to victims. After several years of debate, the British Parliament created an experimental program in 1964.

VICTIM-COMPENSATION PROGRAMS IN THE UNITED STATES. In the United States, interest in victim compensation grew rapidly in the mid-1960s. In 1965 California became the first state to develop a victim-compensation program. The idea spread across the country, with New York (1966), Hawaii (1967), Maryland (1968), Massachusetts (1968), and New Jersey (1971) soon adopting compensation programs.

By the year 2002 all 50 states, the District of Columbia, Puerto Rico, Guam, and the Virgin Islands had victim-compensation programs. Most state laws include reimbursement for medical treatment and physical therapy costs, counseling fees, lost wages, funeral and burial expenses, and loss of support to dependents of homicide victims. Generally, average maximum awards range from $10,000 to $25,000. Some states also require a minimum loss, most often $100, before a victim can be compensated, or a $100 deductible (amount automatically not paid for a claim).

Victim compensation normally does not cover the costs of pain and suffering, future income loss, or property loss and damage (except the loss of eyeglasses, dentures, etc., by the elderly). Compensation is paid only when other resources—private insurance or offender restitution, for example—do not cover the loss.

The federal government maintains the Crime Victims Fund, which is administered by the Office for Victims of Crime (OVC) in the U.S. Department of Justice. The Federal Victims of Crime Act of 1984 (VOCA, PL 98-473) established the fund, which administers two major formula grant programs: Victim Compensation and Victim Assistance. Like the state funds, the victim compensation grants cover medical treatment and physical therapy costs, counseling fees, lost wages, funeral and burial expenses, and loss of support to dependents of homicide victims. Victim assistance funds include money for crisis intervention, counseling, emergency shelter, and criminal justice advocacy. (See below for more information on VOCA.)

Deposits into the fund come from fines, penalty assessments, and bond forfeitures collected from convicted federal criminal offenders. In 2001 legislation was passed allowing the fund to receive gifts, donations, and bequests from private entities. The federal funds from VOCA provide about 20–25 percent of the state compensation programs' total budgets through grants given to each of the states. Of every $140 awarded to a victim, $100 comes from the state and $40 comes from VOCA. This percentage will increase to 60 percent in fiscal year (FY) 2003. When the fund began in FY 1986, $68.3 million was made available. By FY 2001, this amount had reached $550 million. From FY 1986 through FY 2001, $944,794,429 in VOCA compensation grant funds and $2,325,924,323 in VOCA victim assistance grants were distributed from the OVC to the states.

Restitution Programs

Restitution programs require those who have harmed an individual to repay the victim. In the past, the criminal justice system often focused primarily on punishing the criminal, leaving victims to rely on civil court cases to regain damages. By 2000 most states permitted courts to allow restitution payments as a condition of probation and/or parole. About half of the states have laws requiring courts to order restitution or to record the reason for not doing so.

Restitution laws require that the offender be convicted before any restitution can be ordered. Most states allow a victim to claim medical expenses and property damage or loss, and most permit families of homicide victims to claim costs for loss of support. The state of Washington allows courts to determine damages for pain and suffering, as well as "punitive damages" in an amount twice the victim's actual loss. In assessing damages, the courts must take into consideration the offender's ability to pay.

An offender may lose parole privileges and be imprisoned for nonpayment of restitution fees. The courts have upheld the constitutionality of incarcerating offenders for nonpayment, but the Supreme Court, in *Beardon v. Georgia* (461 US 660, 1983), ruled that an offender could not be sent to prison for nonpayment if he or she had made a good-faith effort to pay and could not. Such an action would violate the Fourteenth Amendment. In most cases the offender must prove his inability to make the payments. When offenders prove they cannot pay, the courts can reduce the amount, change the schedule of payments, or suspend payment.

Besides threatening offenders with imprisonment, some jurisdictions have other methods of collection. They can garnishee wages (take the payment amount from wages before the employee receives his salary) or attach (not allow a person to use) the offender's assets (bank accounts, stocks, bonds) until he or she pays the restitution. Some jurisdictions can even sell the offender's home.

Civil Suits

A victim can sue in civil court for damages without the offender having been found guilty of criminal charges.

Victims often follow this route because it is easier to win civil cases. In a criminal case, a jury or judge can find an alleged offender guilty only if the proof is "beyond a reasonable doubt." In a civil case, the burden of proof must be only a "preponderance of the evidence" to find against the accused. One still has to prove a crime was committed, that there were damages, and that the accused is liable to pay for those damages. Even when victims win a civil suit, they often have trouble collecting.

VICTIMS' RIGHTS

State Laws

Victims' rights include the right to attend criminal proceedings, to be notified of proceedings such as parole hearings, and to be free from harassment. The victims' rights movement became active through the 1980s and 1990s. While the movement did not seek to reduce the rights of the accused, it wanted the system to acknowledge that victims also have rights. As a result of this movement, by 2000 almost every state (46) had enacted a "Victims' Bill of Rights," and by 2002, 32 states had passed constitutional amendments for victims' rights.

Recent Federal Legislation

In addition to re-authorizing some $3.3 billion in funding for the Violence Against Women Act, other Federal legislation signed into law from 1999 to 2000 addressed the needs of crime victims.

The Child Abuse Prevention and Enforcement Act (H.R. 764, signed into law March 10, 2000) increased funding for child abuse prevention and victim assistance programs, while the Strengthening Abuse and Neglect Courts Act of 2000 (S. 2272, signed into law on October 17, 2000) provided $25 million in grants to state and local agencies to reduce the backlog of cases and improve efficiency in abuse and neglect courts.

The Insurance Discrimination Provision of the Financial Services Modernization Act (S. 900, signed into law on November 2, 1999) prohibits insurance companies from terminating coverage or raising premiums of victims of domestic violence. The Protecting Seniors from Fraud Act (S. 3164, signed into law on November 22, 2000) authorized $5 million over five years to reduce crime and fraud against the elderly, while Kristen's Act (H.R. 2780, signed into law on November 9, 2000) authorized funding to help organizations find missing adults in cases where foul play is suspected or when the adult suffers from diminished mental capacity.

The Victims of Trafficking and Violence Protection Act (H.R. 3244, signed into law on October 28, 2000) re-authorized the funding of rehabilitation and shelter programs for victims of international trafficking and creates new laws criminalizing forms of human trafficking such as slavery, involuntary servitude, peonage, or forced labor. This would include people who are coerced into sexual or other labor by violence, threat of violence, confiscation of legal documents, and other methods. Prison terms for all slavery violations were increased by 10 to 20 years and life imprisonment was added when the violation involves the death, kidnapping, or sexual abuse of the victim. The law also allows the President to withhold financial aid from governments that do not comply with minimum standards to eliminate such trafficking.

Victims' Participation at Sentencing

Every state allows courts to consider or ask for information from victims concerning the impact of the offense on their lives. Forty-eight states permit victim input at sentencing. Forty-two of these states allow written victim-impact statements (detailing the effect the crime has on the victim or, in the case of murder, on the victim's family). The Child Protection Restoration and Penalties Enhancement Act of 1990 (PL 101-647) permits child victims of federal crimes to present statements commensurate with their age, including drawings. While most impact statements are used at sentencing and parole hearings, victims often have input at bail hearings, pretrial release hearings, and plea-bargaining hearings.

The state legislatures have been quicker to agree on victims' rights legislation than the federal government. California's Proposition Eight, the state's "Victims' Bill of Rights," includes Penal Code Section 1191.1, which states:

> The victim or next of kin has the right to appear, personally or by counsel, at the sentencing proceeding and to reasonably express his or her views concerning the crime, the person responsible, and the need for restitution. The court, in imposing sentence, shall consider the statements of victims and next of kin...and shall state on the record its conclusion concerning whether the person would pose a threat to public safety if granted probation....

Edwin Villamoare and Virginia V. Neto, in *Victim Appearances at Sentencing Hearings Under the California Victims' Bill of Rights* (National Institute of Justice, Washington, D.C., 1987), found that in California there was little effect on the criminal justice system or sentencing when victims appeared at the sentencing proceedings. The victims, rather than wanting to participate in their cases, were generally more concerned with knowing what was going on with their cases. About 80 percent of the victims interviewed indicated that just the existence of the right to participate was most important, not whether they actually made use of that right. Most victims seemed only to want somebody to understand their situation and recognize their rights as victims.

PAYNE V. TENNESSEE. In 1991 the United States Supreme Court, in *Payne v. Tennessee* (501 US 808), ruled that the family of a murder victim could provide victim-impact evidence during the sentencing portion of the trial.

Pervis Payne was convicted of two counts of first-degree murder for killing Charisse Christopher and her two-year-old daughter, and one count of assault with intent to commit murder for attempting to kill her three-year-old son, Nicholas. In arguing for the death penalty, the prosecutor had presented statements from the victims' family. He stated that while there was nothing the jury could do for Charisse Christopher and her daughter, there was something that could be done for Nicholas.

In the *Payne* opinion, written by Chief Justice William Rehnquist, the Supreme Court majority overturned its earlier decisions in two similar cases, *Booth v. Maryland* (482 US 496, 1987) and *South Carolina v. Gather* (490 US 805, 1989). In these two cases the Court held that under the Eighth Amendment ("cruel and unusual punishment shall not be inflicted") a jury could not consider a victim-impact statement in a capital case (one punishable by death). The Supreme Court had found in *Booth* that

> The capital defendant must be treated as a 'uniquely individual human being' and, therefore, the Constitution requires the jury to make an individualized determination as to whether the defendant should be executed based on the character of the individual and the circumstances of the crime.

In *Payne*, the majority found that a victim-impact statement in no way limited the defendant's right to plead his or her case. The addition, "victim's impact evidence is simply another form or method of informing the sentencing authority about the specific harm caused by the crime in question, evidence of a general type long considered by sentencing authorities." The High Court concluded that prohibiting victim-impact statements unfairly weighted the case in favor of the defendant.

Justices John Paul Stevens and Thurgood Marshall, with Justice Harry Blackmun joining, dissented. Fearing that the Court was overturning constitutional liberties, Justice Stevens wrote,

> Until today our capital punishment jurisprudence has required that any decision to impose the death penalty be based solely on evidence that tends to inform the jury about the character of the offense and the character of the defendant. Evidence that serves no purpose other than to appeal to the sympathies or emotions of the juror has never been considered admissible.

According to Stevens the majority had obviously been moved by an argument that had strong political appeal but no proper place in a reasoned judicial argument.

Witnessing Executions

As noted in *FYI: Rights of Survivors of Homicide* (1999), a publication of the National Center for Victims of

Crime (NCVC), various states have statutes allowing victims' family members to be present at executions. As of December 1998 at least 13 states had statutes allowing immediate family members of victims to witness executions: Alabama, Arkansas, California, Delaware, Kentucky, Louisiana, Mississippi, Nevada, Ohio, Oklahoma, South Carolina, Tennessee, and Washington. Other states, though they do not have formal statutes, have informal policies permitting victims' families to view executions: Florida, Illinois, Montana, North Carolina, Pennsylvania, Texas, Utah, and Virginia. Most states limit the viewing to immediate family members and may limit the total number of viewers.

In Delaware in January of 1996 two sons of a victim watched the hanging of their father's murderer. In 1997 relatives of victims murdered in three different states watched the execution of an Ohio man, Michael Lee Lockart. In February of 1998 family members of the two murder victims of Texan Karla Faye Tucker, witnessed her execution by lethal injection. These family members declared that seeing the execution helped put closure to their tragedy. Other witnesses to such executions, however, report that they have yet to find closure.

Just how many victims' immediate family members (over age 18) can be present at executions varies from state to state, depending on the statutes in place. In most states, the number is limited. Some states allow only a few to attend, while others set no limits. Accommodating those family members wishing to be present becomes complicated when executions involve notorious criminals, especially mass murderers.

Such was the case of Timothy McVeigh, who was sentenced to death for bombing the Alfred P. Murrah Federal Building in Oklahoma City on April 19, 1995, killing 168 people and injuring many others. Prior to McVeigh's execution, set for June 11, 2001, more than 250 survivors and victims' relatives asked to witness the execution. In order to accommodate so many, a lottery was established to select 10 victims/family members to watch the sentence performed. Others wishing to see the execution were able to watch the event in a federal prison in Oklahoma City on closed-circuit television.

FEDERAL ACTIONS

The Federal Victim and Witness Protection Act of 1982

In 1982 Congress enacted the Federal Victim and Witness Protection Act, a bill designed to protect and assist victims and witnesses of federal crimes. The law permits victim-impact statements in sentencing hearings to provide judges with information concerning financial, psychological, or physical harm suffered by victims. The law also provides for restitution for victims and prevents victims and/or witnesses from being intimidated by threatening verbal harassment. The law establishes penalties for acts of retaliation by defendants against those who testify against them.

Victims who provide addresses and telephone numbers are to be notified of major events in the criminal proceedings, including the arrest of the accused, the times of any court appearances at which the victim may appear, the release or detention of the accused, and the victim's opportunities to address the sentencing court. The guidelines also recommend that federal officials consult victims and witnesses to obtain their views on such procedures as proposed dismissals and plea negotiations. Officials must not disclose the names and addresses of victims and witnesses.

The President's Task Force on Crime Victims

One dramatic reflection of the increased concern with the rights of crime victims was the creation of the Presidential Task Force on the Victims of Crime. In 1982 the Task Force's final report called for better treatment of victims by all parts of the criminal justice system and greater protection for victims and witnesses. The report recommended fundamental changes in the American judicial system, including the abolition of the exclusionary rule, which throws out any evidence gained as a result of improper police conduct. In addition, the Task Force recommended the abolition of parole so that the offender would be forced to serve the full sentence, reduced only by good-time credits. Other recommendations included:

- Changing the bail laws to permit courts to deny bail to persons found by clear and convincing evidence to present a danger to the community.

- Forbidding the release of those convicted and awaiting sentencing or appeal.

- Passing laws forbidding a criminal to make money from his or her crime through the sale of the story or movie rights about the crime.

Federal Victims of Crime Act (VOCA)

In 1984 Congress passed the Federal Victims of Crime Act (VOCA, PL 98-473), which committed the federal government to promote state and local victim support and compensation programs. The act established the Crime Victims Fund (see above). Two significant changes were made in the VOCA in 1988. To be eligible for federal funds, the 1998 amendments required that state programs must also include compensation for survivors of victims of drunk driving and domestic violence. These two groups had previously been excluded from compensation.

The Comprehensive Crime Control Act of 1990

In 1990 President George Bush signed the Comprehensive Crime Control Act (PL 101-647) that covered many aspects of crime control, including protection for victims of child abuse, penalties for Savings and Loan fraud, and mandatory death penalties. Included in the law is the Victims' Rights and Restitution Act of 1990, which secures victims of federal crimes the right to be treated with fairness and respect, reasonably protected from the accused, notified of court proceedings, afforded an opportunity to meet with a federal prosecutor, and provided with restitution. The act also bars criminals and convicted drunken drivers from declaring bankruptcy to avoid paying restitution.

The Compensation and Assistance to Victims of Terrorism or Mass Violence Act (1996)

In spring of 1996 Congress amended the VOCA (Justice for Victims of Terrorism Act of 1996, PL 104-132). The act authorized compensation for citizens victimized by terrorist acts, both at home and abroad. The law allows the director of the Victims Crime Fund (see above) to make supplemental grants to states to assist residents who are victims of terrorism.

After the terrorist attacks on the United States of September 11, 2001, the October 2001 USA Patriot Act authorized the transfer of emergency supplemental appropriation funding into the Emergency Reserve account to assist victims of the attacks. On April 22, 2002, the OVC announced that it had awarded $40 million to offer mental health counseling for victims of the September 11 attacks, their families, and crisis responders who helped victims of the attacks. The grants included funds to compensate victims for counseling services and to support state and local programs that offer various forms of counseling.

The Air Transportation Safety and System Stabilization Act

On September 22, 2001, the 107th Congress enacted Public Law 107-42, "The Air Transportation Safety and System Stabilization Act." In addition to requiring the federal government to compensate the air carriers for losses incurred as a result of the September 11th attacks, the Act established the "September 11th Victim Compensation Fund of 2001." The fund provides compensation to victims of the attacks who elect not to join in litigation (lawsuits) seeking additional money. The fund compensates any individual who was physically injured, or the families and beneficiaries of victims killed, as a result of the terrorist-related aircraft crashes of September 11th, 2001. The amount of non-economic loss compensation includes a $250,000 non-economic award for each deceased victim as well as $100,000 for the spouse and each dependent of a deceased victim. Though life insurance pay-outs, pensions and retirement accounts may be deducted from the final amount, the Department of Justice stated that it would be very rare that a claimant would receive less than $250,000.

CHAPTER 4

HATE CRIMES AND TERRORISM IN THE UNITED STATES

Crimes committed by hate groups or offenders and those committed by terrorist groups are often very similar, both in method and in effect. For example, a person acting from a motive of religious bias might use an incendiary device (one that causes fire, such as a Molotov cocktail) to burn down a mosque, church, or synagogue. A terrorist group might use the same type of device to burn down a government building. In both cases the results are property damage, intimidation, and possibly even the deaths of or injuries to innocent people.

The primary difference between these types of crime is the motive behind the act. While there are no single, comprehensive definitions for hate crimes and terrorism, the Federal Bureau of Investigation (FBI) uses these working definitions:

- Hate crime (also known as bias crime) is a criminal offense committed against a person, property, or society that is motivated, in whole or in part, by the offender's bias against a race, religion, ethnic/national-origin group, or sexual-orientation group.

- Terrorism is the unlawful use of force or violence against persons or property to intimidate or coerce a government, the civilian population, or any segment thereof, committed to further political or social objectives.

HATE AND TERRORIST GROUPS

The Southern Poverty Law Center (SPLC), a civil-rights advocacy group, reported that 676 hate groups were active in the United States in 2001, an increase of 12 percent from 2000 and nearly 50 percent from the 1990 figure of 457. Figure 4.1 shows the distribution of hate groups across the United States. The SPLC categorizes these groups as Ku Klux Klan (with 109 active groups in 2001), Neo-Nazi (209), Racist Skinhead (43), Christian Identity (31), Black Separatist (51), and Neo-Confederate

(124), plus special-interest groups and publishing houses that endorse hate doctrines (109).

Klan groups are generally related to the Ku Klux Klan in racist ideology if not in organization. The Klan militantly advocates white supremacy. Neo-Nazi groups also generally embrace white-supremacy doctrines. Not all Skinheads are racist or belong to an organized group; only Skinhead groups espousing racial hate doctrines are included in the list. Christian Identity groups are basically racist, anti-Semitic religious organizations opposed to anything they view as a threat to their faith, particularly Jewish people. Black Separatists, a newer category, are ideological groups that support or promote racially-based hate and the separation of the races.

Through the 1990s hate groups increasingly used computer technology to spread their doctrines. In 2000, according to the SPLC, over 300 Web sites on the Internet were dedicated hate sites. The nature of Internet sites and their establishment is such that a single individual may post a Web site and appear to be a large organization.

Militia Groups

Members of the militia movement believe it is imperative they prepare to defend themselves against the federal government and other assumed enemies. On weekends many militias practice military maneuvers to defend themselves against federal troops. They practice survival skills so they can outlast an occupation. Others refuse to pay taxes or appear in court. They frequently resist arrest. Many are members of the Identity religion, a sect that believes whites are God's chosen people and that the federal government is satanic and must be fought as a religious obligation. Many fear the influence of public schools and choose to home-school their children.

While militias have been active in the United States for over a generation, it was the bombing of the Alfred P.

FIGURE 4.1

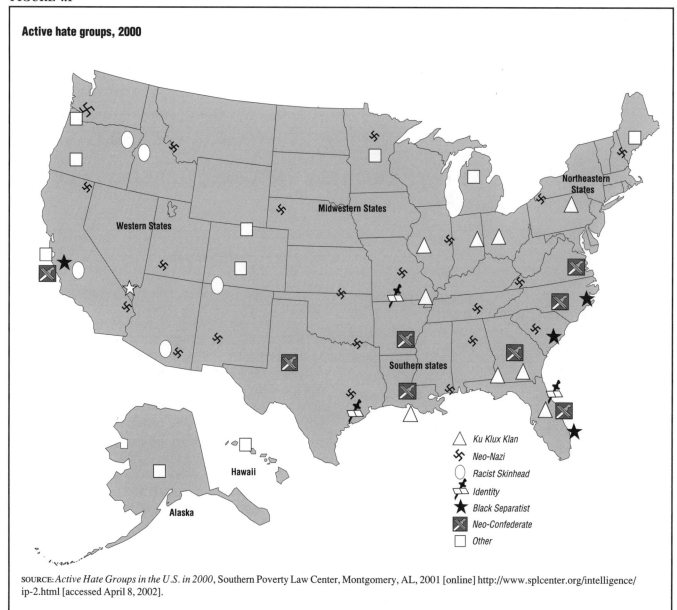

Active hate groups, 2000

Ku Klux Klan
Neo-Nazi
Racist Skinhead
Identity
Black Separatist
Neo-Confederate
Other

Northeastern States
Midwestern States
Western States
Southern states
Hawaii
Alaska

SOURCE: *Active Hate Groups in the U.S. in 2000*, Southern Poverty Law Center, Montgomery, AL, 2001 [online] http://www.splcenter.org/intelligence/ip-2.html [accessed April 8, 2002].

Murrah Federal Building in Oklahoma City on April 19, 1995, that made most Americans aware of their activities. Law enforcement authorities, and many citizens as well, believe that militias are a growing threat to the American people. They fear the paranoid and xenophobic (fearing or hating strangers or foreigners) tendencies of many of these groups will lead to more violence and destruction.

Militia members generally describe themselves as patriots trying to save the nation from an enemy unrecognized by most other Americans. This enemy might be the so-called "New World Order," a unified world government, usually aligned with the United Nations. The North American Free Trade Agreement on Tariffs and Trade (NAFTA) and the General Agreement on Tariffs and Trade (GATT) are also considered evidence of efforts to create a one-world government.

Other perceived enemies include African Americans and Jews, who threaten what the groups consider essential American values. Many recognized racist organizations, such as the Ku Klux Klan, also espouse anti-government rhetoric. In fact many anti-Semitic groups consider the United States a Zionist Occupied Government (ZOG), with Jews occupying and controlling the government and media. Other militias believe themselves the only true Christians and refer to Biblical scripture to justify their beliefs and actions.

Some groups include members who are neither racist nor anti-Semitic, but who believe the federal government is dangerous to individual freedom. Most militia groups consider the federal government an enemy whose goal is to take away individual rights and/or draw the United States into the world government. Therefore, in order to save their perceived way of life, they must destroy the federal government.

Militia leaders and members point to the Brady Handgun Violence Prevention Act of 1993 (PL 103-159), commonly known as the Brady Bill, as evidence of the government's attempts to limit individual rights. The Brady Bill requires a waiting period to purchase handguns. Militias also cite governmental blunders at the Branch Davidian compound outside Waco, Texas, which contributed to the deaths by fire of dozens of cult members, and at Ruby Ridge, Idaho, where authorities shot and killed the son and the wife of Randy Weaver, a militia leader. These events are accepted as evidence of the continuing federal government campaign to destroy individual freedoms. The federal government's environmental policy is seen as a further attempt to restrict individual freedoms.

In addition to using high-powered firearms, militia groups use or threaten to use weapons of mass destruction. In March 1995 a successful attack against a civilian target using weapons of mass destruction occurred when the Japanese religious group Aum Shinrikyo (translated as Aum Supreme Truth) released sarin gas in the Tokyo subway, killing 12 and injuring over 5,000 people. Fearing that similar events could also happen in the United States, in 1997 the FBI initiated more than 100 criminal cases that involved nuclear, biological, and chemical agents. In April of 1997 a package was delivered to the headquarters of the B'nai B'rith, a Jewish organization, in Washington, D.C. The package contained a threatening letter and a glass dish labeled "Anthracis Yersinia," supposedly containing anthrax bacilli, a deadly bacterial toxin. When the substance was tested, it was found to be a hoax. A potentially more dangerous incident was avoided by the September 1997 arrest of an individual for possessing the toxin ricin for use as a weapon.

In 1998 the FBI opened 181 Weapons of Mass Destruction (WMD) criminal cases, 112 of which were biological in nature, and in 1999 there were 123 WMD cases opened by the FBI, 100 of which involved the use of biological agents.

HATE CRIME LEGISLATION

Federal Laws

In 1990 Congress passed the Hate Crime Statistics Act (PL 101-275), which required the attorney general to "acquire data ... about crimes that manifest evidence of prejudice based on race, religion, sexual orientation or ethnicity" and to publish a summary of the data. The Hate Crimes Statistics Act was amended by the Violent Crime and Law Enforcement Act of 1994 (PL 103-322) to include bias-motivated acts against disabled persons. Further amendments in the Church Arsons Prevention Act of 1996 (PL 104-155) directed the FBI to track bias-related church arsons as a permanent part of its duties.

In 1990 only 11 states reported information on hate crimes. By 1994, 7,298 law enforcement agencies in 43 states and the District of Columbia, covering 58 percent of the U.S. population, reported their data. By 2000, hate crime data were reported to the FBI's Hate Crime Collection Program by 11,690 law enforcement agencies, representing 236.9 million (84.2 percent) in population throughout 48 states (Alabama and Hawaii did not participate in reporting) and the District of Columbia.

State Laws

According to recent data, only seven states—Arkansas, Hawaii, Indiana, Kansas, New Mexico, South Carolina, and Wyoming—had no laws that assigned criminal penalties to hate crimes. In six of these states, hate crimes are considered civil matters, not criminal offenses. In Wyoming, there are no laws specifying whether hate crimes require civil actions or criminal penalties. Forty-three states assign enhanced penalties to hate crimes, meaning the penalty for a crime is increased if the prosecutor is able to prove the attack was hate-motivated. (See Figure 4.2.) Most states and the District of Columbia have statutes specifically addressing vandalism of places of worship and cemeteries. Twenty-two states and the District of Columbia included crimes motivated by sexual-orientation bias in their definitions of hate crimes. (See Table 4.1.)

The constitutionality of these laws has been challenged on the grounds they punish free thought. In 1992 the U.S. Supreme Court, in *R.A.V. v. City of St. Paul* (112 S.Ct. 2538), found a Minnesota law outlawing certain "fighting words" unconstitutional. In this case, the defendant had burned a cross "inside the fenced yard of a black family." The Court ruled that

Although there is an important governmental interest in protecting the exercise of the black resident's right to occupy a dwelling free from intimidation, we cannot say that, under the circumstances before us, the government interest is unrelated to the suppression of free expression.

A law limiting pure speech or symbolic speech can only be upheld if it meets the "clear and present danger" standard of *Brandenburg v. Ohio* (395 U.S. 444, 1969). This standard means that speech may be outlawed if it incites or produces "imminent lawless action."

In June 1993, however, the Supreme Court, in *Mitchell v. Wisconsin* (113 S.Ct. 2194), upheld laws that impose harsher prison sentences and greater fines for criminals who are motivated by bigotry. The Court found that such statutes as the Wisconsin law do not illegally restrict free speech and are not so general as to restrict constitutional behavior.

FIGURE 4.2

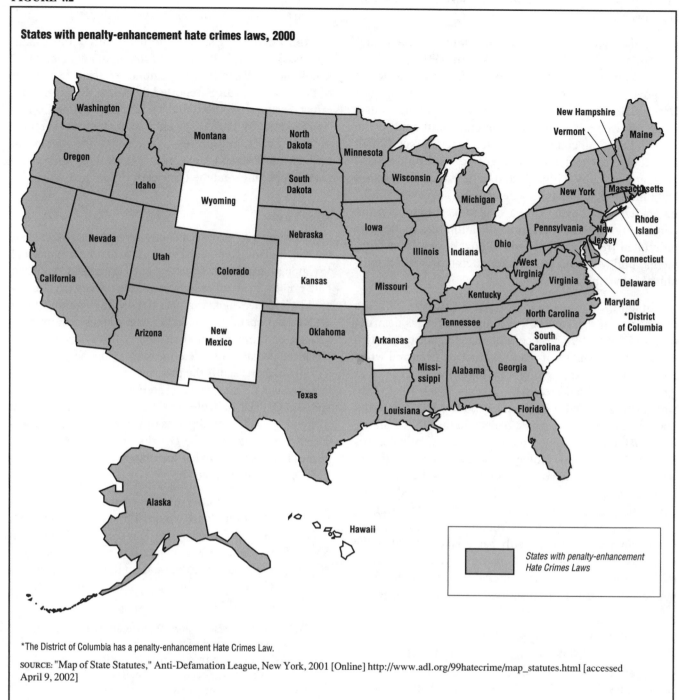

States with penalty-enhancement hate crimes laws, 2000

*The District of Columbia has a penalty-enhancement Hate Crimes Law.

SOURCE: "Map of State Statutes," Anti-Defamation League, New York, 2001 [Online] http://www.adl.org/99hatecrime/map_statutes.html [accessed April 9, 2002]

HATE CRIME OFFENSES

Hate crimes are criminal offenses motivated by the offender's personal prejudice or bias. The FBI has added hate crime to its Uniform Crime Reporting program. Its first reports to include hate-crime data were *Crime in the United States: 1996* (1997), and *Hate Crime Statistics: 1996* (Clarksburg, West Virginia, no date). In the 1994 Violent Crime and Law Enforcement Act, Congress added hate-motivated crimes against disabled persons to the list of bias crimes. The FBI began collecting data on crimes against persons with disabilities on January 1, 1997.

Data on hate crimes are incomplete because many incidents go unreported or cannot be verified as hate crimes. Some victims do not report hate crimes due to fear that the criminal justice system is biased against the group to which the victim belongs and that law enforcement authorities will not be responsive. Many attacks against homosexuals are not reported because the victims do not want to reveal their sexuality to others. In addition, proving that an offender acted from bias can be a long, tedious process, requiring much investigation. Until a law enforcement investigator can find enough evidence

TABLE 4.1

State hate crimes statutory provisions, 1999

Alabama - Missouri

	AL	AK	AZ	AR	CA	CO	CT	DC	DE	FL	GA	HI	ID	IL	IN	IA	KS	KY	LA	ME	MD	MA	MI	MN	MS	MO
Bias-Motivated Violence and Intimidation	✓	✓	✓		✓	✓	✓	✓	✓	✓	✓		✓	✓		✓		✓	✓	✓	✓	✓	✓	✓	✓	✓
Civil Action				✓	✓	✓	✓	✓			✓		✓	✓		✓					✓		✓	✓	✓	✓
Criminal Penalty	✓	✓	✓		✓	✓	✓	✓	✓	✓	✓		✓	✓		✓			✓	✓	✓	✓	✓	✓	✓	✓
Race, Religion, Ethnicity[1]	✓	✓	✓		✓	✓	✓	✓	✓	✓			✓	✓		✓			✓	✓	✓	✓	✓	✓	✓	✓
Sexual Orientation			✓		✓		✓	✓	✓	✓				✓		✓			✓	✓	✓		✓	✓		
Gender		✓	✓		✓			✓						✓		✓				✓	✓					
Other[2]	✓	✓	✓		✓			✓	✓					✓		✓				✓	✓		✓	✓		
Institutional Vandalism	✓		✓	✓	✓	✓	✓	✓	✓	✓	✓	✓		✓	✓		✓	✓	✓	✓	✓	✓	✓	✓	✓	✓
Data Collection[3]			✓		✓		✓	✓		✓			✓	✓		✓		✓	✓	✓	✓	✓	✓	✓		
Training for Law Enforcement Personnel[4]			✓		✓									✓		✓			✓	✓		✓		✓		

Montana - Wyoming

	MT	NE	NV	NH	NJ	NM	NY	NC	ND	OH	OK	OR	PA	RI	SC	SD	TN	TX	UT	VT	VA	WA	WV	WI	WY
Bias-Motivated Violence and Intimidation	✓	✓	✓	✓	✓		✓[5]	✓	✓	✓	✓	✓	✓	✓		✓	✓	✓[6]	✓[7]	✓	✓	✓	✓	✓	
Civil Action		✓	✓	✓						✓	✓	✓	✓	✓		✓	✓			✓	✓	✓			✓
Criminal Penalty	✓	✓	✓	✓	✓			✓	✓	✓	✓	✓	✓	✓		✓	✓	✓	✓	✓	✓	✓	✓	✓	
Race, Religion, Ethnicity[1]	✓	✓	✓	✓	✓			✓	✓	✓	✓	✓	✓	✓		✓	✓			✓	✓	✓	✓	✓	
Sexual Orientation		✓	✓	✓	✓	✓						✓		✓						✓		✓		✓	
Gender		✓	✓	✓	✓	✓		✓						✓						✓		✓	✓	✓	
Other[2]		✓	✓	✓	✓	✓					✓			✓						✓		✓	✓	✓	
Institutional Vandalism	✓		✓		✓	✓		✓		✓	✓	✓	✓	✓	✓		✓	✓			✓	✓		✓	
Data Collection[3]		✓	✓		✓					✓	✓	✓	✓				✓			✓	✓				
Training for Law Enforcement Personnel[4]											✓			✓								✓			

[1] The following states also have statutes criminalizing interference with religious worship: CA, DC, FL, ID, MD, MA, MI, MN, MS, MO, NV, NM, NY, NC, OK, RI, SC, SD, TN, VA, WV.

[2] "Other" includes mental and physical disability or handicap (AL, AK, AZ, CA, DC, DE, IL, IA, LA, ME, MA, MN, NE, NV, NH, NJ, NY, OK, RI, VT, WA, WI), political affiliation (DC, IA, LA, WV) and age (DC, IA, LA, VT).

[3] States with data collection statutes which include sexual orientation are AZ, CA, CT, DC, FL, IL, IA, MD, NV, OR, and WA; those which include gender are AZ, DC, IL, IA, MN, WA.

[4] Some other states have regulations mandating such training.

[5] New York State law provides penalty enhancement limited to the crime of aggravated harassment.

[6] The Texas Statute refers to victims selected "because of the defendant's bias or prejudice against a person or group."

[7] The Utah Statute ties penalties for hate crimes to violations of the victim's constitutional or civil rights.

SOURCE: "State Hate Crimes/Statutory Provisions," *Hate Crimes Laws: 1999*, Anti-Defamation League, New York, 1999 [Online] http://www.adl.org/99hatecrime/provisions.html [accessed April 9, 2002]

---

in a particular case to be sure the offender's actions came, at least in part, from bias, the crime is not counted as a hate crime.

Hate Crimes in 2000

According to the FBI, the number of hate crimes reported to the authorities fluctuated from 7,684 in 1993 to 5,852 in 1994 to 8,759 reported incidents in 1996. In 1998, 7,755 incidents were reported, and by 2000 that number had increased to 8,152 hate crime incidents reported to the FBI. Racial bias motivated 54.7 percent of the hate crimes in 2000; religious bias, 16.5 percent; sexual-orientation bias, 15.9 percent; and ethnic bias, 12.4 percent. (See Figure 4.3.) Among the specific bias types, anti-black incidents accounted for the largest number of single-bias incidents (2,904), followed by 1,119 anti-Jewish incidents and 1,106 anti-gay and anti-lesbian incidents. (See Table 4.2.)

A hate crime may have more than one victim and multiple offenders. To tabulate hate-crime data, the FBI counts one offense for each victim of a crime against persons and one offense for each distinct act of crime against property and crime against society. Therefore, more offenses (9,524) and victims (10,021) were reported than incidents (8,152) in 2000.

In 2000 some 6,397 individuals were victims of single-bias hate incidents. A single-bias incident is a hate crime in which one type of offense (such as assault) is committed as the result of one bias-motivation (such as anti-black sentiment). Individuals were victims of 3,660 racial incidents, 1,190 sexual-orientation incidents, and 811 ethnicity/national-origin incidents. Of institutional-directed hate crimes, 272 churches were targeted in 2000, compared to 219 government institutions and slightly more business/financial institutions. (See Table 4.3.)

Kinds of Crime Motivated by Hate

Hate crimes are categorized in three ways: crimes against persons, crimes against property, and crimes against society. In 2000 about 65 percent of hate offenses

FIGURE 4.3

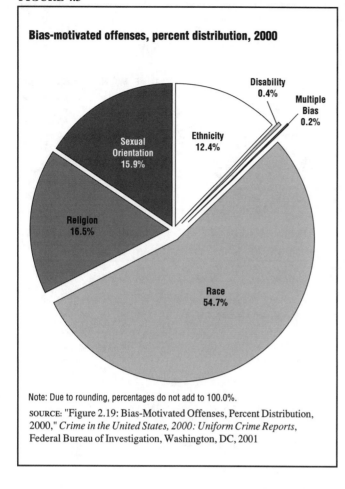

Bias-motivated offenses, percent distribution, 2000

Disability 0.4%
Multiple Bias 0.2%
Ethnicity 12.4%
Sexual Orientation 15.9%
Religion 16.5%
Race 54.7%

Note: Due to rounding, percentages do not add to 100.0%.

SOURCE: "Figure 2.19: Bias-Motivated Offenses, Percent Distribution, 2000," *Crime in the United States, 2000: Uniform Crime Reports*, Federal Bureau of Investigation, Washington, DC, 2001

TABLE 4.2

Number of hate crime incidents, offenses, victims, and known offenders by bias motivation, 2000

Bias motivation	Incidents	Offenses	Victims[1]	Known offenders[2]
Total	**8,152**	**9,524**	**10,021**	**7,642**
Single-Bias Incidents	**8,144**	**9,507**	**10,003**	**7,632**
Race:	**4,368**	**5,206**	**5,435**	**4,498**
Anti-White	886	1,061	1,091	1,182
Anti-Black	2,904	3,433	3,562	2,832
Anti-American Indian/ Alaskan Native	57	62	64	58
Anti-Asian/Pacific Islander	281	317	339	273
Anti-Multiracial Group	240	333	379	153
Religion:	**1,483**	**1,568**	**1,711**	**590**
Anti-Jewish	1,119	1,172	1,280	417
Anti-Catholic	56	61	63	33
Anti-Protestant	59	62	62	23
Anti-Islamic	28	33	36	20
Anti-Other Religious Group	173	188	211	78
Anti-Multireligious Group	44	46	52	18
Anti-Atheism/Agnosticism/etc.	4	6	7	1
Sexual Orientation:	**1,330**	**1,517**	**1,589**	**1,471**
Anti-Male Homosexual	925	1,052	1,089	1,112
Anti-Female Homosexual	181	213	230	173
Anti-Homosexual	182	210	226	153
Anti-Heterosexual	22	22	24	18
Anti-Bisexual	20	20	20	15
Ethnicity/National Origin:	**927**	**1,180**	**1,232**	**1,037**
Anti-Hispanic	567	745	773	711
Anti-Other Ethnicity/ National Origin	360	435	459	326
Disability:	**36**	**36**	**36**	**36**
Anti-Physical	20	20	20	22
Anti-Mental	16	16	16	14
Multiple-Bias Incidents[3]	**8**	**17**	**18**	**10**

[1] The term *victim* may refer to a person, business, institution, or society as a whole.
[2] The term *known offender* does not imply that the identity of the suspect is known, but only that an attribute of the suspect is identified which distinguishes him/her from an unknown offender.
[3] A *multiple-bias incident* is any hate crime in which two or more offense types were committed as a result of two or more bias motivations.

SOURCE: "Table 2.33: Number of Incidents, Offenses, Victims, and Known Offenders, by Bias Motivation, 2000," *Crime in the United States, 2000: Uniform Crime Reports*, Federal Bureau of Investigation, Washington, DC, 2001

were crimes against persons. Of the 6,223 hate crimes against persons, over half (3,294) were acts of intimidation, while 2,890 were assaults (1,616 simple assaults and 1,274 aggravated assaults). (See Table 4.4.)

About one-third (3,242) of hate crimes in 2000 were property crimes, an increase from 2,905 in 1998. Most property crimes (2,766) were acts of destruction, damage, and/or vandalism. Less than 1 percent (59) were crimes against society.

In the wake of the events of September 11, 2001, a surge in attacks against people of Arab descent and Muslims in general was reported, including incidents of fire bombings, shootings, and other acts of violence. In 2000 there were only 33 reported incidents of anti-Islamic hate crimes. In the four months following the attacks, more than 250 incidents against Muslims, Arabs, and South Asians were reported. Some 70 persons were charged on the state and local levels with hate crimes directed at Arab or Muslim Americans as a result of the September 11 terrorist attacks. As of February 2002 the FBI had initiated 318 hate crime investigations involving Americans of Arab, Muslim, and Sikh heritage. As a result of these investigations, eight individuals were charged with federal hate crimes.

Hate-Motivated Murders

The most severe hate-motivated crime against a person is murder. In 2000, 19 bias-motivated murders were reported to the FBI, less than 1 percent of all hate offenses. By their very nature, however, murders motivated by hate or bias are the most horrible and unforgettable to society. The nation was shocked and outraged by the brutal killing of a black man, James Byrd, Jr., near the small town of Jasper, Texas, in June 1998. Two white men convicted in the murder, John William King and Lawrence Russell Brewer, were suspected of ties to white supremacy organizations. A third man, Shawn Allen Berry, was also convicted. These men beat and kicked Byrd and then chained him to the back of a pickup truck and dragged him until his body was torn apart.

TABLE 4.3

Hate crime incidents by victim type and bias motivation, 2000

Bias motivation	Total	Victim type					
		Individual	Business/ financial institution	Government	Religious organization	Society/ public	Other/ unknown/ multiple
Total	**8,063**	**6,404**	**267**	**219**	**272**	**298**	**603**
Single-Bias Incidents	**8,055**	**6,397**	**267**	**219**	**272**	**298**	**602**
Race	4,337	3,660	130	130	25	165	227
Religion	1,472	704	80	52	238	93	305
Sexual Orientation	1,299	1,190	25	27	5	15	37
Ethnicity/National Origin	911	811	32	8	4	23	33
Disability	36	32	0	2	0	2	0
Multiple-Bias Incidents[1]	**8**	**7**	**0**	**0**	**0**	**0**	**1**

[1] A *multiple-bias incident* is a hate crime in which two or more offense types were committed as a result of two or more bias motivations.

SOURCE: "Table 8: Incidents, Victim Type, by Bias Motivation, 2000," *Hate Crime Statistics, 2000*, Federal Bureau of Investigation, Washington, DC, 2001

To "help" the town, the Ku Klux Klan came to Jasper, stating that they were there to protect whites from blacks. The Black Muslims and the New Black Panthers came to protect blacks from whites. Fortunately, law enforcement officers and the townspeople of Jasper were able to prevent further violence. The townspeople repeatedly expressed their sorrow at the murder and begged outsiders to go away and let them try to cope with the crime and its aftermath. The Byrd family issued a written statement asking the public not to use the murder as an excuse for more hatred and retribution. They asked that Americans view the incident as a wake-up call, and that it lead to a time of self-examination and reflection.

Despite the publicity the Byrd case received, the pleas of his family seem to have had little effect on national hate crime murder statistics. Each year, equally shocking cases of hate-motivated murders occur. A man with links to a white supremacist group killed a Filipino-American postal worker after opening fire on a Jewish day care center in Los Angeles, California, in August of 1999. Five people, including an Indian, two Asians, and one African American, were killed in Pittsburgh, Pennsylvania, when an immigration lawyer went on a shooting rampage in April 2000. Also in 2000, in a crime similar to the killing of Byrd in Texas, two teenaged boys beat an African-American gay man and then ran over him with a car repeatedly until he was dead. In Texas, Byrd's death did lead to the passage of the James Byrd Jr. Hate Crimes Act on May 11, 2001. The bill intensifies penalties for crimes motivated by the victim's race, religion, sex, disability, sexual orientation, age, or national origin.

Another famous case of racially-motivated murder came to a close after almost 30 years on May 22, 2002. On that day, Bobby Frank Cherry, 71, a former Ku Klux Klan member, was convicted of four counts of murder stemming from the 1963 bombing of the 16th Street

TABLE 4.4

Number of hate crime offenses, victims, and known offenders, 2000

Offense	Offenses	Victims[1]	Known offenders[2]
Total	**9,524**	**10,021**	**7,642**
Crimes against persons:	6,223	6,223	6,266[3]
Murder and nonnegligent manslaughter	19	19	26
Forcible rape	4	4	5
Aggravated assault	1,274	1,274	1,734
Simple assault	1,616	1,616	2,062
Intimidation	3,294	3,294	2,421
Other[4]	16	16	18
Crimes against property:	**3,242**	**3,739**	**1,653[3]**
Robbery	139	160	327
Burglary	138	158	76
Larceny-theft	114	121	81
Motor vehicle theft	11	12	10
Arson	52	70	48
Destruction/damage/vandalism	2,766	3,193	1,092
Other[4]	22	25	19
Crimes against society[4]	**59**	**59**	**78[3]**

[1] The term *victim* may refer to a person, business, institution, or society as a whole.
[2] The term *known offender* does not imply that the identity of the suspect is known, but only that an attribute of the suspect is identified which distinguishes him/her from an unknown offender.
[3] The actual number of known offenders is 7,642. Some offenders, however, may be responsible for more than one offense and are, therefore, counted more than once in this table.
[4] Includes additional offenses collected in National Incident-Based Reporting System (NIBRS).

SOURCE: "Table 2.34: Number of Offenses, Victims, and Known Offenders, by Offense, 2000," *Crime in the United States, 2000: Uniform Crime Reports*, Federal Bureau of Investigation, Washington, DC, 2001

Baptist Church in Birmingham, Alabama. Four girls were killed—three were 14 years of age and one was 11 years old. Cherry, who had been trained in demolition in the Army, claimed during the trial that he could not have planted the bomb the night before the attack because he was at home watching wrestling on TV with

TABLE 4.5

Hate crime incidents by bias motivation and location, 2000

| Location | Total incidents | Bias motivation | | | | | |
		Race	Religion	Sexual orientation	Ethnicity/ national origin	Disability	Multiple
Total	**8,063**	**4,337**	**1,472**	**1,299**	**911**	**36**	**8**
Air/bus/train terminal	85	50	11	14	10	0	0
Bank/savings and loan	12	7	2	2	1	0	0
Bar/nightclub	147	66	2	63	16	0	0
Church/synagogue/temple	336	40	276	13	7	0	0
Commercial office building	232	125	45	27	33	2	0
Construction site	25	13	7	2	3	0	0
Convenience store	91	56	5	13	16	1	0
Department/discount store	48	29	4	11	4	0	0
Drug store/Dr.'s office/hospital	58	42	6	3	7	0	0
Field/woods	77	41	10	18	8	0	0
Government/public building	101	66	19	9	7	0	0
Grocery/supermarket	42	23	3	6	10	0	0
Highway/road/alley/street	1,441	893	96	267	180	4	1
Hotel/motel/etc.	45	32	3	6	4	0	0
Jail/prison	58	53	0	3	2	0	0
Lake/waterway	20	7	3	8	2	0	0
Liquor store	8	6	0	1	1	0	0
Parking lot/garage	485	286	51	76	67	5	0
Rental storage facility	4	2	0	2	0	0	0
Residence/home	2,590	1,373	445	451	301	17	3
Restaurant	191	113	11	27	38	2	0
School/college	917	518	179	140	77	2	1
Service/gas station	77	46	7	8	16	0	0
Specialty store (TV, fur, etc.)	125	62	21	15	27	0	0
Other/unknown	840	382	266	113	73	3	3
Multiple locations	8	6	0	1	1	0	0

SOURCE: "Table 10: Incidents, Bias Motivation, by Location, 2000," *Hate Crime Statistics, 2000*, Federal Bureau of Investigation, Washington, DC, 2001

his cancer-stricken wife. Prosecutors were able to show that not only was there no wrestling on TV that night, but that Cherry's wife was not diagnosed with cancer until two years after the bombing. Thomas E. Blanton, Cherry's surviving accomplice in the bombing, was convicted in 2001 and sentenced to life in prison. A third accomplice, Robert Chambliss, was convicted in 1977 and later died in prison.

Where Do Hate Crimes Occur?

Of bias incidents in 2000, most (2,590) occurred at the victim's home, compared to 1,441 on highways, streets, roads, and alleys. School and college locations accounted for 917 hate crimes, 485 occurred in parking lots and garages, and 336 occurred in places of worship. (See Table 4.5.)

Who Commits Hate Crimes?

Hate crimes may be committed by an individual, a group of individuals, or an organization with a bias against certain races, religions, or societal groups. The Anti-Defamation League (ADL) states that perpetrators of hate crimes fall into three groups: mission-oriented, reactive, and thrill-seeking.

The mission-oriented perpetrator may or may not be a member of an extremist organization, but always acts from an ideology of bigotry seeking to rid the world of what that individual or group considers evil. This type of perpetrator is the least common type of offender.

Another type of hate-crime perpetrator is the "reactive offender." This type of offender feels that he or she is retaliating against some perceived imminent harm, threat, or danger from the victim, and sees the race, ethnicity, religion, or lifestyle of the victim as responsible for the perpetrator's own problems in life. The offense is usually opportunistic (based on spur-of-the-moment impulses). Frequently, alcohol or drug use is a factor. The reactive offender is the most common type of perpetrator.

In 1997 the Leadership Conference Education Fund (LCEF), a civil-rights advocacy group, published *Cause for Concern: Hate Crimes in America* (Washington, D.C.). Surprisingly, the LCEF found that "youthful thrill-seekers" were also responsible for a large number of hate crimes.

In 2000 whites committed 4,111 of all hate crimes (about 43 percent), blacks were responsible for 1,021 (11 percent), and the offender was unknown in about 35

TABLE 4.6

Hate crime offenses by known offenders race and bias motivation, 2000

Bias motivation	Total offenses	Known offender's race						Unknown offender
		White	Black	American Indian/Alaskan Native	Asian/ Pacific Islander	Multi-racial group	Unknown race	
Total	9,430	4,111	1,021	43	82	177	657	3,339
Single-Bias Incidents	9,413	4,107	1,021	43	82	174	655	3,331
Race:	5,171	2,449	644	26	58	98	358	1,538
Anti-White	1,050	186	527	14	24	32	105	162
Anti-Black	3,409	1,981	72	7	24	50	212	1,063
Anti-American Indian/Alaskan Native	62	33	2	3	1	0	7	16
Anti-Asian/Pacific Islander	317	136	30	2	6	8	20	115
Anti-Multiracial Group	333	113	13	0	3	8	14	182
Religion:	1,556	316	39	3	7	11	117	1,063
Anti-Jewish	1,161	224	19	1	4	5	87	821
Anti-Catholic	61	20	5	0	0	0	5	31
Anti-Protestant	62	16	0	1	0	0	4	41
Anti-Islamic	33	8	4	0	2	0	4	15
Anti-Other Religious Group	187	35	10	1	1	6	12	122
Anti-Multireligious Group	46	12	1	0	0	0	5	28
Anti-Atheism/Agnosticism/etc.	6	1	0	0	0	0	0	5
Sexual Orientation:	1,486	714	168	10	8	45	117	424
Anti-Male Homosexual	1,023	514	117	7	8	38	80	259
Anti-Female Homosexual	211	94	29	3	0	5	11	69
Anti-Homosexual	210	84	18	0	0	2	23	83
Anti-Heterosexual	22	11	1	0	0	0	3	7
Anti-Bisexual	20	11	3	0	0	0	0	6
Ethnicity/National Origin:	1,164	616	159	4	9	19	55	302
Anti-Hispanic	735	403	122	4	5	17	23	161
Anti-Other Ethnicity/National Origin	429	213	37	0	4	2	32	141
Disability:	36	12	11	0	0	1	8	4
Anti-Physical	20	6	6	0	0	1	5	2
Anti-Mental	16	6	5	0	0	0	3	2
Multiple-Bias Incidents[1]	17	4	0	0	0	3	2	8

[1] A *multiple-bias incident* is a hate crime in which two or more offense types were committed as a result of two or more bias motivations.

SOURCE: "Table 5: Offenses, Known Offender's Race, by Bias Motivation, 2000," *Hate Crime Statistics, 2000*, Federal Bureau of Investigation, Washington, DC, 2001

percent of all cases. Racial acts by whites against blacks accounted for 1,981, the largest percentage of all racial incidents. Of the 644 racially motivated attacks by blacks, 527 were directed against whites. (See Table 4.6.)

The Burning of Houses of Worship

A rash of church arsons in the early 1990s—53 black churches were burned between 1990 and June 1996, 23 of them in 1996 alone—created a wave of national concern, and motivated the federal government to commit new resources to investigate the fires. In June 1996 the National Church Arson Task Force (NCATF) was formed to coordinate the efforts of federal, state, and local law enforcement. The FBI and the Bureau of Alcohol, Tobacco, and Firearms (ATF) worked with local and state law officers to investigate church arsons. Other federal groups also pitched in to help rebuild houses of worship and ease community tensions.

From January 1995 to mid-August 2000, the NCATF investigated 945 arsons and bombings of houses of wor-

ship. Almost 33 percent were black churches (310). Over 67 percent were other houses of worship. Of the 486 arsons that occurred in the South, 43.8 percent were aimed at black places of worship. (See Figure 4.4.)

ARRESTS. From 1995 through August 2000, law enforcement officers made arrests in 36.2 percent of 945 investigations. Investigations in 61.8 percent of cases were still pending. (See Figure 4.5.) Of the 342 suspects arrested, 136 were arrested for attacks on black houses of worship and 290 for acts against non-black places of worship.

RACE, AGE, AND SEX OF ARRESTEES. For all of the arsons, over 80 percent of arrestees were white, while 15.1 percent of those arrested were African American and 3 percent were Hispanic. Of attacks on black churches, 62.5 percent of arrestees were Caucasian, 36.8 percent were African American, and less than 1 percent were Hispanic. For all other houses of worship, almost 90 percent of those arrested were Caucasian, while 5.2 percent were

FIGURE 4.4

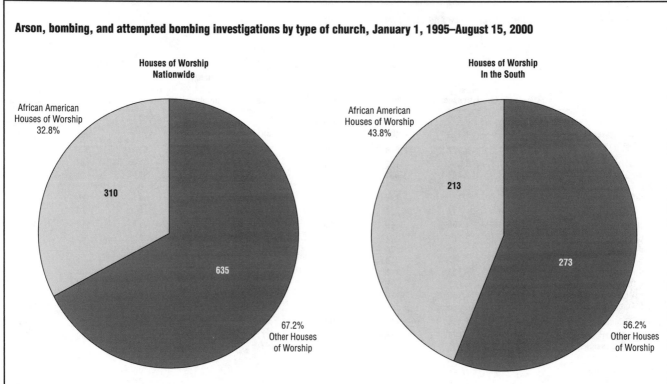

Arson, bombing, and attempted bombing investigations by type of church, January 1, 1995–August 15, 2000

Houses of Worship
Nationwide

African American
Houses of Worship
32.8%

310

635

67.2%
Other Houses
of Worship

Houses of Worship
In the South

African American
Houses of Worship
43.8%

213

273

56.2%
Other Houses
of Worship

Total House of Worship Arsons/Bombings – 945

SOURCE: "Chart A: Breakdown of Arson/Bombing/Attempted Bombing Investigations, January 1, 1995<en>August 15, 2000," *National Church Arson Task Force—Fourth Year Report*, Bureau of Alcohol, Tobacco and Firearms, Washington, DC, 2000 [Online] http://www.atf.treas.gov/pub/gen_pub/report2000/index.htm [accessed April 9, 2002]

African American, 4.1 percent were Hispanic, and one percent were Asian. (See Figure 4.6.)

Males (91.9 percent) ages 14 to 24 (58.2 percent) were the most likely group to be arrested for church arsons and bombings. Only 8.1 percent of those arrested were females. Only 27.6 percent of arrestees were older than age 24. Some 14.2 percent of arrestees (61) were between the ages of 6 and 13. (See Figure 4.7.)

TERRORISM

While no single definition of terrorism is available, the FBI uses the following definitions in its annual report (*Terrorism in the United States, 1999,* Washington, D.C., 2001):

- Domestic terrorism involves groups or individuals who are based and operating entirely within the United States and Puerto Rico without foreign direction. Their acts are directed at elements of the U.S. government or population.

- International terrorism is the unlawful use of force or violence by a group or individual with some connection to a foreign power, or whose acts cross international boundaries. Their aim is to intimidate or coerce

a government, the civilian population, or any segment of these to achieve a political or social objective.

From 1980 to 1999 the FBI recorded 327 incidents, or suspected incidents of terrorism in the United States, that killed 205 people and injured 2,037. Of the 327 incidents, 239 were attributed to domestic terrorists and 88 were international. During the same time period, 130 planned acts of terrorism were prevented by U.S. law enforcement agencies. Of those, 88 were planned by domestic groups or individuals and 47 by international groups or individuals.

According to the FBI, while the overall number of terrorist incidents declined from 1990 to 1999 when compared to the previous ten years, the attacks resulted in greater destruction and numbers of casualties. Of the 60 terrorist attacks between 1990 and 1999, 182 people were killed and nearly 2,000 were injured. By comparison, from 1980 to 1989, there were more than four times as many attacks (267), but the death toll was only 23, with 105 injuries.

According to the U.S. State Department, in 2000 there were 423 international terrorist attacks, an increase of 8 percent from the 392 such attacks recorded in 1999. The number of casualties as the result of these attacks also increased. In 2000, 405 people were killed and 791 were wounded as the result of international terrorist attacks, compared to 233 killed and 706 wounded in 1999.

Incidents of Domestic Terrorism

On April 19, 1995, one of the most deadly acts of domestic terrorism occurred in Oklahoma City when a two-ton truck bomb exploded just outside the Alfred P. Murrah federal building, killing 168 people and injuring 518. Because a day-care center was in the building very near the site of the explosion, many of the victims were children. Federal authorities later arrested Timothy McVeigh for the crime. McVeigh, who was rumored to be associated with an anti-government militia group, was convicted and executed in 2001.

While the toll in lives and property damage was much lower than in the Oklahoma City bombing, the Olympic Games bombing of 1996 created international alarm. In July of 1996, during the Olympic Summer Games in Atlanta, a nail-packed pipe bomb exploded in a large common area. One person was killed and more than 100 injured. Authorities believed the perpetrator may have been affiliated with a so-called Christian Identity group, many of whom see the Olympic Games as part of a satanic New World Order.

Shortly after the attack, suspicion centered on a security guard at Centennial Park, where the blast occurred. He was later cleared and given an official apology. In May of 1998 the FBI added Eric Robert Rudolph to its Top Ten Most Wanted list, seeking him for questioning about the Olympics bombing and two others that followed. Rudolph was also charged with bombing the New Woman All Women Health Care Center (Birmingham, Alabama) in January of 1998. In that blast, an off-duty police officer was killed and a nurse was seriously injured. A $1 million reward was offered by the FBI, the ATF, and the Birmingham Police Department, but Rudolph remained on the run as of May 2002.

In January of 1998 Theodore Kaczynski was sentenced to life imprisonment with no possibility of parole for his actions as the "Unabomber." Over a 17-year period Kaczynski committed 16 bombings in several states. Although he claimed the bombings (usually letter bombs) were directed against the federal government, the victims were generally not directly related to government. Three people were killed and 23 persons injured in the attacks. The manhunt for Kaczynski was one of the longest, most difficult cases in U.S. history, involving hundreds of federal and state law enforcement agents.

Kaczynski was not apprehended until his 56-page "manifesto" was published in *The New York Times* and *The Washington Post* newspapers. His brother, David, read the document and recognized the words as his brother's. Contacting the FBI, David shared his fears that his

FIGURE 4.5

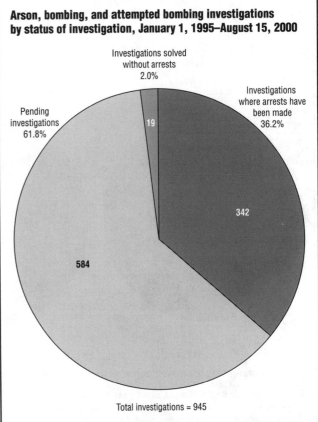

Arson, bombing, and attempted bombing investigations by status of investigation, January 1, 1995–August 15, 2000

Investigations solved without arrests 2.0%

Investigations where arrests have been made 36.2%

Pending investigations 61.8%

19

342

584

Total investigations = 945

SOURCE: "Chart B: Breakdown of Arson/Bombing/Attempted Bombing Investigations, January 1, 1995–August 15, 2000," *National Church Arson Task Force—Fourth Year Report*, Bureau of Alcohol, Tobacco and Firearms, Washington, DC, 2000 [Online] http://www.atf.treas.gov/pub/gen_pub/report2000/index.htm [accessed April 9, 2002]

brother Theodore was the Unabomber. This tip led to the subsequent capture of Theodore, who later pleaded guilty at his trial and received a sentence of life imprisonment without the possibility of parole.

On September 25, 2001, a letter postmarked September 20 from St. Petersburg, Florida, containing a white powdery substance, was handled by an assistant to NBC News anchorman Tom Brokaw. After complaining of a rash, the assistant consulted a physician and tested positive for exposure to the anthrax bacterium (*bacillus anthracis*), an infectious agent which, if inhaled into the lungs, can lead to death. Over the next two months, envelopes testing positive for anthrax were received by various news organizations in the United States and by government offices, including the offices of Senate Majority Leader Tom Daschle and of New York Governor George Pataki. As a result of exposure to anthrax sent via the U.S. mail, five people died, including two postal workers who handled letters carrying the anthrax spores. Hundreds more who were exposed were placed on antibiotics as a preventative measure. Despite an intensive

FIGURE 4.6

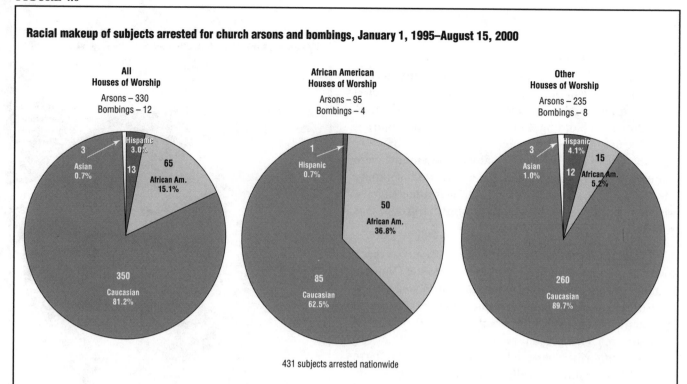

Racial makeup of subjects arrested for church arsons and bombings, January 1, 1995–August 15, 2000

All Houses of Worship
Arsons – 330
Bombings – 12

3 Asian 0.7%
Hispanic 3.0%
13
65 African Am. 15.1%
350 Caucasian 81.2%

African American Houses of Worship
Arsons – 95
Bombings – 4

1 Hispanic 0.7%
50 African Am. 36.8%
85 Caucasian 62.5%

Other Houses of Worship
Arsons – 235
Bombings – 8

3 Asian 1.0%
Hispanic 4.1%
12
15 African Am. 5.2%
260 Caucasian 89.7%

431 subjects arrested nationwide

Note: Five (5) additional Caucasian subjects arrested for arson/bombing of an African American House of Worship and a non-African American House of Worship

SOURCE: "Chart C: Racial Makeup of Subjects Arrested for Church Arsons/Bombings Nationwide, January 1, 1995–August 15, 2000," *National Church Arson Task Force—Fourth Year Report*, Bureau of Alcohol, Tobacco and Firearms, Washington, DC, 2000 [Online] http://www.atf.treas.gov/pub/gen_pub/report2000/index.htm [accessed April 9, 2002]

investigation by the FBI and other law enforcement agencies, no arrests in the case had been made as of May 2002.

In a spree that began on May 3, 2002, 18 pipe bombs were found in rural mailboxes in Illinois, Iowa, Nebraska, Colorado, and Texas, injuring five people. Four days after the first bomb exploded, the FBI arrested 21-year-old college student Luke J. Helder in connection with the bombings. Helder was charged by federal prosecutors in Iowa with using an explosive device to maliciously destroy property affecting interstate commerce and with using a destructive device to commit a crime of violence, punishable by up to life imprisonment. The pipe bombs, some of which did not detonate, were accompanied by letters warning of excessive government control over individual behavior.

Incidents of International Terrorism

In 1993 the World Trade Center in New York, a symbol of American financial wealth and power, was the target of international terrorists, who detonated a bomb in the subterranean parking garage, killing 6 people and injuring 1,000. On September 11, 2001, the World Trade Center's two 110-story office towers were once again the target of a Muslim terrorist group. At 7:59 a.m., American Airlines Flight 11 departed Logan International Airport in Boston bound for Los Angeles. Forty-six minutes later, at

8:45 a.m., the aircraft, diverted by hijackers, crashed into the North Tower of the World Trade Center. At 9:02 a.m., United Airlines Flight 175, also bound for Los Angeles from Boston and also diverted by hijackers, crashed into the South Tower of the World Trade Center. Both towers collapsed shortly thereafter, killing not only thousands of office workers and facility personnel trapped inside, but more than 300 firefighters and rescue workers helping to evacuate them.

By 9:45 a.m., two more domestic airlines had been commandeered by hijackers and crashed. American Airlines Flight 77 crashed into the Pentagon, a symbol of American military power, killing over 100 people who were in that section of the building at the time. United Airlines Flight 93 crashed in a field on the outskirts of Pittsburgh, Pennsylvania, after an attempt by some passengers to wrestle control of the aircraft from the hijackers. There were no survivors on any of the flights. The 19 hijackers were associated with the al-Qaeda group, whose leader Osama Bin Laden went into hiding after U.S.-led attacks on Afghanistan for harboring the terrorist group.

The attacks were the worst acts of international terrorism on U.S. soil in the history of the United States. When the official cleanup and recovery efforts ended with

FIGURE 4.7

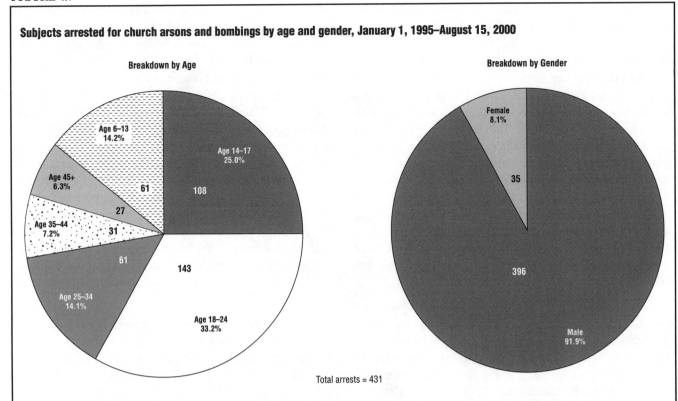

Subjects arrested for church arsons and bombings by age and gender, January 1, 1995–August 15, 2000

Breakdown by Age

Age 6–13
14.2%

Age 14–17
25.0%

61

108

Age 45+
6.3%

Age 35–44
7.2%

27

31

61

143

Age 25–34
14.1%

Age 18–24
33.2%

Breakdown by Gender

Female
8.1%

35

396

Male
91.9%

Total arrests = 431

SOURCE: "Chart D: Demographic Information on Subjects Arrested for Church Arsons/Bombings Nationwide, January 1, 1995–August 15, 2000," *National Church Arson Task Force—Fourth Year Report*, Bureau of Alcohol, Tobacco and Firearms, Washington, DC, 2000 [Online] http://www.atf.treas.gov/pub/gen_pub/report2000/index.htm [accessed April 9, 2002]

a final ceremony on May 30, 2002, the New York City Office of Emergency Management gave the final tolls for the destruction caused by the attacks in that city. Of the 2,823 people killed in the World Trade Center, only 1,102 victims had been identified. An estimated 3.1 million hours of labor were spent on cleanup and 108,342 truckloads, over 1.8 million tons, of debris had been removed.

In addition to all those killed in New York, 64 passengers and crew from Flight 77 and 125 military and civilian personnel from the Pentagon were killed. All 44 passengers and crew on Flight 93 also died in the crash. The total death toll from the September 11 attacks was 3,056 people, including citizens of 78 different countries.

According to the State Department, despite the events of September 11, the 346 international terrorist attacks in 2001 showed a decline from the 426 such attacks in 2000. Of the 346 international terrorist attacks in 2001, 178 (51 percent) were bombings against a multi-national oil pipeline in Columbia. In 2000, there were 152 bombings of the Colombian pipeline, accounting for 40 percent of international terrorist acts in that year.

Yet the casualties inflicted in 2001 far outnumbered those of 2000 or any previous year. In 2000, 409 people

were killed in acts of international terrorism, including only 19 U.S. citizens, of whom 17 were U.S. Navy sailors. The sailors were killed in the attack on the USS Cole in the port of Aden in Yemen on October 12, 2000. The other two U.S. fatalities in 2000 were Carlos Caceres, an aid worker killed by a militia-led mob in West Timor, and Kurt Erich Schork, a journalist killed when rebels in Sierra Leone shot down a U.N. helicopter.

Approximately 3,370 people were killed in international terrorist attacks in 2001, the highest annual death toll from terrorism ever recorded. In addition to those killed or injured in the September 11 attacks, 8 U.S. citizens were killed and 15 were wounded in other international terrorist attacks in 2001.

In the first months of 2002, another U.S. citizen was killed by international terrorists. On January 23, 2002, *Wall Street Journal* reporter Daniel Pearl was abducted in Pakistan while on his way to interview a Muslim fundamentalist leader. A month later the FBI confirmed that it had received a videotape containing "indisputable" confirmation that Pearl, 38, had been killed by his captors. Pearl's killing resulted in the arrest of several people believed to have been involved with the crime, including the alleged ringleader of the group, Ahmed Omar Saeed

Sheikh, who had ties to radical Muslim extremist groups in the region. Pearl's wife, Mariane, who was pregnant at the time of his abduction, gave birth to their son in May 2002.

Aftermath of the Attacks

As a result of the September 11 attacks, the Office of Homeland Security was established by Presidential Executive Order to coordinate federal, state, and local anti-terrorism efforts. Governor Tom Ridge of Pennsylvania was appointed to head the Office, the focus of which is on the detection and prevention of future terrorist attacks, as well as incident management and response and recovery in the event of an attack. In addition, the Homeland Security Council was established to advise the President on all aspects of homeland security. Council members include the Vice President and Attorney General of the United States as well as Secretaries of Defense, Health and Human Services, Transportation, and the Treasury.

On March 12, 2002, the Office of Homeland Security implemented a system of Threat Conditions as a way of providing uniform advisories of possible terrorist threats. The five threat-conditions range from Low (a low risk of terrorist attack) to Severe (a severe risk of terrorist attacks that may necessitate the closing of government offices and the deployment of emergency personnel). Intermediate threat conditions are Guarded (general risk of terrorist attacks), Elevated (significant risk of terrorist attacks), and High (high risk of terrorist attacks).

HOAXES

As of December 20, 2001, the FBI reported that some 40 individuals were charged with staging anthrax hoaxes in the weeks following the discovery of anthrax-laced letters sent to the nation's capitol and to various news organizations. Between October and November 2001, some 750 hoax letters purporting to contain anthrax were received by organizations worldwide, resulting in the closures of U.S. Postal Service offices, schools, and other organizations.

Some 550 anthrax hoax letters were sent to abortion and family planning clinics nationwide. Of those, 300 were received on October 15, 2001—the same day that an anthrax-tainted letter was discovered in the offices of U.S. Senator Tom Daschle. On November 7, 2001, another 250 such letters were received by various family clinics and advocacy groups nationwide. Some of the letters were labeled "Time Sensitive—Urgent Security Notice Enclosed," while others were sent with return addresses fraudulently ascribed to the Planned Parenthood Federation of America or the National Abortion Federation. On December 5, 2001, Clayton Lee Waagner, 44, was arrested near Cincinnati, Ohio, in connection with both waves of anthrax hoax letters sent to abortion and family planning clinics. Waagner, who had escaped from an Illinois jail in February 2001 while awaiting sentencing for weapons possession and auto theft, was expected to stand trial for perpetrating the anthrax hoaxes as early as the summer of 2002.

Others arrested for various anthrax hoaxes across the United States included a Los Angeles City fire captain charged with mailing threatening communication to his ex-wife, a former U.S. Postal Service worker who allegedly sent mail labeled "Anthrax Inclosed" [sic], a former Social Security Administration employee who threatened to use anthrax to "resolve" a dispute regarding his disability payments, and a U.S. Capitol Police Officer. The police officer allegedly placed an anonymous note in a Capitol Police station as a joke on November 7, 2001. The note read: "PLEASE INHALE. YES. THIS COULD BE? CALL YOUR DOCTOR FOR FLU-SYMPTOMS. THIS IS A CAPITOL POLICE TRAINING EXERCISE! I HOPE YOU PASS."

In a press release dated December 20, 2001, FBI Director Robert S. Mueller warned that the FBI "will continue to vigorously investigate and arrest those individuals who commit these crimes." Penalties for such offenses carry a maximum of five years imprisonment and a fine of up to $250,000.

CHAPTER 5

JUVENILE CRIME

JUVENILE ARRESTS

According to the Office of Juvenile Justice and Delinquency Prevention (OJJDP), a branch of the U.S. Department of Justice, an estimated 2.4 million juveniles were arrested in 2000. This number represents decreases of 15 percent from 1996 to 2000 and 5 percent from 1999 to 2000. Juveniles under 15 accounted for the majority of juvenile arrests for arson (65 percent) and for all sex offenses except forcible rape and prostitution (52 percent). They also accounted for about 40 percent of arrests for non-aggravated assault, forcible rape, burglary, larceny-theft, and vandalism. Arrest rates for female juvenile offenders in 2000 were highest for prostitution and commercialized vice (55 percent of all juvenile arrests for these crimes), embezzlement (47 percent), and offenses against family and children (37 percent). (See Table 5.1.)

The proportion of males arrested was significantly higher than the proportion of females. In 2000, 72 percent of arrested juveniles were male, and 28 percent were female. The ratio of juvenile male to female arrests was even higher for violent crime: 82 percent in 2000 were male, and 18 percent were female. From 1991 to 2000 female juvenile arrests increased by 25.3 percent. For violent crimes, female juvenile arrests increased 27.9 percent. For violent offenses, increases for female juvenile arrests were highest for non-aggravated (77.9 percent) and aggravated assaults (44 percent). (See Table 5.2.)

In 2000, juveniles comprised 16 percent of all Violent Crime Index arrests in the United States and 32 percent of all Property Crime Index arrests. Juveniles accounted for 53 percent of arson arrests, 41 percent of arrests for vandalism, 33 percent of motor vehicle thefts, and 25 percent of all robberies in the United States in 2000. (See Figure 5.1.)

Violent Crimes

The rate of juvenile arrests for violent crimes increased dramatically in the late 1980s and early 1990s, peaking in 1994 at over 500 per 100,000 youths ages 10 through 17. Violent crime arrests grew 95 percent between 1980 and 1995 for youth under age 15, compared with 47 percent for older youth. Between 1994 and 2000, juvenile arrests for Violent Crime Index offenses declined by 41 percent to a rate of 309 arrests for every 100,000 persons 10 to 17 years of age. (See Figure 5.2.) While violent crime arrests declined for both adults and juveniles between 1994 and 2000, the declines were greater for juveniles. (See Figure 5.3.) For juveniles 15 to 17 years of age, Violent Crime Index arrests declined by 44 percent, compared to a 24 percent decline for adults 18 to 24 years of age, a 26 percent drop for arrestees 25 to 29 years old, and a 19 percent decline for adult arrestees 30 to 39 years of age.

Over the past few years the largest decline in juvenile violent crime arrests was in the murder rate. Arrests of juveniles for murder peaked in 1993. By 2000, the juvenile arrest rate for murder dropped 74 percent, reaching its lowest level in 20 years and erasing the more than 50 percent rise in juvenile murders from 1986 to 1993. (See Figure 5.4.)

Juvenile arrest rates for forcible rape, robbery, and aggravated assault also declined from their peak levels in the early- to mid-1990s. From 1980 to 1991, the juvenile arrest rate for forcible rape increased by 44 percent. By 2000, the rate had fallen to a level 13 percent lower than in 1980. By 2000 juvenile arrest rates for robbery fell 57 percent from the peak years of 1994–1995. The juvenile arrest rate for aggravated assault fell by 30 percent between 1994 and 2000. However, the 2000 rate was 42 percent higher than it was in 1980, when juvenile arrests for aggravated assault began to rise, more than doubling by 1994. (See Figure 5.4.)

TABLE 5.1

Estimated number of juvenile arrests, 2000

Most Serious Offense	2000 Estimated number of juvenile arrests	Percent of total juvenile arrests		Percent change		
		Female	Under Age 15	1991-00	1996-00	1999-00
Total	**2,369,400**	**28%**	**32%**	**3%**	**-15%**	**-5%**
Crime Index total	617,600	28	38	-28	-27	-5
Violent Crime Index	98,900	18	33	-17	-23	-4
Murder & nonnegligent manslaughter	1,200	11	13	-65	-55	-13
Forcible rape	4,500	1	39	-26	-17	-5
Robbery	26,800	9	27	-29	-38	-5
Aggravated assault	66,300	23	36	-7	-14	-4
Property Crime Index	518,800	30	39	-30	-28	-5
Burglary	95,800	12	39	-38	-30	-5
Larceny-theft	363,500	37	40	-24	-27	-6
Motor vehicle theft	50,800	17	26	-51	-34	-3
Arson	8,700	12	65	-7	-17	-7
Nonindex						
Other assaults	236,800	31	43	37	-1	0
Forgery and counterfeiting	6,400	34	12	-20	-24	-7
Fraud	10,700	32	18	-3	-15	-5
Embezzlement	2,000	47	6	132	48	11
Stolen property (buying, receiving, possessing)	27,700	16	29	-40	-33	-1
Vandalism	114,100	12	44	-21	-19	-4
Weapons (carrying, possessing, etc.)	37,600	10	33	-26	-28	-10
Prostitution and commercialized vice	1,300	55	13	-13	-4	-3
Sex offenses (except forcible rape and prostitution)	17,400	7	52	-4	8	5
Drug abuse violations	203,900	15	17	145	-4	0
Gambling	1,500	4	18	-27	-30	-22
Offenses against the family and children	9,400	37	38	92	-8	2
Driving under the influence	21,000	17	3	14	13	-3
Liquor law violations	159,400	31	10	20	4	-6
Drunkenness	21,700	20	13	-3	-19	-3
Disorderly conduct	165,700	28	38	33	-9	-8
Vagrancy	3,000	23	28	-33	-7	27
All other offenses (except traffic)	414,200	26	28	35	-5	-5
Suspicion	1,200	22	23	-76	-53	-29
Curfew and loitering	154,700	31	28	81	-16	-11
Runaways	142,000	59	39	-18	-29	-6

• In 2000, there were an estimated 1,200 juvenile arrests for murder. Between 1996 and 2000, juvenile arrests for murder fell 55%.
• Females accounted for 23% of juvenile arrests for aggravated assault and 31% of juvenile arrests for other assaults (i.e., simple assaults and intimidations) in 2000. Females were involved in 59% of all arrests for running away from home and 31% of arrests for curfew and loitering violations.
• Between 1991 and 2000, there were substantial declines in juvenile arrests for murder (65%), motor vehicle theft (51%), and burglary (38%) and major increases in juvenile arrests for drug abuse violations (145%) and curfew and loitering violations (81%).
• Youth under the age of 15 accounted for 65% of all juvenile arrests for arson in 2000.

SOURCE: "In 2000, law enforcement agencies made an estimated 2.4 million arrests of persons under the age of 18," in *Statistical Briefing Book,* U.S. Department of Justice, Office of Justice Programs, Office of Juvenile Justice and Delinquency Prevention, Washington, DC, 2001 [Online] http:// ojjdp.ncjrs.org/ojstatbb/html/qa250.html [Accessed April 30, 2002]

Property Crimes

From 1980 to 1991, juvenile arrests for Property Crimes Index offenses rose to a peak of 2,612 arrests per 100,000 persons 10 to 17 years of age. After a period of relative stability in mid-1990s, the juvenile Property Crime Index arrest rates declined by 29 percent from 1997 to 2000, to a 20-year low. (See Figure 5.5.) Consistent with a 20-year trend, in 2000, Property Crime Index arrest rates for all ages were highest for 16-year-olds (2,817.9 arrests per 100,000 population), followed by 17-year-olds (2,785.7), and 15-year-olds (2,540.3). Adults

from 18 to 64 years of age had lower Property Crime Index arrest rates in 2000. (See Figure 5.6.)

In 2000, the juvenile arrest rate for burglary was 291 per 100,000 persons 10 to 17 years of age, a decline of 64 percent from a rate of approximately 800 in 1980, and down by 40 percent (from a rate of about 500) since 1990. After remaining relatively constant between 1980 and 1997, by 2000 the juvenile arrest rate for larceny-theft declined by 29 percent. Females accounted for about one in three juvenile arrests for larceny-theft in 2000, and

TABLE 5.2

Arrest trends by gender, 1991–2000

[6,422 agencies; 2000 estimated population 149,828,555; 1991 estimated population 133,490,609]

| | Males | | | | | | Females | | | | | |
| | Total | | | Under 18 | | | Total | | | Under 18 | | |
Offense charged	1991	2000	Percent change	1991	2000	Percent change	1991	2000	Percent change	1991	2000	Percent change
TOTAL[1]	6,000,210	5,771,866	-3.8	934,971	904,927	-3.2	1,394,668	1,640,428	+17.6	279,782	350,696	+25.3
Murder and nonnegligent manslaughter	10,772	6,237	-42.1	1,737	568	-67.3	1,178	775	-34.2	74	73	-1.4
Forcible rape	20,475	14,382	-29.8	3,158	2,335	-26.1	241	156	-35.3	53	29	-45.3
Robbery	81,000	54,624	-32.6	19,712	13,877	-29.6	7,660	6,188	-19.2	1,792	1,433	-20.0
Aggravated assault	234,479	212,297	-9.5	32,165	27,130	-15.7	36,308	53,088	+46.2	5,677	8,177	+44.0
Burglary	224,420	135,735	-39.5	76,452	45,777	-40.1	23,872	21,930	-8.1	7,481	6,380	-14.7
Larceny-theft	596,714	409,577	-31.4	188,274	127,254	-32.4	283,101	231,793	-18.1	77,532	75,679	-2.4
Motor vehicle theft	106,545	64,825	-39.2	46,604	21,651	-53.5	12,322	12,245	-0.6	6,157	4,448	-27.8
Arson	9,161	7,539	-17.7	4,624	4,176	-9.7	1,347	1,285	-4.6	444	536	+20.7
Violent crime[2]	346,726	287,540	-17.1	56,772	43,910	-22.7	45,387	60,207	+32.7	7,596	9,712	+27.9
Property crime[3]	936,840	617,676	-34.1	315,954	198,858	-37.1	320,642	267,253	-16.7	91,614	87,043	-5.0
Crime Index total[4]	1,283,566	905,216	-29.5	372,726	242,768	-34.9	366,029	327,460	-10.5	99,210	96,755	-2.5
Other assaults	462,154	519,812	+12.5	67,254	83,182	+23.7	92,833	156,507	+68.6	20,972	37,306	+77.9
Forgery and counterfeiting	34,813	35,738	+2.7	2,870	2,292	-20.1	19,040	22,755	+19.5	1,479	1,208	-18.3
Fraud	101,764	84,743	-16.7	3,342	3,152	-5.7	86,336	70,488	-18.4	1,549	1,603	+3.5
Embezzlement	4,381	5,300	+21.0	291	557	+91.4	3,077	5,430	+76.5	179	533	+197.8
Stolen property; buying, receiving, possessing	80,275	55,068	-31.4	23,599	13,173	-44.2	10,891	11,704	+7.5	2,682	2,468	-8.0
Vandalism	156,310	126,935	-18.8	70,764	53,400	-24.5	19,322	23,197	+20.1	6,418	7,551	+17.7
Weapons; carrying, possessing, etc.	116,884	79,704	-31.8	25,629	18,099	-29.4	8,838	6,916	-21.7	1,731	2,034	+17.5
Prostitution and commercialized vice	21,901	18,542	-15.3	396	292	-26.3	35,434	28,939	-18.3	436	435	-0.2
Sex offenses (except forcible rape and prostitution)	55,799	47,792	-14.3	9,575	8,986	-6.2	4,236	3,851	-9.1	587	721	+22.8
Drug abuse violations	468,519	690,873	+47.5	38,296	90,032	+135.1	95,257	151,659	+59.2	4,993	15,961	+219.7
Gambling	6,322	3,555	-43.8	531	381	-28.2	802	465	-42.0	20	23	+15.0
Offenses against the family and children	42,901	53,311	+24.3	1,378	2,539	+84.3	7,968	15,429	+93.6	710	1,476	+107.9
Driving under the influence	844,043	649,243	-23.1	8,263	9,050	+9.5	127,585	126,149	-1.1	1,300	1,838	+41.4
Liquor laws	244,596	264,267	+8.0	49,458	55,923	+13.1	55,551	76,780	+38.2	18,271	25,300	+38.5
Drunkenness	442,460	312,278	-29.4	10,616	9,857	-7.1	50,260	45,763	-8.9	1,946	2,294	+17.9
Disorderly conduct	269,039	225,501	-16.2	46,119	55,055	+19.4	67,379	70,096	+4.0	12,275	22,341	+82.0
Vagrancy	20,933	13,403	-36.0	1,674	1,016	-39.3	3,062	3,605	+17.7	263	280	+6.5
All other offenses (except traffic)	1,264,657	1,584,206	+25.3	123,297	158,794	+28.8	269,971	416,721	+54.4	33,964	54,055	+59.2
Suspicion	7,126	2,220	-68.8	2,063	494	-76.1	1,437	548	-61.9	551	146	-73.5
Curfew and loitering law violations	36,947	62,901	+70.2	36,947	62,901	+70.2	13,525	28,552	+111.1	13,525	28,552	+111.1
Runaways	41,946	33,478	-20.2	41,946	33,478	-20.2	57,272	47,962	-16.3	57,272	47,962	-16.3

[1] Does not include suspicion.
[2] Violent crimes are offenses of murder, forcible rape, robbery, and aggravated assault.
[3] Property crimes are offenses of burglary, larceny-theft, motor vehicle theft, and arson.
[4] Includes arson.

SOURCE: "Table 33: Ten-Year Arrest Trends, by Sex, 1991–2000," *Crime in the United States, 2000: Uniform Crime Reports*, Federal Bureau of Investigation, Washington, DC, 2001

juveniles under 15 years of age comprised 40 percent of all such arrests. Between 1983 and 1990, the juvenile arrest rate for motor vehicle theft rose by 138 percent. By 2000, that rate had declined to 54 percent below the 1990 peak, and was only 10 percent higher than the 20-year low in 1983. Juvenile arson arrests declined by 30 percent between 1994 and 2000. For every juvenile arrested for arson in 2000, 48 were arrested for larceny-theft, 12 for burglary, and 7 for motor vehicle theft. (See Figure 5.7.)

Drug Abuse Violations

After remaining within a limited range from 1980 to 1993, the juvenile arrest rate for drug abuse violations rose by 78 percent between 1993 and 1997. By 2000 the rate was down by 14 percent from its 1997 levels but still far above pre-1993 levels. (See Figure 5.8.) Between 1991 and 2000, juvenile arrests for drug abuse violations rose by 220 percent among females and 135 percent among males.

Race and Ethnicity

As in adult arrest rates, minorities are disproportionately represented in juvenile arrests. While black youths comprise roughly 15 percent of the total juvenile population, of some 1.5 million juvenile arrests in 2000, 389,876 (25 percent) of those arrested were black and 1.1 million (72 percent) were white. (See Table 5.3.) The overall rate of arrest for black youths between 1980 and 2000 rose by 10 percent, compared to a rise of 6 percent for whites and 2 percent for American Indians during the same time period. In 2000, the rate of arrests of blacks and whites did not show as much disparity for property crimes as for violent crimes (2 black arrests per each white versus 3.8 black

FIGURE 5.1

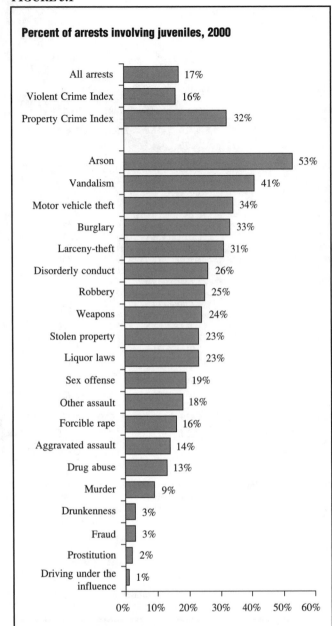

Percent of arrests involving juveniles, 2000

Category	Percent
All arrests	17%
Violent Crime Index	16%
Property Crime Index	32%
Arson	53%
Vandalism	41%
Motor vehicle theft	34%
Burglary	33%
Larceny-theft	31%
Disorderly conduct	26%
Robbery	25%
Weapons	24%
Stolen property	23%
Liquor laws	23%
Sex offense	19%
Other assault	18%
Forcible rape	16%
Aggravated assault	14%
Drug abuse	13%
Murder	9%
Drunkenness	3%
Fraud	3%
Prostitution	2%
Driving under the influence	1%

Note: The violent crime index includes the offenses of murder and nonnegligent manslaughter, forcible rape, robbery, and aggravated assault. The property crime index includes the offenses of burglary, larceny-theft, motor vehicle theft, and arson. Running away from home and curfew and loitering violations are not presented in this figure because, by definition, only juveniles can be arrested for these offenses.

SOURCE: "Juveniles were involved in 16% of all Violent Crime Index arrests and 32% of all Property Crime Index arrests in 2000," in *Statistical Briefing Book,* U.S. Department of Justice, Office of Justice Programs, Office of Juvenile Justice and Delinquency Prevention, Washington, DC, 2001 [Online] http://ojjdp.ncjrs.org/ojstatbb/html/qa251.html [Accessed April 30, 2002]

5.10.) In 2000 arrest rates for Property Crime Index offenses were 37 percent below 1980 levels for black juveniles and 30 percent for white juveniles. Arrests of Asian juveniles for Property Crime Index offenses were half the 1980 levels. (See Figure 5.11.) In 2000, the rate of arrests of blacks and whites did not show as much disparity for property crimes as for violent crimes (2 and 3.8, respectively), though still noticeably disproportionate in both categories.

Gender

Although the juvenile arrest rate for all crimes rose for both females and males from 1983 to 1997, the increase for females was 72 percent compared to 30 percent for males. By 2000, the arrest rate for male juveniles was at or near its 1983 levels, while the rate for females remained 42 percent higher than in 1983. (See Figure 5.12.) Juvenile Violent Crime Index arrests declined from their peak in 1994 to a rate for females of 117 arrests per 100,000 persons 10 to 17 years of age, and a rate for males of 492. While the male juvenile violent crime rate was four times greater than that of females in 2000, the arrest rate for Violent Crime Index offenses for females was 66 percent above the 1980 rate of 70, while the male rate was 16 percent below the 1980 rate of 587. (See Figure 5.13.) For Property Crime Index offenses, the rate of arrest for female juveniles rose by 3 percent between 1980 and 2000, compared to a decline of 46 percent in the number of male juveniles arrested for Property Crime offenses during the same time period. (See Figure 5.14.)

THE CRIMES—COURT STATISTICS

The OJJDP publishes statistics on juvenile court cases (*Juvenile Court Statistics, 1998,* Washington, D.C., 2001) and on juvenile cases sent for trial in adult criminal court. The OJJDP categorizes juvenile crimes in two ways:

- Delinquency offenses—acts that are illegal regardless of the age of the perpetrator

- Status offenses—acts that are illegal only for minors, such as truancy, running away, or curfew violations

DELINQUENCY CASES

Juvenile courts handled almost 1.8 million delinquency cases in 1998, some 3 percent less than in 1997 but 44 percent higher than the level of caseloads in 1989. (See Table 5.4.) A case can include more than one charge. For example, a youth brought on three different robbery charges at the same time is counted as one case. Since 1960, the juvenile court caseload increased over 400 percent, from 1,100 delinquency cases on a given day in 1960 to 4,800 in 1998. (See Figure 5.15.)

Juvenile courts take delinquency cases referred by law enforcement agencies, social service agencies, schools, parents, probation officers, or victims. In 1998 law enforce-

arrests per each white, respectively), though still noticeably disproportionate in both categories. (See Figure 5.9.)

In 1994 Violent Crime Index arrest rates peaked for both black and white juveniles. By 2000, rates declined by 47 percent for black juveniles and 25 percent for white juveniles arrested for violent Crime Index Offenses. (See Figure

FIGURE 5.2

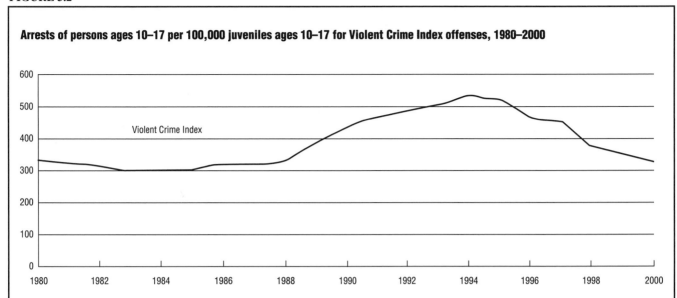

Arrests of persons ages 10–17 per 100,000 juveniles ages 10–17 for Violent Crime Index offenses, 1980–2000

Note: The Violent Crime Index includes the offenses of murder and nonnegligent manslaughter, forcible rape, robbery, and aggravated assault.

SOURCE: "Juvenile arrest rates for Violent Crime Index Offenses, 1980-2000," in *Statistical Briefing Book,* U.S. Department of Justice, Office of Justice Programs, Office of Juvenile Justice and Delinquency Prevention, Washington, DC, 2001 [Online] http://ojjdp.ncjrs.org/ojstatbb/asp/JAR_Display .asp?ID=qa2201002002 [Accessed April 30, 2002]

ment agencies referred 84 percent of delinquency cases to juvenile court. Drug offenses were referred to juvenile court most frequently (92 percent), followed by property offenses (90 percent), person offenses (86 percent), and public order offenses (63 percent). (See Figure 5.16.) Of all juveniles taken into custody by law enforcement agencies in 2000, over 70 percent were referred to juvenile court jurisdiction, 20 percent were handled in the police department and released, and 7 percent of juveniles arrested were referred directly to criminal (adult) court. (See Table 5.7.)

In 1998 property offenses made up about 45 percent of delinquency cases, with the most frequent charge being larceny-theft, which accounted for 21 percent of all delinquency cases handled in 1998. About 23 percent of delinquency cases involved an offense against persons. Public order offenses, such as disorderly conduct, weapons offenses, and liquor law violations, amounted to 20 percent. Drug law violations made up 11 percent of total cases, a 148 percent increase since 1989.

While the number of delinquency cases rose 44 percent from 1989 to 1998, the increases varied by offense. The largest increase occurred in drug law violations (148 percent). Aggravated and simple assault also showed large increases (164 percent, combined). Weapons violations increased 61 percent. Liquor law violations rose 29 percent, and nonviolent sex offenses were up 53 percent.

Age

In 1998, delinquency case rates in juvenile court for drug use and public order offenses increased with the age

FIGURE 5.3

Age-specific Violent Crime Index arrest rates, 1980, 1994, and 2000

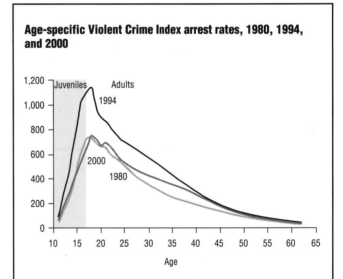

Note: The Violent Crime Index includes the offenses of murder and nonnegligent manslaughter, forcible rape, robbery, and aggravated assault.

SOURCE: "Violent Crime Index arrest rates were higher in 2000 than in 1980 for all adult age groups—for juveniles ages 15–17, 2000 rates were below the rates in 1980," in *Statistical Briefing Book,* U.S. Department of Justice, Office of Justice Programs, Office of Juvenile Justice and Delinquency Prevention, Washington, DC, 2001 [Online] http://ojjdp .ncjrs.org/ojstatbb/html/qa276.html [accessed May 2, 2002]

of the juvenile, while case rates for property crimes peaked with juveniles 16 years of age. (See Figure 5.17.) The rate of delinquency cases in 1998 for offenses against persons was highest among 16-year-olds (23.86 cases per

FIGURE 5.4

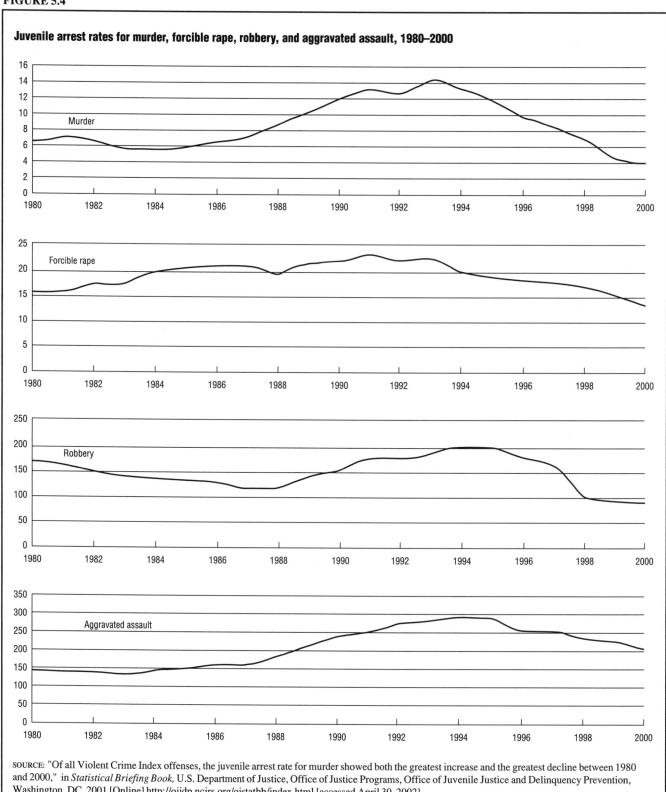

Juvenile arrest rates for murder, forcible rape, robbery, and aggravated assault, 1980–2000

Murder

Forcible rape

Robbery

Aggravated assault

SOURCE: "Of all Violent Crime Index offenses, the juvenile arrest rate for murder showed both the greatest increase and the greatest decline between 1980 and 2000," in *Statistical Briefing Book,* U.S. Department of Justice, Office of Justice Programs, Office of Juvenile Justice and Delinquency Prevention, Washington, DC, 2001 [Online] http://ojjdp.ncjrs.org/ojstatbb/index.html [accessed April 30, 2002]

1,000 juveniles in that age group), followed by 17-year-olds (22.88), and 15-year-olds (21.65). The same pattern was true for property offenses, with a delinquency case rate of 49.45 per 1,000 16-year-olds, 47.45 for 17-year-olds, and 43.31 for juveniles 15 years of age.

Detention

A juvenile court may place youths in a detention facility during court processing. Detention may be needed either to protect the community from the juvenile, to protect the juvenile, or both. Also, detention is sometimes

FIGURE 5.5

Arrests per 100,000 population for Property Crime Index offenses, 1980–2000

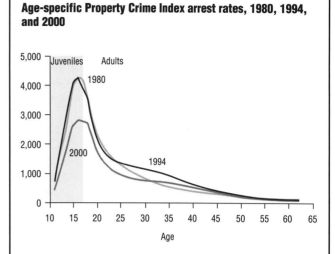

Note: The Property Crime Index includes the offenses of burglary, larceny-theft, motor vehicle theft, and arson.

SOURCE: "Property Crime Index arrest rates were lower in 2000 than in 1980 for persons age 25 or younger," in *Statistical Briefing Book,* U.S. Department of Justice, Office of Justice Programs, Office of Juvenile Justice and Delinquency Prevention, Washington, DC, 2001 [Online] http://ojjdp.ncjrs.org/ojstatbb/html/qa280.html [accessed April 30, 2002]

FIGURE 5.6

Age-specific Property Crime Index arrest rates, 1980, 1994, and 2000

Note: The Property Crime Index includes the offenses of burglary, larceny-theft, motor vehicle theft, and arson.

SOURCE: "Property Crime Index arrest rates were lower in 2000 than in 1980 for persons age 25 or younger," in *Statistical Briefing Book,* U.S. Department of Justice, Office of Justice Programs, Office of Juvenile Justice and Delinquency Prevention, Washington, DC, 2001 [Online] http://ojjdp.ncjrs.org/ojstatbb/html/qa280.html [accessed May 2, 2002]

necessary to ensure a youth's appearance at scheduled hearings or evaluations.

In 1998 youths were held in detention facilities at some point between referral to court intake and case disposition (final outcome of court processing) in 19 percent of all delinquency cases disposed. Property offense cases were the least likely to involve detention (15 percent), and those involving drugs (23 percent) were the most likely to result in detention. Detention was enforced in 22 percent of public order offense and person offense cases. (See Table 5.6.)

Between 1989 and 1998 the number of juveniles detained in drug cases increased by 55 percent. Those detained in person offense cases grew by 63 percent. Overall detained delinquency cases increased by 25 percent, adding to the problems of housing detained juveniles.

Male juveniles charged with a delinquency offense were more likely than females to be held in a secure facility while awaiting the disposition of their cases. In 1998, 20 percent of male juveniles and 14 percent of female juveniles were detained. This represents a 20 percent increase in male juvenile detainees from 1989 to 1998. The number of female juveniles detained increased by 56 percent. Black juveniles were detained in 23 percent of delinquency cases, compared to 17 percent of whites in 1998.

Case Processing

No nationwide uniform procedure exists for processing juvenile cases, but cases do follow similar paths. An intake department first screens cases. The intake department can be the court itself, a state department of social services, or a prosecutor's office. The intake officer may decide that the case will be dismissed for lack of evidence, handled formally (petitioned), or resolved informally (non-petitioned). Formal processing can include placement outside the home, probation, a trial in juvenile court, or transfer to an adult court. Informal processing may consist of referral to a social services agency, a fine, some form of restitution, or informal probation. Both formal and informal processing can result in dismissal of the charges and release of the juvenile. Table 5.7 shows the processing of juvenile delinquency cases in 1998.

In 1998, 57 percent of delinquency cases were handled formally by juvenile courts, meaning that in each case a formal petition containing the allegations against the juvenile offender was filed in juvenile court. Among the 47 percent of non-petitioned cases in 1998, 43 percent were dismissed at intake, usually for lack of legal sufficiency. In the remaining cases the juvenile agreed to informal sanctions such as referral to social service agencies, payment of fines or restitution, or a term of informal probation in which the juvenile is not made an official ward of the juvenile court. (See Figure 5.18.)

Of formally processed delinquency cases in 1998, 63 percent resulted in a finding of delinquency (the equivalent of a verdict of guilty in adult criminal court). About one percent of delinquency cases in 1998 resulted in a

FIGURE 5.7

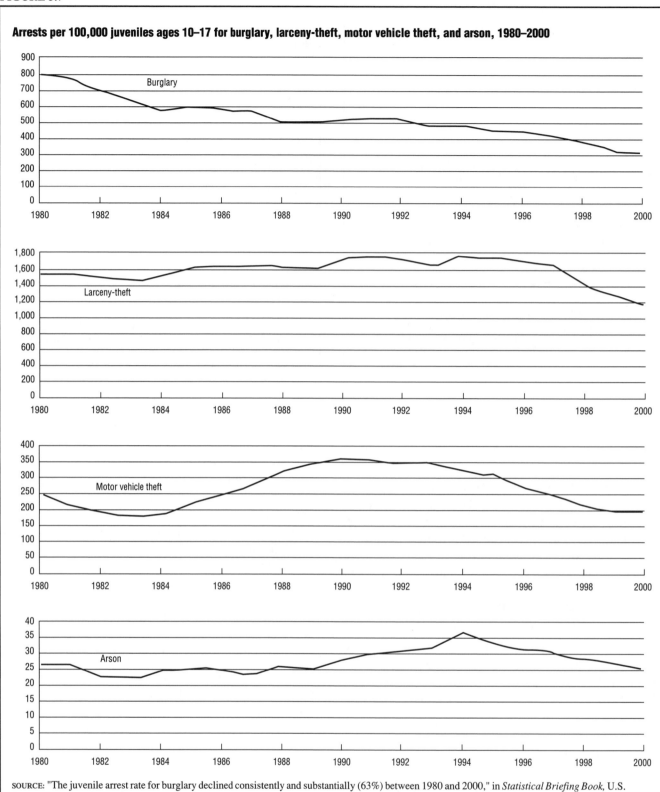

Arrests per 100,000 juveniles ages 10–17 for burglary, larceny-theft, motor vehicle theft, and arson, 1980–2000

SOURCE: "The juvenile arrest rate for burglary declined consistently and substantially (63%) between 1980 and 2000," in *Statistical Briefing Book*, U.S. Department of Justice, Office of Justice Programs, Office of Juvenile Justice and Delinquency Prevention, Washington, DC, 2001 [Online] http://ojjdp.ncjrs. org/ojstatbb/index.html [accessed April 30, 2002]

waiver (or transfer) of the juvenile to adult criminal court. Of all cases referred to the juvenile court in 1998, whether formally or informally processed, some 37 percent resulted in a finding of delinquency or waiver to criminal court.

PROSECUTING MINORS AS ADULTS

Many people believe that some crimes are so terrible that the courts should focus on the type of offense and not the age of the accused. From 1987 to 1993, there was a

FIGURE 5.8

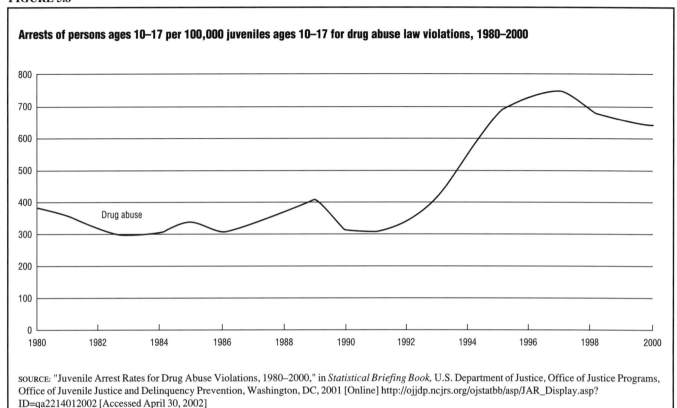

Arrests of persons ages 10–17 per 100,000 juveniles ages 10–17 for drug abuse law violations, 1980–2000

SOURCE: "Juvenile Arrest Rates for Drug Abuse Violations, 1980–2000," in *Statistical Briefing Book,* U.S. Department of Justice, Office of Justice Programs, Office of Juvenile Justice and Delinquency Prevention, Washington, DC, 2001 [Online] http://ojjdp.ncjrs.org/ojstatbb/asp/JAR_Display.asp? ID=qa2214012002 [Accessed April 30, 2002]

dramatic 65 percent increase in the rate of arrests of juveniles for murder. The homicides were overwhelmingly concentrated among black teen-agers in the nation's largest cities. Rates of other violent crimes, like rape, robbery, and aggravated assault, also increased during this time. Most experts believe the increases were related to an upsurge in violent gangs selling crack cocaine and lax controls on access to handguns during this time.

Politicians responded to voter outrage at the increase in violent crime among juveniles and several high-profile murders involving juveniles. By the year 2000 all 50 states and the District of Columbia had one or more laws permitting the transfer of youths to criminal courts to be tried as adults. In recent years many states have also expanded these laws in order to make it easier to prosecute juveniles as adults.

For example, a 1995 Missouri law removed the minimum age limit, which had been 14, for trying children as adults in cases involving drug dealing, murder, rape, robbery, and first-degree assault. The law also permits children 12 years old to be prosecuted as adults for other crimes. A Texas law allows children as young as 10 to be sentenced to up to 40 years' incarceration. In Idaho, criminal courts have jurisdiction over juveniles arrested for carrying concealed weapons on school property.

The number of cases transferred from juvenile to adult courts increased 47 percent between 1987 and 1996,

from 6,800 to 10,000. However, despite increasing numbers, the proportion of transferred cases overall remained fairly constant in the 1990s. In 1992, 1.4 percent of all formally processed delinquency cases were transferred to criminal (adult) court. In 1996 and 1998, 1 percent of all formally processed delinquency cases were waived to adult court.

Does the Practice Make a Difference?

Because the murder rate by juveniles consistently declined from 1994 to 1999, dropping about 68 percent (3,800 juvenile homicides occurred in 1993 versus 1,400 in 1999), some public officials believed that efforts to curb crime by trying children as adults had worked. Yet many experts attribute the decline in the murder rate from 1994 to 1999 to big-city police crackdowns on illegal guns, expanded after-school crime prevention programs, and the decline of crack cocaine and violent gangs.

A Florida study suggested that juveniles tried in adult courts were likely to be rearrested more quickly and more often than juveniles who went through the juvenile court system ("The Transfer of Juveniles to Criminal Court: Does It Make A Difference?," *Crime and Delinquency,* April 1996). The study compared the rearrest rates of juveniles transferred to criminal court to a matched sample (similar crimes, past court experience, age, gender, and race) of those retained in the juvenile system. Thirty

TABLE 5.3

Arrest of persons under 18 by race, 2000

[9,017 agencies; 2000 estimated population 182,090,101]

Offense charged	Arrests under 18					Percent distribution[1]				
	Total	White	Black	American Indian or Alaskan Native	Asian or Pacific Islander	Total	White	Black	American Indian or Alaskan Native	Asian or Pacific Islander
TOTAL	1,554,802	1,120,383	389,876	18,881	25,662	100.0	72.1	25.1	1.2	1.7
Murder and nonnegligent manslaughter	801	377	399	4	21	100.0	47.1	49.8	0.5	2.6
Forcible rape	2,928	1,847	1,036	24	21	100.0	63.1	35.4	0.8	0.7
Robbery	18,262	7,568	10,248	124	322	100.0	41.4	56.1	0.7	1.8
Aggravated assault	43,776	26,658	16,007	453	658	100.0	60.9	36.6	1.0	1.5
Burglary	62,393	45,482	15,334	649	928	100.0	72.9	24.6	1.0	1.5
Larceny-theft	242,878	170,386	63,723	3,479	5,290	100.0	70.2	26.2	1.4	2.2
Motor vehicle theft	33,722	18,658	13,928	433	703	100.0	55.3	41.3	1.3	2.1
Arson	5,613	4,462	1,033	54	64	100.0	79.5	18.4	1.0	1.1
Violent crime[2]	65,767	36,450	27,690	605	1,022	100.0	55.4	42.1	0.9	1.6
Property crime[3]	344,606	238,988	94,018	4,615	6,985	100.0	69.4	27.3	1.3	2.0
Crime Index total[4]	410,373	275,438	121,708	5,220	8,007	100.0	67.1	29.7	1.3	2.0
Other assaults	154,486	100,217	50,527	1,780	1,962	100.0	64.9	32.7	1.2	1.3
Forgery and counterfeiting	4,200	3,242	838	25	95	100.0	77.2	20.0	0.6	2.3
Fraud	6,612	4,194	2,242	54	122	100.0	63.4	33.9	0.8	1.8
Embezzlement	1,296	803	450	2	41	100.0	62.0	34.7	0.2	3.2
Stolen property; buying, receiving, possessing	18,325	11,023	6,826	164	312	100.0	60.2	37.2	0.9	1.7
Vandalism	74,629	61,027	11,800	886	916	100.0	81.8	15.8	1.2	1.2
Weapons; carrying, possessing, etc.	24,802	16,628	7,586	198	390	100.0	67.0	30.6	0.8	1.6
Prostitution and commercialized vice	923	530	363	16	14	100.0	57.4	39.3	1.7	1.5
Sex offenses (except forcible rape and prostitution)	11,319	8,028	3,042	91	158	100.0	70.9	26.9	0.8	1.4
Drug abuse violations	134,200	94,197	37,676	986	1,341	100.0	70.2	28.1	0.7	1.0
Gambling	1,007	118	870	3	16	100.0	11.7	86.4	0.3	1.6
Offenses against the family and children	5,775	4,475	1,141	46	113	100.0	77.5	19.8	0.8	2.0
Driving under the influence	12,898	11,976	603	189	130	100.0	92.9	4.7	1.5	1.0
Liquor laws	101,239	93,042	4,615	2,825	757	100.0	91.9	4.6	2.8	0.7
Drunkenness	14,371	13,106	1,072	86	107	100.0	91.2	7.5	0.6	0.7
Disorderly conduct	109,026	71,807	35,341	958	920	100.0	65.9	32.4	0.9	0.8
Vagrancy	2,033	1,502	507	12	12	100.0	73.9	24.9	0.6	0.6
All other offenses (except traffic)	267,677	201,051	59,681	2,897	4,048	100.0	75.1	22.3	1.1	1.5
Suspicion	781	566	197	3	15	100.0	72.5	25.2	0.4	1.9
Curfew and loitering law violations	105,563	76,233	26,065	1,165	2,100	100.0	72.2	24.7	1.1	2.0
Runaways	93,267	71,180	16,726	1,275	4,086	100.0	76.3	17.9	1.4	4.4

[1] Because of rounding, the percentages may not add to total.
[2] Violent crimes are offenses of murder, forcible rape, robbery, and aggravated assault.
[3] Property crimes are offenses of burglary, larceny-theft, motor vehicle theft, and arson.
[4] Includes arson.

SOURCE: Adapted from "Table 43: Arrests, by Race, 2000," *Crime in the United States, 2000: Uniform Crime Reports*, Federal Bureau of Investigation, Washington, DC, 2001

---

percent of transferred youths were rearrested, compared to only 19 percent of the nontransferred ones. Transferred youths who were rearrested had committed a new offense within 135 days of release, compared to 227 days for youths processed in juvenile courts.

Some of the inherent problems in transferring juveniles to adult court are discussed in the book *Youth on Trial: A Developmental Perspective of Juvenile Justice*, edited by Thomas Grisso and Robert G. Schwartz (University of Chicago Press, Chicago, IL, 2000). According to the research presented in the book, juveniles find it more difficult than adults to make "knowing and intelligent" decisions at many junctures in the criminal justice process. Problems arise in particular in the waiving of Miranda rights, which allow the juvenile to remain silent and talk to a lawyer before responding to questions posed by law enforcement officers. The waiving of these rights can lead to much more serious consequences in adult court than in juvenile proceedings. As the book points out, "questions must be raised regarding the juvenile's judgment, decision-making capacity, and impulse control as they relate to criminal culpability" in adult proceedings. Researchers and experts in child development

FIGURE 5.9

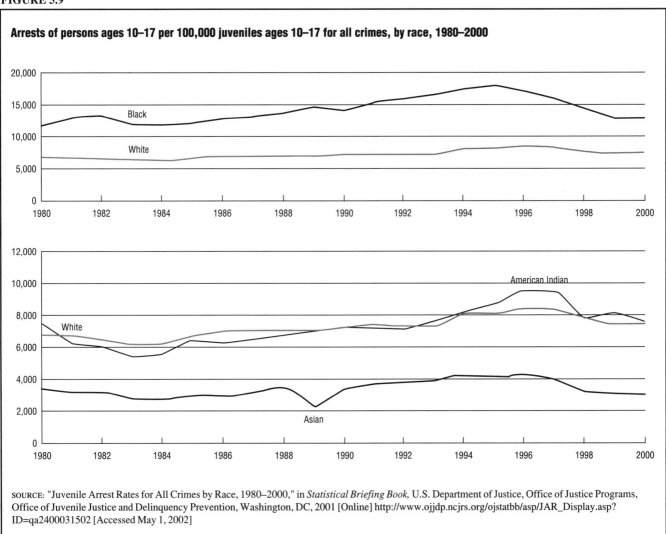

Arrests of persons ages 10–17 per 100,000 juveniles ages 10–17 for all crimes, by race, 1980–2000

SOURCE: "Juvenile Arrest Rates for All Crimes by Race, 1980–2000," in *Statistical Briefing Book,* U.S. Department of Justice, Office of Justice Programs, Office of Juvenile Justice and Delinquency Prevention, Washington, DC, 2001 [Online] http://www.ojjdp.ncjrs.org/ojstatbb/asp/JAR_Display.asp? ID=qa2400031502 [Accessed May 1, 2002]

emphasize the need to understand an adolescent's intellectual, social, and emotional development before deciding if a youth can be held blameworthy as an adult for a particular criminal offense.

Opening Juvenile Records

Many states have begun allowing more openness in juvenile records. According to the National Conference of State Legislatures, in 1995 nine states opened some juvenile criminal records to certain authorities. For example, Georgia allows public access to juvenile court proceedings. A Connecticut law permits law enforcement agencies, school officials, and court officials to view juvenile records. Courts in Virginia must notify school officials when a student is charged with a violent offense. Similar to lowering the age of responsibility for crimes, these laws are intended to make juveniles more accountable for their acts.

STATUS OFFENSE CASES

Status offenses are law violations for which an adult cannot be prosecuted (runaway, truancy, alcohol posses-

sion, ungovernability cases, etc.). In 1997, according to the Office of Juvenile Justice and Delinquency Prevention publication *Juvenile Court Statistics 1997* (2000), there were 5.5 status offense cases for every 1,000 juveniles in the population, up by 34 percent from the 1993 rate of 4.1, and 78 percent from the 1988 rate of 3.1 per 1,000 juveniles. Juvenile courts formally handled an estimated 158,500 status offense cases in 1997, an increase of 41 percent from 112,300 such cases in 1993, and 101 percent from the 79,000 status cases in 1988. Liquor law violations accounted for 40,700 (over 25 percent) of status offense cases in 1997, followed by 40,500 truancy cases (over 25 percent), 24,000 runaway cases (15 percent), and 21,300 ungovernability (also known as incorrigibility) cases (13 percent). There were an additional 32,100 cases of unspecified violations (20 percent).

In many communities, social service agencies rather than juvenile courts have responsibility for accused status offenders. National estimates of informally handled status offense cases are not calculated because of differences in

FIGURE 5.10

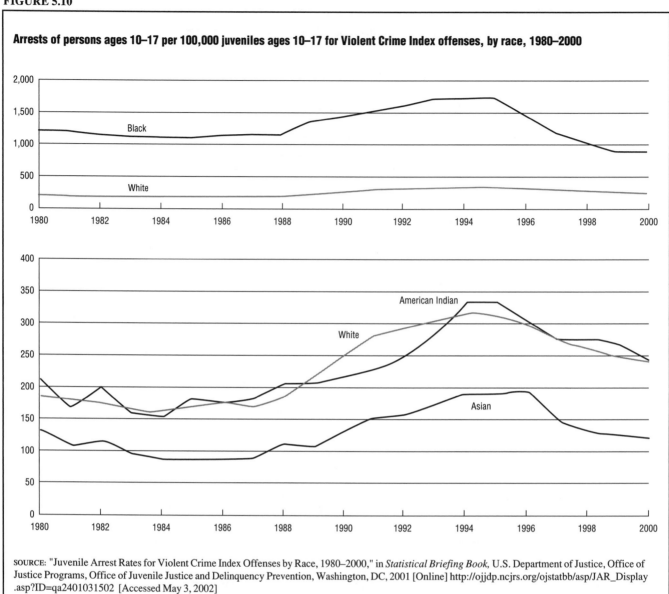

Arrests of persons ages 10–17 per 100,000 juveniles ages 10–17 for Violent Crime Index offenses, by race, 1980–2000

SOURCE: "Juvenile Arrest Rates for Violent Crime Index Offenses by Race, 1980–2000," in *Statistical Briefing Book,* U.S. Department of Justice, Office of Justice Programs, Office of Juvenile Justice and Delinquency Prevention, Washington, DC, 2001 [Online] http://ojjdp.ncjrs.org/ojstatbb/asp/JAR_Display .asp?ID=qa2401031502 [Accessed May 3, 2002]

screening procedures. The statistics, therefore, focus on formally handled (petitioned) status offense cases.

Age, Sex, and Race

Children under 15 accounted for 55 percent of all formally processed status offense cases in 1997. They were involved in 74 percent of all truancy cases, 71 percent of all ungovernability cases, 62 percent of all runaway cases, and 27 percent of status liquor law violations.

In 1997 females were involved in 41 percent of all status offense cases. The offense profiles of male and female status offense cases reflect the relatively high male involvement in liquor law violations and the higher female involvement in runaway cases. Males accounted for 68 percent of all liquor law violations in 1997, while females accounted for 60 percent of all runaway cases in

1997. Males also accounted for 55 percent of all ungovernability cases and 53 percent of all truancy cases.

White youths were involved in 78 percent of the 1997 petitioned status offense cases, which was comparable to their representation in the U.S. youth population. White youths were held in 73 percent of runaway, truancy, and ungovernability cases, and 90 percent of all status liquor law violation cases. (Nearly all youth of Hispanic ethnicity are included in the white racial category.)

In 1997 the petitioned status offense case rate for black juveniles (6.7 per 1,000) was higher than the case rate for white youths (5.4 per 1,000) and the rate among youths of other races (4.0 per 1,000). In all cases except rates for status liquor law violation cases, black juveniles had higher case rates than other youth. The case rate for

FIGURE 5.11

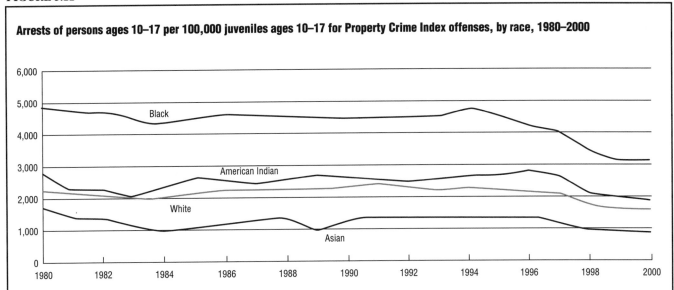

Arrests of persons ages 10–17 per 100,000 juveniles ages 10–17 for Property Crime Index offenses, by race, 1980–2000

SOURCE: "Juvenile Arrest Rates for Property Crime Index Offenses by Race, 1980–2000," *Statistical Briefing Book,* U.S. Department of Justice, Office of Justice Programs, Office of Juvenile Justice and Delinquency Prevention, Washington, DC, 2001 [Online] http://ojjdp.ncjrs.org/ojstatbb/asp/JAR_Display .asp?ID=qa2406031502 [Accessed on May 3, 2002]

alcohol violations by blacks was 0.5 cases per 1,000, as opposed to 1.6 for white youths and 1.1 for other youths.

Detention and Case Processing

The handling of status crimes has changed considerably since the mid-1980s. The Juvenile Justice and Delinquency Prevention Act of 1974 (PL 93-415) offered substantial federal funds to states that tried to reduce the detention of status offenders. The primary responsibility for status offenders was often transferred from the juvenile courts to child welfare agencies. As a result, the character of the juvenile courts' activities changed.

Prior to this change many juvenile detention centers contained a substantial number of young people whose only "crime" was that their parents could no longer control them. By not routinely institutionalizing these adolescents, the courts demonstrated that the youths were seen as deserving the same rights as adults. A logical extension of this has been that children accused of violent crimes are also now being treated legally as if they were adults.

About 53 percent of the 158,500 petitioned status offense cases in 1997 resulted in adjudication (ruling in a court). Fifty-three percent of all cases involving whites were adjudicated, compared to 51 percent of all cases involving blacks. The percentages by gender were 53 percent of all males and 51 percent of all females having cases adjudicated. As in delinquency cases, the courts most frequently issued probation sentences. Of the cases adjudicated, 65 percent of all blacks received probation, while 60 percent of whites received probation. About 64

percent of female adjudicated status offenders received probation, while 59 percent of males received probation. Other dispositions include placement outside of their homes, such as in a detention home or boot camp, and other sanctions, such as restitution or community service.

HOLDING PARENTS RESPONSIBLE

For many decades, civil liability laws held parents at least partly responsible for damages caused by their children. Also, child welfare law included actions against those who contributed to the delinquency of a minor. By the 1990s, in response to rising juvenile crime rates, communities and states passed stronger laws about parental responsibility. Several states have enacted laws making parents criminally responsible for their children's crimes.

For example, in California, parents can be prosecuted for "gross negligence"—failing to supervise their children adequately. If convicted, they can receive a sentence of up to one year in jail and a $2,500 fine. A Louisiana law allows parents to be fined up to $1,000 and imprisoned for up to six months if found guilty of "improper supervision of a minor" (for example, the child is associating with drug dealers, members of a street gang, or convicted felons).

In 1995 Judge Wayne Creech of Family Court in Columbia, South Carolina, ordered a 15-year-old girl chained to her mother for one month. The girl had a history of shoplifting and truancy. In May of 1996 a Michigan jury convicted the parents of a 16-year-old of a criminal misdemeanor for failing to control his behavior. The teenager had broken the law more than once, and his

FIGURE 5.12

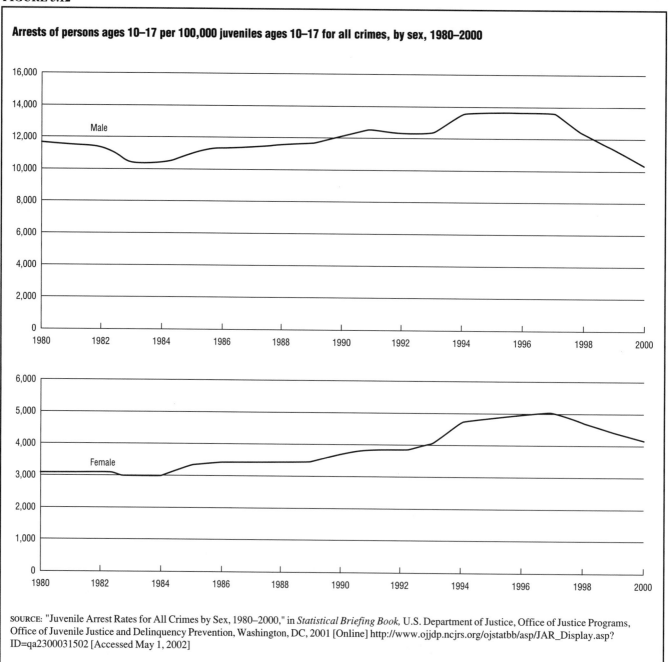

Arrests of persons ages 10–17 per 100,000 juveniles ages 10–17 for all crimes, by sex, 1980–2000

SOURCE: "Juvenile Arrest Rates for All Crimes by Sex, 1980–2000," in *Statistical Briefing Book,* U.S. Department of Justice, Office of Justice Programs, Office of Juvenile Justice and Delinquency Prevention, Washington, DC, 2001 [Online] http://www.ojjdp.ncjrs.org/ojstatbb/asp/JAR_Display.asp? ID=qa2300031502 [Accessed May 1, 2002]

parents claimed that he intimidated them to prevent their interference. Nonetheless the judge fined them $100 each and ordered them to pay court costs of $1,000. Critics of this type of parental liability state that victims are just looking for someone to blame and that U.S. law usually holds people responsible for crimes only if they actively participate. They believe that if standard rules of American law are practiced, the prosecutor of a case should have to prove that the parents intended to participate in a crime in order to be found guilty.

Many states require that parents pay for costs or program fees related to juvenile courts or corrections. For example, Idaho, Indiana, and New Hampshire passed laws

in 1995 making parents pay for the care of their children confined in juvenile facilities. In Alaska, Arizona, Idaho, New Hampshire, North Dakota, and Virginia, parents are responsible for victim restitution. Some states, such as Rhode Island and Texas, require parents to participate with their children in counseling or education programs and at adjudicatory (court) hearings. Based on preliminary findings, involvement of parents in their child's case processing can be effective in deterring repeat offenses.

CURFEWS

Curfews for young people have existed off and on since the 1890s when curfews were enacted to curb crime

FIGURE 5.13

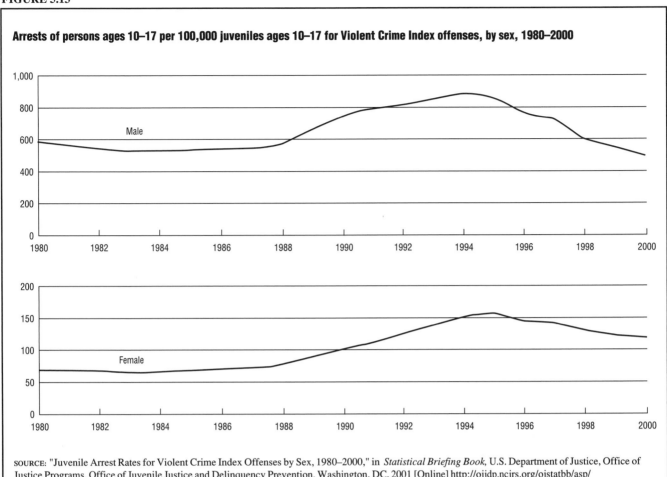

Arrests of persons ages 10–17 per 100,000 juveniles ages 10–17 for Violent Crime Index offenses, by sex, 1980–2000

SOURCE: "Juvenile Arrest Rates for Violent Crime Index Offenses by Sex, 1980–2000," in *Statistical Briefing Book,* U.S. Department of Justice, Office of Justice Programs, Office of Juvenile Justice and Delinquency Prevention, Washington, DC, 2001 [Online] http://ojjdp.ncjrs.org/ojstatbb/asp/JAR_Display.asp?ID=qa2301031031502 [Accessed May 1, 2002]

among immigrant youths. States and cities tend to pass curfew ordinances when citizens perceive a need to maintain more control over juveniles. Because of the rising juvenile crime rates in the late 1980s and early 1990s, more than 1,000 jurisdictions across the United States imposed youth curfews. A U.S. Conference of Mayors survey showed that, by 1997, 276 (78 percent) of the 347 surveyed cities had some sort of a curfew in place. Another 23 cities (6 percent) were considering a curfew law. As a result the OJJDP reported that juvenile curfew and loitering arrests doubled between 1992 and 1998.

Most curfew laws restrict juveniles to their homes or property between the hours of 11 p.m. and 6 a.m. weekdays, allowing them to stay out later on weekends. The laws allow exceptions for young people going to and from school, church events, or work and for those who have a family emergency or are accompanied by their parents.

Critics of curfew ordinances argue that they violate the constitutional rights of children and parents. First, Fourth, Ninth, and Fourteenth Amendment rights, they argue, are endangered by curfew laws—especially the

rights of free speech and association, privacy, and equal protection. The critics also argue that no studies have proven the effectiveness of curfew laws. In 1994 the Supreme Court let stand a lower court ruling (*Qutb v. Bartlett,* F.3rd 488, 62 LW 2343, Rev. 1994) that a Dallas, Texas, curfew law was constitutional.

Are Curfews Successful in Reducing Crime?

Although no statistical studies have concentrated on the effectiveness of curfews, many cities reported declines in juvenile crime and victimization after establishing curfews. John Pionke, a U.S. Conference of Mayors researcher, noted that a number of cities showed a 30 to 50 percent decline in juvenile crime over a period of a year after instituting curfews. The Dallas Police Department recorded an 18 percent decline in juvenile victimization and a 15 percent decline in juvenile arrests during curfew hours. New Orleans, Louisiana and Long Beach, California also reported significant decreases. However, Long Beach and several other cities found that, to some extent, the crime rates had been "displaced"—that is, more juvenile crime was occurring in the non-curfew

FIGURE 5.14

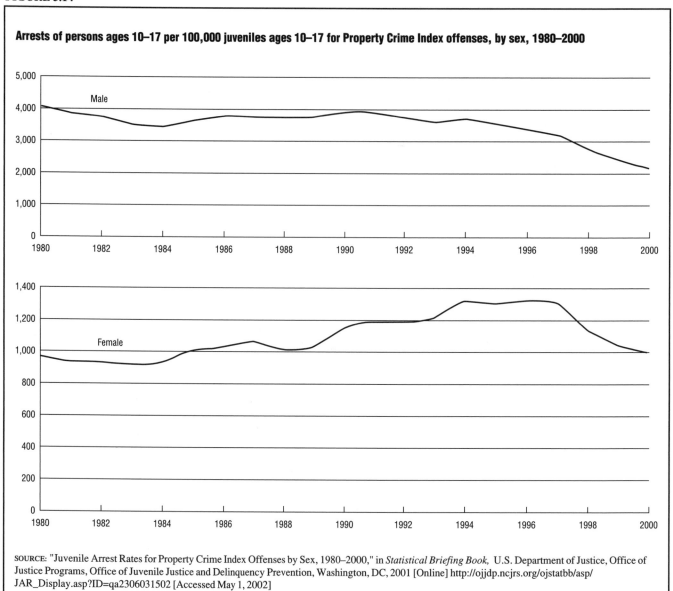

Arrests of persons ages 10–17 per 100,000 juveniles ages 10–17 for Property Crime Index offenses, by sex, 1980–2000

SOURCE: "Juvenile Arrest Rates for Property Crime Index Offenses by Sex, 1980–2000," in *Statistical Briefing Book,* U.S. Department of Justice, Office of Justice Programs, Office of Juvenile Justice and Delinquency Prevention, Washington, DC, 2001 [Online] http://ojjdp.ncjrs.org/ojstatbb/asp/ JAR_Display.asp?ID=qa2306031502 [Accessed May 1, 2002]

hours. Some observers argue that reduction figures are politically motivated by city officials to justify the curfew and that more studies of the information are needed.

To be successful, curfews need sustained enforcement and community support and involvement. Other factors for success include creating recreational, educational, and job opportunities for juveniles, building anti-drug and anti-gang programs, and providing hotlines for community questions or problems.

YOUTH GANGS

Although gangs have been a part of American life since the early eighteenth century, modern street gangs pose a greater threat to public safety and order than ever before. Many gangs originated as social clubs. In the early twentieth century, most street gangs were small groups who engaged in delinquent acts or minor crimes, such as fighting with other gangs. By the late twentieth century, however, they were frequently involved in violence, intimidation, and the illegal trafficking of drugs and weapons. An increasing number supported themselves by the sale of crack cocaine, heroin, and other illegal drugs, and had easy access to high-powered guns and rifles.

What Is a Gang?

A gang can be defined as a group of persons with a unique name and identifiable marks or symbols who claim a territory or turf, associate on a regular basis, and often engage in criminal or antisocial behavior. For gangs whose primary activities include violence and drugs, the FBI uses the term "violent street gang/drug enterprise." These gangs

TABLE 5.4

Delinquency cases, 1998

Most serious offense	Number of cases	Percent change 1989-1998	Percent change 1994-1998	Percent change 1997-1998
Total delinquency	**1,757,400**	**44%**	**5%**	**-3%**
Person offenses	**403,800**	**88%**	**12%**	**1%**
Criminal Homicide	2,000	6	-36	-2
Forcible Rape	6,000	26	-9	-7
Robbery	29,600	29	-23	-12
Aggravated Assault	65,100	36	-22	-6
Simple Assault	262,400	128	33	3
Other violent sex offenses	10,500	53	2	-1
Other person offenses	28,200	87	35	26
Property offenses	**797,600**	**11%**	**-8%**	**-8%**
Burglary	125,800	-7	-14	-9
Larceny-theft	370,500	13	-5	-10
Motor vehicle theft	44,200	-34	-28	-11
Arson	8,400	27	-13	-9
Vandalism	118,700	40	-9	0
Trespassing	64,000	26	-3	-5
Stolen property offenses	34,000	35	0	3
Other property offenses	32,100	37	13	-3
Drug law violations	**192,500**	**148**	**47**	**1**
Public order offenses	**363,500**	**73**	**19**	**0**
Obstruction of justice	152,000	102	38	2
Disorderly conduct	92,100	100	10	-4
Weapons offenses	40,700	61	-20	4
Liquor law violations	19,600	29	32	59
Nonviolent sex offenses	10,900	-13	2	-3
Other public order offenses	48,100	36	34	-10
Violent Crime Index*	**102,600**	**33%**	**-22%**	**-8%**
Property Crime Index**	**548,800**	**3%**	**-10%**	**-10%**

*Includes criminal homicide, forcible rape, robbery, and aggravated assault.
**Includes burglary, larceny-theft, motor vehicle theft, and arson.
Note: Detail may not add to totals because of rounding. Percent-change calculations are based on unrounded numbers.

SOURCE: "In 1998 courts with juvenile jurisdiction disposed more than 1.7 million delinquency cases," in *Statistical Briefing Book*, U.S. Department of Justice, Office of Justice Programs, Office of Juvenile Justice and Delinquency Prevention, Washington, DC, 2001 [Online] http://ojjdp.ncjrs.org/ojstatbb/html/qa179.html [accessed May 1, 2002]

FIGURE 5.15

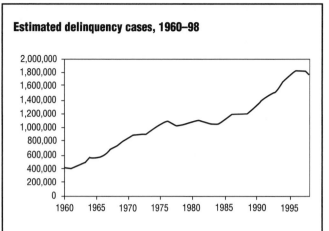

Estimated delinquency cases, 1960–98

SOURCE: "The 1998 juvenile court delinquency caseload was more than 4 times the caseload in 1960," in *Statistical Briefing Book*, U.S. Department of Justice, Office of Justice Programs, Office of Juvenile Justice and Delinquency Prevention, Washington, DC, 2001 [Online] http://ojjdp.ncjrs.org/ojstatbb/html/qa182.html [accessed May 2, 2002]

FIGURE 5.16

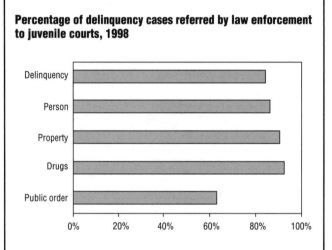

Percentage of delinquency cases referred by law enforcement to juvenile courts, 1998

SOURCE: "The majority of delinquency cases handled in juvenile court in 1998 were referred by law enforcement agencies," in *Statistical Briefing Book*, U.S. Department of Justice, Office of Justice Programs, Office of Juvenile Justice and Delinquency Prevention, Washington, DC, 2001 [Online] http://ojjdp.ncjrs.org/ojstatbb/html/qa181.html [accessed May 2, 2002]

are, in fact, organized criminal conspiracies and can be prosecuted under the federal organized crime statutes. The National Youth Gang Center (NYGC) defines a "youth gang" as a group of youths, ages 10 to 22, who can be classified by local law enforcement agencies as a gang. Law enforcement officials prefer the term "street gang" because it includes both adults and juveniles and indicates where the majority of the gang's activities take place.

The Growth of Youth Gangs

According to the Office of Juvenile Justice and Delinquency Prevention, during the 1970s about 1 percent of all U.S. cities reported having youth gang problems. Cities reporting these problems were referred to as gang cities. By 1998, 7 percent of all U.S. cities were considered gang cities. The biggest growth in gang cities occurred during the 1980s and 1990s, when gangs increased in numbers by 281 percent. Between 1995 and 1998, gang activity was reported in some 1,550 cities and 450 counties where

it had previously gone unreported. In 1999, youth gangs were active in 100 percent of cities with populations of 250,000 or more, 47 percent of suburban counties, 27 percent of cities with populations below 25,000, and 18 percent of rural counties.

The National Youth Gang Survey

Since 1996, the National Youth Gang Center has conducted the National Youth Gang Survey (NYGS), an annual survey of all police and sheriff's departments serving cities and counties with populations of 25,000 or

TABLE 5.5

Police disposition of juvenile offenders taken into custody, 2000

[2000 estimated population]

Population group	Total[1]	Handled within department and released	Referred to juvenile court jurisdiction	Referred to welfare agency	Referred to other police agency	Referred to criminal or adult court
TOTAL AGENCIES: 6,239 agencies; population 135,467,680						
Number	927,112	187,823	656,602	7,507	10,067	65,113
Percent[2]	100.0	20.3	70.8	0.8	1.1	7.0
TOTAL CITIES: 4,612 cities; population 98,274,886						
Number	774,979	162,396	545,860	6,476	8,541	51,706
Percent[2]	100.0	21.0	70.4	0.8	1.1	6.7

[1] Includes all offenses except traffic and neglect cases.
[2] Because of rounding, the percentages may not add to total.

SOURCE: Adapted from "Table 68: Police Disposition, of Juvenile Offenders Taken into Custody, 2000," *Crime in the United States, 2000: Uniform Crime Reports*, Federal Bureau of Investigation, Washington, DC, 2001

FIGURE 5.17

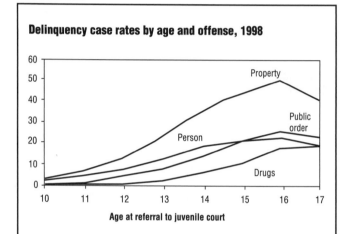

Delinquency case rates by age and offense, 1998

Age at referral to juvenile court

SOURCE: "Delinquency case rates generally increase with the age of the juvenile; however, within offense categories, there are variations in the pattern of age-specific case rates," in *Statistical Briefing Book*, U.S. Department of Justice, Office of Justice Programs, Office of Juvenile Justice and Delinquency Prevention, Washington, DC, 2001 [Online] http://www.ojjdp.ncjrs.org/ojstatbb/html/qa180.html [accessed May 2, 2002]

TABLE 5.6

Deliquency cases involving detention, 1989–1998

Case Type	Percent of all cases involving detention			Percent change in number of cases, 1989–98		Change in number of cases involving detention, 1989–98
	1989	1994	1998	All cases	Detained cases	
Total	**21%**	**18%**	**19%**	**44%**	**25%**	**66,100**
Person	25	23	22	88	63	34,200
Property	17	15	15	11	–6	–7,400
Drugs	36	24	23	148	55	15,600
Public order	26	21	22	73	44	23,800
Male	23%	20%	20%	35%	20%	44,200
Person	27	25	24	71	49	22,800
Property	18	16	16	3	–8	–8,700
Drugs	38	25	23	142	51	12,800
Public order	26	22	22	65	40	17,400
Female	17%	14%	14%	83%	56%	21,900
Person	19	17	18	157	138	11,500
Property	12	10	9	44	8	1,300
Drugs	28	18	19	182	93	2,800
Public order	25	18	19	105	59	6,400
White	18%	16%	17%	43%	33%	49,200
Person	22	20	21	107	95	25,100
Property	15	14	13	8	–8	–5,900
Drugs	23	17	18	192	128	13,100
Public order	24	20	21	68	48	16,900
Black	29%	22%	23%	44%	15%	14,900
Person	30	26	24	63	30	7,800
Property	23	18	19	16	–1	–300
Drugs	56	36	35	80	11	2,000
Public order	30	22	21	86	32	5,400

SOURCE: Paul Harms, "Delinquency cases involving detention, 1989–1998," in *Detention in Delinquency Cases, 1989-1998*, Fact Sheet, U.S. Department of Justice, Office of Juvenile Justice and Deliquency Prevention, January 2002

---

greater. In addition, the NYGS surveys a random sampling of law enforcement agencies serving rural localities with populations between 2,500 and 25,000. Respondents are asked to report information about youth gangs in their jurisdiction, excluding motorcycle gangs, hate or ideology-based groups, prison gangs and adult gangs.

An estimated 24,500 gangs were active in the United States in 2000. Although this represents an overall decline of 5 percent from 1999 levels, cities with populations of over 25,000 reported an increase of 1 percent in the number of gangs, estimated at 12,850, the largest number reported since the survey has been conducted. In 2000 there were some 772,500 active gang members in the United States, an overall decline of 8 percent from 1999. Still, the number of gang members increased by 2 percent to an estimated total of 509,500 in cities with populations of over 25,000. Most youth gang members were males (94 percent), although 39 percent of all youth gangs were reported to have female

TABLE 5.7

Delinquency case processing, 1998

Total deliquency: 1,757,400 estimated cases

Intake decision		Intake disposition		Judicial decision		Judicial disposition	
				Waived	5	Placed	93
						Probation	208
						Other sanction	40
				Adjudicated	361	Released	19
Petitioned	569						
1,000				Nonadjudicated	204	Placed	5
cases						Probation	30
						Other sanction	32
Nonpetitioned	431	Placed	2			Dismissed	137
		Probation	140				
		Other sanction	101				
		Dismissed	187				

Detail may not add to total because of rounding.

SOURCE: "Of every 1,000 delinquency cases handled in 1998, 208 resulted in formal probation and 93 resulted in residential placement following adjudication," in *Statistical Briefing Book,* U.S. Department of Justice, Office of Justice Programs, Office of Juvenile Justice and Delinquency Prevention, Washington, DC, 2001 [Online] http://ojjdp.ncjrs.org/ojstatbb/asp/qa220.asp [accessed May 2, 2002]

FIGURE 5.18

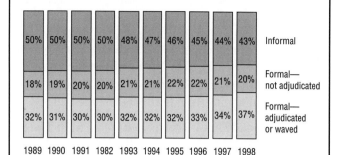

Manner of handling delinquency cases, 1989–98

Note: Detail may not total 100% because of rounding.

SOURCE: "Following the increased use of formal processing, the proportion of delinquency cases that resulted in adjudication or waiver grew between 1989 and 1998," in *Statistical Briefing Book,* U.S. Department of Justice, Office of Justice Programs, Office of Juvenile Justice and Delinquency Prevention, Washington, DC, 2001 [Online] http://ojjdp.ncjrs.org/ojstatbb/html/qa189.html [accessed May 2, 2002]

members. The racial and ethnic composition of gangs changed little over the period of 1996 to 2000, with survey respondents reporting that 47 percent of gang members were Hispanic, 31 percent were African American, 13 percent were white, and 7 percent were Asian.

GANGS AND VIOLENT CRIME. At least one gang-related homicide from 1999 to 2000 was reported in 91 percent of cities with populations over 250,000, 64 percent of cities with populations between 100,000 and 200,000, 55 percent of cities with populations between 50,000 and 100,000, and 32 percent of cities with between 25,000 and 50,000 residents. Among all cities surveyed, 47 percent reported an increase in gang homicides from 1999 to 2000. Among the cities with the highest rate of gang homicides, Los Angeles was ranked second (behind Chicago) with 173 gang homicides in 1998, down by 41 percent from 1996.

Types of Gangs and Activities

The 1995 National Assessment of Gangs study asked prosecutors to indicate the types of gangs operating within their jurisdiction. The study also asked whether or not members of those gangs were involved in drugs or in committing violent crimes. For gangs identified as drug traffickers, the study asked what types of drugs were involved.

Among respondents reporting gang problems, 83 percent in large jurisdictions and 60 percent in small jurisdictions reported the presence of local African American gangs. These gangs originated in that jurisdiction, rather than migrating from California (Crips or Bloods). The second most-prevalent gang types in large jurisdictions were Hispanic gangs (reported by 64 percent of prosecutors), followed closely by motorcycle gangs (62 percent). Forty-nine percent of small jurisdiction prosecutors indicated that motorcycle gangs were present, followed by 43 percent reporting Hispanic gangs.

Approximately 88 percent of large- and 81 percent of small-jurisdiction prosecutors reported that Hispanic gangs in their communities trafficked in drugs. Ninety percent of motorcycle gangs in large jurisdictions and 86 percent in small jurisdictions were reported to be involved in sales of drugs.

In large jurisdictions 50 percent of prosecutors reported the presence of Crips and Bloods, with 90 percent involved in violent crimes and 92 percent involved in drug trafficking. The survey data did not reveal whether local Crips and Bloods had any continuing connection with the Los Angeles gangs. Studies indicate that the names and colors often persist long after dropping any real Los Angeles connection. Caribbean-based gangs were virtually always reportedly involved in drug trafficking. These gangs dealt mainly in cocaine (more than 96 percent).

Asian gangs were more frequently reported to be involved in violent crimes than in drug trafficking. Prosecutors reported the presence of Asian gangs in 52 percent of large jurisdictions but in only 14 percent of small jurisdictions.

Two Studies of Big City Gangs

Two 1995 studies, one funded by the National Institute of Justice (NIJ) and one by the OJJDP, interviewed 50 gang members in each of four communities: Aurora, Colorado; Denver, Colorado; Broward County, Florida; and Cleveland, Ohio. As a control group, 50 youths in each area from the at-risk population who were not gang members were also interviewed. The results of the one-time, confidential interviews showed that gang members were significantly more involved in crime than nonmembers.

According to Dr. C. Ronald Huff (Ohio State University), the principal investigator in the NIJ study, 58 percent of the Colorado and Florida gang members and 45 percent of the Cleveland gang members said they had personally stolen cars. In comparison, control group youths reported much lower car thefts (Colorado and Florida, 12.5 percent; Cleveland, 4 percent). Forty percent of the Cleveland gang members reported participating in a drive-by shooting, compared to only 2 percent of the control group. About 64 percent of the Colorado and Florida gang members stated that members of their gangs had committed homicide, while only 6.5 percent of nonmembers said that their friends had killed someone.

Gang members were also much more likely than nonmembers to own guns. More than 90 percent of gang members in the study communities reported that their peers had carried concealed weapons; more than 80 percent stated that members had taken guns to school. Of the control groups, about half said friends had carried a concealed weapon, and one-third reported friends had taken guns to school.

Gang members were more involved than at-risk nonmembers in drug trafficking. More than 70 percent of gang members reported selling drugs, while only 6 to 9 percent of youths in the control groups said they had sold drugs.

Young Juveniles

In "Early Precursors of Gang Membership: A Study of Seattle Youth" (*Juvenile Justice Bulletin*, Office of Juvenile Justice and Delinquency Prevention, December 2001), Karl G. Hill, Christina Lui, and J. David Hawkins reported on the results of a study in Seattle, Washington, in which fifth-graders were tracked through the age of 18. Of 808 study participants, 124 joined a gang between the ages of 13 and 18. About 69 percent of those belonged to a gang for less than one year, and less than 1 percent of study participants who joined a gang at age 13 were still in a gang at 18 years of age.

According the report, study participants who remained in the gang for several years "were the most behaviorally and socially maladjusted children," often exhibiting "early signs of violent externalizing such as aggression and hyperactivity." Also, study participants who associated with antisocial peers were more than twice as likely to remain in a gang for more than one year. Among the risk factors identified as contributing to gang involvement were learning disabilities, availability of marijuana, low academic achievement, other neighborhood youth in trouble, and youths living with one parent along with other unrelated adults.

JUVENILES AND GUNS

Schools and neighborhoods can be dangerous places for many young Americans. Knives, revolvers, and even shotguns turn up in searches of school lockers. News reports describe incidents of children being shot on playgrounds or of youths firing rifles as they cruise the streets in cars. The use of deadly weapons in violent incidents has increased fear among citizens of all ages.

According to Stuart Greenbaum, a public safety specialist, guns had become readily available to juveniles by the 1980s. In fact, Greenbaum believes that guns are the weapons of choice for youth ("Kids and Guns: From Playgrounds to Battlegrounds," *Juvenile Justice*, vol. 3, no. 2, September 1997). The juvenile arrest rate for weapons law violations increased over 100 percent between 1987 and 1993. Between 1993 and 2000, that rate fell by 48 percent, returning to approximately the same level as in 1987. (See Figure 5.19.)

From 1983 to 1994 gun homicides by juveniles tripled while homicides involving other types of weapons decreased. From 1994 to 1997, however, homicides by youth declined sharply, primarily those involving firearms. Gun suicides also increased in the years from 1983 to 1994. From 1980 to 1994 the suicide rate for persons ages 15 to 19 grew 29 percent; firearms-related suicides accounted for 96 percent of the increase. The risk of suicide is estimated to be five times greater in households where guns are present. Beginning in 1995, the number of firearm-related suicides for persons 19 years of age or younger gradually declined, from 1,450 to 1,078 in 1999. Still, due to the overall decline in all firearm-related deaths during those years (from 5,285 to 3,385), the percentage of firearm-related suicides for persons under 19 rose from 27 percent of all firearm-related deaths in 1995 to 33 percent in 1998, then dropped off slightly to 32 percent in 1999.

According to the U.S. Bureau of Alcohol, Tobacco, and Firearms (ATF), juveniles and youth are more likely than adults to use handguns and semiautomatic weapons in crimes. In 1996 the ATF began the Youth Crime Gun Interdiction, a pilot program in 17 cities throughout the nation aimed at reducing youth violence involving firearms. The cities in the program send information on all "crime guns" to the ATF's National Tracing Center.

In 1997 the ATF announced that four of ten handguns confiscated by law enforcement officers during 1996 were

FIGURE 5.19

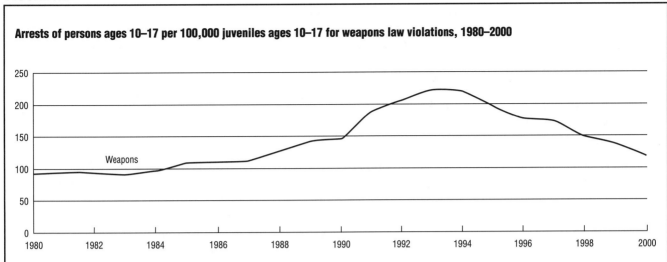

Arrests of persons ages 10–17 per 100,000 juveniles ages 10–17 for weapons law violations, 1980–2000

SOURCE: "Juvenile Arrest Rates for Weapons Law Violations, 1980–2000," in *Statistical Briefing Book,* U.S. Department of Justice, Office of Justice Programs, Office of Juvenile Justice and Delinquency Prevention, Washington, DC, 2001 [Online] http://ojjdp.ncjrs.org/ojstatbb/asp/JAR_Display.asp? ID=qa2213012002 [Accessed April 30, 2002]

collected from persons ages 24 and under. Handguns accounted for 80 percent of the firearms taken from youths and juveniles, compared to 70 percent of guns taken from adults. Six of ten of the handguns confiscated from youths and juveniles were semiautomatic pistols. Most of the guns involved in youth crimes had been obtained from illegal firearms traffickers. About 25 percent of the crime guns wound up in illegal firearms sellers' hands, often as a result of household burglary, within three years of the guns' original legitimate sale through retail channels. This "fast time to crime" indicated the ease with which a criminal can fence a stolen gun, and the pervasiveness of the illegal firearms market.

Guns and Juvenile Homicide Victims

A sharp increase in gun-related juvenile homicides was experienced from the late 1980s until 1993. Most of the homicides of those ages 12 to 17 were male victims killed by males using firearms. Between 1980 and 1997, 3 out of 4 murdered juveniles age 12 or older were killed with a firearm. In 1999, according to the Bureau of Justice Statistics, some 1,990 persons 19 years of age and younger were the victims of firearm-related homicides, down from 2,215 firearm-related homicides in 1998, and from 3,274 in 1991. Among teens 15 to 19 years old, 1,708 were victims of firearm-related homicides, while 282 children 14 and under were victims of firearm-related homicides in 1999. Though the numbers of homicides dropped in 1999, the percentage of those that are firearm-related did not. In 1999, victims of homicide between ages 12 and 17 were usually males (81 percent of all victims), killed by other males (95 percent of all perpetrators), with firearms (86 percent of all deaths).

Weapon Offenses and Offenders

Weapon offenses are violations of statutes or regulations that control deadly weapons. Deadly weapons include firearms and their ammunition, silencers, explosives, and certain knives. Juveniles accounted for 16 percent of those arrested for weapon offenses in 1974 and 24 percent in 1996. Between 1985 and 1993 the number of juvenile arrests increased by more than 100 percent, from just under 30,000 to more than 61,000. From that peak in 1993, however, the rate of arrests declined sharply and steadily. (See Figure 5.19.) Teenage males (25,887) arrested for weapons offenses in 1998 far outnumbered female arrests (2,698). Female arrests nearly doubled from 1989 to 1998.

SCHOOL CRIME

As reported in *Indicators of School Crime and Safety 2001* (jointly published by the Bureau of Justice Statistics and the National Center for Education Statistics, 2001), in 1999 students 12 to 18 years of age were the victims of approximately 2.5 million crimes of violence or theft at school. There were 47 school-related violent deaths in the United States from July 1, 1998 through June 30, 1999. Of those, 38 were homicides (34 of which were students) and 9 were suicides, a decline from a peak of 49 school-related homicides and suicides in the 1995–1996 school year. Of the three remaining school-related violent deaths, one was an unintentional shooting and the other two deaths were those of adults killed as the result of actions taken by law enforcement. There were a total of two multiple-victim homicides at U.S. schools in the 1998–1999 school year, compared to six such incidents during the 1997–1998 academic year. With the exception of the 1993–1994 school year, there has been at least one multiple-victim homicide during each school year since 1992, according to the Office of Juvenile Justice and Delinquency Prevention. In the five years between 1997 and 2002, several school shootings received national media attention:

- March 5, 2001: Two were killed and 13 wounded at Santee High School in Santana, California when a student opened fire from a school bathroom.

- February 29, 2000: A six-year-old student was killed at Theo J. Buell Elementary School near Flint, Michigan, by a fellow student (also six years old) who brought a handgun to school.

- April 20, 1999: Twelve students and a teacher were fatally shot at Columbine High School in Littleton, Colorado, by students Eric Harris, 18, and Dylan Klebold, 17, who eventually killed themselves after their hour-long rampage.

- May 21, 1998: Two students were killed and 22 were wounded at Thurston High School in Springfield, Oregon by student Kip Kingle, who also murdered his parents.

- December 1, 1997: Three students were killed and five were wounded as they participated in a prayer circle at Heath High School in West Paducah, Kentucky.

- October 1, 1997: Two students were killed and seven were wounded by student Luke Woodham, 16, who had earlier killed his mother.

According to the *Youth Risk Behavior Surveillance System 1999 Study* (Centers for Disease Control and Prevention, 2000), a self-report survey of high school students, almost 5 percent of students reported carrying a gun on at least one day in the thirty days prior to the survey. Overall, male students were significantly more likely than females to carry a gun. A total of 17.3 percent of students nationwide reported carrying some type of weapon, such as a gun, knife or club, on at least one day prior to the survey. This represents a decline from 1993, when some 22 percent of students reported carrying a weapon, according to *Indicators of School Crime and Safety: 2001*. In 1999, about 7 percent of students reported carrying a weapon on school property—as opposed to carrying a weapon anywhere—compared to 12 percent in 1993, a reduction of 42 percent. In 1999, 11 percent of males and 3 percent of females reported carrying a weapon on school property. Although students in lower grades were more likely to report carrying a weapon anywhere, the likelihood of carrying a weapon to school was distributed evenly across students in all grades in 1999.

The percentage of secondary school students who reported being threatened or injured at school with a weapon such as a gun, knife, or club fluctuated between 7 and 8 percent from 1993 through 1999, according to *Indicators of School Crime and Safety: 2001*. During that same time period, the percentage of secondary school students who reported carrying a weapon at school fell from 12 to 7 percent. Secondary students in lower grades were more likely than students in higher grades to be threatened with a weapon at school.

Nonfatal School Crimes

In 1999 some 186,000 students ages 12 to 18 were victims of nonfatal serious violent crimes (rape, sexual assault, robbery, and aggravated assault). When simple assault was factored in, the number of school-related victimizations increased significantly, to about 880,000 in 1999. This amounts to about 8 percent of students ages 12 through 18 who reported being victims of nonfatal violent crimes at school in 1999, a decline from 10 percent in 1995.

There were no significant differences in the rates of victimization for students at urban and suburban schools in 1999, although students in urban schools were more likely than suburban students to be victimized away from school. Students between the ages of 12 and 14 were more likely to be victims of school-related crime than were older students 15 through 18 years of age.

Crimes Against Teachers

Some 1.7 million nonfatal crimes at school between 1995 and 1999 were committed against teachers. About one-third of those (635,000) were violent crimes, including rape, sexual assault, robbery, and aggravated or simple assault. Thefts accounted for the remaining 1,073,000 nonfatal crimes against teachers. Between 1995 and 1999, some 342,000 teachers were victims of nonfatal crimes at school, 11 percent of which were serious violent crimes, accounting for a rate of victimization of three serious violent crimes per 1,000 teachers.

Senior and junior high school teachers were more likely to be victimized by violent crimes (usually simple assault) and experienced a higher incidence of theft than elementary school teachers. Male teachers were victimized at a rate of 51 violent crimes per 1,000 teachers, compared to a rate of 22 for female teachers. Teachers in urban schools were victimized at a rate of 39 violent crimes per 1,000 teachers, compared to a rate of 22 in suburban schools and 20 in rural areas.

JUVENILES IN CUSTODY

According to the Bureau of Justice Statistics, on October 29, 1997, some 125,805 juveniles were confined in residential placement facilities in the United States. Residential placements include both public and private detention, correctional, and shelter facilities. Of the 98,913 delinquents (criminal offenders) in residential placement on that date, 35,357 had been involved in person offenses and 26,498 in violent offenses. There were about 6,877 status offenders in residential placement. (Some 20,015 juveniles in residential placement were excluded from the offense category counts because they did not meet the criteria of the Census of Juveniles in Residential Placement.)

CHAPTER 6
SENTENCING AND CORRECTIONS

SENTENCING AND TIME SERVED

In 1998 state and federal courts convicted some 980,000 adults of felonies, according to the Bureau of Justice Statistics. Of those, 927,717 were adults convicted in state courts and 50,494 were convicted in federal jurisdictions. Some 68 percent of convicted felons were sentenced to a period of incarceration in 1998. Of those, 44 percent went to state prisons and 24 percent to local jails. Those in jails were usually confined for less than one year.

In 1998 the average felony sentence imposed by state courts was 39 months in prison. On average, violent offenders served the most time (77 months), compared to averages of 31 months for property and drug offenses, and 29 months for weapons offenses. (See Table 6.1.)

The length of a prison sentence was almost always longer than the time actually served by a convicted felon in 1998. In state prisons, the actual time served was about 47 percent of the overall sentence. Most states (but not the federal system) have parole boards that determine when a prisoner will be paroled (released from prison). In the federal system and in most states, prisoners can earn time credits for good behavior ("good time") to shorten their time in prison.

Sentencing Reform

Because of the variances in sentencing and parole from state to state, the Sentencing Reform Act of 1984 (PL 98-473) created a commission to establish consistent sentencing guidelines. Under the federal guidelines, which went into effect in late 1987, federal prisoners serve a minimum of 85 percent of the actual sentence. After 1986 the average federal prison sentences for violent crimes decreased, but the overall time served increased. The result was a rapidly growing federal prison population.

As of 1993, 46 states had mandatory sentencing laws, requiring prison terms for certain offenses and a minimum number of years offenders must serve. While judges may wish to consider mitigating circumstances and invoke alternative sentencing such as community service, mandatory sentencing laws have taken those options away. In Alabama, for example, a person convicted of selling even a small amount of drugs is sentenced to two years in prison. Another five years are added if the sale occurred within three miles of a school or housing project, and still another five years are added if the sale was within three miles of both.

"Three Strikes" Laws

As of 2002, 40 states had provisions that mandated the lengthening of sentences for repeat offenders. Of those, 26 states had "Three Strikes" laws, which require repeat criminals to serve enhanced prison terms if they are convicted of three violent felonies. Most of these laws were enacted during the 1990s in response to a significant rise in crime, particularly violent crime, during the first half of the decade. The consequence of these new laws was a rise in the prison population, along with its attendant costs.

Opponents of Three Strikes laws argue that the laws demand even more prisons to house prisoners for longer periods. Also, reducing the possibility of parole results in more and more elderly prisoners, who are statistically much less likely to commit crimes than younger prisoners, and who have increasing health-care needs. By the year 2000 many states that had passed Three Strikes laws were wondering how to pay for more prisons and longer incarcerations.

Since 2000 several states have loosened their mandatory minimum sentencing laws or taken other measures to reduce their prison populations. For example, in 2001 Mississippi adopted an early-release provision for nonviolent offenders, and states such as California, Texas, North Carolina, Connecticut, Idaho, and Arkansas have

TABLE 6.1

Lengths of felony sentences imposed by state courts, 1998

Most serious conviction offense	Average maximum sentence length (in months) for felons sentenced to:			
	Incarceration			
	Total	Prison	Jail	Probation
All offenses	39 mo	57 mo	6 mo	40 mo
Violent offenses	77 mo	100 mo	7 mo	47 mo
Property offenses	31 mo	44 mo	5 mo	39 mo
Drug offenses	31 mo	47 mo	5 mo	38 mo
Weapons offenses	29 mo	42 mo	6 mo	35 mo
Other offenses	25 mo	40 mo	6 mo	40 mo

Note: Means exclude sentences to death or to life in prison. Sentence length data were available for 921,328 incarceration and probation sentences.

SOURCE: "Lengths of felony sentences imposed by State courts, 1998" in "Criminal Sentencing Statistics," U.S. Department of Justice, Bureau of Labor Statistics, Washington, DC, February 2002 [Online] http://www.ojp.usdoj.gov/bjs/sent.htm [accessed June 28, 2002]

passed legislation mandating the diversion of non-violent drug offenders to community-based treatment programs.

On April 1, 2002, the United States Supreme Court agreed to consider whether California's Three Strikes law, considered to be one of the toughest in the country, violates the Eight Amendment's ban against cruel and unusual punishment. Over half (57 percent) of California prisoners sentenced under the Three Strikes law were convicted of nonviolent third-strike felonies, including drug possession and petty theft, and are serving mandatory sentences of 25 years to life without the possibility of parole.

THE DEATH PENALTY

Thirty-eight states and the federal Government had laws sanctioning the death penalty in 2002. Of those, 37 states and the federal government allowed the use of lethal injection, and one state (Nebraska) required electrocution as the means of execution. The 37 states that authorized the death penalty by lethal injection were: Alabama, Arizona, Arkansas, California, Colorado, Connecticut, Delaware, Florida, Georgia, Idaho, Illinois, Indiana, Kansas, Kentucky, Louisiana, Maryland, Mississippi, Missouri, Montana, Nevada, New Hampshire, New Jersey, New Mexico, New York, North Carolina, Ohio, Oklahoma, Oregon, Pennsylvania, South Carolina, South Dakota, Tennessee, Texas, Utah, Virginia, Washington, and Wyoming. In addition to lethal injection, nine states permit the use of electrocution, five states allow the use of the gas chamber, and three states permit the use of a firing squad. Delaware, New Hampshire, and Washington permit hanging as a means of execution.

In 2000 some 3,593 prisoners were under the sentence of death in 27 states and in the federal prison system. Eighty-five people, 83 men and 2 women, were

executed in the United States in 2000. Of those, 49 were white (including 6 Hispanics), 35 were African American, and 1 was American Indian. Lethal injection was used in 80 of the executions in 2000, while electrocution was used in 5 executions.

According to the Bureau of Justice Statistics, of the 3,593 prisoners under sentence of death at the end of 2000, 98.5 percent were male and 1.5 percent were female. Slightly more than half (55.4 percent) were white, 42.7 percent were African American, and 1.9 percent of prisoners under death sentence were of other races, including 28 who were self-identified as American Indian and 24 who identified themselves as Asian. Over half of death row inmates (51.7 percent) had dropped out of school by the 11th grade, while 38.2 percent were high school graduates or had completed the GED equivalency, and 10.1 percent had attended college. Some 54 percent of death row prisoners had never married, compared to 22.6 percent who were married and 21 percent who were divorced or separated.

Most prisoners on death row at the end of 2000 were repeat offenders, with 64 percent having prior felony convictions. However, of those, only 8.1 percent had prior homicide convictions. Some 17.6 percent of death row inmates committed their capital offense while on parole, 10.1 percent while on probation, and 7.1 percent while there were other charges pending against them. Sixty percent of death row inmates at year end 2000, reported that they had no pending legal status at the time of their capital offense.

According to "Capital Punishment 2000" by Tracy L. Snell (*Bureau of Justice Statistics Bulletin,* December 2001, revised February 2002), between 1977 and 2000 some 6,588 persons were under the sentence of death in the United States. Of those, some 10 percent (683) were executed, 3 percent died of causes other than executions, and about one-third had their death sentences lifted and received other dispositions. During that time period, 65 percent of the 683 executions occurred in 5 states—Texas (239), Virginia (81), Florida (50), Missouri (46), and Oklahoma (30). In 2001, 18 executions were carried out in Oklahoma and 17 in Texas, accounting for over half of the 66 executions carried out in the United States.

Proponents of the Death Penalty

Some supporters of the death penalty, as a deterrent, look back to 1966 when there was a virtual moratorium on execution at the state level and the murder rate began to increase (until 1980 it was more than twice the 1963 rate). Along with this trend, there was an upswing in the number of felony murders as compared to crimes of passion. By the mid-1990s, when the number of executions had increased, the murder rate dropped again (as it did in the 1930s, when both homicides and executions were at their highest point in national history). Even though the absence of capital punishment doesn't alone cause murder rates to rise, they say, it still plays a major role. Further, they argue, no other punishment can substitute for execution as a deterrent because even life sentences often end early in parole or pardon. Recidivism can occur after release; and innocent victims outnumber prisoners wrongfully executed.

A second reason frequently cited for support of the death penalty, is its function as retribution. This satisfies an emotional need for victims' loved ones, meets the demands of certain moral codes, and contributes to a sort of social cohesiveness (by allowing law-abiding persons to band together and show their support of shared values). Those who feel that punishment should be "proportional" argue that nothing less than the murderer's own death fits the crime of homicide.

Death penalty proponents do not believe that execution methods used in civilized nations like the United States are barbaric. They also point to capital punishment's continuation in most of the Western world until the 1950s and the support it has even today in European countries where it has been abolished. They contend that the Eighth Amendment's prohibition against cruel and unusual punishment does not extend to execution and was never intended to be interpreted that way. In *Furman v. Georgia* (1976), the U.S. Supreme Court found only that the death penalty was used fairly. Plus, they add, the American legal system includes an appeals process, which can stretch on for years after the imposition of a death sentence. Advocates for the death penalty further argue that more capital cases are overturned because of judicial error than due to defendants' innocence.

Troubling Questions

Studies done by the Gallup Poll in 2000 show that though the death penalty is still supported by the majority of Americans (66 percent), support has dropped since its peak in 1994 (80 percent). In the same poll, some 91 percent of respondents said they believed that in the past 20 years at least one person sentenced to death was innocent. These opinions probably have something to do with publicity surrounding several death penalty convictions being overturned due to newly obtained DNA evidence. Other issues, such as erroneous eyewitness accounts, false confessions and testimony, and police or prosecutorial misconduct, have called into question the fairness of capital punishment trials and sentencing of death row inmates.

In Oklahoma in 2001 the discovery of the possible false testimony of state witness forensic chemist, Joyce Gilchrist, left dozens of cases in question. In September 2001 the Department of Justice released a study that documented that race and geography play a role in who is sentenced to death, echoing the findings of several other independent studies across the nation. In Texas, lawyers

of 43 inmates who received the death penalty were later sanctioned for misconduct or even disbarred, according to the *Chicago Tribune*. According to the American Civil Liberties Union (ACLU), nationally there was a 68 percent rate of serious error in death penalty trials.

Because of questions brought about by these cases, several states that allowed the death penalty imposed moratoriums on executions until studies were completed. In Illinois in 2000 Republican Governor George Ryan declared a moratorium after 13 inmates on death row were found innocent within a few months. He put together a commission to review the state's system and offer suggestions for improvements. In April of 2002 85 changes, including reducing the number of capital crimes, videotaping police interrogations, forbidding capital punishment in cases where the conviction is based solely on the testimony of a single eyewitness, and increasing competent counsel protections, were recommended by the commission. In May 2002 Democratic Governor Parris Glendening of Maryland, also declared a moratorium until a study could be completed by the University of Maryland in September 2002, and the state legislature had time to review the results.

According to The Innocence Project, a non-profit legal clinic at the Benjamin N. Cardozo School of Law, from the reinstatement of the death penalty in 1976, until June 24, 2002, 108 people on death row had been exonerated from the crimes for which they had been sentenced to death. The American Bar Association asked for a moratorium on the death penalty in 1997. In 2001 Senators Russell Feingold (D-WI) and Jesse Jackson Jr. (D-IL), proposed the "National Death Penalty Moratorium Act of 2001" (S. 233), calling for a moratorium on the federal death penalty and a federal independent commission on problems within the system.

The Execution of Mentally Retarded Criminals

On June 20, 2002, the United States Supreme Court ruled in favor of Virginia death row inmate Daryl Renard Atkins, who is mentally retarded, and declared that the execution of mentally retarded individuals is unconstitutional. The court, in a 6–3 vote, held that such executions constituted a violation of the Eighth Amendment's ban against cruel and unusual punishment. Until this ruling, some 20 states allowed the execution of mentally retarded persons who were convicted of capital crimes.

In writing for the majority of the court, Justice John Paul Stevens held, "This consensus unquestionably reflects widespread judgement about the relative culpability of mentally retarded offenders, and the relationship between mental retardation and the penological purpose served by the death penalty... Their deficiencies do not warrant an exemption from criminal sanctions, but they do diminish their personal culpability."

In their dissent, Chief Justice William Rehnquist and Justices Antonin Scalia and Clarence Thomas expressed the view that the court went too far in its ruling, which effectively opens the door for inmates with IQs of 70 or less to appeal their death sentences.

Juries Must Decide

In 1972 a U.S. Supreme Court ruling about the constitutionality of capital punishment brought the nation's executions to a halt. The court's decision on *Furman v. Georgia* stated that state death penalty statutes lacked standards and gave too much discretion to individual judges and to juries. After states addressed some of the issues troubling the court, including mandatory death sentences for some crimes, the court ruled in 1976, in *Gregg v. Georgia*, that the death penalty was constitutional.

This decision did not address individual states' laws about who determined sentencing for capital offenses. On June 24, 2002, the U.S. Supreme Court ruled that juries, not judges, must make the final determination to impose the death penalty in a capital case. The ruling, written by Justice Ruth Bader Ginsburg, held that a sentence imposed by a judge violates a defendant's constitutional right to a trial by jury. Joining Justice Ginsburg were Justices John Paul Stevens, Antonin Scalia, Anthony M. Kennedy, David H. Souter, and Clarence Thomas. Justice Stephen Breyer agreed with the majority in a separate opinion. Justice Sandra Day O'Connor wrote the dissenting opinion and was joined by Chief Justice William H. Rehnquist.

The 7 to 2 ruling, which involved the case of an Arizona death row inmate, overturns at least 150 death penalty sentences (not the guilty verdicts) and could potentially affect over 800 death sentences nationwide. The ruling will affect all cases in Arizona, Idaho, and Montana, where a single judge was allowed to decide whether to impose the death penalty. The cases will have to be reconsidered in six other states: Colorado and Nebraska, where panels of judges made sentencing decisions, and Florida, Alabama, Indiana, and Delaware, where a jury can recommend a sentence of death, but a judge ultimately decided on the penalty. The Supreme Court did not decide how the ruling would affect each state. It is possible that the death row inmates' sentences could be commuted to life in prison, or that the inmates could be resentenced, facing the death penalty sentence again.

CORRECTIONS IN THE UNITED STATES

In 2000 about 6.5 million Americans, or about 3 percent of the adult population of the United States, were under some form of correction supervision (prison, jail, probation, and parole). According to the Bureau of Justice Statistics, by June 30, 2000, nearly 2 million persons (1,931,859) were incarcerated in federal, state, and local correctional facilities in the United States. Of those, about two-thirds (1,310,710) were in federal or state custody, while some 621,149 were held in local jails. (See Table 6.2.) The other 4.5 million were either on probation or paroled. Probation and parole consist of court ordered community supervision of convicted offenders by law enforcement agencies, though probation is usually given in place of incarceration and parole is obtained after a period of incarceration. Both usually require the offender to follow specific rules of conduct while in the community. By midyear 2001 there were 1,965,495 million Americans incarcerated: 1,405,531 inmates under state and federal jurisdiction and 702,044 in local jails.

According to the Bureau of Justice Statistics, at midyear 2001 there were 4,848 sentenced African American male inmates per 100,000 African American males in the United States, compared to 1,668 sentenced Hispanic male inmates per 100,000 Hispanic males and 705 white male inmates per 100,000 white males. African American males in their twenties and thirties had much higher rates of incarceration compared to other ethnic and age groups. Of the 1.97 million offenders in local jails or prison on June 30, 2001, some 601,800 (30 percent) were black males between the ages of 20 and 39. In terms of the general population, 12.0 percent of all African American non-Hispanic males in their 20s and early 30s were in prison or jail at midyear 2001, compared to 4.0 percent of Hispanic males, and 1.8 percent of white males in the same age group.

Prisons and Jails—How Do They Differ?

The terms "prison" and "jail" are frequently used interchangeably. Jails, however, are generally city or county institutions while prisons are usually state or federal institutions. Jails are used to confine adults serving short sentences (generally one year or less) or persons awaiting trial or other legal disposition. Prisons, on the other hand, house convicted criminals sentenced to lengthy terms.

The Growth in the Incarceration Rate

From 1980 to 2000 there were increases among all four groups of adult correctional populations in the United States, with the incarceration rate tripling. (See Figure 6.1.) The number of prisoners on death row increased over five times, from 692 to 3,593, in that 20-year period. As of midyear 2001, approximately 690 of 100,000 U.S. residents were in some kind of correctional situation, up slightly from a rate of 686 at midyear 2000. (See Table 6.3.) Annually, between 1995 and 2001, the incarcerated population grew an average of 4 percent, with federal rates rising 8.6 percent, state rates rising 3.4 percent, and local rates rising 3.7 percent.

The United States imprisons a larger share of its population than any other nation, despite a rapidly increasing incarceration rate in Russia. Marc Mauer, in *Americans*

TABLE 6.2

Prisoners under the jurisdiction of state or federal correctional facilities, 2000–01

Region and jurisdiction	Total			Percent change from C		Incarceration rate, 6/30/01[1]
	6/30/01	12/31/00	6/30/00	6/30/00 to 6/30/01	12/31/00 to 6/30/01	
U.S. total	1,405,531	1,391,111	1,390,059	1.1%	1.0%	472
Federal	152,788	145,416	142,530	7.2	5.1	46
State	1,252,743	1,245,695	1,247,529	0.4	0.6	426
Northeast	172,925	174,825	177,965	-2.8%	-1.1%	305
Connecticut[2]	18,875	18,355	18,616	1.4	2.8	384
Maine	1,693	1,679	1,715	-1.3	0.8	126
Massachusetts[3]	10,734	10,722	11,150	-3.7	0.1	247
New Hampshire	2,323	2,257	2,254	3.1	2.9	184
New Jersey[4]	28,108	29,784	31,081	-9.6	-5.6	331
New York	69,158	70,198	71,691	-3.5	-1.5	364
Pennsylvania	37,105	36,847	36,617	1.3	0.7	302
Rhode Island[2]	3,147	3,286	3,186	-1.2	-4.2	179
Vermont[2]	1,782	1,697	1,655	7.7	5.0	221
Midwest	240,213	237,075	236,804	1.4%	1.3%	370
Illinois[4]	45,629	45,281	44,819	1.8	0.8	366
Indiana	20,576	20,125	19,874	3.5	2.2	336
Iowa[5]	8,101	7,955	7,646	6.0	1.8	277
Kansas[4]	8,543	8,344	8,780	-2.7	2.4	317
Michigan	48,371	47,718	47,317	2.2	1.4	484
Minnesota	6,514	6,238	6,219	4.7	4.4	131
Missouri	28,167	27,382	27,292	3.2	2.9	500
Nebraska	3,944	3,895	3,663	7.7	1.3	225
North Dakota	1,080	1,076	1,004	7.6	0.4	158
Ohio[4]	45,684	45,833	46,838	-2.5	-0.3	402
South Dakota	2,673	2,616	2,571	4.0	2.2	353
Wisconsin	20,931	20,612	20,781	0.7	1.5	373
South	563,818	561,373	560,698	0.6%	0.4%	532
Alabama	27,286	26,225	25,786	5.8	4.0	592
Arkansas	12,332	11,915	11,559	6.7	3.5	455
Delaware[2]	7,122	6,921	7,043	1.1	2.9	505
District of Columbia[2]	5,388	7,456	8,575	-37.2	-27.7	592
Florida[5]	72,007	71,319	71,233	1.1	1.0	439
Georgia[5]	45,363	44,232	43,626	4.0	2.6	540
Kentucky	15,400	14,919	15,444	-0.3	3.2	369
Louisiana	35,494	35,207	34,734	2.2	0.8	795
Maryland	23,970	23,538	23,704	1.1	1.8	432
Mississippi	20,672	20,241	18,379	12.5	2.1	689
North Carolina	31,142	31,532	31,070	0.2	-1.2	329
Oklahoma[4]	23,139	23,181	23,009	0.6	-0.2	669
South Carolina	22,267	21,778	22,154	0.5	2.2	526
Tennessee	23,168	22,166	22,566	2.7	4.5	404
Texas	164,465	166,719	168,126	-2.2	-1.4	731
Virginia	30,473	30,168	29,890	2.0	1.0	415
West Virginia	4,130	3,856	3,800	8.7	7.1	225
West	275,787	272,422	272,062	1.4%	1.2%	414
Alaska[2]	4,197	4,173	4,025	4.3	0.6	336
Arizona[5]	27,136	26,510	26,287	3.2	2.4	478
California	163,965	163,001	164,490	-0.3	0.6	468
Colorado[4]	17,122	16,833	16,319	4.9	1.7	388
Hawaii[2]	5,412	5,053	5,051	7.1	7.1	294
Idaho	5,688	5,535	5,465	4.1	2.8	431
Montana	3,250	3,105	3,039	6.9	4.7	359
Nevada	10,291	10,063	9,920	3.7	2.3	485
New Mexico	5,288	5,342	5,277	0.2	-1.0	281
Oregon	11,077	10,580	10,313	7.4	4.7	319
Utah	5,440	5,632	5,450	-0.2	-3.4	235
Washington	15,242	14,915	14,704	3.7	2.2	251
Wyoming	1,679	1,680	1,722	-2.5	-0.1	340

[1] The number of prisoners with a sentence of more than 1 year per 100,000 residents.
[2] Prison and jails form an integrated system. Data include total jail and prison population.
[3] The incarceration rate includes an estimated 6,200 inmates sentenced to more than 1 year but held in local jails or houses of corrections.
[4] "Sentenced to more than 1 year" includes some inmates "sentenced to 1 year or less."
[5] Population figures are based on custody counts.

SOURCE: Allen J. Beck, Jennifer C. Karberg, and Paige M. Harrison, "Table 2. Prisoners under the jurisdiction of State or Federal correctional authorities, June 30 and December 31, 2000 and June 30, 2001," in *Prison and Jail Inmates at Midyear 2001,* U.S. Department of Justice, Bureau of Justice Statistics, Washington, DC, April 2002

FIGURE 6.1

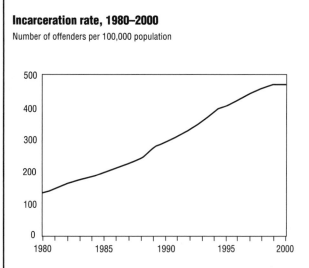

Incarceration rate, 1980–2000

Number of offenders per 100,000 population

SOURCE: "The incarceration rate has more than tripled since 1980," in *U.S. Department of Justice, Bureau of Justice Statistics:* Corrections Statistics, U.S. Department of Justice, Bureau of Justice Statistics, Washington, DC, 2001 [Online] http://www.ojp.usdoj.gov/bjs/glance/corr2.htm [accessed May 3, 2002]

Behind Bars: U.S. and International Use of Incarceration, 1995 (The Sentencing Project, Washington, D.C., 1997), compared prison populations and practices around the world. Statistics provided by the Sentencing Project show that in 2000, the incarceration rate in Russia was 644 per 100,000 persons, while the U.S. rate was 699 per 100,000 persons. The next closest country was South Africa, with an incarceration rate of 400, followed by the United Kingdom (125), Canada, Australia, and Spain (110 each), and Germany, at 95. (See Figure 6.2.) By 2001 Russia's rate had climbed to 676 per 100,000. The U.S. rate, though dropping slightly, was still the world's highest, at 690 per 100,000.

Mauer views a high rate of incarceration as an indication of various problems in a nation. For example, in *Americans Behind Bars*, Mauer observes that a high rate of incarceration may be caused by a high rate of crime, or violent crime, for which large-scale imprisonment is viewed as appropriate or necessary. Incarceration rates that are higher than average could result from more severe punishments for similar offenses in comparable nations. Mauer also notes that high incarceration rates may also be a result of consequences of social policy decisions which affect the population's standard of living and tendency to commit crime.

Underlying the growth in the prison population nationwide has been an increase in the number of arrests for drug offenses. According to the FBI, from 1991 to 2000, the total number of arrests rose by only 0.2 percent, from 7.39 million to 7.41 million. However, during that same time period, arrests for drug abuse violations rose by

TABLE 6.3

Number of persons held in state or federal prisons or local jails, 1990–2001

Year	Total inmates in custody	Prisoners in custody		Inmates held in local jails	Incarceration rate[1]
		Federal	State		
1990	1,148,702	58,838	684,544	405,320	458
1995	1,585,586	89,538	989,004	507,044	601
1996	1,646,020	95,088	1,032,440	518,492	618
1997	1,743,643	101,755	1,074,809	567,079	648
1998	1,816,931	110,793	1,113,676	592,462	669
1999[2]	1,893,115	125,682	1,161,490	605,943	691
2000[3]					
June 30	1,934,990	131,496	1,176,368	621,149	686
December 31	—	133,921	1,175,740	—	
2001[3]					
June 30	1,965,495	140,741	1,187,322	631,240	690
Percent change, 6/30/00 -6/30/01	1.6%	7.0%	0.9%	1.6%	
Annual average increase, 12/31/95 - 6/30/01	4.0%	8.6%	3.4%	3.7%	

Note: Jail counts are for midyear (June 30). Counts for 1994-2001 exclude persons who were supervised outside of a jail facility. State and federal prisoner counts for 1990-99 are for December 31.
—Not available.
[1] Persons in custody per 100,000 residents in each reference year.
[2] In 1999, 15 states expanded their reporting criteria to include inmates held in privately operated correctional facilities. For comparisons with previous years, the state count 1,137,544 and the total count 1,869,169 should be used.
[3] Total counts include federal inmates in non-secure privately operated facilities (5,977 in 2000 and 6,192 in 2001).

SOURCE: Allen J. Beck, Jennifer C. Karberg, and Paige M. Harrison, "Table 1. Number of persons held in State and Federal prisons or in local jails, 1990–2001," in *Prison and Jail Inmates at Midyear 2001*, U.S. Department of Justice, Bureau of Justice Statistics, Washington, DC, April 2002

49.4 percent, from 563,776 to 842,532. This had a significant impact on the prison population, especially in federal correctional facilities. According to the Sentencing Project, a private research and advocacy group, nearly 60 percent of federal inmates were incarcerated for drug offenses as of mid-year 2001, accounting for much of the 7.2 percent rise in the federal prison population from mid-year 2000 to mid-year 2001. This compares to a rise in the state prison population of only 0.4 percent during the same time period, in part because some states, in an effort to reduce their prison rolls, have recently adopted laws that require diversion of drug offenders.

JAIL INMATES

Inmates may be in jails for a variety of reasons:

• They may be individuals waiting for arraignment, trial, conviction, and/or sentencing, or they may be probation, parole, and bail bond violators.

• Juveniles may be temporarily jailed to wait for transfer to juvenile facilities.

• Mentally ill persons are often held in jails pending transfer to mental health facilities.

FIGURE 6.2

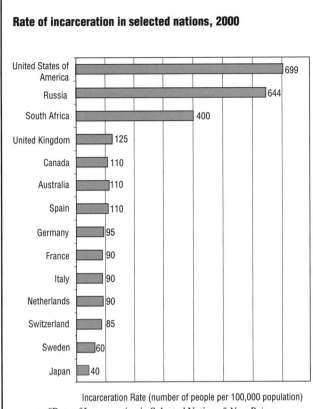

Rate of incarceration in selected nations, 2000

Incarceration Rate (number of people per 100,000 population)

SOURCE: "Rate of Incarceration in Selected Nations," *New Prison Population Figures Show Slowing of Growth but Uncertain Trends*, The Sentencing Project, Washington, DC, 2001

TABLE 6.4

Characteristics of jails

- receive individuals pending arraignment and hold them awaiting trial, conviction, or sentencing
- readmit probation, parole, and bailbond violators and absconders
- temporarily detain juveniles pending transfer to juvenile authorities
- hold mentally ill persons pending their movement to appropriate health facilities
- hold individuals for the military, for protective custody, for contempt, and for the courts as witnesses
- release convicted inmates to the community upon completion of sentence
- transfer inmates to Federal, State, or other authorities
- house inmates for Federal, State, or other authorities because of crowding of their facilities
- relinquish custody of temporary detainees to juvenile and medical authorities
- sometimes operate community-based programs as alternatives to incarceration
- hold inmates sentenced to short terms (generally under 1 year).

SOURCE: Allen J. Beck and Jennifer Karberg, "Jails," in *Prison and Jail Inmates at Midyear 2000*, U.S. Department of Justice, Bureau of Justice Statistics, Washington, DC, 2001

TABLE 6.5

Persons under jail supervision by confinement status and type of program, midyear 1995, 1999–2001

Confinement status and type of program	Number of persons under jail supervision			
	1995	1999	2000	2001
Total	541,913	687,973	687,033	702,044
Held in jail	507,044	605,943	621,149	631,240
Supervised outside a jail facility[1]	34,869	82,030	65,884	70,804
Electronic monitoring	6,788	10,230	10,782	10,017
Home detention[2]	1,376	518	332	539
Day reporting	1,283	5,080	3,969	3,522
Community service	10,253	20,139	13,592	17,561
Weekender programs	1,909	16,089	14,523	14,381
Other pretrial supervision	3,229	10,092	6,279	6,632
Other work programs[3]	9,144	7,780	8,011	5,204
Treatment programs[4]	—	8,500	5,714	5,219
Other/unspecified	887	3,602	2,682	7,729

—Not available.
[1] Excludes persons supervised by a probation or parole agency.
[2] Includes only those without electronic monitoring.
[3] Includes persons in work release programs, work gangs, and other work alternative programs.
[4] Includes persons under drug, alcohol, mental health, and other medical treatment.

SOURCE: Allen J. Beck, Jennifer C. Karberg, and Paige M. Harrison, "Table 9. Persons under jail supervision, by confinement status and type of program, midyear 1995, 1999–2001," in *Prison and Jail Inmates at Midyear 2001*, U.S. Department of Justice, Bureau of Justice Statistics, Washington, DC, April 2002

Table 6.4 lists these and other reasons for holding inmates in jails.

Jails are a generally neglected part of the corrections system. They frequently fail to meet minimum standards for space, care, and staffing and have to mix a wide range of inmates—hardened criminals awaiting trial, those with serious mental problems or addictions, drunks disturbing the peace, and those who are not yet convicted (and may never be). Because the stay in jail is usually brief, medical care, recreation, and opportunities for work or activity are frequently minimal.

Population in the Nation's Jails

On June 30, 2001, 702,044 persons were under some form of jail supervision, either confined in jails or supervised outside jail facilities, up from 687,033 in 2000. Of those, 631,240 were being held in jail, while the remaining persons were in jail-supervised programs such as electronic monitoring or community service or other work programs. (See Table 6.5.)

For the year ending June 30, 2001, the average daily jail population was 625,966, up from 618,319 in 2000 and 408,075 in 1990. Between 1990 and 2001 the average daily population of female jail inmates nearly doubled

from 37,198 to 72,621, while the male population increased from 365,821 to 551,007. (See Table 6.6.) Proportionally the number of female inmates grew from 9.2 percent of the jail inmate population to 11.6 percent, and the number of males decreased from 90.8 percent to 88.4 percent. (See Table 6.7.)

In 2000 minority groups made up about 25 percent of the population of the United States, according to the U.S. Census. Minority groups, however, accounted for a majority (57 percent) of local jail inmates in 2001. Non-Hispanic

TABLE 6.6

Average daily population and the number of men, women, and juveniles in local jails, midyear 1990, 1995, and 2000–01

	1990	1995	2000	2001
Average daily population[1]	408,075	509,828	618,319	625,966
Number of inmates, June 30[2]	405,320	507,044	621,149	631,240
Adults	403,019	499,300	613,534	623,628
Male	365,821	448,000	543,120	551,007
Female	37,198	51,300	70,414	72,621
Juveniles[3]	2,301	7,800	7,615	7,613
Held as adults[4]	—	5,900	6,126	6,757
Held as juveniles	2,301	1,800	1,489	856

Note: Data are for June 30 in 1995 and 2000 and for June 29 in 1990 and 2001. Detailed data for 1995 were estimated and rounded to the nearest 100.

—Not available.

[1] The average daily population is the sum of the number of inmates in a jail each day for a year, divided by the total number of days in the year.

[2] Inmate counts for 1990 include an unknown number of persons who were under jail supervision but not confined.

[3] Juveniles are persons defined by state statute as being under a certain age, usually 18, and subject initially to juvenile court authority even if tried as adults in criminal court. In 1994 the definition was changed to include all persons under age 18.

[4] Includes juveniles who were tried or awaiting trial as adults.

SOURCE: Allen J. Beck, Jennifer C. Karberg, and Paige M. Harrison, "Table 10. Average daily population and the number of men, women, and juveniles in local jails, midyear 1990, 1995, and 2000–2001," in *Prison and Jail Inmates at Midyear 2001*, U.S. Department of Justice, Bureau of Justice Statistics, Washington, DC, April 2002

TABLE 6.7

Gender, race, Hispanic origin, and conviction status of local jail inmates, selected years 1990–2001

Characteristic	Percent of jail inmates			
	1990	1995	2000	2001
Total	**100%**	**100%**	**100%**	**100%**
Gender				
Male	90.8%	89.8%	88.6%	88.4%
Female	9.2	10.2	11.4	11.6
Race/Hispanic origin				
White, non-Hispanic	41.8%	40.1%	41.9%	43.0%
Black, non-Hispanic	42.5	43.5	41.3	40.6
Hispanic	14.3	14.7	15.1	14.7
Other*	1.3	1.7	1.6	1.6
Conviction status (adults only)				
Convicted	48.5%	44.0%	44.0%	41.5%
Male	44.1	39.7	39.0	36.6
Female	4.5	4.3	5.0	4.9
Unconvicted	51.5	56.0	56.0	58.5
Male	46.7	50.0	50.0	51.9
Female	4.8	6.0	6.0	6.6

Note: Detail may not add to total because of rounding.

*Includes American Indians, Alaska Natives, Asians, and Pacific Islanders.

SOURCE: Allen J. Beck, Jennifer C. Karberg, and Paige M. Harrison, "Table 11. Gender, race, Hispanic origin, and conviction status of local jail inmates, midyear 1990, 1995, and 2000–2001," in *Prison and Jail Inmates at Midyear 2001*, U.S. Department of Justice, Bureau of Justice Statistics, Washington, DC, April 2002

whites made up 43 percent of the jail population; non-Hispanic African Americans, 40.6 percent; and Hispanics, 14.7 percent. Other races (Asian Americans, Pacific Islanders, American Indians, and Alaska Natives) accounted for 1.6 percent. Among non-Hispanic African Americans, the jail incarceration rate (703 per 100,000) was more than five times that of non-Hispanic whites (138 per 100,000) and almost three times the rate of Hispanics (263 per 100,000).

Most juveniles in correctional custody were housed in juvenile facilities. However, at mid-year 2001 an estimated 6,757 persons under age 18 were kept in adult jails, most having been tried as adults or awaiting trial as adults in criminal court.

The Growing Jail Population

From 1990 to 2001 the number of jail inmates grew from 405,320 to 631,240, a rise in the jail incarceration rate from 163 to 222 jail inmates per 100,000 U.S. residents. At midyear 1999 jails housed 33 percent of all incarcerated prisoners, the same as at midyear 2001. Since jail sentences remained stable at about seven months, the dramatic growth of the local jail population seemed more related to the increased number of arrests than to longer sentences.

On June 30, 2001, the capacity of all local jails was estimated to be 699,309 inmates, an increase of 21,522 from midyear 2000. Even with this increased capacity, jails were about 90 percent occupied.

STATE AND FEDERAL PRISONS

Persons convicted of murder, burglary, or larceny/theft are most likely to wind up in a state prison. If the crime is a federal offense or was committed outside a state jurisdiction, the offender can be sentenced to a federal prison. Federal offenses include crimes that

- Are committed against a federal institution (bank, post office, or federally insured credit union) or a federal officer (FBI, Drug Enforcement Administration, or U.S. Treasury agent).

- Are committed on the high seas, on government reservations or territories, or in other areas under federal jurisdiction, such as Washington, D.C.

- Involve crossing state lines (kidnapping or transporting stolen automobiles, for example).

- Involve interstate crime, such as telephone or mail fraud.

Prison Population

The BJS regularly surveys the nation's correctional facilities. The June 2001 survey counted 1,965,495 prisoners. State and federal prisons housed two-thirds (1,405,531) of all persons incarcerated in the United States with the other third in local jails. Of those held in prisons, state prisons housed over 89 percent (1,252,743), while federal prisons held about 11 percent (152,788). These figures show a less than 1 percent increase in the state prison population and a 7.2 percent increase in the federal prison population over the previous year. (See Table 6.2.)

PRISONER RATES. Despite a decline in the overall crime rate in the late 1990s, the rate of prisoners per 100,000 population has continued to rise steadily. Since 1980 the incarceration rate more than tripled from 139 per 100,000 to 472 per 100,000 at the end of June 2001. Of those, the number of sentenced federal prisoners per 100,000 residents more than quintupled from 9 to 46 over the same period.

In 2001 the Southern region of the U.S. had the highest incarceration rate, with 532 per 100,000 residents, and the Northeast had the lowest, with 305. Louisiana led the states with 795 prisoners per 100,000 state residents, followed by Texas (731), Mississippi (689), and Oklahoma (669). Mississippi had the highest rate of increase from 2000 (12.5 percent). The District of Columbia had 592 prisoners per 100,000 inhabitants in 2001, a decline of 37.1 percent from midyear 2000.

CHARACTERISTICS OF PRISONERS

Gender

In 2000 women accounted for 91,612 prisoners under state or federal correctional authorities, an increase of 1.2 percent from 1999 and 7.6 percent from 1990. The male prisoner population increased by 1.3 percent from 1999 and 5.9 percent from 1990. The rate of sentenced male prisoners (915 per 100,000 males in the resident population) was significantly higher than the rate for sentenced females (59 per 100,000 females). (See Table 6.8.)

Race and Ethnicity

Increasing percentages of inmates are from racial or ethnic minority groups. In 2001, among young adult U.S.

residents in their 20s and early 30s, 12 percent of black males, 4 percent of Hispanic males and 1.8 percent of white males were behind bars. In 2000, of 1.3 million male prisoners under state or federal correctional authority, 44 percent (572,900) were black, 34 percent (436,500) were white, and 16 percent (206,900) were Hispanic. Of 83,668 females, 45 percent (37,400) were black, 41 percent (34,500) were white, and 12 percent (10,000) were Hispanic in 2000. (See Table 6.9.)

TABLE 6.8

Prisoners under jurisdiction of state or federal correctional authorities by gender, 1990–2000

	Men	Women
All inmates		
Advance 2000	1,290,280	91,612
Final 1999	1,273,171	90,530
Final 1990	729,840	44,065
Percent change, 1999-2000	1.3%	1.2%
Average annual 1990-2000	5.9	7.6
Sentenced to more than 1 year		
Advance 2000	1,237,469	83,668
Final 1999	1,221,611	82,463
Percent change, 1999-2000	1.3%	1.5%
Incarceration rate*		
2000	915	59
1990	572	32

*The number of prisoners with sentences of more than 1 year per 100,000 residents on December 31.

SOURCE: "Table 6. Prisoners under the jurisdiction of State or Federal correctional authorities, by gender, yearend 1990, 1999, and 2000," in Allen J. Beck and Paige M. Harrison, *Prisoners in 2000*, U.S. Department of Justice, Bureau of Justice Statistics, Washington, DC, 2001

TABLE 6.9

Number of sentenced prisoners under state or federal jurisdiction by gender, race, Hispanic origin, and age, 2000

	Number of sentenced prisoners							
	Males				Females			
Age	Total[1]	White[2]	Black[2]	Hispanic	Total[1]	White[2]	Black[2]	Hispanic
Total	1,237,469	436,500	572,900	206,900	83,668	34,500	37,400	10,000
18-19	33,300	8,400	16,300	6,800	1,200	600	500	100
20-24	199,600	56,500	98,100	38,700	7,800	3,300	3,000	1,200
25-29	232,100	67,100	119,100	41,300	14,700	5,300	6,600	2,000
30-34	234,000	81,900	109,400	40,000	21,000	8,300	9,900	2,300
35-39	212,700	79,200	101,700	30,400	18,200	7,600	8,600	2,000
40-44	149,400	58,300	64,600	24,800	10,200	4,100	4,800	1,100
45-54	128,800	60,300	49,200	17,800	8,300	3,800	3,100	1,100
55 or older	42,300	23,700	11,300	6,600	1,900	1,300	600	200

Note: Based on custody counts from National Prisoners Statistics (NPS-1A) and updated from jurisdiction counts by gender at yearend. Estimates by age derived from the Surveys of Inmates in State and Federal Correctional facilities, 1997. Estimates were rounded to the nearest 100.

[1] Includes American Indians, Alaska Natives, Asians, Native Hawaiians, and other Pacific Islanders.
[2] Excludes Hispanics.

SOURCE: Allen J. Beck and Paige M. Harrison, "Table 14. Number of sentenced prisoners under State or Federal jurisdiction, by gender, race, Hispanic origin, and age, 2000," in *Prisoners in 2000*, U.S. Department of Justice, Bureau of Justice Statistics, Washington, DC, 2001

TABLE 6.10

Estimated number of sentenced prisoners under state jurisdiction by offense, gender, race, and Hispanic origin, 1999

Offenses	All	Male	Female	White	Black	Hispanic
Total	**1,189,800**	**1,115,400**	**74,400**	**396,100**	**553,100**	**202,100**
Violent offenses	570,000	548,400	21,600	189,300	266,300	93,800
Murder[1]	141,500	134,900	6,600	44,000	70,700	22,900
Manslaughter	17,500	15,700	1,800	6,200	6,900	3,400
Rape	30,900	30,600	300	14,200	12,400	2,600
Other sexual assault	78,100	77,300	800	44,600	19,300	10,800
Robbery	161,800	156,600	5,200	33,800	97,300	26,200
Assault	115,100	109,700	5,400	35,800	50,500	23,800
Other violent	25,100	23,600	1,500	10,700	9,100	4,200
Property offenses	245,000	225,400	19,600	103,900	98,500	34,100
Burglary	116,600	112,900	3,800	49,200	47,200	16,200
Larceny	46,700	40,500	6,100	17,300	21,000	6,400
Motor vehicle theft	19,900	19,200	700	7,700	7,300	4,400
Fraud	31,700	24,100	7,600	16,000	12,000	2,800
Other property	30,100	28,700	1,400	13,600	11,000	4,200
Drug offenses	251,200	226,100	25,100	50,700	144,700	52,100
Public-order offenses[2]	120,600	112,800	7,800	51,500	42,100	21,300
Other/unspecified[3]	3,000	2,700	300	600	1,500	700

Note: Data are for inmates with a sentence of more than 1 year under the jurisdiction of State correctional authorities. The number of inmates by offense were estimated using the 1997 Survey of Inmates in State Correctional Facilities and rounded to the nearest 100.

[1] Includes nonnegligent manslaughter.
[2] Includes weapons, drunk driving, court offenses, commercialized vice, morals and decency charges, liquor law violations, and other public-order offenses.
[3] Includes juvenile offenses and unspecified felonies.

SOURCE: Allen J. Beck and Paige M. Harrison, "Table 16. Estimated number of sentenced prisoners under State jurisdiction, by offense, gender, race, and Hispanic origin, 1999," in *Prisoners in 2000*, U.S. Department of Justice, Bureau of Justice Statistics, Washington, DC, 2001

Offenses

Of the four offense categories (violent, property, drug, and public-order), the largest growth in state prisoners from 1900 to 1999 was among violent offenders. Property offenders in state prisons increased by some 70,000 during that time period and comprised 14 percent of the state prison population. The rise in drug offenders was 101,500, comprising 20 percent of the state prison population, and public order offenders in state prison increased by 74,800, accounting for 15 percent of state inmates. Between 1990 and 1999 the number of state prisoners sentenced for violent offenses increased by 254,100 and comprised 51 percent of the state prison population nationwide. In 1999 there were 570,000 violent offenders in state prisons nationwide, less than 4 percent (21,600) of whom were female. Just over half of violent offenders in state prison in 1999 were black, 189,300 were white, and 93,800 were Hispanic. In 1999, 48 percent of all state prisoners were violent offenders. About 21 percent were property offenders (245,000) or drug offenders (251,200), and about 10 percent (120,600) of state inmates were serving sentences for public order offenses. (See Table 6.10.)

Among federal prisoners, the number of incarcerated violent offenders rose from 9,557 in 1990 to 13,355 in 1999, for an increase of 39.7 percent. Federal inmates sentenced for property offenses increased by 9.4 percent from 1990 to 1999, from 7,935 to 8,682. The number of drug offenders in federal prisons more than doubled, from 30,470 in 1990 to 68,360 in 1999, accounting for a rise of 124.4 percent. The number of public order offenders in federal prisons increased by 208.2 percent between 1990 and 1999, from 8,585 to 26,456. (See Table 6.11.)

Mental Health

In 2000, 10 percent of all state inmates were receiving psychotropic medications, and one in eight state prisoners were in some type of mental health therapy or counseling, according to the Bureau of Justice Statistics. Some 217,420 prisoners were confined in 155 state facilities specializing in psychiatric confinement.

Of state prison inmates, 22.1 percent of females confined to female-only facilities were receiving psychotropic medication as of mid-year 2000, compared to 8.7 percent of male state prisoners in male-only facilities. Of state prisoners confined to facilities housing both males and females, 15.2 percent of inmates were receiving psychotropic medication as of June 30, 2000. Inmates in female-only facilities were also more likely to receive therapy or counseling in 2000 (27.1 percent), compared to inmates in male-only facilities (11.9 percent), and in institutions that housed both males and females (14.3 percent). (See Table 6.12.)

PROBATION AND PAROLE

At the end of 2000 nearly 4.6 million adults were on probation or parole in the United States, up from 3.2 million at the end of 1990. Of probationers in 2000, 52 percent were convicted of felonies, 46 percent of misdemeanors, and 2 percent of other types of infractions. Twenty-four percent of probationers had drug law violations as their most serious offense. (See Table 6.13.)

Of probationers in 2000, 22 percent were female, compared to 18 percent in 1990. Whites comprised 64 percent of probationers in 2000, down from 68 percent in 1990, while blacks accounted for 34 percent of probationers, up from 31 percent in 1990. In 2000 probationers of Hispanic origin represented 16 percent of all probationers, down from 18 percent in 1990.

In 2000, 725,527 adults were on parole. Almost all offenders on parole (97 percent) had served a felony sentence of one year or more. More than half of parolees in 2000 received mandatory release from prison as the result of a sentencing statute (requirement) or because of good-time provisions. Thirty-seven percent received parole as the result of a decision by a state parole board, 59 percent fewer than in 1990. Twelve percent of all parolees in 2000 were women. Fifty-five percent of adult parolees were white, and 44 percent were black. Hispanics made up 21 percent of parolees. (See Table 6.14.)

RECIDIVISM

The recidivism rate measures the degree to which inmates return to criminal behavior after their release

TABLE 6.11

Number of sentenced inmates in federal prisons by most serious offense, 1990, 1995, and 1999

Offenses	Number of sentenced inmates in federal prisons			Percent change, 1990-99	Percent of total growth, 1990-1999
	1990	1995	1999		
Total	**56,989**	**88,101**	**119,185**	**109.1%**	**100.0%**
Violent offenses	9,557	11,321	13,355	39.7%	6.1%
Homicide[1]	1,233	966	1,498	21.5	0.4
Robbery	5,158	6,341	9,354	81.3	6.7
Other violent	3,166	4,014	2,503	-20.9	-1.1
Property offenses	7,935	7,524	8,682	9.4%	1.2%
Burglary	442	164	195	-55.9	-0.4
Fraud	5,113	5,629	6,553	28.2	2.3
Other property	2,380	1,731	1,934	-18.7	-0.7
Drug offenses	30,470	51,737	68,360	124.4%	60.9%
Public-order offenses	8,585	15,762	26,456	208.2%	28.7%
Immigration	1,728	3,612	10,156	487.7	13.6
Weapons	3,073	7,519	9,494	208.9	10.3
Other public-order	3,784	4,631	6,806	79.9	4.9
Other/unspecified[2]	442	1,757	2,332	427.6%	3.0%

Note: All data are from the BJS Federal justice database. Data for 1990 and 1995 are for December 31. Data for 1999 are for September 30. Data are based on all sentenced inmates, regardless of sentence length.

[1] Includes murder, nonnegligent manslaughter, and negligent manslaughter.
[2] Includes offenses not classifiable or not a violation of the United States Code.

SOURCE: Allen J. Beck and Paige M. Harrison, "Table 19. Number of sentenced inmates in Federal prisons, by most serious offense, 1990, 1995, and 1999," in *Prisoners in 2000*, U.S. Department of Justice, Bureau of Justice Statistics, Washington, DC, 2001

TABLE 6.12

Inmates receiving mental health treatment in state confinement facilities, June 30, 2000

Facility characteristic	Number of inmates receiving —					
	24-hour mental health care		Therapy/ counseling		Psychotropic medications	
	Number	Percent	Number	Percent	Number	Percent
Total[a]	16,986	1.8%	122,376	12.9%	95,114	9.8%
Facility operation						
Public	16,270	1.8%	116,296	13.0%	90,721	10.0%
Private	716	1.3	6,080	10.8	4,393	7.7
Authority to house						
Males only	13,064	1.5%	100,371	11.9%	74,736	8.7%
Females only	830	1.5	14,744	27.1	12,119	22.1
Both	3,092	5.9	7,261	14.3	8,259	15.2
Security level						
Maximum/high	6,928	2.4%	44,637	14.9%	35,069	11.5%
Medium	9,608	1.8	65,726	12.6	52,208	9.8
Minimum/low	448	0.4	11,593	9.3	7,355	5.8
Facility size[b]						
1,500 or more	6,298	1.4%	59,970	12.8%	45,283	9.3%
750-1,499	5,140	1.6	41,953	13.0	31,816	9.9
250-749	4,582	3.5	16,831	13.4	14,866	11.6
100-249	888	3.3	3,309	12.4	2,867	10.9
Fewer than 100	78	2.3	313	11.0	282	8.8

[a] Excludes inmates in mental health treatment in Florida for whom only statewide totals were reported.
[b] Based on the average daily population between July 1, 1999, and June 30, 2000.

SOURCE: Allen J. Beck and Laura M. Maruschak, "Table 4: Inmates receiving mental health treatment in State confinement facilities, by facility characteristic, June 30, 2000," in *Bureau of Justice Statistics Special Report: Mental Health Treatment in State Prisons, 2000*, U.S. Department of Justice, Office of Justice Programs, Washington, DC, July, 2001

TABLE 6.13

Characteristics of adults on probation, 1990 and 2000

	1990	2000
Total	**100%**	**100%**
Gender	100%	100%
Male	82	78
Female	18	22
Race	100%	100%
White	68	64
Black	31	34
Other	1	2
Hispanic origin	100%	100%
Hispanic	18	16
Non-Hispanic	82	84
Status of supervision	100%	100%
Active	83	76
Inactive	9	9
Absconded	6	9
Supervised out of State	2	3
Other	—	3
Adults entering probation	100%	100%
Without incarceration	87	78
With incarceration	8	16
Other	5	6
Adults leaving probation	100 %	100%
Successful completion	69	60
Returned to incarceration	14	15
With new sentence	3	3
With the same sentence	9	8
Type of return unknown	2	4
Absconder	7	3
Discharged to detainer/warrant	2	1
Other unsuccessful	—	11
Death	**	1
Other	7	9
Severity of offense		100%
Felony	—	52
Misdemeanor	—	46
Other infractions	—	2
Most serious offense		100%
Driving under the influence	—	18
Drug law violation	—	24
Other offenses	—	58
Status of probation	100 %	100%
Direct imposition	38	56
Split sentence	6	11
Sentence suspended	41	25
Imposition suspended	14	7
Other	1	1

Note: For every characteristic there were persons of unknown status or type. Detail may not sum to total because of rounding.

—Not available.

**Less than 0.5%.

SOURCE: "Table 5. Characteristics of adults on probation, 1990 and 2000," *National Correctional Population Reaches New High: Grows by 126,400 during 2000 to Total 6.5 Million Adults*, U.S. Department of Justice, Washington, DC, August 26, 2001

TABLE 6.14

Characteristics of adults on parole, 1990 and 2000

Characteristic	1990	2000
Total	**100%**	**100%**
Gender	100%	100%
Male	92	88
Female	8	12
Race	100%	100%
White	52	55
Black	47	44
Other	1	1
Hispanic origin	100%	100%
Hispanic	18	21
Non-Hispanic	82	79
Status of supervision	100%	100%
Active	82	83
Inactive	6	4
Absconded	6	7
Supervised out of State	6	5
Other	—	1
Adults entering parole	100%	100%
Discretionary parole	59	37
Mandatory parole	41	54
Reinstatement	—	6
Other	—	2
Adults leaving parole	100%	100%
Successful completion	50	43
Returned to incarceration	46	42
With new sentence	17	11
Other	29	31
Absconder	1	9
Other unsuccessful	1	2
Transferred	1	1
Death	1	1
Other	—	2
Length of sentence	100%	100%
Less than 1 year	5	3
One year or more	95	97

Note: For every characteristic there were persons of unknown status or type. Detail may not sum to total because of rounding.

Federal parole as defined here includes supervised release, parole, military parole, special parole, and mandatory release.

—Not available.

SOURCE: "Table 6. Characteristics of adults on parole, 1990 and 2000," *National Correctional Population Reaches New High: Grows by 126,400 during 2000 to Total 6.5 Million Adults*, U.S. Department of Justice, Washington, DC, August 26, 2001

from prison. In "Recidivism of Prisoners Released in 1994" (Bureau of Justice Statistics Special Report, June 2002), authors Patrick A. Langan, Ph.D., and David J. Levin, Ph.D., released the findings of a study that tracked 272,111 former inmates three years after their release from prison in 15 states—Arizona, California, Delaware, Florida, Illinois, Maryland, Michigan, Minnesota, New Jersey, New York, North Carolina, Ohio, Oregon, Texas, and Virginia. Of prisoners tracked, over two-thirds (67.5 percent) were rearrested for a new offense during the three years after their release from prison. Of the 272,111 prisoners released in 1994, 46.9 percent were convicted of a new crime, and 25.4 percent were sentenced to prison for the new offense. Almost 52 percent of the 272,111 were back in prison, whether for a new crime or a technical violation of their release.

By offense, the highest rate of rearrest was for motor vehicle theft (78.8 percent), followed by selling stolen property (77.4 percent), larceny (74.6 percent), burglary (74 percent), and robbery (70.2 percent). The sale, use or possession of illegal weapons also accounted for an arrest rate of 70.2 percent. The lowest rates of rearrest in the three years following release from prison in 1994 were for homicide (40.7 percent), sexual assault other than rape

(41.4 percent), rape (46 percent), and driving under the influence (51.5 percent).

Male prisoners released in 1994 were more likely to be rearrested (68.4 percent) than females (57.6 percent). African Americans were more likely to be rearrested (72.9 percent) than were Hispanics (64.6 percent) and whites (62.7 percent). Inmates ages 25 to 29 (22.8 percent) and 30 to 34 (22.7 percent) were most likely to be rearrested, while inmates 45 years of age or older (7.5 percent) were least likely to re-offend in the three years after release from state prison. Of the 211,111 former inmates released in 1994, 7.6 percent were rearrested in a state other than the one that released them.

Arrest history made a difference in recidivism; the more arrests the prisoner had prior to release, the more likely the prisoner's rearrest. Of those with one arrest prior to their release, 41 percent were rearrested. About 47 percent of those with two prior arrests, 55 percent of those with three earlier arrests, and 82 percent of those with more than fifteen prior arrests (18 percent of all released prisoners) were rearrested within a three-year period.

WHAT IS THE SOLUTION?

Is prison the answer to crime? Is prison supposed to punish, or is it supposed to rehabilitate? It is certainly the primary method the government uses to show that it takes crime seriously and will not let it go unpunished. It keeps dangerously violent criminals off the street, which has very likely contributed somewhat to the recent drop in crime.

Prisoners are often considered society's failures, people—mostly men—who have failed in their relationships with their families, schools, and jobs. They suffer disproportionately from physical, drug, and alcohol abuse. They may have low self-esteem and exhibit hostility towards others, especially those in authority. Prisoners bring their own society into prison, which usually revolves around drugs, smuggling, extortion, predatory sexual behavior, and violence.

Many penologists (persons who study prison management and the reformation of criminals) believe that locking up greater numbers of offenders reduces the rate of crime. Mandatory sentencing and habitual-offender laws give longer sentences to those who have broken the law. If criminals are in prison, they are not on the streets committing crimes. Some experts believe longer sentences have acted as a deterrent and played a major role in the recent decline in criminal activity.

Others disagree. In "Reforming Sentencing and Corrections for Just Punishment and Public Safety," (*Sentencing & Corrections*, National Institute of Justice, No. 4, September 1999), authors Michael E. Smith and Walter J. Dickey reported on hearings by the Wisconsin Governor's Task Force on Sentencing and Corrections conducted in 1996,

which focused on a Milwaukee neighborhood where public safety "was in serious disrepair." According to the police testimony at the hearings, at a certain high crime corner some "94 drug arrests were made within a 3-month period.... Despite the two-year prison terms routinely handed down by the sentencing judges (for drug offenses), the drug market continued to thrive at the intersection, posing risks to the safety of all who lived nearby or had to pass through on their way to work or school." According to the testimony, the incarceration of some 100 drug-offense felons "did not increase the public safety at the street corner."

As an alternative to incarceration, programs advocating restorative and community justice are based on principles that address the needs of victims, communities and offenders. As reported by Leena Kurki in "Incorporating Restorative and Community Justice Into American Sentencing and Corrections" (*Sentencing & Corrections*, National Institute of Justice, No. 3, September 1999), the basic principles of restorative justice are that crime involves disruptions in a three-dimensional relationship of victim, offender, and community; that because crime harms the victim and the community, the primary goals should be to repair that harm by healing the victim and community; that the victim, community, and offender should all participate in determining the response to crime; and that case disposition should be based primarily on the victim's and the community's needs.

One example of restorative justice is Victim-Offender Mediation, in which offenders meet with the victim(s) of their crime. These meetings, facilitated by a mediator, focus on the effects of the crime on the life of the victim and on the community at large. A restitution agreement is reached between the offender and the victim. Another example of restorative justice is Family Group Conferencing, which involves the meeting of the victim and the offender plus family, friends, co-workers and teachers of the victim and offender. According to Kurki, family group conferencing originated in New Zealand, where it became part of the juvenile justice system in 1989. As of 1999, about 30 percent of juvenile offenders in New Zealand were sent to family group conferencing instead of to juvenile court.

A Rand Corporation report, *Diverting Children From a Life of Crime: Measuring Costs and Benefits* (1996), found that programs helping children avoid crime were more cost-effective than imprisoning repeat offenders for long periods. The study concluded that a state government could prevent 157 crimes annually by investing $1 million in parent-training programs. They could prevent another 258 crimes by investing $1 million in graduation incentive programs. On the other hand, spending $1 million in constructing and operating new prisons for long-term prisoners would prevent only 60 crimes a year. A cost-benefit comparison seems to favor spending on early crime intervention rather than on construction of prisons.

CHAPTER 7
WHITE-COLLAR CRIME

A DEFINITION

The *Dictionary of Criminal Justice Data Terminology* (Bureau of Justice Statistics) defines white-collar crime as "nonviolent crime for financial gain committed by means of deception by persons...having professional status or specialized technical skills." This definition emphasizes the status of the defendant rather than the nature of the offense. An offense-centered definition used by the Bureau of Justice Statistics (BJS) defines white-collar crime as "nonviolent crime for financial gain committed by deception."

The following is a list of the specific crimes that the Bureau of Justice includes in white-collar crime:

- Counterfeiting is the manufacture or attempted manufacture of a copy of a negotiable instrument (coins, currency, securities, stamps, and official seals) with value set by law or possession of such a copy without authorization and with intent to defraud (cheat).

- Embezzlement is the misappropriation (dishonest use) or illegal disposal of property trusted to an individual with intent to defraud the legal owner or intended beneficiary (someone benefiting). Embezzlement differs from fraud in that it involves a breach (violation) of trust that previously existed between the victim and the offender.

- Forgery is the alteration of something written by another or writing something that claims to be either the act of another or to have been done at a time or place other than was, in fact, the case.

- Fraud is the intentional misrepresentation of fact to unlawfully deprive a person of his or her property or legal rights without damage or threatened or actual injury to persons.

- White-collar regulatory offenses is the violation of federal regulations and laws other than those listed above, including import and export (not including drug offenses), antitrust, transportation, food and drug, labor and agricultural offenses.

HOW MANY CRIMES?

Although the above crimes are not part of the Crime Index total, the FBI keeps statistics on forgery and counterfeiting, fraud, and embezzlement. From 1997 through 1999, some 3.8 percent of all criminal offenses reported to the FBI were white-collar crime, for a total of 5.9 million offenses. Fraud offenses comprised most of the white-collar crimes reported to the FBI between 1997 and 1999, followed by counterfeiting/forgery, embezzlement, and bribery. (See Table 7.1.) Despite the low percentage of white-collar crime out of all crimes, it is speculated that white collar crime can cost far more than street crimes due to the large financial losses incurred by corporate crimes against the government, environment, and society as a whole.

As defined by the FBI, fraud is a somewhat broad category that includes the following offenses: false pretenses, swindles, confidence games, credit card/ATM fraud, impersonation, welfare fraud, and wire fraud. Between 1997 and 1999, there were a reported 61,230 false pretenses/swindle/confidence game offenses, followed by 23,308 credit card/ATM offenses, and 8,689 fraud incidents that involved impersonation. Welfare fraud and wire fraud accounted for 1,289 and 984 reported offenses, respectively, between 1997 and 1999. The Secret Service investigates crimes associated with financial institutions, including bank fraud, access device fraud, fraudulent identification, fraudulent government and commercial securities, and electronic funds transfer fraud.

WHITE-COLLAR CRIME ARRESTS

In 1929 the FBI introduced the Uniform Crime Reporting (UCR) system to collect information about

TABLE 7.1

Economic crime—Group A offenses, 1997–99

	Incidents	Offenses	Victims	Known offenders	Unknown offenders
Total	5,428,613	5,856,985	5,845,031	4,078,106	2,025,419
Fraud offenses					
False pretenses/swindle/confidence game	61,230	61,230	66,095	63,304	6,888
Credit card/ATM fraud	23,308	23,308	26,492	20,568	6,303
Impersonation	8,689	8,689	9,500	8,980	1,019
Welfare fraud	1,289	1,289	1,300	1,344	27
Wire fraud	984	984	1,074	808	281
Bribery	191	191	198	233	5
Counterfeiting/forgery	91,697	91,697	110,545	85,797	21,201
Embezzlement	20,694	20,694	21,356	24,506	1,738
Arson + fraud	10	20	5	23	0

SOURCE: Cynthia Barnett, "Table 2: Economic crime—Group A offenses," in *The Measurement of White-Collar Crime Using Uniform Crime Reporting (UCR) Data,* U.S. Department of Justice, Federal Bureau of Investigation, Criminal Justice Information Services Division,Washington, DC, 2002

TABLE 7.2

Arrest rates for white-collar crimes, 1997–99

	Arrest rate[a]
Total	5317.0
Property crime	635.5
Forgery & counterfeiting	40.7
Fraud	131.5
Embezzlement	6.5

[a]Number of arrests per 100,000 inhabitants

SOURCE: Cynthia Barnett, "Table 1: Arrests reported (Summary)," in *The Measurement of White-Collar Crime Using Uniform Crime Reporting (UCR) Data,* U.S. Department of Justice, Federal Bureau of Investigation, Criminal Justice Information Services Division, Washington, DC, 2002

crimes reported to the police. In 1982 a study of the UCR was completed and a recommendation was made to redesign the system to provide more comprehensive and detailed crime statistics. This resulted in a five-year program to update the system to become the National Incident-Based Reporting System (NIBRS), which collects data on each reported crime incident. The UCR currently reports on cases of homicide, forcible rape, robbery, aggravated assault, burglary, larceny-theft, motor vehicle theft, and arson. Some information about offenses, victims, offenders, and reported arrests for 21 additional crime categories is included. The NIBRS system also provides information on 46 different crimes and 11 lesser offenses, including white-collar crimes.

Under the UCR system, white-collar offenses that are measured only include fraud, forgery/counterfeiting, embezzlement, and a category for "all other crimes." The latter category does not differentiate white-collar crimes from other crimes in this category. The only information available for each of the categories is arrest information,

which includes the age, sex, and race of the arrestee. Because the NIBRS system is still in transition, with some agencies still using the UCR system, the data about other white-collar crimes available from NIBRS in 1997–1999 are not representative of all agencies in the nation.

The rate of arrest for white-collar crimes varied by offense. For fraud offenses (reported most often), the arrest rate was 131.5 arrests per 100,000 inhabitants, while embezzlement had the lowest arrest rate, at 6.5 per 100,000 inhabitants. (See Table 7.2.)

Between 1997 and 1999 fraud offenses had a clearance rate of 33.12 percent. Of fraud cases cleared, 79.52 percent were cleared by arrest. The rate of clearance was highest for bribery (61.78 percent), and lowest for counterfeit/forgery (29.83 percent). (See Table 7.3.)

WHITE-COLLAR CRIME OFFENDERS AND VICTIMS

White-collar crime offenders were usually male, with the exception of embezzlers. Between 1997 and 1999 white-collar crimes were largely perpetrated by whites, who represented 70 percent or more of offenders across all categories of white-collar crime. (See Figure 7.1.)

According to the FBI, between 1997 and 1999 businesses, financial institutions, and government and religious organizations were more likely to be the victims of fraud, counterfeiting, and embezzlement, while individuals were more likely to be the victims of bribery. There were a reported 47,907 incidents of fraud against businesses between 1997 and 1999, followed by individuals (47,826), government (3,844), financial institutions (2,989), society or other (1,357), and religious organizations (70). Businesses were also more likely to be victimized by counterfeiting (55,676 reported incidents) and embezzlement (17,627 incidents). There were some 143

TABLE 7.3

White-collar crime incidents cleared by type, 1997–99

	Percent cleared	Arrests	Death of offender	Prosecution declined	Extradition denied	Refused to cooperate	Juvenile/ no custody
Fraud offenses	33.12%	79.52%	0.15%	12.51%	0.08%	7.40%	0.34%
Bribery	61.78%	93.22%	0.00%	5.93%	0.85%	0.00%	0.00%
Counterfeiting/forgery	29.83%	88.70%	0.13%	7.55%	0.11%	3.20%	0.31%
Embezzlement	38.37%	86.74%	0.08%	6.64%	0.03%	6.04%	0.48%
Total	32.13%	83.80%	0.13%	9.98%	0.09%	5.66%	0.35%

SOURCE: Cynthia Barnett, "Table 7: Incidents cleared by type," in *The Measurement of White-Collar Crime Using Uniform Crime Reporting (UCR) Data*, U.S. Department of Justice, Federal Bureau of Investigation, Criminal Justice Information Services Division, Washington, DC, 2002

FIGURE 7.1

White-collar crime offenders by offense type, 1997–99

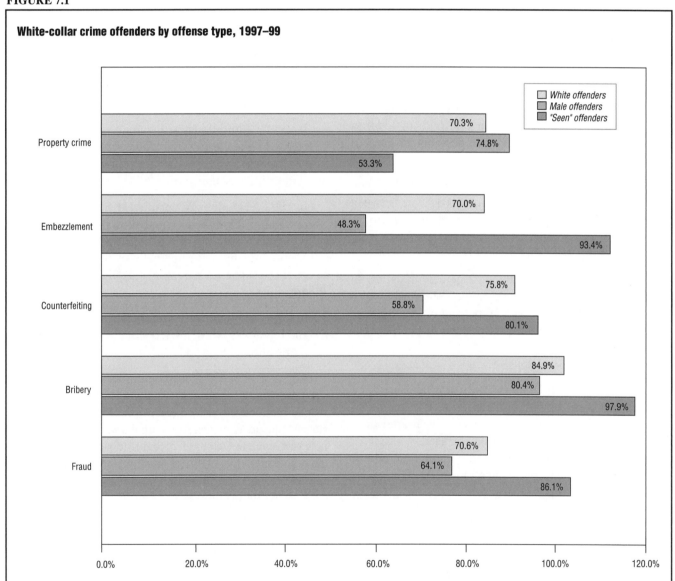

SOURCE: Cynthia Barnett, "Figure 6: Offenders by offense type," in *The Measurement of White-Collar Crime Using Uniform Crime Reporting (UCR) Data*, U.S. Department of Justice, Federal Bureau of Investigation, Criminal Justice Information Services Division, Washington, DC, 2002

incidents of bribery against individuals between 1997 and 1999 according to the FBI, compared to 36 against government organizations and 16 against businesses. (See Table 7.4.)

IDENTITY THEFT

The incidence of identity theft has risen significantly since 1999, when the Federal Trade Commission formed the FTC Identity Theft Hotline and Data Clearinghouse. That year, there were 445 calls per week to the Hotline. By June of 2001 the number of callers to the hotline had increased to 1,800 per week, a rise of about 400 percent.

In 2000 credit card fraud accounted for 54 percent of identity theft, followed by unauthorized use of telephone, utility, and other communications services (26 percent), bank fraud (16 percent), and fraudulent loans (11 percent). (See Table 7.5.) By 2001 some 7 percent of callers to the FTC Hotline reported an identity theft that resulted in the forging of a government document, such as a driver's license. About 21 percent of callers reported that they had experienced more than one type of identity theft. This accounts for the reported percentages exceeding 100 percent.

About 28.4 percent of callers to the FTC Hotline who reported being victimized as of June 2001, were between the ages of 30 to 39, while 26.5 percent were 18 to 25 years of age. Those under 18 and over 65 were least likely to report identity theft. (See Table 7.6.)

According to the FTC, about 21 percent of callers to the Hotline reported having a personal relationship with the suspected offender. Nearly 10 percent of identity theft victims reported a family member as the suspect. Roommates and co-habitants were identified as suspects by 2.4 percent of callers. (See Table 7.5.)

Most callers to the Identity Theft Hotline stated that they did not know how their identities were stolen, and most did not discover the theft until one year after their personal information began to be misused. Victims of identity theft were sometimes unable to obtain credit or financial services, telecommunication services, or utility services as the result of credit problem arising from the identity theft.

CORPORATE CRIME

Tracking white-collar crime, and especially corporate crime, is generally much more complicated than tracking other crimes. There often is no one single offender or one victim to report the crime. White-collar crime is often based on establishing trust between the victim and the offender before any crime is committed. Building trust expands the time frame of the crime, permitting repeated victimizations of an unsuspecting victim.

Different types of ethical violations linked to corporate crime include misrepresentation in advertising, deceptive packaging, the lack of social responsibility in television commercials, the sale of harmful and unsafe products, the sale of virtually worthless products, polluting the environment, kickbacks and payoffs, unethical influences on government, unethical competitive practices, personal gain for management, unethical treatment of workers, stealing of trade secrets, and the victimization of local communities by corporations.

Corporate crime is nothing new. In an article entitled, "Schemers and Scams: A Brief History of Bad Business," in *Fortune Magazine* (March 18, 2002), a brief chronology of corporate malfeasance is given, including some of the more well-known corporate crimes of the past 15 years:

- In 1989 Charles Keating was convicted of fraudulently marketing junk bonds, which led to the collapse of Lincoln Savings and Loan. The cost to taxpayers for the bank's failure was estimated at $3.4 billion. Keating served five years of a twelve-year prison sentence.

- In 1997 Columbia/HCA insurance company was the target of the largest-ever federal investigation into health-care scams. An $840 million Medicare-fraud settlement was agreed to in 2000.

- In 1998 Al Dunlap, nicknamed "Chainsaw Al" in the press after taking over companies and reducing costs by firing people, was fired from Sunbeam for illicitly manufacturing earnings. He overstated revenues, booking sales, for example, on grills neither paid for nor shipped.

- In 2001 Al Taubman, former chairman of Sotheby's auction house, was convicted of conspiracy for price-fixing at Sotheby's and Christie's auction houses.

In November 1998, 46 states collectively settled lawsuits they had brought against cigarette manufacturers to recoup the tobacco-related costs of health care paid out by state Medicaid agencies. Although the sale of tobacco products was legal, the states alleged that tobacco firms knew of the highly addictive nature of smoking yet deliberately concealed their research findings from the general public for decades while promoting tobacco use. According to the terms of the settlement, the tobacco industry agreed to pay out some $206 billion over 25 years. The states of Florida, Texas, Minnesota and Mississippi settled their lawsuits separately for some $40 billion over 25 years.

Between 2001 and 2002 there were a number of verdicts in cases brought against tobacco companies, some of them resulting in million-dollar jury awards. In March 2002 an Oregon jury found Phillip Morris liable for a smoker's death and ordered the company to pay $150 million in punitive damages. In June 2001 a California jury awarded former smoker Richard Boeken $3 billion in

TABLE 7.4

White-collar crime victims by offense type, 1997–99

	Total	Property	Fraud	Bribery	Counterfeiting	Embezzlement
Total victims	5,886,566	4,069,324	103,993	198	110,545	21,356
Individual	3,998,310	2,621,843	47,826	143	45,270	3,006
Business	934,469	934,469	47,907	16	55,676	17,627
Financial institution	11,378	11,378	2,989	0	5,310	182
Government	73,623	73,623	3,844	36	2,949	260
Religious organization	10,794	10,794	70	0	104	35
Society or other	857,992	417,217	1,357	3	1,236	246

SOURCE: Cynthia Barnett, "Table 6: Victims by offense type," in *The Measurement of White-Collar Crime Using Uniform Crime Reporting (UCR) Data*, U.S. Department of Justice, Federal Bureau of Investigation, Criminal Justice Information Services Division, Washington, DC, 2002

TABLE 7.5

Relationship of victim to ID theft suspect, November 1999–June 2001

Type of relationship	Percentage[4]
Family member	9.6
Roommate/co-habitant	2.4
Neighbor	1.3
Workplace co-worker/employer/employee	1.8
Otherwise known	5.6
TOTAL	**20.7**

[4] Percentage is based upon the total number of complaints to the Federal Trade Commission (FTC) Identity Theft Hotline through June 2001 where the consumer reported a relationship with the suspect.

SOURCE: "Figure 7: Type of Relationship," in *Identity Theft Complaint Data: Figures and Trends on Identity Theft, November 1999 through June 2001*, Federal Trade Commission, Washington, DC, 2002

TABLE 7.6

Age distribution of identity theft victims, November 1999–June 2001

Consumer's age	Percentage[3]
65 and over	6.3
60-64	3.3
50-59	12.4
40-49	21.4
30-39	28.4
18-29	26.5
Under 18	1.7
TOTAL	**100.0**

[3] Percentage is based upon the total number of complaints where consumers reported his/her age.

SOURCE: "Figure 2: Consumer's Age," in *Identity Theft Complaint Data: Figures and Trends on Identity Theft, November 1999 through June 2001*, Federal Trade Commission, Washington, DC, 2002

punitive damages, later reduced to $100 million. Also in June of 2001 a New York jury found the U.S. tobacco industry liable for "unfair and deceptive business practices" and awarded some $17.8 million to Empire Blue Cross and Blue Shield of New York for the health costs of smoking-related illnesses.

A Different Type of Crime

Corporate crime can cost billions of dollars, but because these losses are frequently spread out over so many uninformed victims, it usually does not create the same initial public impact as, for example, an armed robbery of a few hundred dollars. There often is no single person to take the blame. Corporations can be so complex and powerful that the rules of justice applied to individuals are often applied differently to business. A board of directors is not imprisoned for a corporate wrongdoing; instead, the corporation may be fined.

Despite their potential to do extensive damage, corporate crimes are not regarded with the same fear as "street crime." Personal attacks are far more frightening, even to persons who have never been physically assaulted, than the seemingly remote possibility of dying a slow death

due to air pollution, or buying defective tires, or using a poorly tested drug. On the other hand, someone who has had a considerable part, or perhaps all, of their savings stolen as the result of fraud or embezzlement can face a painfully insecure future because they may no longer have the money intended to support their later years. Nonetheless, except in certain spectacular cases that receive extensive media coverage such as the savings and loan fraud of the 1980s, the consequences of corporate misbehavior are generally ignored.

CORPORATE ESPIONAGE

Many corporations are becoming concerned about the potential espionage activities of competing corporations. In a computerized global economy where a competitor's advantage can mean life or death for a company, trade secrets, copyrighted information, patents, and trademarks become very important. Most major companies have developed sophisticated security systems to protect their secrets. Stealing classified corporate information has become a major issue for national governments. In a 2001 report by the U.S. General Accounting Office (GAO), it was reported that the American Society for Industrial

Security, which surveys Fortune 500 companies, estimated that potential losses to American businesses from theft of proprietary information were $45 billion in 2000.

Many governments have begun to use their national intelligence organizations to protect local companies from espionage by foreign companies or governments. In the United States, the Central Intelligence Agency (CIA), which with the demise of the Soviet Union in the early 1990s found itself with less to do, has been trying to convince Congress that the agency could be useful in protecting American companies from foreign industrial spies. The Economic Espionage Act of 1996 (PL 104-294) made it a federal crime to steal trade secrets for another country.

STEALING FROM THE DEPARTMENT OF DEFENSE

The U.S. Department of Defense has a long history of lax control of its ordering and payment procedures, a serious problem in a department that spends over $300 billion a year. The U.S. Department of Justice is continually looking for instances in which contractors have defrauded the government. Normally, these investigations end in agreement by the defrauding company to pay a fine.

In March of 1998 the U.S. Department of Justice announced that Unisys Corporation and Lockheed Martin Corporation would pay $3.15 million to settle allegations they had sold spare parts at inflated prices to the Department of Commerce for the NEXRAD Doppler Radar System. During the same month, the Pall Aeropower Corporation agreed to pay $2.2 million to settle allegations that it defrauded the United States by overcharging the Department of the Army for air filters for the AH-1 "Cobra" helicopter. The government also alleged that Pall had defrauded the Department of Defense on other contracts, but the settlement dismissed all allegations.

On March 30, 1998, the U.S. Department of Justice announced that Alliant Techsystems, Inc., and Hercules, Inc., had agreed to pay $4.5 million to settle allegations they illegally overcharged the Navy for labor costs on contracts implementing the Intermediate-Range Nuclear Forces (INF) Treaty. According to the complaint, "managers at Alliant and Hercules regularly directed their employees to mischarge labor time to a number of military contracts even though management knew the employees did not devote as much time to the contract as was charged to the government." On April 23, 1998, the Justice Department reported that M/A-COM, Inc., a division of AMP Incorporated, agreed to pay $3 million to settle claims that it failed to perform some required tests on electronic components.

FALSIFYING CORPORATE DATA

The Securities and Exchange Commission (SEC) reported that falsifying corporate data, especially on financial statements, increased in the 1990s. The falsified reports included statements inflating sales, hiding ownership of the corporation, and embezzlement. This sort of crime continued into the 2000s. The collapse of the Enron corporation was one of the most glaring examples of corporate crime and falsification of corporate data in recent history.

Enron was founded in 1985 in Houston as an oil pipeline company. As electrical power markets were deregulated in the late-1990s, Enron expanded and became an energy broker trading in electricity and other energy commodities. In effect, Enron became the middleman between power suppliers and power consumers. However, instead of simply brokering energy deals, Enron devised increasingly complex contracts with buyers and sellers that allowed Enron to profit from the difference in the selling price and the buying price of commodities such as electricity. In order to service these contracts, which were becoming increasingly speculative due to the instability of unregulated electricity prices, Enron executives created a number of so-called "partnerships"—in effect, "paper" companies whose sole function was to hide debt and make Enron appear to be much more profitable than it actually was.

On December 2, 2001, Enron filed for bankruptcy protection, listing some $13.1 billion in liabilities and $24.7 billion in assets—$38 billion less than the assets listed only two months earlier. As a result, thousands of Enron employees lost their jobs. Perhaps worse, many Enron employees—who had been encouraged by company executives to invest monies from their 401k retirement plans in Enron stock—had their retirement savings reduced to almost nothing as a result of the precipitous decline in value of Enron stock. The stock dropped from $34 dollars a share on October 16, 2001, to pennies per share as of December 2, 2001. Most chilling, Enron executives, who themselves reaped millions in profits from Enron stock, barred employees from cashing in their stock in late October when it still had some value.

According to internal emails and other inter-office communications, warnings were given to Enron executives and to its accounting firm, Arthur Anderson, that Enron was heading for financial disaster as early as a year before Enron declared bankruptcy. The beginning of the end occurred on October 16, 2001, when Enron announced a $638 billion loss for the third quarter. As a result, the value of Enron's stockholders' equity was reduced by $1.2 billion. On November 8, 2001, Enron announced that it had overstated its earnings for the past four years by as much as $585 million. It also owed some $3 billion in obligations—to be paid in company stock—to various partnerships Enron had created to offset its rising debt. By November 28, 2001, Enron's debt instruments were downgraded to junk bond status, making it impossible for Enron to forestall its collapse by borrowing more money to service its debt.

In the wake of Enron's collapse, some 10 committees in the U.S. Senate and House of Representatives began to investigate whether Enron defrauded investors by deliberately concealing financial information. The shredding of financial and inter-office documents by both Enron and its accounting firm, Arthur Anderson, was also under investigation. Meanwhile, numerous lawsuits were filed against Enron, Arthur Anderson, and former Enron executives including former Chairman Kenneth L. Lay and former CEO, Jeffrey Skilling. Former Enron Vice Chairman, Clifford Baxter, was found shot to death in his car on January 15, 2002, in an apparent suicide. News reports linked Baxter's death to his despondency over his role in the Enron scandal.

On June 15, 2002, a New York jury found accounting firm Arthur Anderson guilty of obstructing justice in connection with the Enron collapse. After a six-week trial and 10 days of jury deliberations, Arthur Anderson was convicted of destroying Enron documents during an ongoing federal investigation of the company's accounting practices. During the trial, executives of Arthur Anderson testified that the documents were destroyed as the result of customary housekeeping duties, not as a means to prevent federal investigators from seeing them. As a result of the verdict, Anderson faced a fine of $500,000 and a term of probation of up to 5 years. In the aftermath of the Enron scandal, the 89-year-old accounting firm laid off some 7,000 employees and lost more than 650 of its 2,300 clients.

Other recent examples of alleged falsification of corporate data include the filing for bankruptcy in January 2002 of Global Crossing, a telecommunications company. In February 2002 the Securities and Exchange Commission (SEC) opened an investigation into Global Crossing and its auditor—again, the accounting firm of Arthur Anderson—for questionable accounting practices.

L. Dennis Kozlowski, the former chief executive of Tyco International Ltd., was indicted in June 2002 by a New York grand jury on charges of evading more than $1 million in sales taxes on at least six paintings valued at some $13 million. According to the indictment, Kozlowski allegedly directed New York gallery employees to ship empty cartons to the Tyco corporate headquarters in New Hampshire, where Tyco employees were instructed to sign for the "shipments." The paintings, New York's case claims, eventually ended up in Kozlowski's Manhattan apartment for his own personal use. Kozlowski is accused of trying to evade the New York City taxes that would have been owed on paintings purchased by someone in-state (paintings purchased from out-of-state are not subject to these taxes). On June 26, 2002, the Manhattan district attorney added a charge of evidence-tampering to the other charges against Kozlowski, claiming that he removed a shipping invoice from a crate of documents before it was sent to the district attorney's office. All told,

as of July 2002, Kozlowski faced 12 felony charges and one misdemeanor charge.

According to *Fortune Magazine* (March 18, 2002), between 1992 and 2001, the Securities and Exchange Commission (SEC) filed criminal charges in 609 cases involving stock fraud or other corporate crime. Of the 609 referrals, U.S. Attorney's prosecuted 187 defendants. Of those, 147 defendants were found guilty and 87 went to jail or prison. From 1997 to 2000 the SEC filed some 3,000 civil cases. Of those, 39.1 percent involved securities offerings violations, followed by 16.3 percent for insider trading, 12.2 percent for stock manipulation, 11.5 percent for financial disclosure violations, and 3.1 percent for fraud against consumers. The remaining civil cases brought by the SEC were either for contempt or for other causes of action.

FRAUD AGAINST INSURANCE COMPANIES

Annually, thousands of cases are reported involving acts of fraud against insurance companies, such as faking a death to collect life insurance, setting fire to a house to collect property insurance, or claiming injuries not actually suffered. According to "A Statistical Study of State Insurance Fraud Bureaus: A Quantitative Analysis, 1995 to 2000" (Coalition Against Insurance Fraud, May 2001), insurance fraud bureaus in 41 states received nearly 89,000 referrals involving insurance fraud in 2000, up by 5 percent from 1999. There were 21,000 more cases of fraud reported to insurance fraud bureaus in 2000 than in 1995. Four states—New York, California, New Jersey, and Florida—accounted for 73 percent of all referrals. Referrals may come from insurance companies, consumers, and government and law enforcement agencies.

In 2000 insurance fraud bureaus referred some 3,998 cases of insurance fraud for prosecution, resulting in 2,123 criminal convictions nationwide. Florida reported 386 criminal convictions for insurance fraud in 2000, followed by New York (318), Pennsylvania (276), Arizona (137), and New Jersey (90). In 2000, there were some 1,100 civil actions initiated by insurance bureaus for insurance fraud. This was down somewhat from the 1,200 civil actions brought by insurance bureaus in 1999. Still, the number of civil actions brought by insurance bureaus in 2000 was more than triple the 344 civil actions brought in 1995.

FRAUD BY INSURANCE COMPANIES

In addition to the criminal attempts to swindle insurance companies, insurance companies sometimes defraud their customers. In January of 2002 a preliminary settlement of $59 million was announced in a class action lawsuit brought by automobile policyholders in Georgia against Allstate Insurance Company. Policyholders alleged that Allstate failed to provide payment for the loss of an automobile's market value after an accident when paying for the repair costs of automobiles involved in accidents. Also in January 2002 a final settlement of almost $5.6 million was approved in the class action suit brought by parties in 27 states against United Services Automobile Association (USAA). As in the Allstate action, automobile policyholders alleged that USAA failed to compensate them for the loss of value of vehicles after an accident.

On April 30, 2001, a final settlement was reached in the class action brought against Principal Mutual Life Insurance Company by some 960,000 current and former life insurance policy holders who alleged that they were misled by false and misleading marketing materials when they purchased their policies.

SECURITIES FRAUD

There are many laws regulating the securities markets—which include the New York Stock Exchange (NYSE) and the National Association of Securities Dealers Automated Quotation (NASDAQ)—and the corporations who sell "securities" on the markets. These regulations require corporations to be honest with their investors about the corporations, and stockbrokers to be forthcoming with their clients.

Despite these rules, both the corporate officials who release information about their companies and the stockbrokers who help people invest in securities may knowingly lie to or obscure information from consumers in order to raise the stock level of a company for their own profit. Corporations may commit this type of fraud by releasing false information to the financial markets through news releases, quarterly and annual reports, SEC filings, market analyst conference calls, proxy statements, and prospectuses. Brokers may commit this type of fraud by failure to follow clients' instructions when directed, misrepresentation or omission of information, unsuitable recommendations or investments, unauthorized trades, and excessive trading (churning). Since brokerage analysts' recommendations to clients may affect the fees earned by the firms' investment banking operations, it may be profitable for the analysts to play up the value of certain stocks.

Some 327 federal securities class action lawsuits for securities fraud were filed in 2001, a 60 percent increase from the 204 such filings in 2000, according to the Stanford Law School Securities Class Action Clearinghouse, in cooperation with Cornerstone Research. There were 47 filings in California, 36 filings in New York, and 26 filings in Florida. The number of class actions for securities fraud filed against telecommunications and technology companies increased from 69 in 2000, to 132 filings in 2001.

Of the 96 settlements in securities fraud class actions in 2001, the average amount of the settlement was $16 million. About one-third of cases in 2001 settled for between $1 and $4.9 billion, about the same as in 2000. Some 25 percent of cases settled in 2001 resulted in payments of between $5 and $9.9 million, up from about 20 percent of such actions in 2000. At the high end, less than 5 percent of class actions for securities fraud settled for $75 million or more, down slightly from 2000.

In May 2002 the stock brokerage company Merrill Lynch agreed to settle a case brought against it by the New York Attorney General Eliot Spitzer, for allegedly hyping certain stocks publicly in order to gain banking business while privately criticizing the stocks to others. The settlement amount agreed to by Merrill Lynch was $100 million. In addition to the monetary sum, Merrill Lynch must now include a warning on its stock recommendations to advise investors that it may be doing business with the companies whose stock it is rating.

Oil and Gas Investment Frauds

While many oil and gas investments are legitimate, this area is well-known for fraudulent offers. Oil- and gas-well deals are sometimes offered by "boiler rooms," or fly-by-night operations that consist of nothing more than bare office space and a dozen or so desks and telephones. Boiler room operators employ telephone solicitors trained to use high-pressure sales tactics. These con artists make repeated unsolicited telephone calls in which they follow a carefully scripted sales pitch that guarantees high profits. Some swindlers surround themselves with the trappings of legitimacy, including professionally designed color brochures.

In a fraudulent oil and gas scheme, scam artists promoting the investment often offer limited partnership interests to prospective investors who live outside the state where the well is located and outside the state the scam artists are calling from. This distance reduces chances for an investor to visit the site of a well or what may be nonexistent company headquarters.

Individuals subjected to a high-pressure sales pitch in an unsolicited telephone call should watch for the following tip-offs that they may be dealing with a swindler:

- The oil well investment "can't miss."

- Very little risk is involved.

- The promoter has hit oil or gas on every other well previously drilled.

- A lot of oil or gas has been found in an adjacent field.

- A large reputable oil company is already operating near the company's leased property, or planning to do so.

- A decision must be made immediately to invest in order to assure the purchase of one of the few interests remaining unsold.

- The deal is only available to a few lucky and specially chosen investors.

- The salesperson has personally invested in the venture himself.

- A tip from a reputable geologist has given the company a unique opportunity to make this venture a success.

One can reduce the risk of being swindled by being suspicious of any deal that promises a fantastic return at little risk.

TELEMARKETING FRAUD

Telemarketing is a form of direct marketing in which representatives from companies call consumers or other businesses in order to sell their goods and services. Telemarketing services may also be tied in with other forms of direct marketing such as print, radio, or television marketing. For example, an advertisement on the television may request the viewer to call a toll-free number. The overwhelming majority of telemarketing operations are legitimate and trustworthy.

The National Fraud Information Center (NFIC) is a project of the National Consumers League, a non-profit organization founded in 1992. The NFIC considers itself "a vital resource for consumers and law enforcement agencies in the fight against telemarketing fraud." The National Fraud Information Center reported the following swindles as the top 10 telemarketing frauds for 2001.

- Work-At-Home (20 percent). The swindler offers expensive kits to launch work-at-home businesses, such as envelope stuffing, that seldom generate much, if any, income.

- Prizes/Sweepstakes (19 percent). Prize awards, often phony, are offered in exchange for a certain amount of money paid up front.

- Credit Card Issuing (17 percent). Individuals who would normally have difficulty getting a credit card are offered the chance to do so for a fee paid up front. Often, the credit card is never issued.

- Advance Fee Loans (9 percent). Similar to credit card scams, for an up-front fee, loans that seldom materialize are offered to individuals who would normally not qualify for a loan through a legitimate lender.

- Magazines (7 percent). Bogus magazine subscriptions are offered for an up-front fee.

- Telephone Slamming (4 percent). Telephone customers are tricked into switching their telephone companies, often without knowing that they have agreed to the change.

- Buyers Clubs (3 percent). Membership to non-existent buyers clubs that purport to offer deeply discounted prices are offered for an up-front fee.

- Credit Card Loss Protection (2 percent). Non-existent protection against credit card fraud is offered for a fee up front.

- Telephone Pay-Per-Call Services (2 percent). Various services are offered over 900 numbers without disclosing that there are often exorbitant charges for the use of the 900 number.

- Nigerian Money Offers (2 percent). Perpetrated via U.S. Mail or, increasingly, via e-mail or Internet chat rooms, targeted victims receive a plea from someone purportedly in an African city who is desperate to remove hidden funds, often in the millions of dollars, from their country to a U.S. bank. The intended victim is offered a percentage of the funds if they are willing to have them transferred to their bank account. In order to participate, the intended victim must provide his or her bank account number and other personal information, which is then used fraudulently.

Characteristics of Telemarketing Fraud Schemes

The United States Postal Inspection Service (USPIS) investigates and enforces over 200 federal statutes related to crimes against the U.S. Mail, the Postal Service, and its employees. It investigates any crime that uses the U.S. Mail to further a scheme, no matter where it originated: via phone, mail, or Internet. The USPIS offers a list of guidelines that can help prevent a person from being victimized by a fraudulent telemarketing scheme. This list can be applied to any type of offer, not just telemarketing offers.

- *The offer sounds too good to be true.* An unbelievable-sounding deal probably is not legitimate.

- *High-pressure sales tactics.* A swindler often refuses to take no for an answer; he has a sensible-sounding answer for your every hesitation, inquiry, or objection.

- *Insistence on an immediate decision.* Swindlers often say you must make a decision "right now," and they usually give a reason, like, "The offer will expire soon."

- *You are one of just a few people eligible for the offer.* Don't believe it. Swindlers often target hundreds of thousands—and sometimes millions—of solicitations to consumers across the nation.

- *Your credit card number is requested for verification.* Do not provide your credit card number (or even just its expiration date) if you are not making a purchase, even if you are asked for it for "identification" or "verification" purposes, or to prove "eligibility" for the offer. If you give your card number, the swindler may make unauthorized charges to your account, even if you decide not to buy anything. Once that is done, it may be very hard to get your money back.

- *You are urged to provide money quickly.* A crook may try to impress upon you the urgency of making an immediate decision by offering to send a delivery service to your home or office to pick up your check. This may be to get your money before you have a chance to think carefully about the offer and change your mind, or to avoid the possibility of mail fraud charges in the future.

- *There is no risk.* All investments have some risk, except for U.S. Government obligations. And if you are dealing with a swindler, any "money-back guarantee" he or she makes will simply not be honored.

- *You are given no detailed written information.* If you must send money or provide a credit card number before the telemarketer gives you the details in writing, be skeptical. Do not accept excuses such as, "It's such a new offer we don't have any written materials yet," or "You'll get written information after you pay."

- *You are asked to trust the telemarketer.* A swindler, unable to get you to take the bait with all of his other gimmicks, may ask you to "trust" him. Be careful about trusting a stranger you talk to on the phone.

- *You are told you have won a prize, but you must pay for something before you can receive it.* This payment can either be a requirement to purchase a minimum order of cleaning supplies or vitamins, or it can be a shipping/handling charge or a processing fee. Do not deal with a promoter who uses this tactic.

MAIL CRIME

In 2001 the USPIS made some 1,691 arrests for mail fraud in 2001, resulting in 1,477 criminal convictions. The USPIS also investigates many other types of crimes perpetrated through the U.S. Mail. For example, in 2001, the USPIS was responsible for 6,364 arrests for mail theft, which includes the theft or possession of stolen mail. Of those arrests, there were 5,384 convictions. The mailing of controlled substances such as narcotics, steroids, and drug paraphernalia accounted for 1,662 arrests by the USPIS in 2001, and resulted in 1,477 criminal convictions. Other crimes investigated by the USPIS in 2001, included the use of counterfeit postage, money orders, child exploitation (child pornography), and the mailing of obscene matter and sexually oriented advertisements.

COMPUTER CRIME

Types of Computer Crime

By the 1990s computer-assisted crime had became a major element of white-collar crime. Like corporate crime, computer crime often goes unrecorded. The National Institute of Justice defines three different types of computer crimes:

- Computer abuse is a broad range of intentional acts that may or may not be specifically prohibited by criminal statutes. Any intentional act involving knowledge of computer use or technology...if one or more perpetrators made or could have made gain and/or one or more victims suffered or could have suffered loss.

- Computer fraud is any crime in which a person uses the computer either directly or as a vehicle for deliberate misrepresentation or deception, usually to cover up embezzlement or theft of money, goods, services, or information.

- Computer crime is any violation of a computer crime law.

Computer crime is faceless and bloodless, and the financial gain can be huge. A common computer crime involves tampering with accounting and banking records, especially through electronic funds transfers. These electronic funds transfers, or wire transfers, are cash management systems that allow the customer electronic access to an account, automatic teller machines, and internal banking procedures, including on-line teller terminals and computerized check processing.

Computers and their technology (printers, modems, computer bulletin boards, e-mail) are used for credit card fraud, counterfeiting, bank embezzlement, theft of secret documents, vandalism, and other illegal activities. Experts place the annual value of computer crime at anywhere from $550 million to $5 billion a year. Even the larger figure may be underestimated, because many victims try to hide the crime. Few companies want to admit their computer security has been breached and their confidential files or accounts are vulnerable. No centralized databank exists for computer crime statistics. Computer crimes are often counted under other categories such as fraud and embezzlement.

According to the FBI, economic crime accounted for 42 percent of all crimes involving the use of a computer between 1997 and 1999. Of economic crimes, larceny-theft accounted for 31 percent of all crimes involving the use of a computer; fraud offenses accounted for 9 percent; and embezzlement accounted for 2 percent. (See Figure 7.2.)

The first state computer crime law took effect in Florida in 1978. An Arizona law took effect two months later. Other states soon followed, and by 2000, Vermont was the only state without a specific computer crime provision.

In 1986 Congress passed the Computer Fraud and Abuse Act (PL 99-474) that makes it illegal to perpetrate fraud on a computer. The Computer Abuse Amendments of 1994 (PL 103-322) make it a federal crime "through means of a computer used in interstate commerce of communication...[to] damage, or cause damage to, a computer, computer system, network, information, data, or program...with reckless disregard" for the consequences of those actions to the computer owner. This law refers to someone who maliciously destroys or changes computer records or knowingly distributes a virus that shuts down a computer system.

CORPORATIONS AND COMPUTER CRIME. The Computer Security Institute in San Francisco, California conducted "The 2002 Computer Crime and Security Survey" with the participation of the FBI's San Francisco Computer Intrusion Squad. The study found that of 503 computer security practitioners from major U.S. corporations, government agencies, financial and medical institutions, and universities, some 90 percent had detected computer security breaches within the last 12 months. Some 80 percent of respondents stated that their institution had suffered financial losses due to computer breaches. Of those, 223 respondents (about 44 percent) reported collective financial losses of over $455 million due to computer security breaches.

According to the survey, the most serious financial losses resulted from the theft of proprietary information, with 26 respondents reporting total losses of over $170 million. Still, despite these significant financial losses, only 34 percent of respondents reported the computer intrusions to law enforcement. In part, this low level of reporting of computer crime to law enforcement may have to do with an unwillingness to reveal the proprietary nature of the information breached.

Survey respondents reported various types of attacks on or unauthorized uses of their computer systems. Some 78 percent of respondents stated they had detected employee abuse of Internet access privileges, such as downloading pornography or pirating software. Eighty-five percent of respondents reported the detection of computer viruses, and 70 percent stated that computer attacks had resulted in vandalism to their system or web site. Twelve percent of respondents reported the theft of transaction information through computer attacks, and 6 percent reported financial fraud, up from only 3 percent in 2000.

HOLDING A COMPANY HOSTAGE. For a company, the most feared type of computer crime involves the sabotage or threatened sabotage of the company's computer system. It is almost impossible to determine how often this happens since very few companies ever report the incidents.

Most American companies of any size have become totally dependent on their computers. Management is generally unaware of how computers work and are fully dependent on their systems administrator or the person responsible for keeping the computers running. In fact, in many companies, the systems administrator might be considered the most powerful person in the company,

FIGURE 7.2

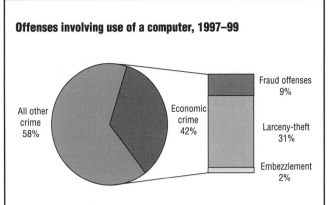

Offenses involving use of a computer, 1997–99

All other crime 58%

Economic crime 42%

Fraud offenses 9%

Larceny-theft 31%

Embezzlement 2%

SOURCE: Cynthia Barnett, "Figure 2: Offenses involving use of a computer," in *The Measurement of White-Collar Crime Using Uniform Crime Reporting (UCR) Data,* U.S. Department of Justice, Federal Bureau of Investigation, Criminal Justice Information Services Division, Washington, DC, 2002

although his or her salary and title might not indicate it. While the computer system might have a sophisticated security system, these are often only a hindrance to an experienced systems analyst.

In the computer age, several new scenarios of employee threats have generated increasing concern. A disgruntled employee might want to take revenge on the company. A systems administrator responsible for the running of the company computer system might feel unappreciated. A discontented employee might create a "logic bomb" that explodes a month after he or she has left and destroys most of the company records, bringing the company's operations to a complete halt. An unhappy or overly ambitious systems administrator might walk into the company president's office and inform her that he wants a huge bonus or the computer system will cease to exist the next morning. The company cannot fire him or her for fear he or she will carry out the threat. They cannot hurriedly bring in a replacement because, by the time he or she could understand what had been done, the system could be destroyed.

Experts recommend that to avoid such potential disasters, a company should make sure no one person has complete knowledge and responsibility for a computer system. While this strategy would provide no guarantee against catastrophe, at least such incidents would be somewhat less likely. Many companies planning to fire a systems analyst often contact computer security firms beforehand to see what they can do. Although it appears cold, callous, and humiliating (and it often is), many companies now escort laid off or fired employees to their desks, helping them collect their possessions, and then accompany them to the door. They hope this harsh procedure will eliminate any opportunity for the former employee to do harm to the company's computer system. While it may be necessary, this tactic is particularly hard on honest workers who have worked many years for the company and see this severe treatment as their reward.

Although infrequent, charges have at times been brought against those who destroy a company's computer system. In February of 1998 the U.S. Department of Justice brought charges against a former chief computer network program designer of Omega, a high-tech company that did work for NASA and the U.S. Navy. The designer had worked for the company for 11 years. After he was terminated, it was alleged that in retaliation he "intentionally caused irreparable damage to Omega's computer system by activating a 'bomb' that permanently deleted all of the company's sophisticated software programs." The loss cost the company at least $10 million in sales and contracts.

Juvenile Computer Hacking is No Joke

Illegal accessing of a computer, known as hacking, is a crime committed frequently by juveniles. When it is followed by manipulation of the information of private, corporate, or government databases and networks, it can be quite costly. Another means of computer hacking involves creation of what has become known as a "virus" program. The virus program is one that resides inside another program, activated by some predetermined code to create havoc in the host computer. Virus programs can be transmitted either through the sharing of disks and programs or through electronic mail.

Cases of juvenile hacking have been going on for at least two decades and have included: six teens gaining access into more than 60 computer networks, including Memorial Sloan-Kettering Cancer Center and Los Alamos National Laboratory in 1983; several juvenile hackers accessing AT&T's computer network in 1987; and teens hacking into computer networks and Web sites for NASA, the Korean Atomic Research Institute, America Online, the U.S. Senate, the White House, the U.S. Army, and the U.S. Department of Justice in the 1990s.

In 1998 the U.S. Secret Service filed the first criminal case against a juvenile for a computer crime. The computer hacking of the unnamed perpetrator shut down the Worcester, Massachusetts, airport in 1997 for six hours. The airport is integrated into the Federal Aviation Administrative traffic system by telephone lines. The accused got into the communication system and disabled it by sending a series of computer commands that changed the data carried on the system. As a result, the airport could not function. (No accidents occurred during that time.) According to the Department of Justice, the juvenile pled guilty in return for two years probation, a fine, and community service.

United States Attorney Donald K. Stern, lead attorney on the case against the juvenile observed that:

Computer and telephone networks are at the heart of vital services provided by the government and private industry, and our critical infrastructure. They are not toys for the entertainment of teenagers. Hacking a computer or telephone network can create a tremendous risk to the public and we will prosecute juvenile hackers in appropriate cases....

On December 6, 2000, 18-year-old Robert Russell Sanford pled guilty to six felony charges of breach of computer security and one felony charge of aggravated theft in connection with cyber attacks on U.S. Postal Service computers. Sanford, a Canadian, was placed on 5 years probation, although he could have been sentenced to up to 20 years in prison. Sanford was also ordered to pay over $45,000 in restitution fines for the cyber attacks.

On September 21, 2000, a 16-year-old from Miami entered a guilty plea and was sentenced to six months detention for illegally intercepting electronic communications on military computer networks. The juvenile admitted that he was responsible for computer intrusions in August and October of 1999 into a military computer network used by the Defense Threat Reduction Agency (DTRA), an arm of the Department of Defense. The DTRA is responsible for reducing the threat against the United States from nuclear, biological, chemical, conventional and special weapons.

Vulnerability of the Defense Department

Investigators from the U.S. General Accounting Office (GAO), in a report prepared for two Congressional committees, observed that the Pentagon experienced as many as 250,000 "attacks" on its computers in 1995, probably by computer hackers cruising the Internet. The Pentagon figures imply that in 65 percent of the attempts, hackers were able to gain entry into a computer network. The investigators warned, "the potential for catastrophic damage is great, especially if terrorists or enemy governments break into the Pentagon's systems." The report stated that the military's current security program was "dated, inconsistent and incomplete."

Even after this warning, in 1998, hackers broke into unclassified Pentagon networks and altered personnel and payroll data, in what Deputy Defense Secretary John Hamre called "the most organized and systematic attack the Pentagon has seen to date." In 1999, there were a reported 22,124 cyber attacks against the Department of Defense alone, costing the government an estimated $25 billion to bolster computer security procedures in order to ward off future attacks.

Internet Fraud

The Internet is no different than any other form of potential commerce. While most businesses are honest, potential frauds abound. In one example, in 1997 KRW

Internet Sales and Marketing offered refurbished cellular phones on an online auction. None of the phones worked. Any scam that a deceitful telemarketer or dishonest mailer (see above) can offer, a deceiving swindler on the Internet can offer as well.

ROBBING THE COMPANY

In March of 1998 Gabriel Sagaz, former president of Domecq Importers, Inc., a subsidiary of Allied Domecq, P.L.C., the world's second-largest liquor company, pled guilty to fraud and avoiding income taxes. From 1989 through 1996 Sagaz and other top executives at Domecq Importers embezzled over $13 million from the company and received another $2 million in kickbacks from outside vendors.

Cooperative outside vendors would bill Domecq Importers, Inc. for goods never produced and services never performed. Sagaz and his fellow embezzlers would approve the payment of these invoices. The outside vendors would then deposit the money in accounts the criminals had set up in offshore banks. In addition Sagaz and the others took kickbacks from outside vendors to steer contracts to those vendors.

THE COMPANY ROBBING THE CONSUMER

Throughout most of the early 1990s, nine corporations colluded to fix the price of and to control an estimated $1 billion market for lysine, a widely used additive for animal feed. In September of 1998 three former executives of the Archer Daniels Midland Corporation (ADM) were found guilty of having secretly met with other lysine producers to divide up marketing territories and establish prices.

Scott R. Lassar, the United States Attorney in Chicago, characterized the case as "one of the hardest-fought trials that I have ever been involved in, in terms of the firepower brought in by both sides." The case involved Michael D. Andreas, the son of ADM's owner and the one-time heir apparent to the $9.2 billion, privately owned food industry giant. In 1999 Andreas and Terrance S. Wilson were each sentenced to two years in jail and each ordered to pay a $350,000 fine. This could have been more, since the government is legally allowed to seek twice the amount gained in the crime or lost by the victims. The prosecutors asked for $25 million from Andreas; the judge set the lower fine amount instead. In September 2000 the sentences of Andreas and Wilson were changed from two years to three years and from two years to nine months, respectively. Appeals brought by the two men were rejected by the U.S. Supreme Court in November 2000. Marc Whitacre, the other executive charged, was given immunity for his help taping conversations for the FBI, but later had it revoked after it was discovered that he also embezzled $9 million from the

company. He was given a nine-year sentence, which had 20 months added to it in 1999.

The U.S. government's investigation of the food and feed additive industries resulted in eight criminal cases against nine corporations. Virtually all the companies pled guilty and paid almost $200 million in fines. In 1996 ADM agreed to pay $100 million in fines. In that deal, ADM was granted immunity against charges of price-fixing in the sale of high-fructose corn syrup, a major ADM product, if it cooperated with the federal government in its investigation of the industry.

By fixing prices for lysine, the animal feed bought by poultry and animal producers cost more than if there had been a free market in lysine. The food producers then passed this increased price on to consumers. Some estimated the cost of the price-fixing to the nation's consumers as high as $170 million. Although ADM and the other companies paid fines, and the convicted ADM executives were likely also to pay fines, none of this loss will likely ever be directly recovered by an individual consumer.

TAX FRAUD

For most Americans, failure to pay the correct amount of taxes to the Internal Revenue Service (IRS) results in agreement to pay off the taxes in some manner. However, when the IRS believes it has found a pattern of deception designed to avoid paying taxes, criminal charges can be brought. In 2002 the Criminal Investigations Division of the IRS initiated 1,753 cases. Of those, the IRS recommended prosecution in 917 cases, and in 821 cases criminal charges were filed or brought by indictment. In 2002 the IRS reported 964 convictions for tax fraud (more than the 821 cases filed because some cases involved more than one defendant). Of those, 933 individuals (81.6 percent) were sent to prison.

BRIBERY

Some U.S. companies often feel they operate at a disadvantage in other countries because American law prohibits U.S.-based companies from using bribes to get foreign contracts, while some forms of bribery are allowed in most other industrialized countries. Until recently, the United States was the only major national economy with such laws. In fact, many foreign companies often deducted bribes as business expenses. In many countries, especially in Asia, the unwritten rule is that a senior official will get 5 percent of a $200,000 contract and a head of state requires 5 percent of a $200 million contract. The percentage increased in the 1990s, as some officials were demanding 10 to 15 percent before a bid for services or goods could be accepted.

Many businesses and diplomats from several European countries believe that changes in their tax laws would reduce the amount of bribery; others believe that because of stiff competition, businesses would find loopholes. Some American businesses hire middlemen to conduct the bribery of foreign officials; others invite prospective clients on junkets to the United States.

FORGERY AND COUNTERFEITING

As technology advances, forgers are able to use sophisticated computers, scanners (a machine that "reads" a document and transfers it to computer coding), and laser printers to make copies of more and more documents, including counterfeit checks, identification badges, driver's licenses, even dollar bills (though the bills may not have the right feel, they can be inserted into a stack of currency and an overworked bank teller may not catch the forgery).

The manufacturing of counterfeit United States currency or altering of genuine currency to increase its value is punishable by a fine of up to $5,000 and imprisonment of up to 15 years, or both. Possession of counterfeit U.S. currency is also a crime, punishable by a fine of up to $15,000, or imprisonment of up to 15 years, or both. Counterfeiting is not limited to paper money. The illegal manufacturing of a coin in any denomination above five cents is subject to the same penalties as counterfeiting paper currency, and increasing the numismatic value of a coin is punishable by a fine of up to $2,000, or imprisonment of up to 5 years, or both.

In response to the growing use of computer-generated counterfeit money, the U.S. Department of the Treasury redesigned the $50 and $100 bills in the 1990s. Noting that the $20 bill was the one most counterfeited, the Department of the Treasury introduced new $5, $10, and $20 dollar bills between 1998 and 2000. These bills contain a watermark making them harder to accurately copy.

According to the Department of the Treasury, advances in home computer technology and desktop publishing software have made counterfeiting easier than ever, despite the new designs of U.S. currency intended as safeguards against counterfeiting. In the past, fake money required some understanding of inks and how to mix them to achieve the exact tones needed to create authentic-looking currency. With advances in ink-jet printing, however, so-called P-notes (printer notes) require no such knowledge about inks or printing. From 1995 to 2000 the Department of the Treasury reported a steady decline in arrests for counterfeiting using the old methods. However, arrests for P-notes have increased from 37 in 1995 to 4,500 in 2000.

Perhaps because of the ease of using computers and printers, overall arrests for counterfeiting have risen sharply, from 1,800 in 1995 to 5,400 in 2001. Meanwhile, tracking counterfeiters has become more difficult because, increasingly, bills are made in smaller batches, often to be used only occasionally.

According to the General Accounting Office report *International Crime Control* (U.S. General Accounting Office, Washington, D.C., 2001), about one-third of U.S. counterfeit currency distributed in the United States from 1999 to 2001 originated in Columbia. Other international counterfeiting schemes included reproducing financial instruments including commercial checks, traveler's checks, and money orders. Advanced reprographic capabilities made possible through computer technology, plus the growth of the worldwide Web, have extended counterfeiting knowledge to criminals throughout the world.

Counterfeit Products

Counterfeiting popular name brand products is a multi-billion-dollar white-collar crime. Fake Chanel purses and Nike athletic shoes have been seized all over the world. In 2001 the GAO reported an International Chamber of Commerce estimate that counterfeit trademarked products account for 8 percent ($200 billion) of all world trade annually. Online counterfeit sales may account for $25 billion. In 1999 U.S. Customs seized a record $98.5 billion in counterfeit merchandise, reflecting an increase of $22 billion over the previous year. Relations between the United States and the People's Republic of China became strained due to the manufacture of counterfeit products in China, as well as the production of copyrighted software and compact disks. The Chinese government claimed to be initiating criminal action against such violators, but many observers wondered whether the few resulting arrests of copyright violators was nothing more than show.

MONEY LAUNDERING

The U.S. General Accounting Office defines money laundering as "the disguising or concealing of illicit income to make it appear legitimate." Money laundering involves transferring illegally received monies into legal accounts so that when money is withdrawn from those accounts, it appears to the police or other government authorities to be legal earnings of the account or the business. When a money-laundering scheme is successful, the criminals can spend their illegally acquired money with little fear of being caught. Many of the techniques that launderers use would be perfectly legal business transactions if the source of the cash were not illegal activities.

The money-laundering scheme may be as simple as mailing a box of cash to an accomplice in another country where there is very little bank regulation. The accomplice deposits it in the local bank. The sender then writes a check on that bank and can use the money without fear of anyone knowing where the money came from. Other schemes may involve bribing a bank officer to permit illegal monies to be put in good accounts and then drawing the monies out. However, banking regulations (Bank

Secrecy Act of 1970 and its implementing regulations; PL 91-508) require banks to report all deposits over $10,000.

The GAO reported in 2001 that it estimates the amount of money laundered worldwide each year to be as high as $1 trillion. Drug traffickers launder an estimated $300 to $500 billion each year, often using supposedly respectable financial institutions. Other crimes that need money laundered are fraud offenses, securities (stocks and bonds) manipulation, illegal gambling, bribery, extortion, tax evasion, illegal arms sales, political payoffs, and terrorism. Money laundering may account for as much as 2 to 5 percent of the world's gross domestic product, according to a former Managing Director of the International Monetary Fund.

The GAO, in *Money Laundering: Rapid Growth of Casinos Makes Them Vulnerable* (Washington, D.C., 1996), found that gambling was expanding rapidly across the United States. Along with this growth came a large increase in the amount of cash wagered at all casinos, which totaled about $439 billion in 1996. With this much cash changing hands, casinos may be particularly vulnerable to money laundering in the form of money from illegal activities being placed into legal gaming transactions.

Money laundering is a global problem requiring collective international efforts to combat. The United States has promoted multilateral efforts to combat money laundering. The United States and over 120 other nations signed the United Nations Convention on Transnational Organized Crime in order to combat money laundering as well as other international crimes in 2000.

The State Department is required by law (the International Narcotics Control Act of 1992, PL 102-583) to identify major money-laundering countries and to provide certain specific information for each country. The Department of State works with agencies of the Departments of the Treasury and Justice to put this information together. Countries are categorized by the degree to which they are at risk of money-laundering activities. Canada, Cayman Islands, Columbia, Germany, Hong Kong, Thailand, the United Kingdom, the United States, and Venezuela are examples of the countries placed on the high priority list.

RETAIL STORE THEFT

In the *2001 National Retail Security Survey Final Report* (University of Florida, Gainesville, FL, 2002), an annual survey of retail theft prepared for the National Retail Federation, authors Richard Hollinger, Ph.D., and Jason L. Davis found that the average retail store surveyed in 2001 lost about 1.8 percent of its inventory to shrinkage (the industry term for the difference between the recorded value of inventory bought and sold and the value of the actual inventory at the end of the year). The shrinkage rate

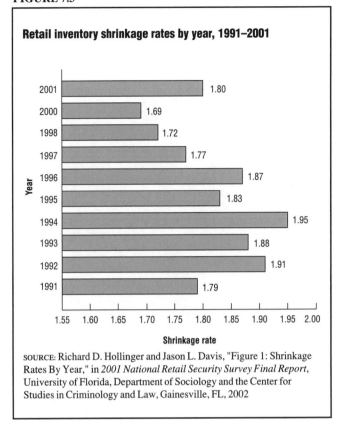

FIGURE 7.3

Retail inventory shrinkage rates by year, 1991–2001

SOURCE: Richard D. Hollinger and Jason L. Davis, "Figure 1: Shrinkage Rates By Year," in *2001 National Retail Security Survey Final Report*, University of Florida, Department of Sociology and the Center for Studies in Criminology and Law, Gainesville, FL, 2002

in 2001 was the highest since 1996, when the rate was 1.87 percent. (See Figure 7.3.)

Shrinkage is generally attributed to shoplifting, employee theft, administrative error, or vendor fraud. Respondents to the 2001 survey reported that 45.9 percent of their losses were due to employee theft (up from 44.5 percent in 2000), 30.8 percent to shoplifting (down from 32.7 percent in 2000), 17.5 percent to administrative errors (the same as 2000), and 5.9 percent to vendor fraud (up slightly from 5.1 percent in 2000). (See Figure 7.4.)

As in previous surveys, employee theft was reported as the single most significant source of inventory shrinkage among retailers, accounting for some $15.2 billion in losses (nearly half of the total $33.2 billion in losses due to inventory shrinkage in 2001.) The highest rate of inventory shrinkage due to employee theft in 2001, was experienced in supermarkets and grocery stores (62 percent), followed by shoe retailers (60 percent). Both consumer electronics/appliances retailers and discount stores reported that 54.6 percent of their inventory shrinkage was due to employee theft. The lowest rates of employee theft occurred among book and magazine vendors (20 percent), followed by household furnishing retailers (32 percent), and music/video retailers (34.1 percent) (See Figure 7.5.)

Responses to employee theft include apprehension and termination of the employee, prosecution, and civil demand or recovery. In 2001, there were 30.3 employee

FIGURE 7.4

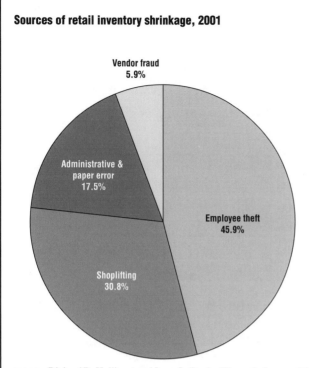

Sources of retail inventory shrinkage, 2001

Vendor fraud
5.9%

Administrative &
paper error
17.5%

Employee theft
45.9%

Shoplifting
30.8%

SOURCE: Richard D. Hollinger and Jason L. Davis, "Figure 3: Sources Of Inventory Shrinkage," in *2001 National Retail Security Survey Final Report*, University of Florida, Department of Sociology and the Center for Studies in Criminology and Law, Gainesville, FL, 2002

theft apprehensions for every $100 million in sales among retailers. About 23 percent of all apprehensions resulted in criminal prosecution. The rate of employee theft prosecutions was 11.5 for each $100 million, and the rate of civil court actions as the result of employee thefts was 37 for every $100 million in sales. The average amount stolen by each employee theft incident was about $1,445.

Shoplifting, the second highest source of inventory shrinkage in 2001, accounted for $10.2 billion in losses to American retailers in 2001. Though employee theft accounts for a larger amount of total monetary loss, there are more incidents of shoplifting than there are of employee theft. There were 131.6 shoplifting apprehensions for every $100 million in sales, 92.8 shoplifting prosecutions, and 133.7 civil demands as the result of shoplifting. (See Figure 7.6.)

PUBLIC CORRUPTION

A broad definition of public corruption includes a public employee asking for money, gifts, or services in exchange for doing something such as giving a city contract or voting in a certain way. This abuse of public trust may be found wherever the interest of individuals or business and government overlap. It ranges from the health inspector who accepts a bribe from a restaurant owner or the police officer who "shakes down" the drug dealer, to the councilman or legislator who accepts money to vote a certain way. These crimes are often difficult to uncover, as often few willing witnesses are available.

Congressional Post Office Scandal

The postmaster of the congressional post office was found guilty in 1994 of giving congressmen and senators cash while making it seem that they were buying stamps for official use. This misuse of funds hurt the political futures of many of the involved congressmen.

In 1996 Dan Rostenkowski, a congressman for 36 years and chairman of the powerful Ways and Means Committee in the 1980s and early 1990s, became the most prominent lawmaker to go to prison for official corruption. He pled guilty to two charges of mail fraud. In the plea bargain, charges of embezzlement from the House post office were dropped. He also pled guilty to sending official payroll checks from his Washington office to people in his Chicago office who did personal services for him, and to mailing an official check to pay for a personal gift. Both acts, he insisted, were "well-accepted" practices in Congress. He was indicted on 13 other counts including embezzlement from the House post office and using his official expense account to buy cars for his personal use. Rostenkowski served a 17-month prison sentence and paid $100,000 in fines and restitution.

Bribes, Kickbacks, and Racketeering

In April 2002 U.S. Representative James A. Traficant was convicted of taking bribes and kickbacks from businessmen and his office staff. The nine-term Ohio Democrat was found guilty of 10 federal charges, including racketeering, bribery, and fraud, and was ordered to forfeit some $96,000 acquired as the result of illegal activities. As a result of the felony conviction, Traficant faced the possibility of being expelled from the U.S. House of Representatives. Expulsion would require a two-thirds vote by House members. The only such expulsion in recent history was in 1980, when Representative Michael Myers, a Democrat from Pennsylvania, was expelled for accepting money from undercover FBI agents posing as foreign dignitaries looking to buy influence in Congress.

The charges against Traficant included filing false tax returns, receiving gifts and free labor from business persons in return for political favors, and taking cash kickbacks from members of his staff. During the trial, prosecutors also accused Traficant of lobbying for contractors in exchange for free work, including paving a barn floor, fixing a drainage system, and removing trees at Traficant's farm.

In June 2002 Providence, Rhode Island mayor, Vincent A. Cianci Jr., was found guilty by a federal jury of conspiring to run a criminal enterprise from City Hall,

FIGURE 7.5

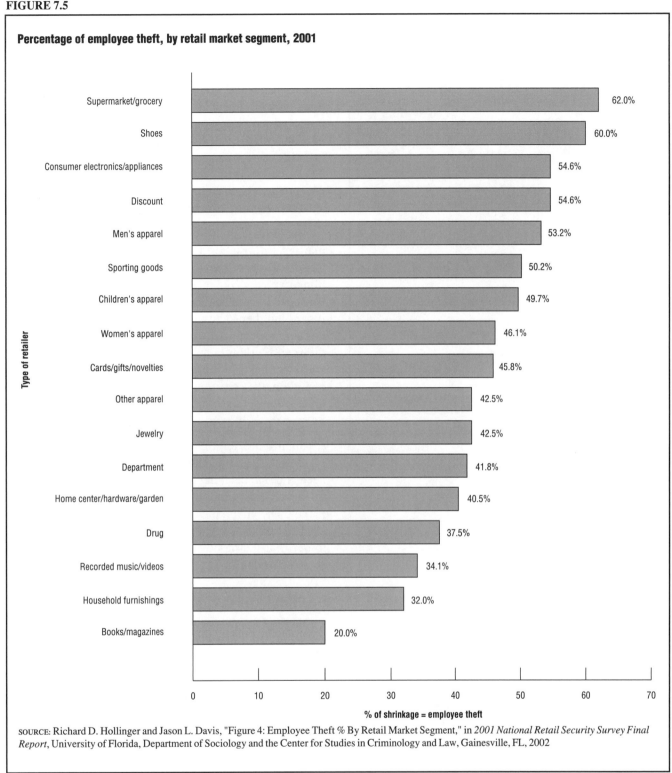

Percentage of employee theft, by retail market segment, 2001

SOURCE: Richard D. Hollinger and Jason L. Davis, "Figure 4: Employee Theft % By Retail Market Segment," in *2001 National Retail Security Survey Final Report*, University of Florida, Department of Sociology and the Center for Studies in Criminology and Law, Gainesville, FL, 2002

although he was acquitted of 11 other charges against him. Cianci's conviction for racketeering conspiracy carried a maximum penalty of 20 years in prison and up to $250,000 in fines, or both. Two co-defendants in the case were also found guilty of racketeering conspiracy.

In May 2000 former Louisiana Governor, Edwin Edwards, was convicted of racketeering, extortion, mail fraud, and wire fraud in connection with a scheme to extort bribes from applicants for riverboat casino licenses. Edwards was convicted on 17 counts and his son, Stephen, was convicted on 18 counts involving the extortion of some $3 million. Two of the charges for which former Governor Edwards was convicted carried prison terms of up 20 years and fines of up to $250,000.

FIGURE 7.6

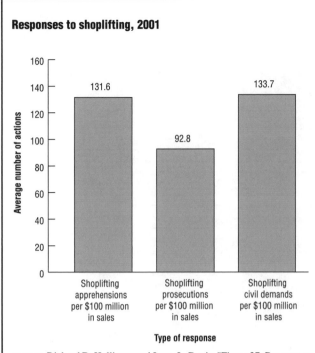

Responses to shoplifting, 2001

SOURCE: Richard D. Hollinger and Jason L. Davis, "Figure 27: Responses To Shoplifting," in *2001 National Retail Security Survey Final Report*, University of Florida, Department of Sociology and the Center for Studies in Criminology and Law, Gainesville, FL, 2002

SCAMS ON THE ELDERLY

Because senior citizens are often retired and living on fixed incomes and savings, the promise of economic security can be very alluring. As a consequence, the elderly can be particularly vulnerable to economic crimes such as fraud and confidence schemes.

Seniors are particularly vulnerable to con artists. Often, they are lonely, isolated from their families, and sometimes more willing than in earlier years to believe what they are told. Some suffer mental or physical frailties that leave them less able to defend themselves against high-pressure tactics. In addition, they may be financially insecure and may want to believe the con artist's promises of future wealth and security. Since many elderly are too embarrassed to admit that they have been fooled, many of these crimes are not reported.

Statistics on fraud against the elderly, sometimes called elder scams, are not collected by the major crime reporting agencies. In 2002 the National Fraud Information Center estimated that there were 14,000 illegal telemarketing operations in the United States, and that the elderly fell prey to unscrupulous telemarketers to the tune of $40 billion per year. Additionally, surveys conducted by the AARP (formerly the American Association of Retired Persons) indicated that most victims of telemarketing fraud were 50 years of age or older.

Because the elderly are more likely to suffer from health-related problems such as diabetes, hypertension, arthritis, and heart disease, they can be especially susceptible to fraudulent claims for products marketed as treatments or cures for diseases. In 2001 the Federal Trade Commission initiated legal action against eight companies that used the Internet to fraudulently market medical devices, herbal products, and dietary supplements as treatments or cures for Alzheimer's disease, diabetes, arthritis and other diseases that affect senior citizens. The actions were the result of the FTC's Operation CureAll. The initiative was to identify deceptive and misleading Internet promotions of products and services that purportedly treat or cure various diseases.

Another popular scam involves con artists calling or mailing information to elderly people announcing that they have won a free prize, but must pay postage and handling to receive them. They are told a credit card number is needed to pay these costs. The thieves then use the credit card number to buy items and to get cash. The elderly are also susceptible to repairmen who stop by and say they can fix their homes. The workers may do the repair work, but it is shoddy and overpriced. If the elderly try to complain, the repairmen are no longer in the area, possibly not even in the state.

A more elaborate scam involves a con artist, acting as a bank official, telling the elderly person that a particular bank teller is giving out counterfeit bills and that the bank needs help in catching the teller. The elderly person goes to the teller's window and withdraws a large sum of money. The victim then gives the money to the "bank official" to be examined. The "bank official" assures the customer that the money will be redeposited in his or her account; of course, it never is.

ENVIRONMENTAL CRIME

Environmental crime is a serious problem for the United States, even though the immediate consequences of an offense may not be obvious or immediately severe. Environmental crimes do have victims. The cumulative costs in environmental damage and the long range toll in illness, injury, and death may be considerable.

—Theodore M. Hammett and Joel Epstein, "Prosecuting Environmental Crime: Los Angeles County," *National Institute of Justice Program Focus,* 1993

Environmental crime involves illegally polluting the air, water, or ground. Sometimes firms dump hazardous materials and waste. To investigate properly, local, state, national, and international agencies often need to cooperate. It is not unusual for environmental criminals to transport hazardous waste across state or international borders for disposal in places with less stringent environmental enforcement.

According to the National Institute of Justice, several obstacles exist in prosecuting environmental crime.

1. Some prosecutors feel unprepared to tackle environmental cases, which are perceived as hopelessly complicated and impossible to win.

2. Some corporate defendants regard civil penalties and one-time cleanup costs as part of doing business. Many prosecutors are now turning to civil suits only when criminal remedies are not available.

3. Some judges are not well-informed on environmental laws or are not sensitive to the seriousness of the crimes.

4. Individual juries may be reluctant to convict a community's business leaders and significant employers if the alleged environmental damage does not have immediate consequences.

The more common means of enforcing environmental laws is through regulatory action by the government's responsible agencies and the application of civil penalties to those who violate the regulations.

According to the U.S. Environmental Protection Agency (EPA), in fiscal year 2001 criminal charges were brought against 372 defendants for violations of environmental laws nationwide. Those found guilty were fined some $95 million and were sentenced collectively to 256 years in prison. One example of a successful criminal prosecution in fiscal year (FY) 2001 reported by the EPA, is the case of David D. Nuyen of Silver Springs, Maryland. In July 2001 Nuyen pled guilty to violations of the Lead Hazard Reduction Act and the Toxic Substances Control Act. Nuyen, who owned 15 low-income rental properties in Washington, D.C., admitted that he failed to notify tenants of lead paint hazards in one of his buildings. Nuyen was sentenced to two years in prison and fined $50,000.

In addition, the EPA reported the settlement of 222 civil actions in FY 2001, resulting in $125 million in civil penalties plus $25.5 million in settlements shared with states, including a multi-state enforcement case involving Morton International, Inc. In October 2001 the company agreed to resolve charges of violating clean air, water, and hazardous waste laws at its Moss Point, Mississippi facility. Under the terms of the settlement, Morton International agreed to pay $20 million in penalties and to spend up to $16 million on projects to enhance the environment.

In another civil action in FY 2001, the EPA reached settlements with four major refineries—Koch Petroleum, BP Amoco, Marathon Ashland Petroleum, and Motiva/Equilon/Shell. The settlements involved a total of 27 refineries in violation of hazardous air pollution laws. The EPA did not disclose the terms of the settlements. As a result of criminal prosecutions, civil actions, and administrative penalties, the EPA reported that in FY 2001 environmental violators paid a total of $4.3 billion for pollution controls and environmental clean-up.

In March 2002 the EPA and the Department of Justice announced that they had filed a civil action against Shell Pipeline Company LP and Olympic Pipeline Company in connection with a gasoline pipeline rupture near Bellingham, Washington, in 1999. The rupture released a three-inch thick layer of gasoline over a 1.33-mile stretch of creek water, resulting in a massive explosion that caused the deaths of three people, including two 10-year-old boys. The resulting fire destroyed some 2.5 miles of vegetation and created a burn zone encompassing 26 acres.

On May 13, 2002, Ashland, Inc., of Covington, Kentucky, pled guilty to negligent endangerment under the Clean Air Act for failing to properly seal a manhole cover on a sewer used to transport flammable hydrocarbons, resulting in an explosion that injured five people, one of them severely. Ashland, Inc., agreed to pay a total of $10.7 million in fines and payments to compensate the injured parties.

In April 2002 the Miami, Florida-based Carnival Company, which operates some 40 cruise ships, pled guilty to falsifying oil record books on several of its ships and agreed to pay $18 million in fines. The falsification of records occurred when Carnival employees ran fresh water past oil water separators, resulting in artificially low oil concentration readings that were officially recorded in the ships' oil records books. As a consequence, bilge water with higher levels of oil concentration than allowed under the law was released, threatening surrounding ocean life.

CHAPTER 8

CRIME, ALCOHOL, AND DRUGS

The connection between criminal activity and the use of drugs and alcohol has long been an issue in American society. Even before federal laws were passed in 1914 to control narcotics and other drugs, observers claimed that drug use and criminal activity were strongly linked. Drugs and alcohol are thought to encourage criminal behavior in several ways. Their use can reduce inhibitions, stimulate aggression, and interfere with critical thinking and motor skills (such as driving or operating machinery), all of which may also reduce a person's ability to earn an income. Illegal drug users may more frequently find themselves exposed to situations that encourage crime. For those using addictive drugs, the need to get money to support a drug habit may take priority over any other consideration.

For the poor and underprivileged, drug and alcohol abuse can become an additional negative social condition within their environment. The same circumstances leading a person to commit crimes may also lead to drug use. In addition, the same conditions limiting employment opportunity may also contribute to both drug abuse and criminal behavior. Table 8.1 shows the relationship between drugs and crime.

SUBSTANCE-RELATED ARRESTS

In *Crime in the United States, 2000* (Washington, D.C., 2001), the Federal Bureau of Investigation (FBI) reported that of the 13.9 million estimated arrests in 2000, drug abuse violations accounted for 1.6 million arrests, or about 11 percent, making drug abuse violations the highest single category of arrest. The same was true in 1999, when the FBI reported 1.53 million arrests for drug abuse violations, followed by 1.51 million arrests for driving under the influence, 1.3 million for simple assault, and 1.2 million for larceny/theft. (See Table 8.2.)

Drug-Related Arrests

The federal government passed a number of anti-drug and anti-crime bills in the 1980s—the Comprehensive

TABLE 8.1

How are drugs and crime related?

Drugs and crime relationship	Definition	Examples
Drug-defined offenses	Violations of laws prohibiting or regulating the possession, use, distribution, or manufacture of illegal drugs.	Drug possession or use. Marijuana cultivation. Methamphetamine production. Cocaine, heroin, or marijuana sales.
Drug-related offenses	Offenses in which a drug's pharmacologic effects contribute; offenses motivated by the user's need for money to support continued use; and offenses connected with drug distribution itself.	Violent behavior resulting from drug effects. Stealing to get money to buy drugs. Violence against rival drug dealers.
Interactional circumstances	Drug use and crime are common aspects of a deviant lifestyle. The likelihood and frequency of involvement in illegal activity is increased because drug users and offenders are exposed to situations that encourage crime.	A life orientation with an emphasis on short-term goals supported by illegal activities. Opportunities to offend resulting from contacts with offenders and illegal markets. Criminal skills learned from other offenders.

SOURCE: *Drugs, Crime and the Justice System,* U.S. Department of Justice, Bureau of Justice Statistics, Washington, DC, 1992

Crime Control Act of 1984 (PL 98-473), the Anti-Drug Abuse Act of 1986 (PL 99-570), and the Anti-Drug Abuse Act of 1988 (PL 100-690). Each of these requires increased mandatory sentencing (see below), harsher sentencing, preventive detention, and even the death penalty for certain drug-related crimes. These laws were a major factor in the rising rate of drug arrests and prison sentences for drug convictions in the late 1980s and 1990s. (See Figure 8.1.)

Eighty-one percent of drug abuse violations in the United States in 2000 were for possession of drugs and 19 percent were for the sale or manufacturing of drugs.

TABLE 8.2

Estimated totals of top 7 arrest offenses, 1999

Type of arrest	Number of arrests*
Total arrests*	14,031,100
Drug abuse violations	**1,532,200**
Driving under the influence	1,511,300
Simple assaults	1,294,400
Larceny/theft	1,189,400
Drunkenness	656,100
Disorderly conduct	633,100
Liquor laws	657,900

*Arrest totals are based on all reporting agencies and estimates for unreported areas.

SOURCE: "Estimated totals of top 7 arrest offenses, United States, 1999," in *Drugs and Crime Facts,* U.S. Department of Justice, Bureau of Justice Statistics, Washington, DC, 2001

TABLE 8.3

Arrests for drug abuse violations by region, 2000

Drug abuse violations	United States Total	North-eastern States	Mid-western States	Southern States	Western States
Total	**100.0**	**100.0**	**100.0**	**100.0**	**100.0**
Sale/Manufacturing:	19.0	26.0	19.5	17.0	17.0
Heroin or cocaine and their derivatives	9.3	18.1	5.0	9.1	6.7
Marijuana	5.6	6.3	9.3	4.8	4.7
Synthetic or manu-factured drugs	1.1	0.7	0.7	2.0	0.8
Other dangerous non-narcotic drugs	3.0	1.0	4.4	1.2	4.9
Possession:	81.0	74.0	80.5	83.0	83.0
Heroin or cocaine and their derivatives	24.2	26.5	14.0	24.2	26.8
Marijuana	40.9	42.0	52.1	50.5	28.5
Synthetic or manu-factured drugs	2.2	1.5	1.8	2.7	2.3
Other dangerous non-narcotic drugs	13.6	3.9	12.6	5.5	25.5

Note: Because of rounding, the percentages may not add to total.

SOURCE: "Table 4.1: Arrests for Drug Abuse Violations, by Region, 2000, " *Crime in the United States, 2000: Uniform Crime Reports*, Federal Bureau of Investigation, Washington, DC, 2001

Possession of marijuana accounted for almost 41 percent of drug abuse violations in 2000. Heroin or cocaine and their derivatives accounted for 24.2 percent of arrests for possession and 9.3 percent of arrests for the sale or manufacture of drugs. (See Table 8.3.) These patterns were nearly identical to 1999 arrests for drug abuse violations nationally. Across the four main regions of the United States, statistics were usually similar to the national data, but in the Northeast, the figures for sale or manufacturing were significantly higher, at almost 27 percent of all drug abuse arrests. (See Table 8.4.) Since 1982, arrests for possession of drugs have far outpaced arrests for their manufacture and sale. (See Figure 8.2.)

FIGURE 8.1

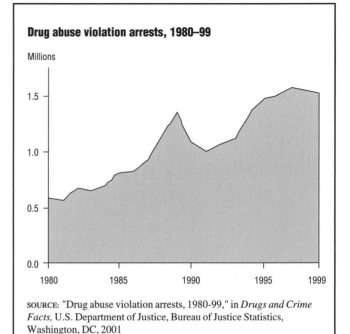

Drug abuse violation arrests, 1980–99

SOURCE: "Drug abuse violation arrests, 1980-99," in *Drugs and Crime Facts,* U.S. Department of Justice, Bureau of Justice Statistics, Washington, DC, 2001

DEMOGRAPHICS. Arrests for drug abuse violations in 2000 were prevalent among younger persons. A total of 48 percent (505,057) of those arrested for drug abuse violations were under age 25. Those under age 21 accounted for 32.2 percent (335,529) of arrests for drug violations while juvenile offenders under age 18 made up 12.9 percent (134,580) of arrests. Persons under age 15 accounted for 2.1 percent (22,237) of drug abuse arrests. Still, from 1970 to 1999, the number of adults arrested for drug abuse violations increased much more steeply than the number of juveniles. (See Figure 8.3.)

From 1991 to 2000 drug abuse arrests increased for all ages by 49.4 percent. Arrests of those under age 18 rose 144.8 percent, and the number of females arrested for drug offenses rose 59.2 percent between 1991 and 2000. Males continued to make up an overwhelming majority of drug abuse arrestees. In 2000 males accounted for about 691,000 arrests for drug abuse violations, compared to about 152,000 for females.

In 2000 whites accounted for 64.2 percent of all arrests for drug abuse in the United States, while African Americans accounted for 34.5 percent of all arrests. American Indians/Alaskan Natives (0.5 percent) and Asian/Pacific Islanders (0.7 percent) represented a very small proportion of total drug abuse arrests.

Alcohol-Related Arrests

In 2000 there were 775,000 arrests for driving under the influence of alcohol, down some 20 percent from the 971,628 arrests for DUI's in 1991. Similarly, arrests for drunkenness were down by 27.3 percent, from a total of

TABLE 8.4

Arrests for drug abuse violations, by geographic region, 1999

Type of violations	U.S. total	Percent of arrests for drug abuse violations			
		Northeast	Midwest	South	West
Total*	100.0%	100.0%	100.0%	100.0%	100.0%
Sale/manufacture*	**19.5%**	**26.7%**	**19.8%**	**16.6%**	**18.3%**
Heroin or cocaine	10.0	19.6	6.6	8.5	7.5
Marijuana	5.5	5.7	8.2	4.7	5.0
Synthetic or manufactured drugs	1.2	0.7	0.7	2.1	0.8
Other dangerous nonnarcotic drugs	2.9	0.7	4.2	1.2	4.9
Possession*	**80.5%**	**73.3%**	**80.2%**	**83.4%**	**81.7%**
Heroin or cocaine	24.5	29.2	15.1	22.0	27.4
Marijuana	40.5	39.7	51.2	52.8	27.8
Synthetic or manufactured drugs	1.9	1.3	1.5	2.4	2.0
Other dangerous nonnarcotic drugs	13.5	3.0	12.5	6.2	24.5

*Because of rounding, percentages may not add to total.

SOURCE: "Arrests for drug abuse violations, by geographic region, 1999," in *Drugs and Crime Facts,* U.S. Department of Justice, Bureau of Justice Statistics, Washington, DC, 2001

FIGURE 8.2

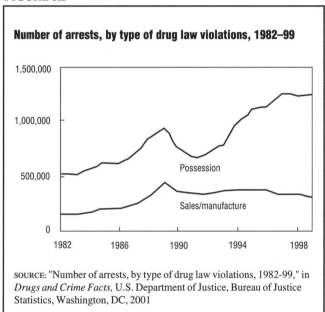

Number of arrests, by type of drug law violations, 1982–99

SOURCE: "Number of arrests, by type of drug law violations, 1982-99," in *Drugs and Crime Facts,* U.S. Department of Justice, Bureau of Justice Statistics, Washington, DC, 2001

FIGURE 8.3

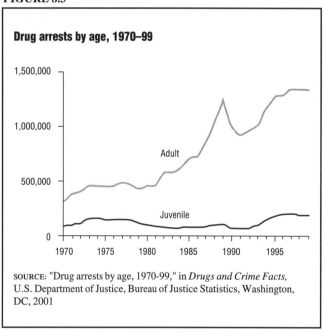

Drug arrests by age, 1970–99

SOURCE: "Drug arrests by age, 1970-99," in *Drugs and Crime Facts,* U.S. Department of Justice, Bureau of Justice Statistics, Washington, DC, 2001

492,720 in 1991, to 358,041 in 2000. Arrests for liquor law violations increased from 300,147 in 1991 to 341,047 in 2000, a gain of 13.6 percent. Liquor law violations are more common among juvenile offenders, as it is illegal for juveniles to possess or purchase alcoholic beverages. Among persons under 18 years of age in 2000, arrests for liquor law violations rose by nearly 20 percent, compared to a rise of 11.8 percent among arrestees 18 or older.

White offenders are consistently involved in more arrests for alcohol violations than other races. In 1998 white arrests made up 86.9 percent of driving under the influence offenses, 85.4 percent of the liquor law viola- tions, and 82.1 percent of drunkenness arrests. American Indians/Alaskan Natives accounted for 2.6 percent of liquor law arrests and 2.3 percent of drunkenness arrests.

Increased Arrests Prove Ineffective

A General Accounting Office study (*The War on Drugs: Arrests Burdening Local Criminal Justice Systems*, Washington, D.C., 1991) found that increasing arrests without also expanding the capacity of the crimi- nal justice system has been ineffective in deterring drug crime. The nation's criminal justice system has become overburdened with crowded court schedules, overworked attorneys and prosecutors, and overflowing jails, prisons, and drug treatment centers. The report stated,

> For the criminal justice system to have an impact, it should convey to potential drug offenders that they would be held accountable for their illegal activities. Although generating additional prison capacity would appear to be the simplest solution, it is becoming a less feasible option as fiscal constraints are imposed at every level of government.

Efforts by states to cope with the increased number of arrests have led to more plea-bargaining, probation, parole, and early release programs, even among those accused or convicted of non-drug, and often violent, crimes. These alternatives are less costly than incarceration, but some observers believe they also reduce the offender's accountability for his or her crime and therefore weaken the criminal justice system.

PRESENCE OF DRUGS AT THE TIME OF ARREST

In 1987 the National Institute of Justice introduced the Drug Use Forecasting program (DUF) to determine the nature and extent of drug abuse in the nation by monitoring drug use of arrestees in 23 cities across the United States. In 1993 the DUF was criticized for producing data that were not generalized. This led to the redesign of the study, now called the Arrestee Drug Abuse Monitoring Program, or ADAM, and expansion to include 27 cities. The new program added elements to make the collected data more accurate and valuable to the local sites in monitoring local drug trends. The NIJ also plans to eventually expand the program to 75 cities. The data, collected quarterly in central booking facilities of each city, comes from voluntary and anonymous interviews and urine specimens from selected arrestees. Except for marijuana and PCP, which can remain in the system for several weeks, all the other drugs had been used by arrestees in the preceding two or three days.

Adult Arrestees

In 2000 the 27 cities collected data from adult male arrestees and published the results in *ADAM Preliminary 2000 Findings on Drug Use and Drug Markets—Adult Male Arrestees*, (National Institute of Justice, Washington, D.C., 2001). The percentage of male arrestees who tested positive for any drug use ranged from 79 percent in New York, NY to 51 percent in Des Moines, Iowa, with a median (half of the cities had higher percentages testing positive, half had lower) of 65 percent. (See Table 8.5.)

The findings are viewed as conservative estimates of drug use, since self-report studies tend to understate actual drug use. Urinalysis revealed that some 20 percent of arrestees in about half of the cities had used more than one drug. The use of more than one drug per arrestee ranged from 30 percent in Tucson, Arizona, to 10 percent in Anchorage, Alaska. In most of the reporting cities,

TABLE 8.5

Drug test results, by site, for adult male arrestees, January–September, 2000

Primary City	Percent of Arrestees Who Tested Positive
New York, NY	79%
Philadelphia, PA	74
Sacramento, CA	73
Cleveland, OH	72
Oklahoma City, OK	72
Atlanta, GA	70
New Orleans, LA	69
Tucson, AZ	69
Birmingham, AL	67
Indianapolis, IN	66
Minneapolis, MN	66
Albuquerque, NM	65
San Diego, CA	65
Seattle, WA	65
Denver, CO	63
Miami, FL	63
Phoenix, AZ	63
Portland, OR	61
Omaha, NE	60
Laredo, TX	57
Las Vegas, NV	56
Spokane, WA	56
San Antonio, TX	55
Salt Lake City, UT	54
Anchorage, AK	53
San Jose, CA	52
Des Moines, IA	51
Median	65%

*The NIDA–5 drugs are cocaine, opiates, marijuana, methamphetamines, and PCP. The National Institute on Drug Abuse (NIDA) established this list as a standard panel of commonly used illegal drugs.

SOURCE: Bruce G. Taylor et. al., "Table 1: Drug Test Results—Any NIDA–5 Drug, by Site—Adult Male Arrestees," in *ADAM Preliminary 2000 Findings on Drug Use & Drug Markets: Adult Male Arrestees,* U.S. Department of Justice, Office of Justice Programs, National Institute of Justice, Washington, DC, December 2001

adult male arrestees were 32 years of age or older, with the mean age between 30 (in Minneapolis, Minnesota) and 35 (in Atlanta, Georgia). In half the study sites 30 percent or more of arrestees did not have a high school diploma. The frequency of drug arrestees who were high school dropouts ranged from 55 percent in Anchorage, Alaska, to 20 percent in San Jose, California. Some of the arrestees reported having no fixed address, ranging from 27 percent in Portland, Oregon, and Denver, Colorado, to 5 percent in Laredo, Texas.

Data from the *1999 Annual Report on Drug Use Among Adult and Juvenile Arrestees* (National Institute of Justice, 2000), show the range of drug use among arrestees in 34 U.S. cities in 1999. Among white male arrestees, the highest rate of use of any drug was in Philadelphia, Pennsylvania (72.6 percent), while the highest rate among African American male arrestees was 83.3 percent in Albuquerque, New Mexico. Use of drugs among Hispanic male arrestees was highest in New York City, New York where the rate was 73.7 percent.

TABLE 8.6

Drug use by adult arrestees in 34 cities by type of drug, race, ethnicity, and gender, 1999

(Percent testing positive)

City	Any drug[a]			Cocaine			Marijuana			Opiates		
	Black	White	Hispanic	Black	White	Hispanic	Black	White	Hispanic	Black	White	Hispanic
Male												
Albuquerque, NM	83.3%	61.9%	67.1%	61.9%	33.9%	47.0%	61.9%	31.4%	38.8%	14.3%	10.2%	16.1%
Anchorage, AK	67.4	57.3	52.2	45.7	27.1	13.0	35.9	39.6	47.8	1.1	4.2	8.7
Atlanta, GA	78.7	61.2	60.0	53.2	35.7	50.0	45.9	35.7	20.0	3.6	7.0	10.0
Birmingham, AL	67.2	51.6	(b)	40.3	23.6	(b)	40.3	35.7	(b)	2.8	7.6	(b)
Chicago, IL	81.6	58.5	63.6	45.3	31.9	38.9	49.9	34.2	33.5	25.1	11.0	10.2
Cleveland, OH	75.5	53.4	66.7	43.0	30.8	29.6	45.9	33.6	37.0	3.5	6.8	11.1
Dallas, TX	69.5	53.9	48.9	39.4	25.3	33.9	47.7	35.3	26.1	4.8	5.0	3.3
Denver, CO	78.1	62.4	61.3	54.0	29.3	39.0	46.3	43.7	40.8	1.6	4.9	4.3
Des Moines, IA	69.9	52.1	43.3	34.9	8.1	10.0	51.8	41.3	36.7	1.2	1.3	0.0
Detroit, MI	67.3	58.9	58.3	27.0	28.0	33.0	49.3	43.4	33.0	7.5	13.1	0.0
Fort Lauderdale, FL	67.1	61.3	52.0	40.1	43.0	34.0	46.1	31.5	36.0	0.5	2.9	0.0
Houston, TX	69.0	58.0	41.9	40.9	35.0	26.3	45.8	37.8	23.3	8.5	4.2	3.0
Indianapolis, IN	74.0	52.7	(b)	45.4	19.8	(b)	51.1	44.9	(b)	2.9	1.8	(b)
Laredo, TX	(b)	52.9	58.4	(b)	35.3	42.2	(b)	35.3	32.5	(b)	5.9	11.5
Las Vegas, NV	69.4	55.4	54.0	50.8	17.8	31.0	28.4	29.5	21.4	2.2	6.0	6.3
Los Angeles, CA	80.6	65.0	52.0	46.8	25.4	34.3	47.7	30.8	25.0	4.0	10.3	4.8
Miami, FL	71.8	64.3	50.6	57.0	39.8	40.4	37.7	39.4	25.3	2.4	6.4	2.4
Minneapolis, MN	72.7	47.8	30.8	39.9	18.9	3.8	50.9	36.5	26.9	5.9	1.3	0.0
New Orleans, LA	70.1	68.1	(b)	46.1	33.3	(b)	38.7	47.1	(b)	13.7	13.8	(b)
New York, NY	77.2	69.3	73.7	48.0	44.7	39.0	40.4	37.0	43.3	11.3	17.5	22.5
Oklahoma City, OK	72.1	62.2	50.0	37.7	18.2	24.0	51.1	48.6	34.0	1.1	1.9	2.0
Omaha, NE	71.7	53.0	58.3	29.2	13.0	33.3	63.2	42.0	37.5	0.5	0.5	0.0
Philadelphia, PA	67.7	72.6	72.7	36.9	40.9	47.3	43.1	38.4	41.8	6.5	22.6	30.9
Phoenix, AZ	76.3	63.9	66.9	51.3	22.1	43.6	40.0	37.0	35.0	4.4	8.2	8.9
Portland, OR	76.0	64.2	39.2	48.0	13.7	25.5	40.0	35.4	21.6	8.0	14.2	19.6
Sacramento, CA	75.2	67.6	60.9	31.4	6.7	9.6	50.4	40.5	40.4	5.0	4.3	4.5
Salt Lake City, UT	68.7	62.4	55.9	43.3	19.2	28.8	32.8	34.7	34.1	13.4	9.8	5.9
San Antonio, TX	59.4	49.4	48.0	30.2	18.2	23.2	38.7	39.5	32.8	2.8	9.6	11.3
San Diego, CA	66.7	67.2	59.0	40.3	8.9	11.0	36.1	45.2	27.5	4.9	9.3	13.0
San Jose, CA	74.0	58.0	54.4	27.4	9.7	13.4	57.5	38.2	32.2	5.5	4.6	4.3
Seattle, WA	77.4	62.6	(b)	47.1	27.6	(b)	45.2	37.2	(b)	12.7	14.6	(b)
Spokane, WA	82.8	59.4	72.0	40.9	14.3	12.0	52.7	42.2	48.0	9.7	6.5	12.0
Tuscon, AZ	80.9	64.5	68.8	62.6	29.5	45.6	49.6	46.5	42.0	5.2	9.4	9.3
Washington, DC	72.0	(b)	(b)	37.6	(b)	(b)	38.7	(b)	(b)	15.1	(b)	(b)

Among females, use of any drug by white arrestees was highest in New York City (85.1 percent), while the largest proportion of African American female arrestees were found to have used drugs in Albuquerque (89.5 percent), and the largest proportion of Hispanic female arrestee drug users was found in Fort Lauderdale, Florida (84.6 percent). (See Table 8.6.)

Juvenile Arrestees

Drug use by male juvenile arrestees tested in nine U.S. cities in 1999 ranged from 68.5 percent in Phoenix, Arizona to 43.3 percent in Portland, Oregon. Marijuana use occurred with the most frequency in all nine cities, with the highest use in Phoenix (62.2 percent) and the lowest in Portland, Oregon (40.9 percent). (See Table 8.7.) Marijuana is the drug most commonly used by both male and female juvenile detainees, as reported in the *1999 Arrestee Drug Abuse Monitoring Program Report* (National Institute of Justice, 2000).

Generally, the older the juvenile arrestee, the more likely he was to test positive for drug use. The highest rate of male juvenile arrestees 17 to 18 years of age testing positive for drug use (81 percent) was found in Phoenix, Arizona. The highest rate among 15- to 16-year-olds was 67.6 percent in Denver, Colorado. The highest rate among those aged 13 to 14 years old (61.6 percent) was also found in Phoenix.

JUVENILE DRUG USE

In 2000 juveniles who regularly smoked cigarettes were more likely to use alcohol or illicit drugs, according to the *2000 National Household Survey on Drug Abuse* (Department of Health and Human Services, Substance Abuse and Mental Health Services, 2001). The survey also reported that in 2000 almost 10 percent of juveniles between the ages of 12 and 17 reported that they currently used illicit drugs.

Nationwide, according to the *2001 Monitoring the Future Study* conducted by the University of Michigan, 54 percent of all teenagers reported in 2001 that they had tried at least one illicit drug before they graduated from high school. The *2001 Monitoring the Future Study (MFS)*, is an annual self-report survey of some 50,000 students between the eighth and twelfth grades in public and private schools, sponsored by the National Institute on Drug Abuse (2002).

TABLE 8.6

Drug use by adult arrestees in 34 cities by type of drug, race, ethnicity, and gender, 1999 [CONTINUED]

(Percent testing positive)

City	Any drug[a]			Cocaine			Marijuana			Opiates		
	Black	White	Hispanic	Black	White	Hispanic	Black	White	Hispanic	Black	White	Hispanic
Female												
Albuquerque, NM	89.5	66.7	80.4	78.9	51.1	60.8	36.8	13.3	25.8	21.1	20.0	42.3
Anchorage, AK	82.4	58.6	(b)	64.7	47.1	(b)	29.4	27.1	(b)	0.0	1.4	(b)
Atlanta, GA	77.5	78.7	(b)	62.5	63.9	(b)	34.4	29.5	(b)	3.2	11.5	(b)
Birmingham, AL	52.6	56.3	(b)	28.2	50.0	(b)	28.2	21.9	(b)	2.6	6.3	(b)
Chicago, IL	82.0	60.9	63.2	69.0	47.8	57.9	27.5	24.3	21.1	36.5	22.6	15.8
Cleveland, OH	68.5	66.7	(b)	52.7	43.8	(b)	26.5	32.3	(b)	5.4	14.6	(b)
Dallas, TX	61.3	54.5	26.1	46.4	33.3	21.7	29.8	26.3	8.7	5.0	12.1	0.0
Denver, CO	80.1	60.8	63.8	64.5	42.2	44.0	34.8	29.4	37.1	0.7	5.9	2.6
Des Moines, IA	52.4	52.7	(b)	38.1	18.7	(b)	33.3	33.0	(b)	0.0	3.3	(b)
Detroit, MI	68.6	(b)	(b)	43.1	(b)	(b)	29.4	(b)	(b)	15.7	(b)	(b)
Fort Lauderdale, FL	60.9	73.9	84.6	43.5	61.4	46.2	32.9	22.2	53.8	0.6	7.2	7.7
Houston, TX	44.5	48.0	33.6	21.1	30.9	19.8	25.5	22.3	15.5	9.6	4.6	1.7
Indianapolis, IN	71.0	67.4	(b)	52.1	36.8	(b)	34.1	42.5	(b)	4.6	5.2	(b)
Laredo, TX	(b)	(b)	21.9	(b)	(b)	20.3	(b)	(b)	9.4	(b)	(b)	1.6
Las Vegas, NV	78.5	72.1	45.8	66.9	41.5	33.3	24.4	23.2	20.8	4.7	12.1	4.2
Los Angeles, CA	71.4	73.8	34.8	48.6	36.1	22.5	31.4	19.3	7.9	2.7	16.8	6.7
Minneapolis, MN	65.3	45.7	(b)	44.0	27.1	(b)	36.0	17.1	(b)	13.3	5.7	(b)
New Orleans, LA	57.2	65.2	(b)	41.4	40.9	(b)	23.0	31.8	(b)	4.3	18.2	(b)
New York, NY	81.9	85.1	79.3	65.9	66.9	63.1	26.8	19.5	29.0	14.9	37.7	27.9
Oklahoma City, OK	75.9	63.6	30.8	46.9	30.4	15.4	44.8	38.8	15.4	1.4	5.1	0.0
Omaha, NE	71.1	56.8	(b)	33.3	32.4	(b)	42.2	32.4	(b)	0.0	0.0	(b)
Philadelphia, PA	77.7	71.0	(b)	65.7	44.9	(b)	25.1	24.6	(b)	5.1	31.9	(b)
Phoenix, AZ	80.0	63.4	69.3	63.1	35.6	52.5	33.8	20.6	28.7	1.5	12.4	18.8
Portland, OR	71.6	68.4	(b)	55.2	25.4	(b)	23.9	24.4	(b)	9.0	21.8	(b)
Sacramento, CA	81.6	73.2	65.7	59.2	12.2	11.4	35.0	35.0	20.0	4.9	4.9	8.6
Salt Lake City, UT	(b)	67.9	57.1	(b)	20.7	47.6	(b)	23.6	23.8	(b)	14.3	14.3
San Antonio, TX	31.0	30.6	30.1	19.0	15.7	19.4	19.0	17.6	13.3	4.8	6.5	12.8
San Diego, CA	71.0	70.7	56.9	48.4	15.5	13.7	32.3	27.6	27.5	8.1	12.1	15.7
San Jose, CA	60.0	81.1	37.5	30.0	18.9	16.7	40.0	37.8	8.3	10.1	21.6	4.2
Seattle, WA	77.6	69.0	(b)	67.1	41.3	(b)	30.3	27.0	(b)	17.1	22.2	(b)
Spokane, WA	61.5	71.4	(b)	23.1	30.6	(b)	46.2	32.0	(b)	0.0	14.3	(b)
Tuscon, AZ	77.5	57.5	56.4	55.0	41.3	39.6	37.5	16.2	30.7	5.0	10.2	7.9

Note: The racial category "other" has been omitted because of the small number of sample cases at most sites.

[a] Includes cocaine, marijuana, opiates, methamphetamine, and phencyclidine (PCP).

[b] Base figure is less than 10 cases.

SOURCE: "Table 4.31. Drug use by adult arrestees in 34 U.S. cities, By type of drug, race, ethnicity, and sex, 1999," *Sourcebook of Criminal Justice Statistics 2000*, U.S. Department of Justice, Bureau of Justice Statistics, Washington, DC, 2000

The 2001 study also reported that if inhalants were considered to be illicit drugs, 35 percent of teens had tried a drug prior to eighth grade. Because most inhalants are legal aerosols or volatile solvents (like airplane glue, shoe polish, or gasoline) which give off gases or fumes, access and abuse was fairly easy for those in this age group. The use of inhalants generally declined from 1995 to 2001, though the decline was only statistically significant for 12th graders. Marijuana use among twelfth graders, which had peaked in 1979, when 51 percent reported they had used it, dropped to 22 percent by 1992, but gained steadily in the 1990s. In 2001 it was almost 40 percent.

So-called "club drugs" such as Ecstasy (MDMA), Rohypnol (known as the date rape drug), GHB, and ketamine have become popular among teenagers at dance clubs and "raves" in recent years. Because each of these club drugs is now scheduled under the Controlled Substances Act (Title II of the Comprehensive Drug Abuse Prevention and Control Act of 1970), they are illegal and their use constitutes a criminal offense.

Some 2.6 percent of 12- to 17-year-olds reported lifetime use (use at any time during their lifetime, rather than just within the past year) of Ecstasy, according to the *2000 National Household Survey on Drug Abuse*. In 2000 some 8.2 percent of twelfth graders, 5.4 percent of tenth graders, and 3.1 percent of eighth graders reported that they had used Ecstasy within the past year, as reported in the *2000 Monitoring the Future Study*. In the *2001 Monitoring the Future Study*, MDMA use continued to climb, but the rate of increase was less than it had been from 1999 to 2000. The slowed rate of incline may have been due to perceived danger, since the number of twelfth graders responding that they felt its use was a "great risk" was 8 percent higher than in the previous year. Use of most other drugs, like heroin (without a needle), cocaine, and LSD remained at levels similar to or slightly less than those in 1997, a year in which their use peaked.

MORE DRUG OFFENDERS BEHIND BARS

At all levels—local, state, and federal—the number of drug offenders in prisons and jails increased dramatically

TABLE 8.7

Drug use by male juvenile arrestees and detainees in 9 cities by type of drug and age, 1999

(Percent testing positive)

City	Any drug[a]	Cocaine	Marijuana	Opiates	Metham-phetamine	PCP	Multiple drugs
Total							
Birmingham, AL	45.3%	4.3%	42.7%	0.0%	0.0%	0.0%	1.7%
Cleveland, OH	62.0	9.3	59.7	0.3	0.0	6.4	12.5
Denver, CO	62.2	9.3	58.8	0.3	0.3	0.0	6.5
Los Angeles, CA	53.9	8.0	51.9	0.7	2.2	1.0	9.2
Phoenix, AZ	68.5	15.9	62.2	2.4	5.6	2.1	18.5
Portland, OR	43.3	2.5	40.9	2.5	4.9	0.0	6.4
San Antonio, TX	56.1	7.0	53.1	2.6	0.4	0.0	6.6
San Diego, CA	56.8	2.5	52.5	0.4	15.8	0.7	14.0
Tucson, AZ	55.8	11.6	53.1	0.7	0.7	0.0	9.9
13 to 14 years							
Birmingham, AL	18.2	0.0	18.2	0.0	0.0	0.0	0.0
Cleveland, OH	49.3	4.3	47.8	0.0	0.0	1.4	2.9
Denver, CO	52.6	5.3	47.4	0.0	1.8	0.0	1.8
Los Angeles, CA	42.6	4.9	42.6	0.0	0.0	1.6	6.6
Phoenix, AZ	61.6	9.3	61.6	1.2	0.0	0.0	10.5
Portland, OR	15.9	0.0	15.9	0.0	0.0	0.0	0.0
San Antonio, TX	47.1	5.9	45.9	2.4	0.0	0.0	7.1
San Diego, CA	37.5	4.2	35.4	0.0	10.4	2.1	12.5
Tucson, AZ	42.0	3.4	42.0	0.0	0.0	0.0	3.4
15 to 16 years							
Birmingham, AL	49.1	7.3	45.5	0.0	0.0	0.0	3.6
Cleveland, OH	64.2	12.8	60.8	0.7	0.0	5.4	14.2
Denver, CO	67.6	7.9	66.2	0.0	0.0	0.0	6.5
Los Angeles, CA	56.7	10.0	55.7	1.0	1.0	0.5	10.9
Phoenix, AZ	65.0	16.0	57.1	3.1	6.1	3.1	17.8
Portland, OR	51.5	1.0	48.5	2.1	5.2	0.0	5.2
San Antonio, TX	67.2	8.6	62.9	3.4	0.9	0.0	7.8
San Diego, CA	66.2	3.1	62.3	0.0	21.5	0.8	20.0
Tucson, AZ	67.5	15.4	64.1	1.7	0.0	0.0	13.7
17 to 18 years							
Birmingham, AL	57.9	2.6	55.3	0.0	0.0	0.0	0.0
Cleveland, OH	73.3	8.1	72.1	0.0	0.0	12.8	18.6
Denver, CO	63.1	14.3	58.3	1.2	0.0	0.0	10.7
Los Angeles, CA	62.4	8.0	57.6	0.0	5.6	1.6	8.8
Phoenix, AZ	81.0	21.6	71.6	2.6	8.6	1.7	25.0
Portland, OR	52.5	6.8	49.2	5.1	8.5	0.0	13.6
San Antonio, TX	(b)	(b)	(b)	(b)	(b)	(b)	(b)
San Diego, CA	55.7	1.0	49.5	1.0	11.3	0.0	7.2
Tucson, AZ	64.1	20.3	57.8	0.0	3.1	0.0	15.6

Note: Data on male juvenile arrestees/detainees are collected at nine Arrestee Drug Abuse Monitoring (ADAM) sites throughout the United States. Six of the nine sites also collected data on female juvenile arrestees/detainees; however, these data are omitted because the sample sizes at each site were generally small. The "9 to 12 year" age category has been omitted because of the small number of sample cases within each drug type.

[a] Includes cocaine, marijuana, opiates, methamphetamine, and phencyclidine (PCP).
[b] Base figure is less than 10 cases.

SOURCE: "Table 4.32: Drug use by male juvenile arrestees/detainees in 9 U.S. cities, by type of drug and age, 1999," *Sourcebook of Criminal Justice Statistics 2000*, U.S. Department of Justice, Bureau of Justice Statistics, Washington, DC, 2000

from 1980 to 1993, far outstripping the generally sharp increase in the overall prison and jail populations. During this period, the total number of state prisoners almost tripled, and the number of federal prisoners increased fourfold. Over the same period, the number of drug offenders in state and federal prisons each grew tenfold. While the rate of increase slowed from 1990 to 1996, the proportion of drug offenders out of all inmates continued to increase dramatically.

From 1990 to 1999 the number of drug offenders in state prisons rose by 69 percent, from 148,600 to 251,200. (See Figure 8.4.) During that time period, female drug offenders accounted for one-third of the increase in total growth (35 percent) of female state prisoners sentenced, compared to a 28 percent growth in female violent offenders, and 21 percent growth in female property crime offenders. In comparison, male drug offenders accounted for only 19 percent of the total growth of male state prison populations, with 53 percent of the growth attributed to male violent offenders. (See Table 8.8.) From 1990 to 1999 there was an increase of 64,900 African American drug offenders in state prisons, accounting for 27 percent of the total growth of sentenced black prisoners under state jurisdiction. There were 21,100 additional white drug offenders in state prison and 13,400 more Hispanic drug offenders, representing 14 percent of the total growth of white prisoners and 15 percent of the total growth of Hispanic prisoners. (See Table 8.9.)

According to the Bureau of Justice Statistics, in 1997 some 19 percent of state prisoners and 16 percent of federal prisoners reported that they committed their current offense to obtain money for drugs, as did 61,000 convicted jail inmates in 1998. In 1999 13.3 percent of all jail inmates were incarcerated for offenses committed to buy drugs. Of property crimes, 24.4 percent were committed to obtain money to buy drugs, as well as 14 percent of all drug offenses (such as the sale or trafficking in drugs), 11.5 percent of violent offenses, and 3.3 percent of public order offenses. (See Table 8.10.) In 1999, of 12,658 homicides, 4.5 percent were drug-related, a slight decrease from 4.8 percent in 1998 but higher than the 1986 rate of 3.9 percent. (See Table 8.11.) Of crime victims in 1999, about 28 percent reported that they believed the offender was using drugs, either alone or in combination with alcohol. (See Figure 8.5.)

Crime-Related Costs of Drug Use

According to the Office of National Drug Control Policy in Washington, DC, the crime-related costs of drug abuse rose from $60.8 billion in 1992 to over $100 billion in 2000. (See Figure 8.6.) From 1992 to 1998 the cost of drug-related crime-victim health care rose by 5.4 percent, the cost of incarceration by 9.1 percent, and the cost of police protection by 9.3 percent. (See Table 8.12.)

Drug Offender Sentences

Federal and state laws consider a number of factors in establishing penalties for violators of drug laws. In general, the penalties for drug violations are determined by:

- The dangerousness of the drug
- Whether the violation is for drug possession or drug trafficking
- The amount of the drug involved
- The criminal history of the offender
- The location of the transaction, such as near a school or in a crack house
- The ages of the buyer and seller

Figure 8.7 shows the mean (average) and median (half were more; half were less) lengths of prison

FIGURE 8.4

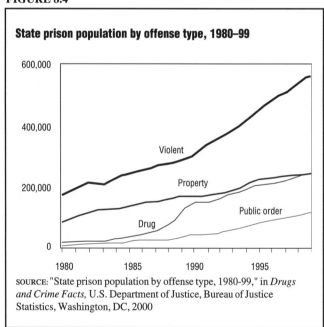

State prison population by offense type, 1980–99

SOURCE: "State prison population by offense type, 1980-99," in *Drugs and Crime Facts,* U.S. Department of Justice, Bureau of Justice Statistics, Washington, DC, 2000

TABLE 8.8

Percent of total growth of sentenced prisoners under state jurisdiction, by offense and gender, 1990–99

	Male	Female
Total	100%	100%
Violent	53	28
Property	13	21
Drug	**19%**	**35%**
Public-order	15	16

SOURCE: "Percent of total growth of sentenced prisoners under State jurisdiction, by offense and gender, 1990–99," in *Drugs and Crime Facts,* U.S. Department of Justice, Bureau of Justice Statistics, Washington, DC, 2001

TABLE 8.9

Total growth of sentenced prisoners under state jurisdiction, by offense, race, and Hispanic origin, 1990–99

	White		Black		Hispanic	
	Increase, 1990-99	Percent of total	Increase, 1990-99	Percent of total	Increase, 1990-99	Percent of total
Total	152,700	100%	238,400	100%	86,800	100%
Violent	71,700	47	120,200	50	50,100	58
Property	28,700	19	27,600	12	9,900	11
Drug	**21,100**	**14**	**64,900**	**27**	**13,400**	**15**
Public-order	31,800	21	25,500	11	13,000	15

SOURCE: "Total growth of sentenced prisoners under state jurisdiction, by offense, race, and Hispanic origin, 1990–99," in *Drugs and Crime Facts,* U.S. Department of Justice, Bureau of Justice Statistics, Washington, DC, 2001

TABLE 8.10

Percent of jail inmates who committed offense to get money for drugs, 1996 and 1999

Offense	1996	1999
Total	15.8%	13.3%
Violent	8.8	11.5
Property	25.6	24.4
Drugs	23.5	14.0
Public-order	4.2	3.3

SOURCE: "Percent of jail inmates who committed offense to get money for drugs," in *Drugs and Crime Facts,* U.S. Department of Justice, Bureau of Justice Statistics, Washington, DC, 2001

FIGURE 8.5

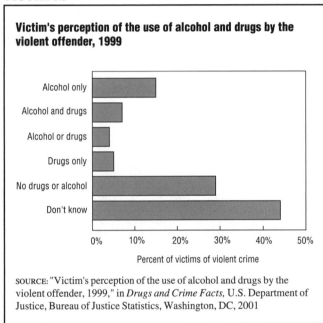

Victim's perception of the use of alcohol and drugs by the violent offender, 1999

SOURCE: "Victim's perception of the use of alcohol and drugs by the violent offender, 1999," in *Drugs and Crime Facts,* U.S. Department of Justice, Bureau of Justice Statistics, Washington, DC, 2001

TABLE 8.11

Drug-related homicides, 1986–99

Year	Number of homicides	Percent drug related
1986	19,257	3.9%
1987	17,963	4.9
1988	17,971	5.6
1989	18,954	7.4
1990	20,273	6.7
1991	21,676	6.2
1992	22,716	5.7
1993	23,180	5.5
1994	22,084	5.6
1995	20,232	5.1
1996	16,967	5.0
1997	15,837	5.1
1998	14,276	4.8
1999	12,658	4.5

Note: The percentages are based on data from the Supplementary Homicide Reports (SHR) while the totals are from the Uniform Crime Reports (UCR). Not all homicides in the UCR result in reports in the SHR.

SOURCE: "Drug related homicides," in *Drugs and Crime Facts,* U.S. Department of Justice, Bureau of Justice Statistics, Washington, DC, 2001

FIGURE 8.6

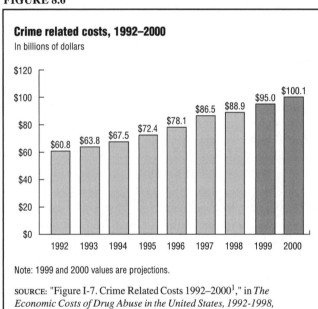

Crime related costs, 1992–2000

In billions of dollars

Note: 1999 and 2000 values are projections.

SOURCE: "Figure I-7. Crime Related Costs 1992–2000[1]," in *The Economic Costs of Drug Abuse in the United States, 1992-1998,* Executive Office of the President, Office of National Drug Control Policy, Washington, DC, September 2001

sentences for each drug type in fiscal year 2000. The highest mean and median sentences were for crack cocaine (119.5 months and 97 months, respectively), followed by methamphetamine, with a mean of 87.8 months and a median sentence of 70 months. The lowest mean and median sentences (36.4 months and 24 months) were for the most widely used illicit drug, marijuana.

MANDATORY MINIMUM SENTENCING. Mandatory minimum sentences limit the sentencing discretion of the judge. While the law sets the minimum length of time to which a convicted felon can be sentenced, it does allow judges to impose sentences longer than the mandatory minimums. A first-time offender in a federal court facing a 10-year mandatory minimum sentence could receive anything from 10 years up to and including life imprisonment. For example, offenders convicted of possessing at least five grams of crack cocaine for their first conviction, three grams for their second conviction, and one gram for

their third conviction are sentenced to a mandatory minimum prison sentence of 5 years and a maximum sentence of 20 years.

Many law enforcement officials think some mandatory sentences are too harsh for the crime. As a result, some prosecutors charge the accused with lesser crimes than those for which they were arrested, and some judges ignore the mandatory sentencing and apply lesser punishments. In 2002 the U.S. Supreme Court agreed to decide on the constitutionality of mandatory sentencing as

TABLE 8.12

Crime related costs, 1992 and 1998

In millions of dollars

Cost Categories	1992	1998	Annualized Percentage Change
Health Care Costs			
Crime Victim Health Care Costs	$92	$127	5.4%
Productivity Losses			
Productivity Loss of Victims of Crime	$2,059	$2,165	0.8%
Incarceration	$17,907	$30,133	9.1%
Crime Careers	$19,198	$24,627	4.2%
Cost of Other Effects			
Criminal Justice System and Other Public Costs			
Police Protection	$5,348	$9,096	9.3%
Legal Adjudication	$2,716	$4,489	8.7%
State and Federal Corrections	$7,495	$11,027	6.6%
Local Corrections	$1,333	$1,660	3.7%
Federal Spending to Reduce Supply	$4,126	$4,827	2.6%
Private Costs			
Private Legal Defense	$365	$548	7.0%
Property Damage for Victims of Crime	$193	$186	-0.5%
Total	**$60,832**	**$88,887**	**6.5%**

SOURCE: "Table I-4. Crime Related Costs, 1992 and 1998," in *The Economic Costs of Drug Abuse in the United States, 1992-1998,* Executive Office of the President, Office of National Drug Control Policy, Washington, DC, September 2001

TABLE 8.13

Total federal drug control budget, fiscal years 1981–2001

	(in millions)
FY 1981 actual	$1,531.8
FY 1989 actual	6,663.7
FY 1990 actual	9,758.9
FY 1991 actual	10,957.6
FY 1992 actual	11,565.2
FY 1993 actual	11,936.2
FY 1994 actual	11,962.4
FY 1995 actual	12,981.1
FY 1996 actual	12,988.0
FY 1997 actual	14,353.7
FY 1998 actual	15,178.6
FY 1999 actual	17,124.2
FY 2000 final budget authority	17,940.3
FY 2001 enacted	18,053.1

SOURCE: "Total Federal drug control budget," in *Drugs and Crime Facts,* U.S. Department of Justice, Bureau of Justice Statistics, Washington, DC, 2001

applied in California's Three Strikes law. The high court's decision will effectively establish legal precedent in all 50 states.

MANDATORY LIFE TERM UPHELD. In June of 1991 the U.S. Supreme Court in *Harmelin v. Michigan* (501 US 957) upheld a Michigan law that imposed a mandatory life sentence without parole for possession of more than 650 grams of cocaine. Harmelin's attorney argued that the mandatory sentence violated the Eighth Amendment's prohibition against cruel and unusual punishment. He claimed the sentence was "grossly disproportionate" to the crime. Also, the state law did not permit the judge to use his own discretion to reduce a sentence based on other mitigating factors, such as the fact that Harmelin had no prior felony convictions.

In a sharply divided 5–4 decision, the majority declared that the Eighth Amendment does not require a sentencing judge to be given discretion to reduce a sentence. The Court ruled that "cruel and unusual" came from the English Declaration of Rights of 1689 and was intended to prevent sentences of being burned or drawn and quartered (the criminal's hands and feet were tied to horses, which then pulled the victim to pieces). Although Harmelin's sentence was the second most severe penalty permitted by law (death is the most severe), the Court did not find it grossly inconsistent.

Driving Under the Influence

In 2000, according to the National Highway Traffic Safety Administration, there were 16,653 alcohol-related traffic fatalities, 4 percent more than in 1999 but 25 percent less than in 1990, when alcohol-related fatalities numbered 22,084. Fatalities in alcohol-related crashes comprised 40 percent of all traffic fatalities in 2000. Some 310,000 people were injured in crashes in which law enforcement reported that alcohol was present. The rate of alcohol-related fatal crashes was more than three times higher at night (61 percent) than during the day (18 percent). For all crashes, the rate of alcohol involvement was four times as high at night (17 percent) than during the day (4 percent). The highest intoxication rates in fatal crashes in 2000 were recorded among drivers 21 to 24 years of age (27 percent), followed by drivers 25 to 34 years of age (24 percent), and 35 to 44 years of age (22 percent).

In 1983, the peak year for DUI arrests and fatalities, 33 states allowed persons under age 21 to purchase and sell alcoholic beverages. Since then, changes in the federal laws governing the way federal highway funds are distributed caused states to raise the legal drinking age to age 21. As of the year 2000, all states and the District of Columbia have a 21-year minimum drinking age. Observers link this change to the lowered incidence of DUI arrests and fatalities. In addition, social attitudes toward drinking and driving have changed through the 1980s and 1990s. By the end of the twentieth century, driving after several drinks was considered far less socially acceptable than just a generation earlier.

THE FEDERAL GOVERNMENT'S ROLE

The federal government has addressed the drug problem in two ways: reduction of supply through

FIGURE 8.7

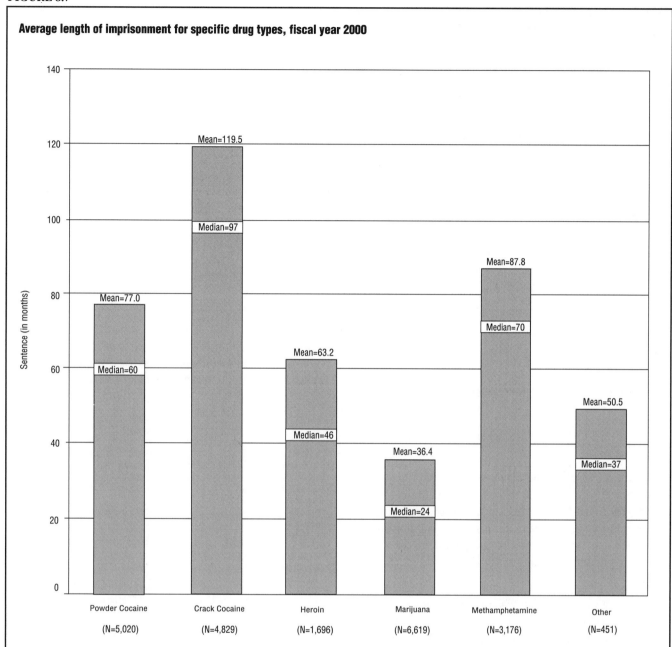

Average length of imprisonment for specific drug types, fiscal year 2000

Of the 59,846 cases, 23,542 were sentenced under USSG Chapter Two, Part D (drugs). Of these, 23,424 were sentenced under §§2D1.1, 2D1.2, 2D1.5, 2D1.6, 2D1.8, or 2D2.1 as depicted in this figure. Additionally, 1,263 with zero months prison ordered were excluded. Of the remaining 22,161 cases, 370 were excluded due to one or both of the following reasons: (37) missing drug type or (334) missing sentencing information.

SOURCE: "Figure J: Average length of imprisonment for each drug type, Fiscal Year 2000," *2000 Sourcebook of Federal Sentencing Statistics*, U.S. Sentencing Commission, Washington, DC, 2001

enforcement and interdiction, and reduction of demand through education, prevention, and treatment. According to the Office of National Drug Control Policy, actual federal spending on drug control programs increased from $1.5 billion in 1981 to $18.1 billion in 2001. From 1981 to 1991 alone, the drug control budget increased sevenfold, from $1.5 billion to almost $11 billion. (See Table 8.13.) As of 1999 spending on drug control leveled off somewhat, with $17.1 billion spent that year, $17.9 billion spent in 2000, and $18.1 billion in 2001. Some $19.2 billion was proposed for fiscal year (FY) 2002. (See Figure 8.8.)

The enacted FY 2001 federal budget included $18.1 billion for drug control. Drug control spending by department for FY 2001 included $8.1 billion allocated to the Justice Department, $3.3 billion to the Department of Health and Human Services, $1.5 billion to the Department of the

TABLE 8.14

Drug spending by federal government department, fiscal years 2000–02

Budget Authority ($ Millions)

Department	Fiscal year 00 Final BA	Fiscal year 01 Enacted	Fiscal year 02 Request	Fiscal year 01-02 Change	% Change
Defense	1,273.3	1,047.1	1,069.1*	22.0	2.1%
Education	598.0	633.2	633.2	0.0	0.0%
Health and Human Services	3,022.0	3,333.2	3,622.0	288.7	8.7%
Justice	7,357.5	8,148.8	8,338.1	189.4	2.3%
Office of National Drug Control Policy	464.4	499.8	519.1	19.2	3.8%
State	1,301.3	289.1	904.5	615.4	212.9%
Transportation	814.9	691.2	816.8	125.6	18.2%
Treasury	1,348.8	1,539.7	1,595.1	55.3	3.6%
Veterans Affairs	554.6	572.9	580.8	7.9	1.4%
All Other	1,205.5	1,298.1	1,100.2	(197.9)	(15.2%)
Total	**17,940.3**	**18,053.1**	**19,178.8**	**1,125.7**	**6.2%**

*Tentative, pending Defense strategy review.

SOURCE: "Table 1: Drug Spending by Department," *2002 National Drug Control Strategy*, Office of National Drug Control Policy, Washington, DC, 2002

FIGURE 8.8

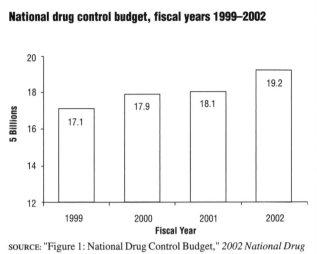

National drug control budget, fiscal years 1999–2002

SOURCE: "Figure 1: National Drug Control Budget," *2002 National Drug Control Strategy*, Office of National Drug Control Policy, Washington, DC, 2002

TABLE 8.15

Federal drug control budget by function, fiscal years 2000–01

	2000 (in millions)	2001 (in millions)
Total	**$17,940.3**	**$18,053.1**
Drug treatment	$2,915.2	$3,168.3
Drug prevention	2,338.6	2,515.7
Criminal justice system	8,429.0	9,357.7
International	1,892.9	609.7
Interdiction	1,965.9	1,950.4
Research	89.6	106.1
Intelligence	309.1	345.2
International (U.S. Support for Plan Colombia & the Andean Region)		954.4

SOURCE: "Fiscal Year 2000 and 2001 Federal drug control budget by function," in *Drugs and Crime Facts*, U.S. Department of Justice, Bureau of Justice Statistics, Washington, DC, 2001

Treasury, and $1 billion to the Department of Defense. (See Table 8.14.)

Of the $18.1 billion in actual drug control spending in 2001, some $9.4 billion was allocated to the criminal justice system, followed by $3.2 billion for drug treatment, and $2.5 billion for various programs aimed at drug prevention. Proportionally, these figures are comparable to the allocation of drug control spending in 2000. (See Table 8.15.)

Federal drug seizures, as reported by five federal law enforcement agencies, increased for most types of drugs from 1989 to 2000. According to the Office of National Drug Control Policy, in 1989 about 1.3 million pounds of drugs were seized, compared to 2.9 million in 2000. The largest rise in drug seizures occurred for marijuana, more than doubling from 1.1 million pounds in 1989 to 2.6 million pounds seized in 2000. In FY 2000, drug interdiction efforts by the federal government accounted for the seizure of 234,863 pounds of cocaine, 3,119 pounds of heroin, and

23,988 pounds of hashish. Seizures of hashish in 2000 showed a marked decline from the 51,625 pounds seized in 1989 and from the peak of 178,211 in 1991, but showed an equally dramatic increase from the 1,678 pounds seized in 1999 and the 596 pounds seized in 1998. (See Table 8.16.)

TABLE 8.16

Federal drug seizures, fiscal years 1989–2000

| Fiscal year | Pounds seized[1] | | | | |
	Total	Heroin	Cocaine	Marijuana	Hashish
1989	1,343,702	2,415	218,697	1,070,965	51,625
1990	738,004	1,704	235,885	483,353	17,062
1991	926,700	3,067	246,325	499,097	178,211
1992	1,093,366	2,552	303,289	783,477	4,048
1993	1,045,997	3,516	244,315	772,086	26,080
1994	1,355,678	2,898	309,710	1,041,445	1,625
1995	1,576,865	2,569	234,105	1,308,171	32,020
1996	1,718,552	3,373	253,297	1,429,786	32,096
1997	1,796,863	3,121	252,329	1,488,362	53,051
1998	2,047,558	3,499	266,029	1,777,434	596
1999	2,615,636	2,732	292,234	2,318,992	1,678
2000	2,856,462	3,119	234,863	2,594,492	23,988

Note: The Federal-wide Drug Seizure System (FDSS) contains information about drug seizures made within the jurisdiction of the United States by the Drug Enforcement Administration, Federal Bureau of Investigation, U.S. Customs Service, and U.S. Border Patrol as well as maritime seizures made by the U.S. Coast Guard. Drug seizures made by other Federal agencies are included in the FDSS database when custody of the drug evidence was transferred to one of these five agencies.

[1]Figures are rounded to the nearest pound.

SOURCE: "Table 4.37. Federal drug seizures: By type of drug, fiscal years 1989-2000," in *Sourcebook of Criminal Justice Statistics, 2000,* U.S. Department of Justice, Bureau of Justice Statistics, Washington, DC, 2001 [Online] http://www.albany.edu/sourcebook/1995/pdf/t437.pdf [Accessed May 06, 2002]

CHAPTER 9

LAW ENFORCEMENT, CRIME PREVENTION, AND PUBLIC OPINIONS ABOUT CRIME

After a crime has been committed, the justice system of the United States goes into action. The system has three major components that work together:

- Law enforcement agencies gather evidence and capture suspected perpetrators.

- The judicial system tries perpetrators in a court of law and, if they are found guilty, sentences them to a period of incarceration or some other form of punishment, restitution, and/or treatment.

- Correction agencies house convicted criminals in prisons, jails, treatment centers, or other places of confinement.

CITY, COUNTY, AND STATE LAW ENFORCEMENT

In 2000 the United States had 13,535 city, county, and state police agencies and 9 major federal law enforcement agencies. As of October 31, 2000, there were 926,583 full-time police employees. Of the total, 654,601 were sworn police officers. Civilian employees accounted for 271,982. Almost 90 percent of police officers were male, while 62.7 percent of civilian employees were female. Suburban counties employed 246,992 police personnel, and the 68 cities in the nation with populations of 250,000 or more employed 205,032 police personnel. The 10 cities with populations of 1 million or more employed 113,827 police personnel. (See Table 9.1.)

Killed in the Line of Duty

Wearing a badge is a dangerous profession.... While progress is being made, violence remains a serious threat to those who have sworn to protect society.

—The Federal Bureau of Investigation, *Law Enforcement Officers Killed and Assaulted, 1996*

From 1991 through 2000, felons killed 644 law enforcement officers, an average of about 64 officers per year. In 2000, 51 law enforcement officers were killed in the line of duty, up from 42 in 1999. (See Table 9.2.) Law enforcement murders were higher in the mid-1990s. From a peak of 79 in 1994, the number of officers killed declined to 61 in 1996, rose to 71 in 1997 and dropped again in 1998 to 61.

In 2000, 12 officers were killed during arrest situations, such as drug-related arrests. Six officers died while investigating suspicious persons or circumstances. Eight were killed answering disturbance calls, and 13 died in traffic stops or pursuits. Being in a one-officer vehicle was the most dangerous situation: 19 officers were in one-officer vehicles without assistance when they were killed. (See Table 9.3.)

WEAPONS USED. Firearms claimed the lives of 601 of the 644 officers killed in the line of duty from 1991 through 2000. Of these murders, 452 were committed with handguns, 114 with rifles, and 35 with shotguns. Bombs killed 11 officers, while knives (8), personal weapons (3), and other weapons (21) killed the remainder of officers. (See Table 9.4.) During 2000, firearms were used in 47 of the 51 slayings, and handguns were used in 33 of those killings. One officer was shot with his own service weapon.

ASSAILANTS. In 2000, 65 suspects were arrested for the murders of law enforcement officers; 63 were male and 2 were female. Forty-seven of the arrestees were white, and 16 were black. Thirty-seven assailants were under the age of 31, and 21 were ages 18 to 24. (See Table 9.5.)

Among the 845 persons arrested and charged for killing officers from 1991 to 2000, the average age was 28. Some 542 had been previously arrested for criminal activities, and 385 had been convicted, while 163 were on parole at the time of the killings.

FEDERAL LAW ENFORCEMENT

According to a Bureau of Justice Statistics (BJS) survey, in June of 2000 federal agencies employed more than

TABLE 9.1

Full-time law enforcement employees by gender and population group as of October 31, 2000

[2000 estimated population]

Population group	Total police employees Total	Percent Male	Percent Female	Police officers (sworn) Total	Percent Male	Percent Female	Civilian employees Total	Percent Male	Percent Female
TOTAL AGENCIES: 13,535 agencies; population 264,813,489	**926,583**	**73.8**	**26.2**	**654,601**	**89.0**	**11.0**	**271,982**	**37.3**	**62.7**
TOTAL CITIES: 10,386 cities; population 177,721,567	**550,971**	**75.6**	**24.4**	**425,860**	**89.1**	**10.9**	**125,111**	**30.0**	**70.0**
GROUP I									
68 cities, 250,000 and over; population 50,410,355	205,032	71.3	28.7	156,205	83.8	16.2	48,827	31.5	68.5
10 cities, 1,000,000 and over; population 23,597,803	113,827	70.8	29.2	86,926	83.0	17.0	26,901	31.4	68.6
22 cities, 500,000 to 999,999; population 14,230,170	52,751	72.4	27.6	40,444	84.1	15.9	12,307	34.0	66.0
36 cities, 250,000 to 499,999; population 12,582,382	38,454	71.3	28.7	28,835	85.7	14.3	9,619	28.2	71.8
GROUP II									
161 cities, 100,000 to 249,999; population 23,931,099	60,802	74.0	26.0	46,100	89.5	10.5	14,702	25.5	74.5
GROUP III									
376 cities, 50,000 to 99,999; population 25,637,085	59,338	77.1	22.9	46,080	91.7	8.3	13,258	26.3	73.7
GROUP IV									
743 cities, 25,000 to 49,999; population 25,673,349	59,491	78.6	21.4	46,836	92.6	7.4	12,655	27.0	73.0
GROUP V									
1,795 cities, 10,000 to 24,999; population 28,276,838	68,251	80.0	20.0	54,533	93.5	6.5	13,718	26.2	73.8
GROUP VI									
7,243 cities, under 10,000; population 23,792,841	98,057	79.9	20.1	76,106	92.6	7.4	21,951	35.9	64.1
SUBURBAN COUNTIES									
879 agencies; population 56,867,728	246,992	70.5	29.5	149,700	87.2	12.8	97,292	44.7	55.3
RURAL COUNTIES									
2,270 agencies; population 30,224,194	128,620	72.5	27.5	79,041	91.9	8.1	49,579	41.5	58.5
SUBURBAN AREA*									
6,357 agencies; population 108,189,602	395,878	73.9	26.1	266,124	89.6	10.4	129,754	41.6	58.4

*Includes suburban city and county law enforcement agencies within metropolitan areas. Excludes central cities. Suburban cities and counties are also included in other groups.

SOURCE: "Table 74: Full-Time Law Enforcement Employees as of October 31, 2000, Percent Male and Female by Population Group," *Crime in the United States, 2000: Uniform Crime Reports,* Federal Bureau of Investigation, Washington, DC, 2001

88,000 full-time officers authorized to make arrests and carry guns. This figure reflects an almost 6 percent increase from June of 1998. Of the major federal employers in 2000, the Immigration and Naturalization Service (INS) employed the most officers (17,973), almost half of whom were Border Patrol agents. The Federal Bureau of Prisons (BOP) accounted for 13,714 officers, the FBI for 11,712, and the U.S. Customs Service for 10,820. (See Table 9.6.)

In 2000, 85.6 percent of federal officers were male. The Internal Revenue Service (IRS), one of the agencies with 500 or more officers, had the largest proportion of female agents, at 27 percent. The DEA (Drug Enforcement Agency) had the smallest proportion of female officers, only 8.4 percent. Racial or ethnic minorities filled 30.5 percent of all federal law enforcement positions. Hispanics, who can be of any race, accounted for 15.2 percent of federal officers, and non-Hispanic blacks made up another 11.7 percent. Asian/Pacific Islanders (2.2 percent) and American Indians (1.2 percent) were also represented in the federal force. (See Figure 9.1.)

Federal Officers Assaulted and Killed

From 1996 to 2000 a total of 2,992 federal officers were assaulted. (The 1996 data for the National Park Service were not reported, so the actual total may be higher.) The assaults resulted in 12 fatalities, none of which occurred in 2000. Of the 528 Federal officers assaulted in

TABLE 9.2

Law enforcement officers feloniously killed, by circumstance at scene of incident, 1991–2000

Circumstance at scene of incident	Total	1991	1992	1993	1994	1995	1996	1997	1998	1999	2000
Total	**644**	**71**	**64**	**70**	**79**	**74**	**61**	**71**	**61**	**42**	**51**
Disturbance calls	**103**	17	11	10	8	8	4	14	16	7	8
Bar fights, persons with firearms, etc.	**42**	8	2	5	4	2	1	3	7	6	4
Family quarrels	**61**	9	9	5	4	6	3	11	9	1	4
Arrest situations	**211**	14	27	28	33	21	26	22	16	12	12
Burglaries in progress/ pursuing burglary suspects	**27**	3	5	1	4	4	3	5	0	0	2
Robberies in progress/ pursuing robbery suspects	**80**	4	11	9	17	7	12	11	3	4	2
Drug-related matters	**33**	3	3	3	4	4	3	1	7	2	3
Attempting other arrests	**71**	4	8	15	8	6	8	5	6	6	5
Civil disorders (mass disobedience, riot, etc.)	**0**	0	0	0	0	0	0	0	0	0	0
Handling, transporting, custody of prisoners	**26**	6	2	1	1	4	0	4	4	2	2
Investigating suspicious persons/circumstances	**106**	10	7	15	15	17	13	10	6	7	6
Ambush situations	**89**	11	7	5	8	14	6	12	10	6	10
Entrapment/premeditation	**37**	5	5	3	1	6	2	5	4	4	2
Unprovoked attacks	**52**	6	2	2	7	8	4	7	6	2	8
Mentally deranged assailants	**8**	0	0	1	4	1	1	1	0	0	0
Traffic pursuits/stops	**101**	13	10	10	10	9	11	8	9	8	13

SOURCE: "Table 19: Law Enforcement Officers Feloniously Killed, Circumstance at Scene of Incident, 1991–2000," *Crime in the United States, 2000: Uniform Crime Reports*, Federal Bureau of Investigation, Washington, DC, 2001

2000, personal weapons (hands, feet, etc.) were used in 171 incidents. Firearms were used in 56 incidents, and threats accounted for 52 incidents. (See Table 9.7.) In 1995 seven federal officers were killed in the bombing of the Edward P. Murrah building in Oklahoma City, Oklahoma.

In July of 1998 the nation was shocked by a shooting in the Capitol Building in Washington, D.C. Russell E. Weston, Jr., was charged with fatally shooting two Capitol police officers, Jacob J. Chestnut and John M. Gibson. Both men were buried with honors in Arlington National Cemetery. Weston himself was wounded in the gunfire exchange but recovered. Also wounded was a young female tourist.

CRIME PREVENTION

Crime prevention programs implemented by state and local agencies receive over $3.2 billion in U.S. Department of Justice grant funds each year. In 1996 the United States Congress issued a mandate to the Attorney General to authorize an evaluation of the effectiveness of these programs. The University of Maryland's Department of Criminology and Criminal Justice was selected to conduct the evaluation and issue a report. That report, "Preventing Crime: What Works, What Doesn't, What's Promising," was published in July 1998 as a *Research in Brief* by the National Institute of Justice (Office of Justice Programs, U.S. Department of Justice, Washington, DC).

In evaluating crime prevention programs throughout the United States, researchers looked at both the process employed by each program (how it was designed to work), and the impact of each program on reducing crime in a number of categories, such as in schools, families, communities, businesses, and high-crime areas. Based on ratings of between one (weakest) and five (strongest) in each category, researchers divided crime prevention programs into those that worked and those that didn't work. Programs that worked had ratings of three or higher in at least two categories, while those that didn't work had ratings of less than three in all categories or in all but one category. Crime prevention programs were rated as "promising" if there was no conclusive evidence of overall success or failure but the program received a level three evaluation or higher in at least one category and was "found to be effective by the remaining evidence."

What Worked

For small children, frequent home visits to infants under the age of 2 by trained nurses or aides reduced the incidence of child abuse as well as other injuries to children, and an arrest by age 15 occurred less frequently among preschoolers under the age of 5 who received weekly home visits from teachers. Among adolescents, risk factors for delinquency such as aggression and hyperactivity were more effectively dealt with by parents who

TABLE 9.3

Law enforcement officers feloniously killed, by type of assignment and circumstance at scene of incident, 2000

Circumstance at scene of incident	Total	2-Officer vehicle	1-Officer vehicle		Foot patrol		Other*		Off duty
			Alone	Assisted	Alone	Assisted	Alone	Assisted	
Total	51	8	19	12	0	0	2	5	5
Disturbance calls	8	1	3	3	0	0	0	0	1
Bar fights, persons with firearms, etc.	4	0	1	2	0	0	0	0	1
Family quarrels	4	1	2	1	0	0	0	0	0
Arrest situations	12	3	1	3	0	0	1	3	1
Burglaries in progress/ pursuing burglary suspects	2	0	0	1	0	0	0	1	0
Robberies in progress/ pursuing robbery suspects	2	1	0	0	0	0	0	0	1
Drug-related matters	3	0	0	0	0	0	1	2	0
Attempting other arrests	5	2	1	2	0	0	0	0	0
Civil disorders (mass disobedience, riot, etc.)	0	0	0	0	0	0	0	0	0
Handling, transporting, custody of prisoners	2	0	1	0	0	0	0	1	0
Investigating suspicious persons/circumstances	6	1	2	1	0	0	1	0	1
Ambush situations	10	2	3	2	0	0	0	1	2
Entrapment/premeditation	2	0	1	0	0	0	0	1	0
Unprovoked attacks	8	2	2	2	0	0	0	0	2
Mentally deranged assailants	0	0	0	0	0	0	0	0	0
Traffic pursuits/stops	13	1	9	3	0	0	0	0	0

*Includes detectives, officers on special assignments, undercover officers, and officers on other types of assignments that are not listed.

SOURCE: "Table 20: Law Enforcement Officers Feloniously Killed, Type of Assignment by Circumstance at Scene of Incident, 2000," *Crime in the United States, 2000: Uniform Crime Reports*, Federal Bureau of Investigation, Washington, DC, 2001

TABLE 9.4

Law enforcement officers feloniously killed, by type of weapon, 1991–2000

Year	Total	Handgun	Rifle	Shotgun	Total firearms	Knife or cutting instrument	Bomb	Personal weapons	Other
Total	644	452	114	35	601	8	11	3	21
1991	71	50	14	4	68	0	1	0	2
1992	64	44	9	2	55	1	1	1	6
1993	70	51	13	3	67	0	0	0	3
1994	79	66	8	4	78	0	0	0	1
1995	74	43	14	5	62	2	8	0	2
1996	61	50	6	1	57	1	0	1	2
1997	71	50	12	6	68	2	0	1	0
1998	61	40	17	1	58	1	1	0	1
1999	42	25	11	5	41	0	0	0	1
2000	51	33	10	4	47	1	0	0	3

SOURCE: "Table 4: Law Enforcement Officers Feloniously Killed, Type of Weapon, 1991–2000," *Crime in the United States, 2000: Uniform Crime Reports*, Federal Bureau of Investigation, Washington, DC, 2001

had participated in some type of family therapy or parenting classes.

Several types of school-based programs were identified as being effective. A combination of consistency with school rules, reinforcing positive behavior among students, and implementing school-wide programs such as anti-bullying campaigns reduced the incidence of crime and delinquency. Long-term programs such as Life Skills Training in the areas of stress control, anger management, and problem solving helped to reduce delinquency and substance abuse, as did the use of behavior modification techniques in teaching thinking skills to juveniles at high risk of delinquency.

Police programs rated effective in reducing crime included extra police patrols in high-crime areas and the use of specialized units that identified and monitored repeat offenders once they were released into the community. The study found that the arrest of employed domestic abusers reduced the rate of future incidents of domestic abuse by the same individuals.

Among other programs, the threat of filing civil actions against landlords for not reporting drug offenses helped to reduce the incidence of drug crime on their premises, while drug treatment programs in prison reduced the rate of repeat drug offenses by prison parolees. Treatment also proved effective in reducing overall repeat offender rates among both juveniles and adults when the treatment program was targeted at risk factors related to the underlying criminal offense, such as aggression or childhood abuse.

What Didn't Work

Despite their popularity and widespread use, gun buyback programs, Drug Abuse Resistance Education (D.A.R.E.), and "Scared Straight" programs that brought juvenile offenders face-to-face with hardened prison inmates were among programs rated ineffective by researchers. Among other popular programs, boot camps using military-like discipline and regimentation failed to reduce the rate of repeat offenders among both juveniles and adults. Similarly, shock probation, shock parole, and split sentences under which offenders were briefly incarcerated before being released to a supervised community setting did not reduce the incidence of repeat offending any more than programs that placed similar offenders directly under community supervision without an initial period of incarceration.

According to the report, the incarceration of serious offenders at high risk of re-offending was effective in preventing future crimes; however, the less serious the offender, the less likely incarceration was to have a demonstrable impact on future crimes.

As discussed earlier, the arrest of employed domestic abusers reduced repeat offenses of domestic abuse; however, the opposite occurred among domestic abusers who were unemployed. According to the report, "Arrests of unemployed suspects for domestic assault caused higher rates of repeat offending over the long term than nonarrest alternatives" that addressed the underlying problems that contributed to the unemployment, such as substance abuse.

Summer-job and subsidized work programs also failed to reduce crime or arrests, as did police newsletters with local crime information.

What Was Promising

The report lists the following programs as among those that are potentially helpful in reducing certain types of criminal activity or repeat offending:

TABLE 9.5

Law enforcement officers feloniously killed, profile of known assailants, 1991–2000

Known assailants	2000	1991–1995	1996–2000	1991–2000
Total	65	493	352	845
Age				
Under 18 years	4	71	28	99
18 - 24 years	21	180	134	314
25 - 30 years	12	82	81	163
31 - 40 years	9	77	52	129
Over 40 years	15	52	50	102
Age not reported	4	31	7	38
Average years of age	32	27	28	28
Sex				
Male	63	460	346	806
Female	2	14	6	20
Sex not reported	0	19	0	19
Race				
White	47	245	190	435
Black	16	211	129	340
Asian/Pacific Islander	0	5	9	14
American Indian/Alaskan Native	0	4	10	14
Race not reported	2	28	14	42
Criminal history				
Prior criminal arrest	52	288	254	542
Convicted on prior criminal charge	30	194	191	385
Prior arrest for crime of violence	20	168	101	269
On parole or probation at time of killing	12	82	81	163
Prior arrest for murder	3	12	11	23
Prior arrest for drug law violation	15	128	119	247
Prior arrest for assaulting an officer or resisting arrest	9	76	59	135
Prior arrest for weapons violation	20	139	109	248

SOURCE: "Table 25: Law Enforcement Officers Feloniously Killed, Profile of Known Assailants, 1991–2000," *Crime in the United States, 2000: Uniform Crime Reports*, Federal Bureau of Investigation, Washington, DC, 2001

- Proactive drunk driving arrests with breath tests may reduce accident deaths.

- Community policing, including meetings with area residents, may reduce inaccurate perceptions of crime.

- Mailing arrest warrants to domestic violence suspects who leave the scene before police arrive may reduce repeat offenses.

- Battered women's shelters may help some women reduce the likelihood of being victimized again.

- Gang monitoring by community workers and probation and police officers may reduce criminal gang activity.

- Community-based mentoring by Big Brothers/Big Sisters of America may prevent drug abuse.

- Schools that group students into smaller units, like a school within a school, may prevent school crime.

- Job Corps residential training programs for at-risk youth may reduce the incidence of felony offenses.

TABLE 9.6

Federal agencies employing 500 or more full-time officers with arrest and firearm authority, June 2000

Agency	Number of officers*	Gender		White	American Indian	Black or African American	Asian or Pacific Islander	Hispanic or Latino of any race
		Male	Female					
Immigration and Naturalization Service	17,973	88.7%	11.3%	58.2%	0.5%	5.3%	2.2%	33.2%
Federal Bureau of Prisons	13,714	86.9	13.1	60.8	1.4	24.5	1.1	12.1
Federal Bureau of Investigation	11,712	82.9	17.1	83.6	0.5	6.2	2.7	7.1
U.S. Customs Service	10,820	80.9	19.1	64.5	0.8	7.4	3.5	23.8
Drug Enforcement Administration	4,201	91.6%	8.4%	82.1%	0.0%	8.0%	1.9%	7.3%
U.S. Secret Service	4,039	90.9	9.1	79.5	0.8	12.4	1.8	5.6
U.S. Postal Inspection Service	3,456	84.1	15.9	64.3	0.4	23.6	3.6	8.2
Internal Revenue Service	2,742	72.7	27.3	79.0	1.1	9.6	3.5	6.8
U.S. Marshals Service	2,777	88.0%	12.0%	82.1%	0.6%	7.9%	1.9%	7.5%
National Park Service	2,195	86.5	13.5	86.9	2.0	5.2	2.2	3.7
Ranger Activities Division	1,551	84.7	15.3	89.4	2.7	2.5	2.0	3.4
U.S. Park Police	644	90.8	9.2	80.9	0.3	11.6	2.6	4.5
Bureau of Alcohol, Tobacco and Firearms	1,983	88.0	12.0	80.3	1.2	9.9	1.6	7.0
U.S. Capitol Police	1,199	82.2	17.8	67.4	0.3	28.8	1.1	2.5
U.S. Fish and Wildlife Service	895	86.6%	13.4%	86.8%	3.9%	2.1%	1.5%	5.7%
GSA - Federal Protective Service	809	91.1	8.9	55.6	0.4	32.4	1.5	10.1
Bureau of Diplomatic Security	617	90.3	9.7	92.9	0.2	3.7	1.6	1.6
USDA Forest Service	586	83.1	16.9	81.7	8.0	3.1	1.0	6.1

Note: Data on gender and race or ethnicity of officers were not provided by the Administrative Office of the U.S. Courts. Detail may not add to total because of rounding.

*Includes employees in U.S. territories.

SOURCE: "Table 5. Gender and race or ethnicity of Federal officers with arrest and firearm authority, agencies employing 500 or more full-time officers, June 2000," *Federal Law Enforcement Officers, 2000*, U.S. Department of Justice, Bureau of Justice Statistics, Washington, DC, 2001

- Prison-based vocational education programs for adult inmates in Federal prisons may reduce repeat offending.

- Adding a second clerk in a convenience store that was previously robbed may reduce store robberies.

- Drug courts may reduce repeat drug offending.

- Drug treatment in jails with follow-up urine testing in the community may reduce the rate of drug re-offenses.

- Intensive supervision and aftercare of juvenile offenders may reduce the rate of re-offending for both minor and serious crimes.

- Community-based after-school recreation programs may reduce local juvenile crime.

Neighborhood Watch

According to the report, "neighborhood watch programs organized with police failed to reduce burglary or other target crimes, especially in higher crime areas where voluntary participation often fails." The latter point on voluntary participation was echoed by The National Sheriff's Association, which founded the current National Neighborhood Watch Program in 1972 with funding from the Law Enforcement Assistance Administration. According to information provided by the National Sheriff's

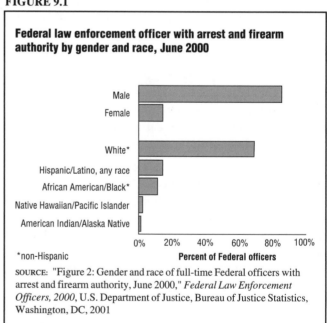

FIGURE 9.1

Federal law enforcement officer with arrest and firearm authority by gender and race, June 2000

*non-Hispanic

SOURCE: "Figure 2: Gender and race of full-time Federal officers with arrest and firearm authority, June 2000," *Federal Law Enforcement Officers, 2000*, U.S. Department of Justice, Bureau of Justice Statistics, Washington, DC, 2001

Association, "communities that need neighborhood watches the most are the ones that find it the hardest to keep them. This is particularly the case with lower income neighborhoods. Typically, adults in these neighborhoods

TABLE 9.7

Assaults on federal officers, by type of weapon and extent of injury, 1996–2000

Extent of injury	Total	Firearm	Knife or cutting instrument	Blunt object	Bomb	Vehicle	Personal weapons	Threat	Other
Total	**2,992**	**450**	**50**	**39**	**36**	**307**	**1,013**	**459**	**638**
1996˙	556	113	11	3	2	43	162	159	63
Killed	3	2	0	0	0	0	1	0	0
Injured	116	22	2	2	0	14	69	0	7
Not injured	437	89	9	1	2	29	92	159	56
1997	628	115	10	8	28	67	193	69	138
Killed	2	2	0	0	0	0	0	0	0
Injured	157	9	6	5	6	16	89	0	26
Not injured	469	104	4	3	22	51	104	69	112
1998	653	66	9	13	1	92	253	88	131
Killed	6	6	0	0	0	0	0	0	0
Injured	175	3	0	4	0	26	129	0	13
Not injured	472	57	9	9	1	66	124	88	118
1999	627	100	13	9	0	55	234	91	125
Killed	1	1	0	0	0	0	0	0	0
Injured	171	32	3	4	0	13	108	0	11
Not injured	455	67	10	5	0	42	126	91	114
2000	528	56	7	6	5	50	171	52	181
Killed	0	0	0	0	0	0	0	0	0
Injured	124	5	1	4	0	12	80	0	22
Not injured	404	51	6	2	5	38	91	52	159

*Information on officer assaults for the National Park Service is not available for 1996.

SOURCE: "Table 45: Assaults on Federal Officers, Type of Weapon by Extent of Injury, 1996–2000," *Crime in the United States, 2000: Uniform Crime Reports*, Federal Bureau of Investigation, Washington, DC, 2001

work multiple jobs with odd hours, making it difficult to schedule meetings and organize events. It also makes it difficult for neighbors to get to know and care about one another in a way that makes them feel comfortable watching out for one another."

Still, according to the National Sheriff's Association, the National Neighborhood Watch Program has proved successful in reducing crime in many neighborhoods across the country. For example, in Minnesota in the late 1990s, existing Neighborhood Watch programs mobilized in response to a rise in crime and assisted local police in clearing an average of 25 percent of cases. Similarly, in the late 1990s, with the help of Neighborhood Watch programs in Fairfax County, Virginia, burglary rates dropped by 90 percent.

According to the National Sheriff's Association, "Although not all Neighborhood Watches report success, and most of the time they fail to fully mobilize the residents, most of these programs are successful. Further, these programs often produce positive results beyond reducing crime, such as social interaction or cleaning up the neighborhood."

THE FEAR OF CRIME

The fear of becoming a victim of crime can undermine community relationships. People may withdraw physically and emotionally, losing contact with their neighbors and weakening the social fabric of their lives and communities. In a 2001 Gallup Poll, 9 percent of those polled named crime and violence as the most important problem facing the country. This percentage was down significantly from 37 percent in 1994. The percent of those naming crime and violence as the most important issue has steadily decreased since 1994, down to 17 percent in 1999 and 13 percent in 2000. Yet the 9 percent of those polled in 2001 who named crime as the nation's most important problem was still a higher figure than at any time during the 1980s, and was nine times higher than in 1990 (1 percent). (See Table 9.8.)

More Crime or Less Crime Today?

Another Gallup Poll reported that in 2000 47 percent of Americans thought there was more crime in the United States than in the year before. (See Table 9.9.) That figure is lower than the 52 percent of respondents in 1998 who felt there was more crime than the year before, and the 64 percent of respondents in 1997 who felt the same. In 1992, 89 percent of respondents felt there was more crime that the year before.

In 2000 more women (54 percent) felt there was more crime than there had been the year before than did men (40 percent). Fifty-two percent of African Americans thought so, compared to 46 percent of whites. Fifty-six

TABLE 9.8

Attitudes toward the most important problem facing the country, 1982–2001

QUESTION: "WHAT DO YOU THINK IS THE MOST IMPORTANT PROBLEM FACING THIS COUNTRY TODAY?"

	Oct. 15-18, 1982	Oct. 7-10, 1983	Feb. 10-13, 1984	Jan. 25-28, 1985	July 11-14, 1986	Apr. 10-13, 1987	Sept. 9-11, 1988	May 4-7, 1989	July 19-22, 1990	Mar. 7-10, 1991	Mar. 26-29, 1992	Jan. 8-11, 1993	Jan. 15-17, 1994	Jan. 16-18, 1995	May 9-12, 1996	Jan. 10-13, 1997	Apr. 17-19, 1998	Sept. 14-15, 1998	May 23-24, 1999	Mar. 10-12, 2000	Jan. 10-14, 2001
High cost of living; inflation; taxes	18%	12%	10%	11%	4%	5%	2%	3%	2%	2%	8%	4%	4%	7%	11%	6%	7%	5%	3%	13%	6%
Unemployment	61	41	29	20	23	13	9	6	3	8	25	22	18	15	13	NA	5	4	4	2	4
International problems; foreign affairs	2	7	11	NA	NA	NA	4	4	NA	1	3	8	3	2	4	3	4	6	3	4	4
Crime; violence	3	5	4	4	3	3	2	6	1	2	5	9	37	27	25	23	20	10	17	13	9
Guns/gun control	NA	NA	NA	NA	NA	NA	NA	NA	NA	NA	NA	NA	NA	(a)	NA	NA	1	(a)	10	7	1
Fear of war/nuclear war; international tensions	3	14	11	27	22	23	5	2	1	2	NA	NA	NA	(a)	NA	NA	NA	NA	2	NA	(a)
Ethics, moral, family decline	3	5	7	2	3	5	1	5	2	2	5	7	8	6	14	9	16	15	18	15	13
Excessive government spending; Federal budget deficit	4	4	12	18	13	11	12	7	21	8	8	13	5	14	15	8	5	2	1	4	1
Dissatisfaction with government	3	2	2	NA	NA	5	NA	2	1	NA	8	5	6	5	12	7	8	14	5	11	9
Economy (general)	11	4	5	6	7	10	12	8	7	24	42	35	14	10	12	21	6	12	3	6	7
Poverty; hunger; homelessness	NA	NA	NA	6	6	5	7	10	7	10	15	15	11	10	7	10	10	6	7	5	4
Drugs; drug abuse	NA	NA	NA	2	8	11	11	27	18	11	8	6	9	6	10	17	12	9	5	5	7
Trade deficit; trade relations	NA	NA	NA	NA	NA	NA	3	3	1	1	4	3	2	1	2	1	1	1	1	1	(a)
Education; quality of education	NA	NA	NA	NA	NA	NA	2	3	2	2	8	8	7	5	13	10	13	13	11	16	12
Environment; pollution	NA	NA	NA	NA	NA	NA	NA	4	5	2	3	3	1	1	3	1	2	1	2	2	2
AIDS	NA	NA	NA	NA	NA	NA	NA	1	2	(a)	3	2	2	1	(a)	1	1	(a)	(a)	(a)	(a)
Abortion	NA	NA	NA	NA	NA	NA	NA	(a)	NA	NA	NA	NA	NA	1	0	1	1	1	(a)	2	1
Health care	NA	4	4	NA	NA	NA	NA	NA	NA	NA	12	18	20	12	10	7	6	6	5	8	7
No opinion; don't know	2	4	4	3	3	4	12	7	5	NA	2	2	2	7	7	6	4	8	2	6	8

Note: Exact wording of response categories varies across surveys. Multiple responses are possible; the Source records up to three problems per respondent. Some problems mentioned by a small percentage of respondents are not included in the table. Sample sizes vary from year to year; the data for 2001 are based on telephone interviews with a randomly selected national sample of 1,004 adults, 18 years of age and older, conducted Jan. 10-14, 2001.
[a]Less than 0.5%.

SOURCE: Results of polling conducted by The Gallup Organization, Inc., Princeton, NJ, adapted for "Table 2.1: Attitudes toward the most important problem facing the country, United States, 1982–2001," Sourcebook of Criminal Justice Statistics 2000, U.S. Department of Justice, Bureau of Justice Statistics, Washington, DC, 2000

TABLE 9.9

TABLE 9.10

Attitudes toward level of crime in the United States, selected years 1989–2000

QUESTION: "IS THERE MORE CRIME IN THE U.S. THAN THERE WAS A YEAR AGO, OR LESS?"

	More	Less	Same[a]	No opinion
1989	84%	5%	5%	6%
1990	84	3	7	6
1992	89	3	4	4
1993	87	4	5	4
1996	71	15	8	6
1997	64	25	6	5
1998	52	35	8	5
2000	47	41	7	5

[a] Response volunteered.

SOURCE: Results of polling conducted by The Gallup Organization, Inc., Princeton, NJ, adapted for "Table 2.36: Attitudes toward level of crime in the United States, United States, selected years 1989–2000," *Sourcebook of Criminal Justice Statistics 2000*, U.S. Department of Justice, Bureau of Justice Statistics, Washington, DC, 2000

Attitudes toward level of crime in own area, selected years 1972–2000

QUESTION: "IS THERE MORE CRIME IN YOUR AREA THAN THERE WAS A YEAR AGO, OR LESS?"

	More	Less	Same[a]	No opinion
1972	51%	10%	27%	12%
1975	50	12	29	9
1977	43	17	32	8
1981	54	8	29	9
1983	37	17	36	10
January 1989	47	21	27	5
June 1989	53	18	22	7
1990	51	18	24	8
1992	54	19	23	4
1996	46	24	25	5
1997	46	32	20	2
1998	31	48	16	5
2000	34	46	15	5

Note: Percents may not add to 100 because of rounding.
[a] Response volunteered.

SOURCE: Results of polling conducted by The Gallup Organization, Inc., Princeton, NJ, adapted for "Table 2.38: Attitudes toward level of crime in own area, United States, selected years 1972–2000," *Sourcebook of Criminal Justice Statistics 2000*, U.S. Department of Justice, Bureau of Justice Statistics, Washington, DC, 2000

percent of the youngest respondents (18 to 29 years of age) and 49 percent of the oldest (65 or older) felt that there was more crime in the United States than the year before. Those who were less educated and had more limited earnings were more likely to feel that there was more crime in the United States than the year prior.

Some 34 percent of respondents in another Gallup Poll said that they believed there was more crime in their area in 2000 than there was a year ago. This is up slightly from the 31 percent who perceived more crime in their area in 1998, but well below the over 50 percent during the years from 1989 to 1992 and the 46 percent in 1996 and 1997. (See Table 9.10.)

Feeling Afraid

In 2000 the Gallup Poll found that about one in three Americans (34 percent) was afraid to walk alone at night. The same proportion of Americans felt that way in 1965. Through the 1970s, 1980s, and early 1990s the proportion increased to between 40 and 45 percent, and has declined steadily since 1993. (See Table 9.11.)

Asked if they engaged in selective behaviors because of concern over crime, 56 percent of Gallup Poll respondents in 2000 reported avoiding going to certain places or neighborhoods, 39 percent had special locks installed in their homes, 32 percent kept a dog for protection, 23 percent had a burglar alarm, and 22 percent reported buying a gun for protection. (See Table 9.12.)

JUVENILES AND CRIME

Worrying About Crime

Each year the Institute for Social Research at the University of Michigan conducts the *Monitoring the Future*

TABLE 9.11

Respondents reporting fear of walking alone and feeling unsafe at home at night, selected years 1965–2000

QUESTION: "IS THERE ANY AREA NEAR WHERE YOU LIVE—THAT IS, WITHIN A MILE—WHERE YOU WOULD BE AFRAID TO WALK ALONE AT NIGHT? HOW ABOUT WHEN YOU'RE AT HOME AT NIGHT—DO YOU FEEL SAFE AND SECURE, OR NOT?"

	Afraid to walk alone at night	Feel unsafe at home at night
1965	34%	NA
1967	31	NA
1972	42	17%
1975	45	20
1977	45	15
1981	45	16
1983	45	16
1989	43	10
1990	40	10
1992	44	11
1993	43	NA
1996	39	9
1997	38	9
2000	34	NA

Note: Sample sizes vary from year to year.

SOURCE: Results of polling conducted by The Gallup Organization, Inc., Princeton, NJ, adapted for "Table 2.40: Respondents reporting fear of walking alone and feeling unsafe at home at night, United States, selected years 1965–2000," *Sourcebook of Criminal Justice Statistics 2000*, U.S. Department of Justice, Bureau of Justice Statistics, Washington, DC, 2000

survey of students and young adults. Primarily, the survey asks questions about social behaviors, such as sexual activity, drug use, violence, and crime. In 2000, 83.5 percent of high school seniors said that they often or sometimes worried about crime and violence. Female stu-

TABLE 9.12

Respondents reporting whether they engaged in selected behaviors because of concern over crime, 2000

QUESTION: "NEXT, I'M GOING TO READ SOME THINGS PEOPLE DO BECAUSE OF THEIR CONCERN OVER CRIME. PLEASE TELL ME WHICH, IF ANY, OF THESE THINGS YOU, YOURSELF, DO OR HAVE DONE."

	Yes	No
Avoid going to certain places or neighborhoods you might otherwise want to go to	56%	44%
Had special locks installed in your home	39	60
Keep a dog for protection	32	68
Had a burglar alarm installed in your home	23	76
Bought a gun for protection of yourself or your home	22	78
Carry mace or pepper spray	18	82
Taken a self-defense course	18	82
Carry a gun for defense	12	87
Carry a knife for defense	10	90

Note: The "no opinion" category has been omitted; therefore percents may not sum to 100.

SOURCE: Results of polling conducted by The Gallup Organization, Inc., Princeton, NJ, adapted for "Table 2.43: Respondents reporting whether they engaged in selected behaviors because of concern over crime, United States, 2000," *Sourcebook of Criminal Justice Statistics 2000*, U.S. Department of Justice, Bureau of Justice Statistics, Washington, DC, 2000

dents (90.2 percent) were more likely to worry than were male students (76 percent). African American students (91.1 percent) were more worried about crime and violence than white students (82.6 percent). These proportions were generally consistent with results from previous years back to 1988. (See Table 9.13.)

According to the same study, when asked how often they worried about certain major problems facing the nation, high school seniors in the class of 2000 said they worried about crime and violence the most (83.5 percent), followed by drug abuse (60.9 percent), hunger and poverty (54.4 percent), and pollution (53.3 percent). From 1988 to 2000 crime and violence was the number one worry of high school seniors participating in the study.

Juvenile Punishment

In 1995 the Survey Research Program of the College of Criminal Justice at Sam Houston State University (Huntsville, Texas) asked for opinions about trying juveniles as adults. A significant majority of respondents said they believed that a juvenile should be tried as an adult if the juvenile was charged with:

• A serious property crime (62.6 percent)

• Sale of illegal drugs (69.1 percent)

• A serious violent crime (86.5 percent)

Persons with less than a high school diploma (71.6 percent) were most likely to feel that juvenile property offenders should be tried in adult courts. Males (68.3 per-

cent), persons over age 60 (68.2 percent), and Hispanics (66.2 percent) were more likely than others to approve of treating juvenile property offenders as adults. For juveniles charged with selling illegal drugs or murder, the responses were more uniform.

In 2000, 65 percent of respondents to a national Gallup Poll thought that juveniles between the ages of 14 and 17 who commit violent crimes should be tried as adults. Male respondents were more likely to feel that way than females (69 percent to 61 percent, respectively). Those 65 years and older were less likely to believe juveniles over 14 should be treated as adults (61 percent) than were those ages 50 to 64 (67 percent). Sixty-eight percent of those interviewed who had "some college" education believed juveniles should be tried as adults, while only 55 percent of those with post-college graduate education felt that way. (See Table 9.14.)

THE DEATH PENALTY

A Gallup Poll found that although a majority of Americans still favored the death penalty in 2000, the percentage of those supporting the death penalty was 66 percent, the lowest level since 1981. (See Figure 9.2.) In the same poll, some 91 percent of respondents said they believed that in the past 20 years at least one person sentenced to death was innocent. Still, a poll conducted by the National Law Journal in 2000 found that almost half of potential jurors (47 percent) in 2000 agreed that the current procedure for reviewing death penalty sentences is adequate. (See Figure 9.3.)

CONFIDENCE IN THE CRIMINAL JUSTICE SYSTEM

Each year the Gallup Organization, Inc., asks the American people about their confidence in the major institutions of society. In 2000 only 24 percent of those polled said that they had a great deal or quite a lot of confidence in the criminal justice system. (See Table 9.15.) The question about the criminal justice system was first asked in 1993, and responses have remained relatively stable through 2000.

In 2000 one-third of all respondents had either very little or no confidence in the criminal justice system. The responses were remarkably uniform across all demographic groups. Fewer whites (31 percent) than African Americans (37 percent) had little or no confidence in the system. Fewer Republicans (28 percent) than Democrats (32 percent) expressed a lack of confidence in the criminal justice system. The poor (40 percent) were more likely than the rich (27 percent) to feel little or no confidence in the system.

CONFIDENCE IN THE POLICE

In the 2000 Gallup Poll, Americans expressed much more confidence in the police than they did in the criminal justice system. Fifty-seven percent stated they had a great

TABLE 9.13

High school seniors reporting that they worry about crime and violence, 1988–2000

QUESTION: "OF ALL THE PROBLEMS FACING THE NATION TODAY, HOW OFTEN DO YOU WORRY ABOUT. . .CRIME AND VIOLENCE?"

(Percent responding "sometimes" or "often")

	Class of 1988 (N=3,326)	Class of 1989 (N=2,849)	Class of 1990 (N=2,595)	Class of 1991 (N=2,595)	Class of 1992 (N=2,736)	Class of 1993 (N=2,807)	Class of 1994 (N=2,664)	Class of 1995 (N=2,646)	Class of 1996 (N=2,502)	Class of 1997 (N=2,651)	Class of 1998 (N=2,621)	Class of 1999 (N=2,348)	Class of 2000 (N=2,204)
Total	**83.9%**	**86.3%**	**88.8%**	**88.1%**	**91.6%**	**90.8%**	**92.7%**	**90.2%**	**90.1%**	**86.5%**	**84.4%**	**81.8%**	**83.5%**
Sex													
Male	76.0	80.9	84.8	82.6	87.6	85.7	88.4	85.8	84.8	79.4	76.5	74.4	76.0
Female	91.8	92.2	93.4	93.6	95.7	95.6	96.5	95.1	95.4	93.7	91.7	89.5	90.2
Race													
White	82.8	84.6	88.1	86.6	90.5	89.4	92.9	90.0	89.5	84.5	83.5	80.8	82.6
Black	88.2	91.8	92.7	94.5	96.9	95.1	90.7	93.0	92.9	90.4	85.7	84.8	91.1
Region													
Northeast	81.9	83.0	87.7	86.0	92.0	90.6	91.0	91.7	89.4	83.2	83.1	85.4	82.2
North Central	81.7	83.0	87.0	88.8	87.6	90.2	93.2	86.7	87.4	85.1	80.7	80.0	84.6
South	86.1	89.4	90.4	88.4	93.8	91.2	93.3	91.3	91.1	88.7	87.0	81.1	85.8
West	85.4	88.2	89.4	89.0	93.0	91.4	92.4	92.2	93.4	88.2	85.4	82.0	79.3
College plans													
Yes	85.4	88.0	89.8	89.9	93.1	92.4	94.1	92.6	91.6	88.4	85.3	84.5	85.0
No	80.8	82.8	88.0	83.9	87.7	85.8	89.4	84.0	86.2	80.7	82.2	72.3	77.9
Lifetime illicit drug use													
None	85.8	88.8	90.6	90.7	92.9	91.9	94.1	91.8	90.5	89.1	86.8	84.3	85.4
Marijuana only	83.9	86.6	87.1	85.4	89.6	91.1	91.5	90.9	91.9	85.7	82.3	82.8	85.8
Few pills	83.7	85.2	87.6	86.6	89.4	90.7	95.6	92.6	91.0	88.3	84.6	84.3	79.1
More pills	81.2	81.7	85.7	84.8	90.6	87.4	89.5	84.1	87.4	81.0	83.3	75.6	79.9

Note: These data are from a series of nationwide surveys of high school seniors conducted by the Monitoring the Future Project at the University of Michigan's Institute for Social Research from 1975 through 2000. The survey design is a multistage random sample of high school seniors in public and private schools throughout the continental United States. All percentages reported are based on weighted cases; the Ns that are shown in the tables refer to the number of weighted cases. Data are given for those who identify themselves as white or Caucasian and those who identify themselves as black or African-American because these are the two largest racial/ethnic subgroups in the population. Data are not given for the other ethnic categories because each of these groups comprises a small portion of the sample in any given year. "College plans" distinguishes those seniors who expect to graduate from a 4-year college from those who expect to receive some college training or none. The four drug use categories are based on an index of seriousness of involvement. The "pills" category indicates use of any of a number of drugs including some that usually are not taken in pill form. Respondents indicating the use of one or more of a number of illicit drugs but who had not used any one class of them on three or more occasions and did not use heroin at all fall into the "few pills" category. Respondents indicating such use on three or more occasions and who did not use heroin at all fall into the "more pills" category. Respondents reporting heroin use were included in a separate category that is not presented here due to the small number of respondents indicating such use.

Response categories were "never," "seldom," "sometimes," and "often."

SOURCE: Lloyd D. Johnston, Jerald G. Bachman, and Patrick M. O'Malley, *Monitoring the Future 1998*, University of Michigan, Institute for Social Research, Ann Arbor, MI, as updated in "Table 2.87: High school seniors reporting that they worry about crime and violence, by sex, race, region, college plans, and illicit drug use, United States, 1988–2000," *Sourcebook of Criminal Justice Statistics 2000*, U.S. Department of Justice, Bureau of Justice Statistics, Washington, DC, 2000

deal or quite a lot of confidence in the police, and 31 percent said they had some confidence. Only 12 percent claimed to have little or no confidence in the police. (See Table 9.16.)

Blacks (38 percent) were significantly less likely than whites (59 percent) to have a high level of confidence in the police. Rural dwellers (62 percent) and Republicans (67 percent) were more likely than urban residents (51 percent) and Democrats (57 percent) to express high levels of confidence. A strong majority in all demographic groups had at least some confidence in the police.

GUNS

Guns in the Home

In 2000, 42 percent of Americans told the Gallup Poll they had guns in their homes, up from 36 percent in 1999. The proportion of gun ownership stayed relatively stable the last four decades of the twentieth century, ranging

from a low of 36 percent in 1999 to a high of 51 percent in October 1993. (See Table 9.17.) A survey by the National Opinion Research Center (The Roper Center for Public Opinion Research, University of Connecticut, 2000) reached a different conclusion about levels of gun ownership in the nation. The Roper survey found that about 32 percent of Americans—compared to 42 percent in the Gallup poll—had a firearm in their home in 2000.

In 2000 the most likely people to own guns were male (42 percent), high school graduates (36 percent), aged 50 or older (38 percent), making $50,000 or more (43 percent), and living in the South or Midwest (37 percent).

Laws Governing Firearm Sales

The regulation of gun sales remained a controversial issue for the nation's citizens through the 1990s. In 2000 the Gallup Poll reported that 62 percent of those polled

TABLE 9.14

Attitudes toward the treatment of juveniles who commit violent crimes, 2000

QUESTION: "IN YOUR VIEW, HOW SHOULD JUVENILES BETWEEN THE AGES OF 14 AND 17 WHO COMMIT VIOLENT CRIMES BE TREATED IN THE CRIMINAL JUSTICE SYSTEM—SHOULD THEY BE TREATED THE SAME AS ADULTS, OR SHOULD THEY BE GIVEN MORE LENIENT TREATMENT IN A JUVENILE COURT?"

	Same as adults	More lenient treatment	Tougher[a]	Depends[a]	Don't know/ refused
National	65%	24%	1%	9%	1%
Sex					
Male	69	21	1	8	1
Female	61	27	2	9	1
Race					
White	67	22	1	9	1
Black	52	35	2	10	1
Nonwhite[b]	55	33	3	8	1
Age					
18 to 29 years	65	25	2	7	1
30 to 49 years	66	23	2	8	1
50 to 64 years	67	22	1	8	2
50 years and older	64	23	1	10	2
65 years and older	61	23	1	11	4
Education					
College postgraduate	55	32	3	10	(c)
College graduate	63	29	0	8	0
Some college	68	21	1	9	1
High school graduate or less	66	22	2	8	2
Income					
$75,000 and over	60	27	3	9	1
$50,000 to $74,999	69	20	2	9	0
$30,000 to $49,999	68	20	2	9	1
$20,000 to $29,999	61	24	0	13	2
Under $20,000	64	28	(c)	6	2
Community					
Urban area	59	29	1	11	(c)
Suburban area	69	20	2	7	2
Rural area	65	24	1	8	2
Region					
East	60	26	2	9	3
Midwest	71	19	(c)	8	2
South	62	26	2	10	(c)
West	68	23	1	7	1
Politics					
Republican	67	19	2	10	2
Democrat	60	31	1	6	2
Independent	68	19	2	10	1

[a]Response volunteered.
[b]Includes black respondents.
[c]Less than 0.5%.

SOURCE: Results of polling conducted by The Gallup Organization, Inc., Princeton, NJ, adapted for "Table 2.58: Attitudes toward the treatment of juveniles who commit violent crimes, by demographic characteristics, United States, 2000," *Sourcebook of Criminal Justice Statistics 2000*, U.S. Department of Justice, Bureau of Justice Statistics, Washington, DC, 2000

TABLE 9.15

Reported confidence in the criminal justice system, 2000

QUESTION: "I AM GOING TO READ YOU A LIST OF INSTITUTIONS IN AMERICAN SOCIETY. PLEASE TELL ME HOW MUCH CONFIDENCE YOU, YOURSELF, HAVE IN EACH ONE—A GREAT DEAL, QUITE A LOT, SOME, OR VERY LITTLE: THE CRIMINAL JUSTICE SYSTEM?"

	Great deal/quite a lot	Some	Very little	None[a]
National	24%	42%	30%	3%
Sex				
Male	28	38	32	2
Female	21	45	28	4
Race				
White	25	42	29	2
Black	18	43	28	9
Nonwhite[b]	18	43	30	7
Age				
18 to 29 years	28	39	28	4
30 to 49 years	22	43	31	4
50 to 64 years	20	45	33	2
50 years and older	24	43	29	2
65 years and older	28	40	25	2
Education				
College postgraduate	25	44	29	1
College graduate	27	48	22	2
Some college	20	46	30	3
High school graduate or less	26	37	31	4
Income				
$75,000 and over	24	48	25	2
$50,000 and over[c]	22	47	29	2
$30,000 to $49,999	28	38	31	3
$20,000 to $29,999	25	51	19	4
Under $20,000	25	33	35	5
Community				
Urban area	23	40	31	4
Suburban area	27	40	30	2
Rural area	20	46	29	3
Region				
East	25	43	27	4
Midwest	21	41	35	2
South	28	40	27	3
West	20	45	30	4
Politics				
Republican	28	42	27	1
Democrat	25	43	28	4
Independent	20	41	34	4

Note: The "don't know/refused" category has been omitted; therefore percents may not sum to 100.

[a]Response volunteered.
[b]Includes black respondents.
[c]Includes $75,000 and over category.

SOURCE: Results of polling conducted by The Gallup Organization, Inc., Princeton, NJ, adapted for "Table 2.14: Reported confidence in the criminal justice system, by demographic characteristics, United States, 2000, "*Sourcebook of Criminal Justice Statistics 2000*," U.S. Department of Justice, Bureau of Justice Statistics, Washington, DC, 2000

---

felt that laws covering firearm sales should be stricter. Thirty-one percent favored keeping the laws as they were, and only 5 percent believed the gun laws should be less strict. Seventy-two percent of females and 81 percent of Democrats supported stricter laws, compared to 52 percent of males and 44 percent of Republicans. Sixty-seven percent of persons living in urban areas felt that firearm sales laws should be stricter. (See Table 9.18.)

FIGURE 9.2

Public opinion about the death penalty

QUESTION: "ARE YOU IN FAVOR OF THE DEATH PENALTY FOR A PERSON CONVICTED OF MURDER?

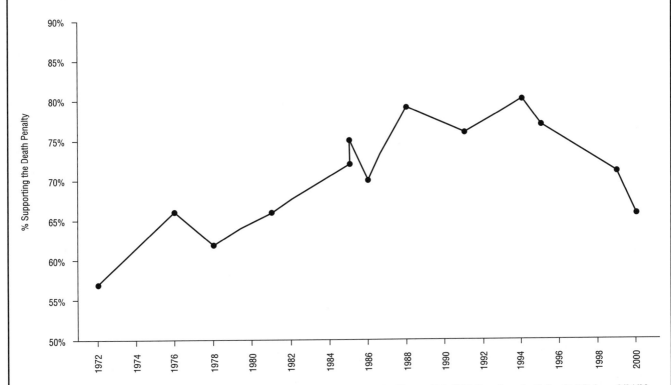

SOURCE: "Public Opinion About the Death Penalty," Death Penalty Information Center, Washington, DC, 2002. Data from the Gallup Poll Release 2/24/00 [Online] http://www.deathpenaltyinfo.org/Polls.html#2/24/00 [Accessed May, 06, 2002]

FIGURE 9.3

Opinion on current procedure for reviewing death penalty sentences

DO YOU AGREE THAT THE CURRENT PROCEDURE FOR REVIEWING DEATH PENALTY SENTENCES IS ADEQUATE?

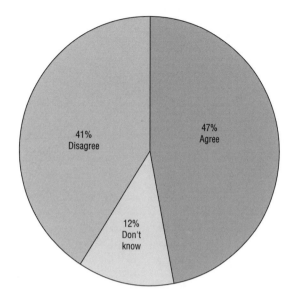

SOURCE: "Do you agree that the current procedure for reviewing death penalty sentences is adequate?" Death Penalty Information Center, Washington, DC, 2002. Data from The National Law Journal, 12/11/00 [Online] http://www.deathpenaltyinfo.org/Polls.html#NLJ/DQ [Accessed May, 06, 2002]

TABLE 9.17

Respondents reporting having a gun in their home, selected years 1959–2000

QUESTION: "DO YOU HAVE A GUN IN YOUR HOME?"

	Yes	No
1959	49%	51%
1965	48	52
1968	50	50
1972	43	55
1975	44	54
1980	45	53
1983	40	58
1985	44	55
1989	47	51
1990	47	52
1991	46	53
March 1993	48	51
October 1993	51	48
1996	38	60
1997	42	57
1999	36	62
2000	42	57

Note: Sample sizes vary from year to year; the data for 2000 are based on telephone interviews with a randomly selected national sample of 1,006 adults, 18 years of age and older, conducted Apr. 7-9, 2000. The "don't know/refused" category has been omitted; therefore percents may not sum to 100.

SOURCE: George Gallup, Jr. and Alec Gallup, *The Gallup Poll Monthly*, number 416, May 2000, page 53, adapted for "Table 2.68: Respondents reporting having a gun in their home, United States, selected years 1959–2000," *Sourcebook of Criminal Justice Statistics 2000*, U.S. Department of Justice, Bureau of Justice Statistics, Washington, DC, 2000

TABLE 9.16

Reported confidence in the police, 2000

QUESTION: "I AM GOING TO READ YOU A LIST OF INSTITUTIONS IN AMERICAN SOCIETY. PLEASE TELL ME HOW MUCH CONFIDENCE YOU, YOURSELF, HAVE IN EACH ONE—A GREAT DEAL, QUITE A LOT, SOME, OR VERY LITTLE: THE POLICE?"

	Great deal/quite a lot	Some	Very little	None[a]
National	57%	31%	11%	1%
Sex				
Male	56	30	11	2
Female	58	31	11	(b)
Race				
White	59	29	10	1
Black	38	43	19	0
Nonwhite[c]	44	39	16	1
Age				
18 to 29 years	45	27	25	1
30 to 49 years	59	32	8	1
50 to 64 years	60	31	7	2
50 years and older	60	31	8	1
65 years and older	60	31	9	0
Education				
College postgraduate	57	34	7	2
College graduate	61	30	8	1
Some college	56	31	13	(b)
High school graduate or less	57	29	12	1
Income				
$75,000 and over	66	28	4	(b)
$50,000 and over[d]	62	30	7	(b)
$30,000 to $49,999	58	32	8	2
$20,000 to $29,999	57	29	13	1
Under $20,000	48	32	19	1
Community				
Urban area	51	34	13	2
Suburban area	58	31	9	1
Rural area	62	25	13	(b)
Region				
East	53	34	10	2
Midwest	57	29	13	1
South	57	31	10	2
West	59	28	12	0
Politics				
Republican	67	26	7	(b)
Democrat	57	31	11	1
Independent	47	35	15	2

Note: The "don't know/refused" category has been omitted; therefore percents may not sum to 100.

[a]Response volunteered.
[b]Less than 0.5%.
[c]Includes black respondents.
[d]Includes $75,000 and over category.

SOURCE: Results of polling conducted by The Gallup Organization, Inc., Princeton, NJ, adapted for "Table 2.16: Reported confidence in the police, by demographic characteristics, United States, 2001," *Sourcebook of Criminal Justice Statistics 2000*, U.S. Department of Justice, Bureau of Justice Statistics, Washington, DC, 2000

TABLE 9.18

Attitudes toward laws covering the sale of firearms, 2000

QUESTION: "IN GENERAL, DO YOU FEEL THAT THE LAWS COVERING THE SALE OF FIREARMS SHOULD BE MADE MORE STRICT, LESS STRICT, OR KEPT AS THEY ARE NOW?"

	More strict	Less strict	Kept as they are now
National	62%	5%	31%
Sex			
Male	52	8	39
Female	72	2	24
Race			
White	61	5	32
Black	84	0	15
Nonwhite[a]	74	2	23
Age			
18 to 29 years	69	6	24
30 to 49 years	64	5	29
50 to 64 years	49	6	44
50 years and older	57	4	37
65 years and older	64	2	31
Education			
College postgraduate	68	6	25
College graduate	67	7	24
Some college	59	5	35
High school graduate or less	62	4	32
Income			
$75,000 and over	65	5	29
$50,000 and over[b]	62	6	31
$30,000 to $49,999	62	5	33
$20,000 to $29,999	62	4	33
Under $20,000	70	6	21
Community			
Urban area	67	5	27
Suburban area	65	5	28
Rural area	53	4	42
Region			
East	76	3	20
Midwest	59	5	35
South	59	5	35
West	57	7	33
Politics			
Republican	44	9	44
Democrat	81	2	16
Independent	61	4	33

Note: The "no opinion" category has been omitted; therefore percents may not sum to 100.

[a] Includes black respondents.
[b] Includes $75,000 and over category.

SOURCE: "Table 2.76: Attitudes toward laws covering the sale of firearms, by demographic characteristics, United States, 2000," in *Sourcebook of Criminal Justice Statistics 2000*, U.S. Department of Justice, Bureau of Justice Statistics, Washington, DC, 2000. Data from the Gallup Organization, Inc.

IMPORTANT NAMES AND ADDRESSES

American Civil Liberties Union
125 Broad Street, 18th Floor
New York, NY 10004
(212) 234-3005
E-mail: infoaclu@aclu.org
URL: http://www.aclu.org

Anti-Defamation League
823 United Nations Plaza
New York, NY 10017
(212) 885-7700
FAX (212) 867-0779
E-mail: webmaster@adl.org
URL: http://www.adl.org

Bureau of Alcohol, Tobacco, and Firearms
650 Massachusetts Ave. NW, Room 8290
Washington, DC 20226
(202) 927-7970
FAX (202) 927-7756
E-mail: atfmail@atfhq.atf.treas.gov
URL: http://www.atf.treas.gov

Bureau of Engraving and Printing
Department of the Treasury
14th and C Streets SW
Washington, DC 20228
(202) 874-3019
URL: http://www.bep.treas.gov

Bureau of Justice Statistics
810 7th Street NW
Washington, DC 20531
(202) 307-0765
E-mail: askbjs@ojp.usdoj.gov
URL: http://www.ojp.usdoj.gov/bjs

Bureau of Labor Statistics
Postal Square Building
2 Massachusetts Ave., NE
Washington, DC 20212-0001
(202) 691-5200
Fax on Demand: (202) 691-6325
E-mail: feedback@bls.gov
URL: http://www.bls.gov/home.htm

Coalition for Juvenile Justice
1211 Connecticut Ave. NW, Suite 414
Washington, DC 20036-2072
(202) 467-0864
FAX (202) 887-0738
E-mail: info@juvjustice.org
URL: http://www.juvjustice.org

Drug Enforcement Administration
2401 Jefferson Davis Highway
Mailstop AXS
Alexandria, VA 22301
(202) 307-1000
FAX (202) 307-7335
URL: http://www.usdoj.gov/dea

Federal Bureau of Investigation
935 Pennsylvania Ave., NW #7116
Washington, DC 20535-0002
(202) 324-3444
FAX (202) 324-4705
URL: http://www.fbi.gov

**Federal Bureau of Investigation:
Terrorism and Violent Crime**
935 Pennsylvania Ave., NW, #5222
Washington, DC 20535-0002
(202) 324-4664
FAX (202) 324-1524
http://www.fbi.gov

Federal Bureau of Prisons
320 1st St. NW
Washington, DC 20534
(202) 307-3198
E-mail: webmaster@bop.gov
URL: http://www.bop.gov

Federal Trade Commission
600 Pennsylvania Ave., NW
Washington, DC 20580
(202) 326-2222
URL: http://www.ftc.gov

Highway Loss Data Institute
1005 North Glebe Rd., Suite 800
Arlington, VA 22201
(703) 247-1600
FAX (703) 247-1595
URL: http://www.hwysafety.org

**Internal Revenue Service Criminal
Investigation Division**
Washington, DC 20066-6096
(202) 283-9665
(800) 829-0433
URL: http://www.ustreas.gov/irs/ci

**National Association for the Advancement
of Colored People**
4805 Mt. Hope Drive
Baltimore, MD 21215
(800) NAACP-98
E-mail: dcbureau@naacp.org
URL: http://www.naacp.org

National Center for Victims of Crime
2000 M Street NW, Suite 480
Washington, DC 20036
(202) 467-8700
FAX (202) 467-8701
E-mail: webmaster@ncvc.org
URL: http://www.ncvc.org

National Conference of State Legislatures
1560 Broadway, #700
Denver, CO 80202
(303) 830-2200
E-mail: Info@ncsl.org
URL: http://www.ncsl.org

National Consumers League
1701 K St. NW, Suite 1200
Washington, DC 20006
(202) 835-3323
FAX (202) 835-0747
E-mail: info@nclnet.org
URL: http://www.nclnet.org

National Crime Prevention Council
1000 Connecticut Avenue, NW, 13th Floor
Washington, DC 20036
(202) 466-6272
FAX (202) 296-1356
URL: http://www.ncpc.org

National Criminal Justice Association
720 7th Street, 3rd Floor
Washington, DC 20001-3716
(202) 628-8550
FAX (202) 628-0080
E-mail: info@ncja.org
URL: http://www.ncja.org

**National Criminal Justice
Reference Service**
P.O. Box 6000
Rockville, MD 20849-6000
(301) 519-5500
FAX (301) 519-5212
(800) 627-6872
E-mail: askncjrs@ncjrs.org
URL: http://ncjrs.org/

**National Highway Traffic
Safety Administration**
400 7th St. SW
Washington, DC 20590
(202) 366-0123
(800) 424-9393
URL: http://www.nhtsa.dot.gov

National Institute of Justice
810 7th St. NW
Washington, DC 20531
(202) 307-2942
FAX (202) 307-6394
URL: http://www.ojp.usdoj.gov/nij

**National Organization for
Victim Assistance**
1730 Park Rd. NW
Washington, DC 20010
(202) 232-6682
FAX (202) 462-2255
Information Hotline: (800) 879-6682
E-mail: nova@try-nova.org
URL: http://www.try-nova.org

National Youth Gang Center
P.O. Box 12729
Tallahasee, FL 32317
(850) 385-0600
E-mail: nygc@iir.com
URL: http://www.iir.com/nygc

Office for Victims of Crime
810 7th St. NW, 8th Floor
Washington, DC 20531
(202) 307-5983
FAX (202) 514-6383
E-mail: askovp@ojp.usdoj.gov
URL: http://www.ojp.usdoj.gov/ovc

**Office of Juvenile Justice and
Delinquency Prevention**
810 7th St. NW, 6th floor
Washington, DC 20531
(202) 307-5911
FAX (202) 307-2093
Juvenile Justice Clearinghouse (800) 638-8736
E-mail: askjj@ncjrs.org
URL: http://www.ojjdp.ncjrs.org

Office of National Drug Control Policy
Drug Policy Information Clearinghouse
P.O. Box 6000
Rockville, MD 20849-6000
(800) 666-3332
FAX: (301) 519-5212
Email: ondcp@ncjrs.org
URL: http://www.whitehousedrugpolicy.gov

The Sentencing Project
514 10th St. NW
Washington, DC 20004
(202) 628-0871
FAX (202) 628-1091
E-mail: staff@sentencingproject.org
URL: http://www.sentencingproject.org

Southern Poverty Law Center
400 Washington Ave.
Montgomery, AL 36104
(334) 956-8200
URL: http://www.splcenter.org

Supreme Court of the United States
One 1st St. NE
Washington, DC 20543

(202) 479-3211
URL: http://www.supremecourtus.gov

U.S. Census Bureau
Washington, DC 20233
(301) 457-1722
E-mail: webmaster@census.gov
URL: http://www.census.gov

U.S. Department of Justice
950 Pennsylvania Ave., NW
Washington, DC 20530-0001
(202) 353-1555
E-mail: askdoj@usdoj.gov
URL: http://www.usdoj.gov

U.S. Postal Inspection Service
P.O. Box 96096
Washington, DC 20066-6096
(202) 636-2300
FAX: (202) 636-2287
URL: http://www.usps.com/postalinspectors

U.S. Secret Service
Office of Liaison and Public Affairs
950 H Street NW, Suite 8400
Washington, DC 20223
(202) 406-5708
URL: http://www.treas.gov/usss

U.S. Securities and Exchange Commission
450 5th St., NW
Washington, DC 20549
(202) 942-7040
E-mail: help@sec.gov
URL: http://www.sec.gov

U.S. Sentencing Commission
Office of Public Affairs
1 Columbus Circle NE
Washington, DC 20002-8002
(202) 502-4500
E-mail: pubaffairs@ussc.gov
URL: http://www.ussc.gov

Violence Policy Center
1140 19th St., NW, #600
Washington, DC 20036
E-mail: info@vpc.org
URL: http://www.vpc.org

RESOURCES

The various agencies of the U.S. Department of Justice are the major sources of crime and justice data in America. The Bureau of Justice Statistics (BJS) compiles statistics on virtually every area of crime and reports that data in a number of publications. The annual BJS *Sourcebook of Criminal Justice Statistics*, prepared by the Hindelang Criminal Justice Research Center, State University of New York at Albany, is a comprehensive compilation of criminal justice statistics. The annual BJS *National Crime Victimization Survey* provides data for several studies, the most important of which is *Criminal Victimization in the United States*. Other valuable BJS publications include *Federal Law Enforcement Officers, 2000* (2001), *Prison and Jail Inmates at Midyear 2001* (2002), *Age Patterns in Violent Victimizations, 1976–2000* (2002), *Mental Health Treatment in State Prisons, 2000* (2002), *Prisoners in 2000* (2001), and *Drug Crime Facts* (2001).

The Federal Bureau of Investigation (FBI) collects crime data from state law enforcement agencies through its Uniform Crime Reports program. The FBI annual *Crime in the United States* is the most important source of information on crime reported to law enforcement agencies. Other important annual publications include *Law Enforcement Officers Killed and Assaulted, Terrorism in the United States, Hate Crime Statistics*, and *The Measurement of White Collar Crime Using Uniform Crime Reporting (UCR) Data*.

The Office of Juvenile Justice and Delinquency Prevention (OJJDP) published the following: *Short- and Long-Term Consequences of Adolescent Victimization* (2002), *Juvenile Court Statistics, 1998* (2001), *Highlights of the 2000 National Youth Gang Survey* (2002), *National Youth Gang Survey Trends, 1996 to 2000* (2002), *Statistical Briefing Book (online)* (2002), and *Detention in Delinquency Cases, 1989–1998* (1996). The OJJDP *Juvenile Justice Bulletin* is a major source of current information about juvenile crime; its "Juvenile Arrests 2000" (Howard N. Snyder, 2002) was also helpful.

The Bureau of Alcohol, Tobacco, and Firearms (ATF) of the U.S. Department of the Treasury provides data on bombings, arson, and weapons offenses. Of special importance was the *First Year Report for the President* (1997) of the National Church Arson Task Force, which is jointly headed by the FBI and the ATF. The Office of National Drug Control Policy provided information from its report, *National Drug Control Strategy* (2002) and *The Economic Costs of Drug Abuse in the United States, 1992–1998* (2001). The National Criminal Justice Association (Washington, DC) monitors crime legislation and issues, as reported in its periodical *Justice Bulletin*.

The Federal Trade Commission, through its Identify Theft Clearinghouse, published *Figures and Trends on Identity Theft, November 1999 through June 2001* (2001). The National Institute of Justice provided information on drug use among persons arrested in three reports: *ADAM Preliminary 2000 Findings on Drug Use and Drug Markets—Adult Male Arrestees* (2001), the *1999 Annual Report on Drug Use Among Adult and Juvenile Arrestees* (2000), and the *1999 Arrestee Drug Abuse Monitoring Program Report* (2000).

Several organizations are devoted to combating prejudice and civil rights abuses in the United States. The Anti-Defamation League produced *Map of State Statutes for Hate Crimes* (New York, 2001) as a reference guide on the nation's hate crime legislation. The Southern Poverty Law Center (Montgomery, Alabama) publishes data on hate crimes in its periodical *Intelligence Report*.

The Sentencing Project conducts research on criminal justice issues and promotes sentencing reform. They published *Americans Behind Bars: U.S. and International Use of Incarceration, 1995* (Marc Mauer, updated 2001). Key information was also acquired from polling results reported by the Gallup Organization. Also used was the *Monitoring the Future Study National Results on Adolescent Drug Use: Overview of Key Findings 2001* (2002), completed by the Survey Research Center of the Institute for Social Research at the University of Michigan (Ann Arbor). The National Law Journal provided valuable survey data on Americans' opinions of the death penalty. The Violence Policy Center reported on the use of guns in high-profile shootings in its report, *Where'd They Get Their Guns? An Analysis of the Firearms Used in High-Profile Shootings, 1963 to 2001* (2002).

Other publications used in this book include the *2001 National Retail Security Survey* (Richard Hollinger et al., University of Florida, Gainesville, FL, 2001). The Highway Loss Data Institute provided valuable information on trends in motor vehicle thefts.

INDEX

Murder
    arrests, 22, 24
    circumstances, 21–22, 23t, 24t
    decline in rate, 19–20
    hate-motivated, 58–60
    juvenile, 67, 75
    offender demographic characteristics, 21,
        22(t2.3)
    regional trends, 21, 21t
    urban rates, 5, 7
    victim/offender relationship, 22(t2.4), 23t
    victims, 25(t2.7), 31t
    weapons, 21–22, 25(t2.7), 31t
    See also Homicide
Muslims, hate crimes against, 58

N

National Assessment of Gangs, 85
National Crime Victimization Survey, 37–39,
    44–46
National Institute of Justice youth gang
    study, 86
National Sheriff's Association, 145–146
National Youth Gang Survey, 83–85
Native Americans and Alaska Natives
    arrests, 11t
    federal law enforcement officers, 144f
    hate crimes offenders, 61t
    juvenile arrests, 76t, 77f, 78f, 79f
Native Hawaiian/Pacific Islander American
    federal law enforcement officers, 144f
Neighborhood watch programs, 144–145

O

Offenders
    death row inmates, 92
    drug, 128–129, 128t, 130–132
    hate crime, 58–59, 59(t4.4), 60–62, 61t
    juvenile weapons offenses, 87
    murder, 21, 22(t2.3), 22(t2.4), 23t
    restitution programs, 49
    victim/offender relationship, 43–44, 46t
    victim's perception of use of alcohol and
        drugs by the violent offender, 133(f8.5)
    white-collar crime, 106, 107f, 108
    See also Corrections; Sentencing
Offenses cleared by arrest, 11, 12f
Office of Homeland Security, 66
Office of Juvenile Justice and Delinquency
    Prevention youth gang study, 86
Office of National Drug Control Policy,
    135–136
Ohio, Brandenburg v. (1969), 55
Oil and gas investment fraud, 112–113
    See also White-collar crime
Oklahoma City bombing, 63
Olympic Pipeline Company, 123
Omega, 116

P

Parents of juvenile offenders, 79–80
Parole. *See* Corrections; Probation and
    parole
Payne v. Tennessee (1991), 50
Pearl, Daniel, 65–66

Petroleum refineries and environmental
    crime, 123
Pipe bombs, 64
Police. *See* Law enforcement
Polluters, corporate, 122–123
Presidential Task Force on the Victims of
    Crime, 51
"Preventing Crime: What Works, What
    Doesn't," 141–144
Prevention programs. *See* Crime prevention
    programs
Price fixing, 117
    See also White-collar crime
Principal Mutual Life Insurance Company, 112
Prison. *See* Corrections
Probation and parole, 100–101, 102t
    See also Corrections
Projections, crime rate, 3
Property crime
    age specific arrest rates, 73(f5.6)
    arrests, 73f
    arson, 30–31, 30(t2.14), 61–62, 62f, 63f,
        64f, 65f
    burglary, 27–28, 27f
    increase in, 4
    juvenile, 68–69, 74f, 79f, 82f
    larceny-theft, 28–29, 28f, 28t, 29t,
        30(t2.13), 42(t3.4), 44t
    motor vehicle theft, 28t, 29, 29t,
        30(t2.13)
    personal theft rates by gender, age, race,
        and Hispanic origin, 42(t3.4)
    race and ethnicity of victims, 41–43
    rates, 45–46, 47(f3.4)
    recovery rate, 12, 14t
    reporting, 40
    robbery, 25–26, 26t
    urban rates, 7
    value of losses, 12, 14t, 26, 27, 28–29
    victimization, 39, 43t
Public opinion
    capital punishment, 148, 151f
    criminal justice system, public
        confidence in, 150(t9.15)
    death penalty review, 152f
    fear of crime, 37, 145–147, 147(t9.11),
        148t, 149t
    firearms, 149–150, 153t
    juvenile crime, 148, 150(t9.14)
    law enforcement, confidence in,
        148–149, 152(t9.16)
    level of crime, 147(t9.9), 147(t9.10)
    problems facing the country, 146t

R

R.A.V. v. City of St. Paul (1992), 55
Race and ethnicity
    arrests, 9–11, 11t
    hate crime offenders, 61t
    juvenile crime, 69–70, 76t, 77f
    murder offenders, 22(t2.3)
    murder victim/offender relationship by,
        22(t2.4)
    prisoners, 99
    property crime victimization, 41–43
    status offenders, 78–79
    victims, 41–43

See also Specific race/ethnicity
Rape, 24–25, 25(t2.8)
Recidivism, 75–76, 101–103
Records, juvenile, 77
Recovery rate of stolen property, 12, 14t
Regions, geographic
    aggravated assault, 27t
    crime trends, 4, 6f, 7, 21, 21t
    drug abuse violation arrests, 126(t8.3),
        127t
    drug use by arrestees, 128t, 129t–130t
    incarceration, 95t
    robbery, 26t
    victimization, 43, 43t, 44t
Reporting crime, 39–41, 42(t3.3)
Restitution programs, 49
Restorative justice, 103
Retail store theft, 119–120, 119f, 120f, 121f,
    122f
    See also White-collar crime
Revictimization, 48
Robbery, 25–26, 26t
Rostenkowski, Dan, 120

S

Sagaz, Gabriel, 117
Sanford, Robert Russell, 116
School crime, 87–88
Securities and Exchange Commission
    (SEC), 110–111
Securities fraud, 112
    See also White-collar crime
Sentencing
    drug offenses, 132–134
    felony sentence lengths imposed by state
        courts, 92t
    life terms for drug offenses, 134
    mandatory, 91, 133–134
    reform, 91, 103
    restorative justice, 103
    Sentencing Reform Act of 1984, 91
    "Three Strikes" laws, 91–92
    victim participation, 50
    See also Capital punishment;
        Corrections; Offenders
Sentencing Reform Act of 1984, 91
September 11 attacks, 64–66
Shell Pipeline Company LP, 123
Shoplifting. *See* Retail store theft
Southern Poverty Law Center (SPLC), 53
States
    corrections budgets, 14
    death penalty, 92, 93
    felony sentence lengths imposed by state
        courts, 92t
    hate crimes legislation, 55, 56f, 57t
    parental responsibility for juvenile crime,
        79–80
    sentencing reform, 91–92
    victims' rights laws, 49, 50–51
Statistical information
    adolescent victims of violence, 45f
    age of arrestees, 8t, 9t
    age specific property crime rates, 73(f5.6)
    aggravated assault, 27t
    arrests by crime, 7t